THE

AMERICAN WEST

THE AMERICAN WEST

The Reader

WALTER NUGENT *and*
MARTIN RIDGE, *editors*

INDIANA UNIVERSITY PRESS
Bloomington and Indianapolis

This book is a publication of

Indiana University Press

601 North Morton Street

Bloomington, Indiana 47404-3797 USA

www.indiana.edu/~iupress

Telephone orders 800-842-6796

Fax orders 812-855-7931

Orders by e-mail iuporder@indiana.edu

© 1999   by Indiana University Press

The paper used in this publication meets the minimum
requirements of American National Standard for Information
Sciences—Permanence of Paper for Printed Library
Materials, ANSI Z39.48-1984.

Manufactured in the United States of America

Library of Congress Cataloging-in-Publication Data

The American West : the reader / Walter Nugent, Martin Ridge,
editors.

      p.   cm.

    Includes index.

    ISBN 0-253-33530-2 (alk. paper). — ISBN 0-253-21290-1 (pbk. :
alk. paper)

    1. West (U.S.)—History.   I. Nugent, Walter T. K.   II. Ridge,
Martin.

F591.A425   1999

978—dc21   99-19404

1 2 3 4 5   04 03 02 01 00 99

FOR
Erika Katherine Yngve
Kevin Arthur Yngve
Walter T. K. Nugent III
Matthew Ari Nugent
Natalie Rose Nugent
Hannah Rose Ronich
—W. N.

FOR
Lukas Ridge
Hannah Ridge
Kelsey Ridge
Martin (Max) Ridge
—M. R.

CONTENTS

Acknowledgments   xi

Timeline   xiii

General Introduction   I

PART I: DEFINING THE WEST

ARE WE TALKING ABOUT A PLACE? WHAT IS IT? WHERE IS IT?

1. Where Is the American West? Report on a Survey   II
   Walter Nugent

2. The American West: From Frontier to Region   24
   Martin Ridge

3. Frontiers and Empires in the Late Nineteenth Century   39
   Walter Nugent

PART II: THE EIGHTEENTH CENTURY

CALIFORNIA WOMEN, 1769–1848

4. Rancheras and the Land: Women and Property Rights in
   Hispanic California   59
   Gloria Ricci Lothrop

PART III: THE NINETEENTH CENTURY

EXPLORATION, THE FUR TRADE, AND NATIONAL IDENTITY, 1807–1845

5. Mountain Man as Jacksonian Man   83
   William H. Goetzmann

INDIANS, ANIMALS, AND THE GREAT PLAINS, 1800–1850
6. Bison Ecology and Bison Diplomacy: The Southern Plains
   from 1800 to 1850   97
     Dan Flores

THE MEXICAN-AMERICAN WAR, 1846–1848
7. Mexican Opinion, American Racism, and the War of 1846   120
     Gene M. Brack

THE LATTER-DAY SAINTS, 1830–1890
8. Mormon "Deliverance" and the Closing of the Frontier   133
     Martin Ridge

INDIANS, THE ARMY, AND SETTLERS, 1864
9. Sand Creek   147
     Janet LeCompte

COWBOYS AS WAGE WORKERS, 1880s
10. Cowboy Strikes and Unions   164
     David E. Lopez

HOMESTEADING, 1880S–1930s
11. "Everything I Want Is Here!": The *Dakota Farmer*'s Rural
    Ideal, 1884–1934   179
      Paula M. Nelson

PART IV: THE TWENTIETH CENTURY

MEXICAN, "ANGLO," AND EUROPEAN MINERS AND CAPITAL, 1900–1915
12. "The Men Have Become Organizers": Labor Conflict and
    Unionization in the Mexican Mining Communities of
    Arizona, 1900–1915   203
      Phil Mellinger

THE GREAT DEPRESSION IN THE NORTHWEST, 1929–1941
13. Idaho and the Great Depression   225
      Leonard J. Arrington

WORLD WAR II AND THE METROPOLIS, 1941–1945
14. The Impact of the Second World War on Los Angeles   234
      Arthur C. Verge

JAPANESE-AMERICAN WOMEN AND THE INTERNMENT OF 1942–1945
15. Japanese-American Women during World War II   255
      Valerie Matsumoto

AFRICAN AMERICANS IN THE WEST, 1541–1993
16. From Esteban to Rodney King: Five Centuries of African
    American History in the West								274
        Quintard Taylor

THE PACIFIC NORTHWEST SINCE 1945
17. Regional City and Network City: Portland and Seattle in
    the Twentieth Century										295
        Carl Abbott

Index													325

ACKNOWLEDGMENTS

The editors wish to thank Patricia Parrish of the staff of the Henry E. Huntington Library; the staff of the Humanities and Social Science Division of the California Institute of Technology; and the Theodore M. Hesburgh Library of the University of Notre Dame, for much-appreciated assistance. We also thank the various journals and photographic collections whose essays and visiual materials are reprinted here for their permission to do so.

The essays have not been changed from their original appearance, except for a very few emendations, particularly as regards punctuation, to conform to the preferences of Indiana University Press.

The editors also gratefully thank their wives, Sally Ridge and Suellen Hoy, for unending moral support and encouragement.

Martin Ridge
Walter Nugent
November 1998

The editors gratefully acknowledge permission to reprint material previously published as follows:

Chapter 1, Walter Nugent, "Where Is the American West?," *Montana: The Magazine of Western History*, Vol. 42 (Summer 1992), pp. 2–23.

Chapter 2, Martin Ridge, "The American West: From Frontier to Region," *New Mexico Historical Review*, Vol. 64 (April 1989), pp. 125–141.

Chapter 3, Walter Nugent, "Frontiers and Empires in the Late Nineteenth Century," *The Western Historical Quarterly*, Vol. 20 (November 1989), pp. 393–408.

Chapter 4, Gloria Ricci Lothrop, "Rancheras and the Land: Women and Property Rights in Hispanic California," *Southern California Quarterly*, Vol. 76 (Spring 1994), pp. 59–84.

Chapter 5, William H. Goetzmann, "Mountain Man as Jacksonian Man," *American Quarterly*, Vol. XV (Fall 1963), pp. 402–415.

Chapter 6, Dan Flores, "Bison Ecology and Bison Diplomacy: The Southern Plains from 1800 to 1850," *Journal of American History*, Vol. 78 (September 1991), pp. 465–485.

Chapter 7, Gene M. Brack, "Mexican Opinion, American Racism, and the War of 1846," *The Western Historical Quarterly*, Vol. 1 (April 1970), pp. 161–174.

Chapter 8, Martin Ridge, "Mormon 'Deliverance' and the Closing of the Frontier," *Journal of Mormon History*, Vol. 18 (Spring 1992), pp. 137–152.

Chapter 9, Janet LeCompte, "Sand Creek," *The Colorado Magazine*, Vol. XLI, No. 4 (1964), pp. 315–334.

Chapter 10, David E. Lopez, "Cowboy Strikes and Unions," *Labor History*, Vol. 18 (Summer 1977), pp. 325–340.

Chapter 11, Paula M. Nelson, " 'Everything I Want Is Here!': The *Dakota Farmer*'s Rural Ideal, 1884–1934," *South Dakota History*, Vol. 22 (Summer 1992), pp. 105–135.

Chapter 12, Phil Mellinger, " 'The Men Have Become Organizers': Labor Conflict and Unionization in the Mexican Mining Communities of Arizona, 1900–1915," *The Western Historical Quarterly*, Vol. 23 (August 1992), pp. 323–347.

Chapter 13, Leonard J. Arrington, "Idaho and the Great Depression," *Idaho Yesterdays* (Summer 1969), pp. 2–8.

Chapter 14, Arthur C. Verge, "The Impact of the Second World War on Los Angeles," *Pacific Historical Review*, Vol. 63 (August 1994), pp. 289–314. Copyright © 1994 by the American Historical Association, Pacific Coast Branch.

Chapter 15, Valerie Matsumoto, "Japanese-American Women during World War II," *Frontiers*, Vol. VIII, No. 1 (1984), pp. 6–14.

Chapter 16, Quintard Taylor, "From Esteban to Rodney King: Five Centuries of African American History in the West," *Montana: The Magazine of Western History*, Vol. 46 (Winter 1996), pp. 2–17.

Chapter 17, Carl Abbott, "Regional City and Network City: Portland and Seattle in the Twentieth Century," *The Western Historical Quarterly*, Vol. 23 (August 1992), pp. 293–322.

TIMELINE

Date	North America	American West
1492	Columbus reaches West Indies	
1519–1521		Cortés conquers the Aztec Empire in central Mexico
1598		Oñate leads 400 soldiers and settlers through El Paso del Norte into New Mexico
1607	Jamestown, Virginia founded	
1609		Sante Fe created as capital of New Mexico
1630	Mass. Bay colony (Boston)	
1680		Pueblo Revolt; Spanish return in 1692
1700		Kino founds San Xavier mission near future Tucson
1716		San Antonio (Texas) missions and presidio
1769		Serra and Portola found San Diego mission and presidio
1776	United States declares independence from Britain	San Francisco mission founded
1781		Los Angeles founded
1783	Treaty of Paris recognizes U.S.	
1785	Land Ordinance by Congress creates U.S. public domain	
1804–1806		Lewis and Clark expedition
1807–1845		Era of the Mountain Men
1819	U.S. acquires Florida, fixes boundary to Pacific	

Date	North America	American West
1819–1836		Austin and followers settle on land grants in Texas; gain in numbers; win independence
1829–1837	Presidency of Andrew Jackson	
1835–1838	"Trail of Tears": eastern Indians removed to Kansas and Oklahoma	
1839		Johann August Sutter builds fort at present Sacramento
1841		Bidwell-Bartleson party become first Americans to cross Sierras, settle in northern California
1845	U.S. annexes Texas	
1846	U.S. acquires Oregon south of 49th parallel in treaty with Britain	
1846	U.S. invades Mexican territory, begins war with Mexico	
1847		Mormons migrate to Salt Lake area
1848	Treaty of Guadalupe Hidalgo with Mexico	U.S. acquires California and the Southwest
1849–1852		California Gold Rush
1859		Comstock lode (silver) in Nevada; gold rush to Colorado (Pike's Peak and Denver)
1861–1865	Civil War between Union and Confederacy	Oklahoma Indian slaveholders side with Confederacy
1862	Homestead Act	
1864		Sand Creek massacre of Colorado Indians
1866–1873		Long cattle drives from Texas to Abilene, Wichita, Dodge City, and other Kansas towns
1867	Alaska purchased from Russia	

Date	North America	American West
1869	Transcontinental railroad opens	
1872		Yellowstone becomes first national park
1876	U.S. celebrates centennial of independence	Lakota and Cheyenne defeat Custer at Little Bighorn
1879		"Powell Report" on "Lands of the Arid Region"
1885–1911		William F. Cody's "Wild West and Congress of Rough Riders" plays everywhere
1887	Dawes Severalty Act shifts Indians from tribal to individual land	Severe winter kills cattle herds on northern Plains
1890		"Battle" of Wounded Knee, South Dakota; death of Sitting Bull
1893	World's Columbian Exposition held in Chicago	Frontier declared closed after 1890 census; F. J. Turner essay on "significance of the frontier"
1898	Hawaii annexed to U.S.	
1902	Owen Wister's *The Virginian*, first major western novel	Newlands Reclamation Act
1910–1921	Mexican Revolution	
1913		Peak year for homestead entries (11,000,000 acres); Los Angeles aqueduct opens
1917		Striking miners deported from Bisbee, Ariz.
1920		Los Angeles passes San Francisco, is largest city in West; reaches 1.2 million in 1930
1929–1941	Great Depression	
1933–1943	Franklin Roosevelt President; his New Deal includes, for the West: Tribal Reorganization Act and Taylor Grazing Act, 1934	Dust bowl at its worst

Date	North America	American West
1936–1937		Oakland-Bay and Golden Gate bridges completed in San Francisco
1939		Arroyo Seco Freeway (later Pasadena Freeway) opens in Los Angeles, the first freeway
1941–1945	World War II (1939–1945 in Europe)	Internment of Japanese Americans
1942–1965	The Baby Boom	
1947–1989	The Cold War	
1954	U.S. Supreme Court decides against school segregation in *Brown* v. *Board of Education of Topeka*	
1962	Rachel Carson publishes *Silent Spring*	
1965	Immigration Act repeals national origins quotas, admits Asians and Latin Americans	Watts riots in Los Angeles
1970	Earth Day	
1979–1981		Sagebrush Rebellion
1986	Immigration Reform and Control Act results in expanded Asian and Latin-American immigration	
1992		Los Angeles: acquittal of police in Rodney King trial triggers uprising in South Central

THE
AMERICAN
WEST

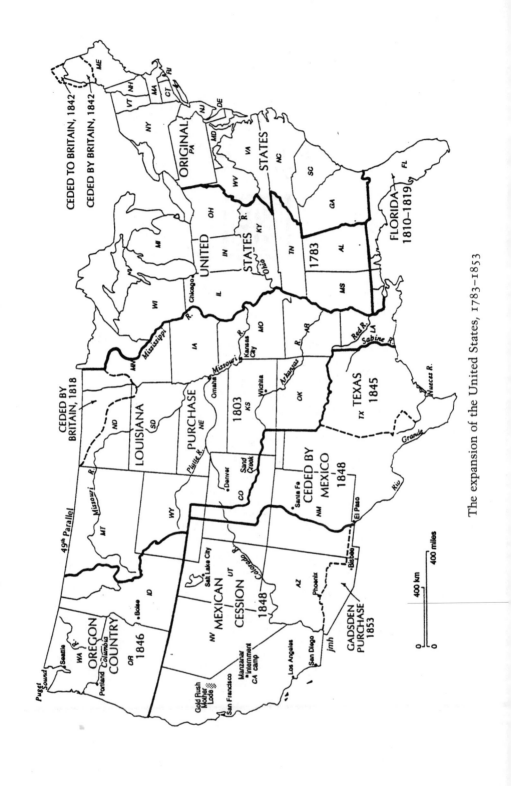

The expansion of the United States, 1783–1853

GENERAL INTRODUCTION

The United States acquired the Trans-Mississippi West through purchase, war, and diplomacy. The stories of the Louisiana Purchase, the Mexican War, and the ousting of the British from the Oregon country, along with the tales of high adventure by explorers, soldiers, travelers, and fur traders, are a significant part of the narrative history of the United States. This book is neither a retelling of that story nor an effort to write a single western narrative. It does not seek to identify a unifying western culture. It brings together a group of essays that deal with the dreams, experiences, values, and ideas of the diverse groups of people who made their lives in different parts of the West. The essays are, in part, cautionary tales about what happens when a modernizing commercial and industrial economy functions in a regional setting, and what happens when different cultures intersect in an underdeveloped region of vast resources. The collection of essays should be not be seen as a jeremiad or as a series of disparate heroic episodes. Taken together, they tell an ambiguous yet valuable and rewarding story. Their purpose is both to impart information and to challenge the reader to think beyond the facts. To know *what* some people in the West did is only half a history; to know *why* they did it and to what effect is of equal or greater importance.

The West, most scholars agree, encompasses an incredibly diverse climatological and geographic landscape that spans the nation's girth. The ore-rich mountain ranges, semi-arid plains, lush forests, well-watered valleys, and true deserts play a genuine role in the region's history. They are not merely the stage for human actions. People in the West, whether native or alien, never lacked for a sense of place.

Many Native Americans in the West felt the impact of European culture long before they directly encountered the Spaniards from Mexico or the traders from French and, later, British North America. European diseases, against which the Indians had little or no resistance, moved with deadly and debilitating effect along Indian trade routes far in advance of the white presence. Spanish horses, stolen or traded in New Mexico, revolutionized the lives of western Indians, just as the demands of the European fur market and the growth of white settlement changed intertribal warfare in the East and forced displaced Indians onto the lands of their neighbors. The artifacts of white material culture—weapons, utensils, traps, ornaments, cloth, and tools—introduced into Indian life melded the economic interests and material cultures of Indians and whites who may never have seen each other.

When the Spaniards entered the Southwest, they came initially as missionaries and wealth seekers. Although some Catholic missionaries had personal shortcomings, they believed that they were doing divine work in spreading Christianity and introducing the native population to a superior culture. They would have been astonished to learn that a later generation would condemn them for trying to root out the indigenous religious practices that played a vital part in Indian life. The Spanish-speaking pioneers in the Southwest, who followed in the wake of the missionaries gradually, despite conflicts, reached an accommodation with the sedentary peoples of the region. The Indians of the High Plains, who had horses and sufficient weapons to wreak havoc among settled Mission Indian and Mexican pioneer communities, blocked Spanish expansion, as did deserts and mountains. Farther west, in California, despite their worthy intentions, missionaries, soldiers, and Mexican settlers contributed to disaster as the Native Americans with whom they came in contact died off by the thousands.

Racism proved an important factor in the Southwest. Tension existed between Indians and Mexican settlers, although many Spanish-speaking pioneers were of mixed Indian, Spanish and African American blood. Abolition of slavery occurred in Mexico long before it did in the United States. In fact, the slave-owning southerners in Texas rebelled rather than give up their chattel. Race remained an issue in the Southwest after the United States annexed the region.

By the time native-born English-speaking people from the United States moved into the West, they brought with them a clearly defined social and material culture. For example, in both law and custom, the patriarchy, or male-dominated family, proved the rule. Males controlled family property. Because women had limited legal control of their assets, they lacked opportunities for individual economic advancement. During the nineteenth century, the idea of separate spheres for women and men—that is, men working outside the home in a cash economy and women working without income in the home—gradually took hold in the commercial and industrial East. It did not affect rural or western women who worked side by side with men on farms or labored on farms alone. Families tended to be large in a farm economy because children were an economic asset. After the Civil War, the gender-neutral Homestead Act allowed some women, regardless of color, to claim land in their own right. An increasing number of white women in the West enjoyed the luxury of being housewives. Poor native-born white and immigrant women, along with women of color, often worked at menial jobs if they lived in large cities or in burgeoning agricultural towns and mining centers. Some men in the West granted high status to middle-class white women, especially in the mining and milling towns, because of the skewed sex ratio. This was not the case in larger cities with more balanced sex ratios. In the Southwest, Mexican-American women, who had enjoyed many rights under Spanish law, lost most of these rights after the United States annexed the region. They, as well as other women, regardless of color, retained as a legacy of Spanish law the benefit of community property rights, something women in northern states did not possess. White women in Wyoming and Utah were among the first to win the vote. Aside from these unique privileges and the relaxation of laws pertaining to divorce, the status of most women in the West has differed little from those in other parts of the nation since the beginning of the nineteenth century.

The native-born whites who entered the West differed sharply from the Native Americans on how they viewed the land. Many Indians believed in the sacredness of land and incorporated parts of the landscape in their tribal myths and religious rituals. They believed that tribes held land in common for mutual use, and found the idea of selling or buying it alien. Many Indians believed that no one could actually own land.

Whites saw land as a commodity that could be bought, sold, or traded away for profit. Whites were land-hungry. The wealthy wanted land as a long-term investment or an asset for immediate use in the most profitable manner. The rural landless poor often believed that unfenced or unoccupied land—even if already owned by someone—was empty and, therefore, free for the taking. Poor whites, often squatters, wantonly took up land, cut down trees, and raised corn, tobacco, and swine. When the real owner appeared or when the government put the land up for sale, these squatters bought it or, more likely, moved on to begin again. Even many successful middle-western farmers sold their land, picked up their possessions, and moved farther west on the basis of rumors of better or cheaper land in Texas, Missouri, California, or Oregon. Southern slave-holders, too, abandoned their worked-out fields and took their whole estates to the virgin lands in the West. Only the most successful or the indigent elements of the population stayed behind. The Federal land policy became increasingly liberal during the nineteenth century, gradually alienating millions of acres to railroads, speculators, farmers, ranchers, and miners at practically no cost. Most western territories and states, eager to trade land for people, used land as an inducement to commercial, industrial, and agricultural development. These policies led to boom-and-bust economic cycles. Farmers took up marginal western lands during periods of unusually heavy rainfall only to fail in times of drought. Ranchers, pursuing a similar policy, went bankrupt during the 1880s when intense blizzards and prolonged drought killed off untended herds on the open range.

The native-born whites who went west in the early 1800s virtually "breathed a spirit" of militant national expansion and white hegemony. Even government officials, who paid lip service to the idea that Native Americans had legitimate claims of land ownership, believed that such lands would ultimately be surrendered to whites. Constant pressure on the Indians to give up increasingly larger parts of their land base resulted in both wars of Indian extermination and the establishment of reservations. For the remnants of once-powerful Indian peoples, reservations seemed like concentration camps. Moreover, these reservations became targets of opportunity for white farmers and ranchers. Even reformers, most of whom were zealous Protestants, believed, like the Spanish missionaries, that they had the Native Americans' best interests at heart. They urged the Indians to convert to Christianity, abandon their way of life, and become part of white society. In fact, reformers did not hesitate in trying to achieve these goals through political means. In the 1880s they embraced the idea that, if they could end the Indian communal lifestyle, the Indian would accept white ways. The reformers pushed through a severalty act that broke up tribal holdings, and in the process opened large tracts previously held as tribal land to white settlement. By 1900 Native Americans occupied only small pockets of land in most western states. The Indians were marginalized in the dominant white society, and their total population fell to 237,000, its lowest level.

Pro-Indian advocates, who thought that Native Americans should determine their own destinies, lacked influence until the Indian New Deal in the 1930s. Many whites continued to insist that Indians should leave their reservations and meld into white society. In the 1950s the Eisenhower administration encouraged, with limited success, the movement of Indians from reservations to large cities. The Native American population has been growing steadily since 1900 and approached 2,000,000 by the 1990s. There has been a revival of cultural identity among many Indian groups. The current status of western Indians is ambiguous: casino gambling has made some very rich, while others remain trapped on impoverished reservations.

Politicians in the 1840s, espousing the doctrine of Manifest Destiny, the idea that it was the God-given right and duty of the United States not only to spread its democratic form of government from sea to sea but also to rule the continent, dictated the nation's foreign policy. They found ready support among merchants engaged in the China trade, slave-holders, and land-hungry middle-western farmers who wanted to drive Mexico and Great Britain out of the West. Their idea of national superiority, closely linked to racism and color consciousness, prevailed during the Mexican War. The "spread eagle" rhetoric of major political leaders disparaged the Mexicans as a "mongrel race"—people who could be easily brushed aside by the advance of "Anglo-Saxon" Americans.

The idea of the "whiteness" of people allowed both native-born whites and European immigrants to denounce Mexicans and Chinese miners as unwelcome aliens during and after the California gold rush. Ironically, at the same time that Irish laborers and railroad workers rioted against the Chinese in San Francisco and Rock Springs, Wyoming, Irish Catholic immigrants in the East fell victim to religious and "racial" discrimination. The problems of a modernizing nation, urban growth, commercial and industrial expansion, the rapid construction and completion of the transcontinental railroads, and the occupation of arable land exacerbated racial and ethnic tensions. The opportunity to gain industrial work or to secure farms brought hordes of people to the West, not only from the eastern and middle-western states but also from Europe. Xenophobic outbreaks in the West came as regularly as the boom-and-bust cycles in the economy. Racial, ethnic, and religious tensions became and remained a part of western life.

By 1900, the nature of the western economy made the West a heavily urbanized region. Most of the population lived in commercial, mining, and processing factory towns. Western agriculture tended to disperse people on large-scale farms and ranches. The modest-sized towns and cities of the West at the turn of the century probably reflected the nation's urban society as much as did the great cities of New York, Chicago, Philadelphia, St. Louis, and Boston. Western cities often contained polyglot populations as diverse in their ethnicity and racial makeup as those in large eastern cities. Only smaller western agricultural communities may have been more homogeneous. As the nation's major port of entry, New York's Ellis Island greeted millions of immigrants, but Galveston, Texas, also received its share of immigrants from central Europe, and San Francisco continued to process Chinese immigrants, despite the legislative restrictions of the 1880s.

The western economy during the latter part of the nineteenth century became so thoroughly integrated into that of the nation that it proved highly vulnerable to national and international business cycles. Although western entrepreneurs and boosters often boasted that their economy suffered less from industrial strife, national depressions, foreign competition, and financial panics, the opposite was true. Labor, after the Civil War, as likely confronted capital behind barricades in the West as in the East. Intense violence frequently marked railroad and mining strikes. Mine owners lobbied the government to keep buying silver for coinage as the price of the white metal fell steadily on the world market. Farmers supported these efforts in the belief that a silver-based currency would bring inflation and result in higher prices for farm products. Western sheep growers sought tariff protection, and sugar beet growers, fearing foreign cane sugar imports, did the same. Western wheat farmers followed prices in Liverpool's grain exchange, just as ranchers watched the cattle trading prices at the Chicago stock yards.

In the twentieth century, the West, as much as or more than the rest of the nation, felt the impact of wars, depressions, and panics. Although western politicians continued to speak in terms of individualism, entrepreneurs, and free enterprise, they lobbied hard in Congress for massive construction projects, such as hydroelectric dams, highways, canals, irrigation systems, military bases, defense plants, and airports. From the 1930s on federal money played a vital role in sustaining and building the western economy.

The free-wheeling habits of the nineteenth-century frontier business community, encouraged by a supportive and paternalistic national government that allowed for slash-and-burn forestry, soil-depleting agriculture, overstocked cattle ranges, and highly destructive hydraulic mining, gave way after 1900 to demands by middle-class reformers for increased state protection, regulation, and conservation. A more developed and mature urban society became increasingly conscious of the fragility of parts of the western landscape. Many people looked with horror on the remnants of the frontier era and helped to create an environmental movement. Slowly, over the course of the twentieth century, they demanded that slag heaps, toxic settling basins, and other sources of pollution be eliminated. They also insisted that newer mines and electrical power plants be environmentally safe. Water, the most critical commodity in the arid portions of the West, became a subject of such intense legal adjudication that the controversies in mining law paled in comparison. Today, people in virtually every western state argue not only about who is entitled to use water but also about how to protect pure water and what to do with waste in an industrial age. The environmental movement has produced head-on collisions between pro-growth elements and passionate advocates of preservation and restoration of forests, rivers, and wildlife.

Some business leaders and railroad promoters recognized quite early that the vast scenic areas of the West, too rugged for farming, unsuited for logging, and devoid of minerals, could be turned into tourist meccas. The Grand Canyon, Glacier National Park, and the Grand Tetons drew thousands of people to the West. The monumental figures on Mount Rushmore, man-made icons, serve the same purpose. What pioneering people had seen as obstacles to progress and profit became economic assets. Businessmen also learned that the Rocky Mountains, like the Swiss Alps, attracted health seekers, mountain climbers, naturalists, and city people in search of an outing. The West, like the East, developed a service economy as thousands of people found employment in tourism, summer and ski resorts, and tuberculosis sanitariums. Restored abandoned mining camps and rebuilt "old towns" that attracted the motoring public in quest of the "frontier West" proved the salvation of many dying villages.

Capitalizing on the legendary frontier era came early. The pioneering generation on the plains had not yet passed away in 1882 when William "Buffalo Bill" Cody organized "The Old Glory Blow Out," in North Platte, Nebraska. This original extravaganza launched his famous wild west show. Cody's productions, which played widely in the United States as well as in Europe, embodied a sanitized and mythic West. Cody incorporated and created popular western stereotypes that captured the public's historical imagination for more than a century. The gold prospector, the United States Cavalry, the stagecoach, the buffalo, the cowboy, the cattle stampede, the prairie schooner, the sharpshooter, the lonely settler's cabin, and the Indian attack all had a role in Cody's western saga. He employed Annie Oakley, the best trick shooter in the nation, and turned the Sioux warrior Sitting Bull into a household name and perhaps America's best-known Indian. The frontier West of Cody's imagination also became, in part, the forerunner of the modern rodeo, which turned a cowhand's hard work into showmanship, and western historical events into popular public festivals. Invariably, after 1900 these frontier festivals depicted a unifying heroic pageant, much to the chagrin of Indians. The early romanticized version of the West, later picked up by popular novelists, reinforced both stereotypes and myths. American filmmakers recognized the marketability of the West. From the rugged realism of early western film star William S. Hart to the cynical realism of contemporary films, producers usually retained a basic formula that mixed the tragedy and promise of the West. These films remain a staple of the industry. The Disney Company, the ultimate exploiter of western myths, created frontier legends and marketed them on film and in theme parks.

After the Second World War, the West enjoyed continued and rapid population growth. It continued to suffer all of the problems of a society in transition. Nevertheless, it remains, in the public's mind, a self-conscious region, despite its obvious diversity of place, culture, race, and identity. Increasingly, however, it serves as a synecdoche for the nation as well as for modern societies everywhere. The cultures of New England and the South remain specific to them. The behavior of western people, whether on the sun-drenched beaches of California, the open prairies of Montana, the mountain slopes of Colorado, great bridges over coastal harbors, or clogged urban freeways are widely recognized thanks to television and film. Not only do today's fashion trends in Los Angeles, Denver, and Dallas quickly gain acceptance worldwide but the symbols of the "Old West" also continue to represent the whole United States. The nineteenth-century immigrant miners and laborers who bought Levi Strauss's work pants and the ranchers and cowhands who owned Stetsons would be astonished to learn that today these work-a-day objects are denounced as symbols of American cultural imperialism by foreign governments whose people buy them. For working men and women, the West is not a socially constructed myth; it is where they live out often conflicted lives. Their story is in part told in the essays that follow.

PART I

DEFINING
THE WEST

1

WHERE IS THE AMERICAN WEST?
REPORT ON A SURVEY

Walter Nugent

*The answer to the question "Where is the American West?"
seems obvious—but in very different ways to different people.
Some answer immediately, "It's out here," or "It's out there," pointing
to the western third, half, or two-thirds of the United States as it appears on a map. Others answer just as quickly, "It's part of our minds
and culture." One definition is steadfastly geographical; the other is
defiantly mental and mythical. In this essay, the author reports on a
survey he conducted in 1991 of several hundred historians, fiction
writers, and journalists. He asked them three questions: Where are the
boundaries of the West? Where do you think you have to go to get in or
out of the West? And why do you think so—what are its distinguishing
characteristics, making it different from the Midwest, South, and Northeast?*

*The historians generally gave geographical answers, most of them
setting the eastern boundary at the Mississippi or the Great Plains, and
the other boundaries at the Canadian and Mexican borders and the
Pacific. The writers, as often as not, refused to put "the West" on the
map and insisted it lives only in our minds and myths. In each group,
the majority insisted that the West can't be defined without reference
to time, because it moved across the West (and in our minds) over
time; and a minority said that the Pacific Coast, especially California
and the big coastal cities, is not western at all (although those who
lived in those cities insisted they were both at the edge and the center
of the West).*

*Where do you think the West is, or was? Is it a geographical or a
mythical entity? What, to you, makes the West western?—editors*

DISAGREEMENTS ABOUT how to define "West" and "frontier" and
how to distinguish the two terms are nothing new to historians of
both. The urgency of these problems has ebbed and flowed. Lately it has
flooded like a spring torrent, fed by the assertions of some "new western
historians" that the West is a place, not a Turnerian process. Before the
day is done, the torrent may further swell by the melting snowpack from

"old western historians" who think that process remains very much part of the story.

But new western historians have raised the place-versus-process issue, and hence, questioned anew the definition of "the West." They have stated their premises clearly in several recent publications.[1] Among these premises (though not every new western historian agrees on all of them) are these: that western history hardly stopped in 1890 or 1893 or any other years; that it has been marked less by "progress" than by "conquest" and conflict; that the West is a place where this conquest has taken place, a definite place on the map, rather than the process that Frederick Jackson Turner stated was essential to the frontier idea. As Patricia Nelson Limerick wrote in *Legacy of Conquest*, "De-emphasize the frontier and its supposed end, conceive of the West as a place and not a process, and Western American history has a new look."[2] Richard White, in his massive new history of the western region, avoids the term "frontier." In the set of essays edited by William Cronon, George Miles, and Jay Gitlin, Limerick explains that

> To Frederick Jackson Turner and his followers in conventional western history, the frontier (and, by extension, the West) was a process, not a place; a concept, not an actual geographical location. In this way of thinking, the West is wherever the American mind puts it— a pretty vague and ephemeral target for "image" analysis.[3]

It seemed to me, since the new western history continued to gain attention and generate controversy, that it would be interesting and useful to know how widely the "place versus process" antinomy operates in people's minds, and where people believe the *true* West to be. That question leads, of course, to what the West signifies. Since the frontier idea, as William Goetzmann and others have said, has been our great American creation myth, the question touches not just on images of the West but on conceptions of the whole of America.

But does not the question of "where" the West is also suggest "when" the West was? And this suggests yet another question—do frontiers end, do regions come and go, and if so how can we tell? That last question must wait for another occasion. It is enough for now to inquire of people seriously interested in the West, from different perspectives, how they feel about the place-versus-process argument. I have also been curious, long before the new western history appeared, about the simple question of where other people began to sense westernness as they traveled from east to west across the country (or where they no longer felt "western" if they were leaving the region). The answers should help define regionalism.

What interested parties think about place-versus-process and where one starts or stops feeling "western" are questions resolvable by a survey. Therefore, in the spring of 1991, I designed and mailed out nearly five hundred questionnaires to members of the Western History Association, a list of editors and publishers of newspapers and magazines from Colorado to California, and members of the Western Writers of America. The response was remarkable for size, vehemence, and content. The results appear below.

THE QUESTIONS

The questionnaire consisted of three short questions: (1) "How would you describe the boundaries of 'the West' (on the east, south, north, and west)?"; (2) "Where are you now (i.e. in what section of the country), and where would you have to go to get to the edge of the West?"; (3) "What characteristics set apart the West, as you have defined it, from other regions?" Each person also received a personal data form so that answers could be linked to age, sex, place of residence, and occupation.[4] The three questions are increasingly open ended. The first asks for a specific geographic response; the second for a more personal but still presumably geographic response; while the third is almost completely open, and to it many people have several answers—Wests of geography, climate, myth, history, imagination, and more.

The cover letter explained that various people have defined the West differently. Bernard DeVoto and Joan Didion said it starts "where rainfall drops below twenty inches a year." But that excludes San Francisco and the coast north of it. An "eminent historian of the West who lives in New England" felt "western," so he once told me, when he crossed Indiana. The columnist Richard Reeves said he "got the notion that Chillicothe, Ohio, was where the West really began."

On the back of the data sheet was a map, and it contained one of the two major biases in the questionnaire—both unavoidable but also not without malice aforethought. The map was of the continental United States, with insets of Hawaii, Alaska, and Puerto Rico. State boundaries were indicated but rivers and other natural features were not, nor were Canada or Mexico. The map was therefore skewed toward a political response and against including Canada or Mexico. My alternative was to provide a map of North America, but that, I thought, would have introduced an even stronger bias toward including Canada and Mexico. The very presence of a map invited responses that were geographical and also presentist. It discouraged responses that located or defined the West as it may have been at any past time, or as it may now exist in people's minds.

Despite these biases, many respondents insisted on including Canada and/or Mexico; many insisted that the "West" must be defined not only by "where," but also by "when?"; and many pronounced it not a geographical entity at all, but a cultural one. Many insisted, explicitly, on the West as process rather than just as place. One respondent, in a personal letter, upbraided me for the questionnaire's "refusal to situate itself in time," but concluded, "My suspicion is that you probably share a number of the reservations [about defining the West exclusively as place] I've expressed . . . [and] your strategy in framing the questions as you have is no doubt clev-

1. Judith Basin homestead, about 1910.
Courtesy of Robert Lacy.

erer and sneakier than I've realized." True. Also, given the geographic and
presentist bias of the questionnaire, we can assume that historical and cultural definitions are even stronger in the respondents' minds than the nu-
merical results indicate.

THE QUESTIONNAIRE

The questionnaire went to three groups of people. The first and largest
was a roughly one-fifth sample, basically random, of the members of the
Western History Association (WHA)—307 people.[5] The second was a group
of 97 editors and publishers ranging from metropolitan dailies to special
interest magazines.[6] The third was a roughly one-fifth sample, 76 people,
of the Western Writers of America (WWA). These 480 questionnaires were
mailed in March and April 1991.

THE RESPONSES

By the end of June we received 251 responses: 188 from WHA members (61 percent); 25 from journalists (26 percent); and 38 from WWA
members (50 percent).[7] The WHA responses were especially gratifying.
Reading them was like arriving at a WHA meeting on an October Thurs-
day and actually having time to talk with almost two hundred friends

and colleagues about an ostensibly casual but really quite complex question.[8] Clearly the great majority of respondents regarded these as serious questions.[9] The respondents had lived, on average, nineteen years in their state of present residence, and divided about equally among large, medium, and small cities, and rural places.[10] The WWA people were more reclusive—fully a quarter of them live on farms, ranches, and in villages, compared to only 4 percent of historians and none of the journalists. Two-thirds were between thirty and sixty years old, most of the rest were over sixty, and only 2 percent were under thirty. Of the WWA group, 43 percent were female compared to 19 percent of the WHA group and 20 percent of the journalists. Only 8 percent of the WHA and WWA respondents—but 21 percent of the journalists!—asked not to be quoted.

The personal data sheets were not dry profiles. To the question, "how long have you lived in your present state of residence" and how long elsewhere, Michael Harrison answered, "57 years in California (present), plus 10 in Arizona, 3 in New Mexico, and 25 in New Jersey; total 95." A WWA member from Buena Vista, Colorado, replied that "I've lived here as a child, student, teacher, wife, widow, mother, journalist, writer, camper, rockhound" and another, from Santa Fe, wrote, "I write under a man's name. Please don't use my real name. Ladies don't sell westerns." One WWA member, Lauran Paine of Siskiyou County, California, wrote,

> I have worked and lived in most Far Western and Southwestern
> states. Cattle ranching, wild horse trapping, blacksmithing, even
> sank so low as to become a motion picture rider, and upon discover-
> ing that none of these vocations would provide the income I aspired
> to . . . I began writing. Total published books to date 912 of which
> 714 Westerns have been for one publisher.

But now for the meat and potatoes. Where do these people think the West is, and why?

Question 1:
Where are the West's boundaries?

The answers may be summed up in these ten points:

1. Respondents focused much more on the eastern boundary than the other three. Everyone made a choice, and only about 5 percent were unclear (10/211). Regarding the western boundary, again only 5 percent were unclear, but 22 percent gave no response.

2. Respondents were more indecisive, or just inattentive, about the northern and southern boundaries. Many probably took the Canadian and Mexican borders for granted. In both cases 5 percent answered unclearly; and 25 percent simply did not state a northern boundary and 27 percent did not state a southern one. Differences were not great among the three groups (WHA, journalists, WWA).

3. A number of people identified only an eastern boundary, perhaps having mentally exhausted themselves in so doing. And a few who were reluctant to set any geographical boundaries said, well, if you insist, I'd place the eastern one at X or Y, then left it at that.

4. About one out of 6 (40/251=15.9%) refused to name any geographical boundaries. Instead they said the West is a "state of mind," an "idea," "myth," or "mental construct," or something similar. Of the three groups, about one-eighth of the WHA members took this position (23/187= 12.3%), only one of the editors did so (1/25 = 4%), but nearly half of the western writers (16/39 = 41%). The writers, or many of them, believe the West is myth, and they write about and perpetuate the myth.

Many of them are genre writers and adamantly oppose the whole idea of demythologizing. Many in this group also reject the idea that the West is a contemporary, twentieth-century matter. I can think of other fiction writers who would scarcely agree—Ivan Doig and Tom King, for example, whose material is twentieth century. But the Western Writers of America largely work with material from, or redolent of, the past. Their livelihood depends on the myths. It's not that they are necessarily more romantic about the West (though some are deeply attached to it) but that they write and sell what is romantic to many readers.

5. Regarding the eastern boundary, geographical responses were as follows. WHA members chose the Mississippi River in 22 percent of the cases, sometimes reluctantly, but because that is where many begin the courses they teach. The largest group, 29 percent, picked the north–south line of the Red, Missouri, and Sabine rivers. But combining the 16.5 percent who chose the 98th meridian and the 15 percent who chose the 100th, fully 31 percent locate it at the eastern edge of the Great Plains, often with a verbal bow to Walter Prescott Webb. Only 5 percent chose the Rockies or close by, with 13 percent giving unclear or other responses, from the Atlantic Coast to eastern Idaho.

The editors, all from Colorado to California, opted strongly—46 percent—for the Rockies or the eastern borders of states in the front range of the Rockies (Montana, Wyoming, Colorado, New Mexico), with only 8 percent choosing the Mississippi River.

The writers—the slight majority who gave geographical responses— stuck to the traditional Mississippi River or Missouri River two-thirds of the time (65 percent).

6. Regarding the western boundary, most of the historians and journalists clearly opted for the Pacific Coast, but a minority of about one in six excluded all or parts of California, Oregon, and Washington. The writers were again more traditional; 40 percent of them excluded all or parts of the coastal states, and several refused to include any large cities, or what one called "plastic places" such as Vail, Aspen, and Las Vegas.

The exclusion of the coastal states, coastal strip, or cities, is a minority view but a significant one. Interestingly, most of those who hold it do not live in those areas. People who do live there, quite definitely those who live in Los Angeles, regard themselves as being not only in the West but in the center of the West.

7. As to whether Alaska and Hawaii are western: both appeared on the map circulated with the questionnaire, so it was hard to ignore them. Yet many did. Of the 70 (27.8 percent) who did refer to Alaska, 83 percent think it is indeed part of the West, wherever else they place the western or northern boundaries of the region. Of the 47 (18.7 percent) referring to Hawaii, the split was close—49 percent including it, 51 percent saying it is not western. The divisions on Alaska and Hawaii were nearly the same among all three respondent groups, except that the writers (WWA) were less inclined than the historians (WHA) to include Alaska.

8. Many took the northern boundary for granted. The map I provided showed the United States only, so a respondent had to go slightly against the grain to include Canada. But many did. More historians (62) said; "include some parts of it," than said, "stop at the border" (57). The writers split about evenly. The journalists strongly (13 to 1) preferred to use the United States border than to include any part of Canada. Had I circulated a map of North America rather than of the United States, I suspect more would have included Canada. The tilt of the historians may indicate—so their comments often suggest—that, influenced by Webb, James Malin, and perhaps Turner, they think more in terms of environment and physiography than the other groups do, and more in terms of prairie settlement patterns than of political boundaries.

9. The southern boundary brought more non-responses than the other three. Many probably take the Rio Grande and the line across the Sonoran desert as a given. Some of the historians, especially those living in Arizona or New Mexico or who specialize in borderlands history, pointed out that the border arbitrarily divides people and geography that are better thought of as a unit. Thus, 24 percent of the historians, 26 percent of the writers, and only 8 percent of the editors consider parts of northern Mexico as being in the West.

10. A consensus? Not quite. On the east, about half see the West as beginning at the Mississippi River or Missouri River, the other half at the eastern edge of the Great Plains or, in a few cases, the Rockies' front range. On the west, most stop at the Pacific Ocean but a sizeable minority leave out the coast and its cities. On the north, historians divide, slightly in favor of including western Canada, the rest stopping at the border. On the south, most of those saying anything at all stop at the border, though a goodly minority of historians would include parts of northern Mexico, especially the desert. But, to repeat, fully one-sixth (and nearly half of the writers) refused to identify any geographical boundaries at all, and many others stated them under protest. These people remain convinced that "West" and "frontier" are not that separable, and that process remains more important than present place.

RESPONSES TO QUESTION I

Who responded?	WHA	Press	WWA	Total
Total, each group	187	25	39	251
Gave non-geographical response	23	1	16	40
Geographical responses	164	24	23	211

Place the Eastern boundary at:

	WHA	Press	WWA	Total
Mississippi River	36	2	7	45
Red-Missouri-Sabine Rrs.	40	8	6	54
Same, but exclude east Texas or other small area	7	0	2	9
98th meridian	27	2	1	30
100th meridian	24	1	2	27
Eastern borders of MT-NM	4	6	0	10
Rockies (east face)	5	5	1	11
Other (often includes Old Northwest, or "between" Miss. & Mo. 98th & 100th)	15	0	0	15
Unclear	6	0	4	10
Blank	0	0	0	0

Northern Boundary:

	WHA	Press	WWA	Total
Border, 49th parallel	57	13	6	76
Include parts of Canada	54	1	6	61
Arctic Circle or Ocean	8	0	1	9
Other	1	0	0	1
Unclear	6	1	4	11
Blank	38	9	6	53

Include Alaska? (at northern or western boundary)

	WHA	Press	WWA	Total
Yes	52	2	4	58
No	10	0	2	12

Include Hawaii?

	WHA	Press	WWA	Total
Yes	20	1	2	23
No	22	0	2	24

Southern boundary:

	WHA	Press	WWA	Total
Border or "Gulf"	75	11	7	93
Include parts of Mexico	40	2	6	48
Other	1	1	1	2
Unclear	6	1	4	11
Blank	42	9	6	57

Western boundary:

	WHA	Press	WWA	Total
Pacific Ocean	97	10	6	113
Pacific, with exclusions	12	1	3	16
(Exclude large cities:	3	0	1	4)

southern Calif.	0	0	1	1)
all of Calif.	3	1	0	4)
Pacific NW	3	0	0	3)
"coastal strip"	3	0	1	4)
Cascades-Sierras	9	3	5	17
Exclude Calif.-Ore.-Wash.	4	0	0	4
Other	3	1	0	4
Unclear	6	1	4	11
Blank	3	8	5	46

Question 2:
Where do you have to go to get to the West?

Replies to this question were not always consistent with replies to question 1. Here, respondents often placed the eastern edge farther west. Many seem to have answered #1 mindful of how they teach, but #2 in more personal terms. For example, the same person might say "Mississippi River" to #1, but "Grand Island, Nebraska" to #2.

Unanimously, everyone east of the plains states, when asked about the edge, identified an eastern edge. So did most of the Texans, but two of them and one Kansan referred only to a western edge (the Pacific). The farther west the respondent's residence, the more often she or he mentioned the Pacific or some other western border, rather than an eastern border. A few in the Southwest, assuming they should choose the closest edge, mentioned "somewhere in Mexico" or, specifically, Nogales (either Arizona or Sonora).

A few non-Californians put the edge at the California-Nevada line— that is, west of that is no longer "the West"—but only 4 of the 37 Californians (WHA) did so. The other 33 Californians in the WHA group regarded themselves as inside the West; eight expressly said, "I'm at the edge of the West." Thus, although some (especially among the writers) wanted California declared outside the region, the Californians nearly all dealt themselves in. One wrote that, being in Los Angeles, she was at the edge and the center simultaneously.

Everybody in the WHA living east of the Missouri River regards themselves as outside the West. (This is despite the fact that 34 respondents, from all over, placed the eastern edge at the Mississippi, not the Missouri; but nobody actually living between the Mississippi and Missouri rivers— in Minnesota, Iowa, Missouri, Arkansas, and Louisiana—claimed to be within the West.) On the other hand, respondents from Oklahoma, Texas, Colorado, Wyoming, Montana, and everywhere farther west said they were inside, except one Texan and six Californians.

The states whose respondents split over whether their state was part of the West—and most of them said the boundary was somewhere within their own state—were Kansas, Nebraska, and South Dakota. The Kansans split, five thinking themselves inside, two outside, with three ambiguous. The "outsiders" live in Lawrence and Topeka and said the edge was at Dodge City, or west of Salina and Wichita; two said they were half in, half out (Emporia and the Flint Hills); six said they were inside (they live in Lawrence, Topeka, Manhattan, Wichita, and Dodge City) and would have to go to the Pacific, to Ohio, to St. Louis, or to Micronesia to get to the edge. The respondent from Dodge City, Betty Braddock, who manages a cultural resource center there, wrote that the edge of the West is "In Dodge City—on the 100th meridian."

As for the ten Nebraskans and South Dakotans, all but one placed the edge somewhere within their states. Two wrote "I'm there"; they live in Lincoln. Another Lincolnian said he was right on the edge. Two others (from Lincoln or Omaha) said the edge was 90 or 100 miles west of Omaha; one named Grand Island, another North Platte. The two South Dakotans both named the 100th meridian; one lives on it, the other a bit east and hence declared himself outside. The sole North Dakotan also named the 100th meridian. So, as identified by those closest to it and most conscious of it, the eastern edge of the West consists of the eastern borders of Texas and Oklahoma, and it either continues straight north along the Missouri and Red Rivers or jumps somewhere to a north-south line through the middle of Kansas, Nebraska, and the Dakotas.

The replies to question 2 were more personal, less cerebral, less insistent that the West cannot be identified geographically. Thus, question 2 (rather unintentionally—I sought primarily a personal feeling of when one gets there or gets out of it) served as a validity check on question 1.

A few places received several mentions. St. Louis was often claimed to be the eastern edge, East St. Louis as just outside; others drew lines between Kansas City, Missouri, and Kansas City, Kansas; Omaha and Council Bluffs; and Dallas and Forth Worth (five respondents) in the same way.[11] Kearney and North Platte, Nebraska, and Topeka, Kansas, each got two votes. Five chose Grand Island, Nebraska, and five others Fort Smith, Arkansas.[12]

The more imperialistic (or cosmopolitan) respondents placed the western and northern edges (one vote each) at Kamchatka, Attu Island, Japan, Micronesia, the North Pole, or the Arctic Ocean. The farthest eastward placement of the eastern boundary was western New England.

Does residence or previous experience have much to do with where people put the boundaries? Initially I suspected so but it seems to have minimal influence except in a couple of ways. I had expected that people in, say, New York would say Chicago is West (as people did when I was a child in northern New York) and that people on the plains would consider Chicago and Indiana as East (as my wife's graduate school roommate, a South Dakotan, did). But not many did so. It is true that eastern people picked the Mississippi River or St. Louis more often than did people living in the middle of the country (in Kansas, for example), but so did Californians, looking from the other direction. Haziness about distant geography played some role—Californians were happy with any place from the Missouri River to Ohio, while some easterners think that not much separates the Rockies from the Sierras or the Pacific. That aside, there were few differences that seem based solely on residential experience.

Question 3:
What are the West's characteristics?

This was the most open-ended of the three questions. Question 1 directed the reply toward four compass directions; question 2 asked for specific locations on the "edge" of the West. But question 3 did not limit responses. The result was that many people gave more than one defining characteristic.[13] They fall into two broad categories: geographical definitions such as aridity, scenery, open space, lack of population density, or environment; and cultural definitions such as openness, friendliness, or other attitudes; a common and recent frontier history; or that the West is a myth or state of mind. Clearly, here, as in the replies to the other two questions, historians were more geographically minded; editors and, above all, writers more culturally minded. While 61 percent of the WHA group mentioned cultural definitions, virtually all of the writers did so. The historians often said that a definition of the West depends on *when* one is talking about—the term means nothing without a time frame. The writers often said that the West exists in the past, and in the mind; very few of them seem to think that there is such a thing as a twentieth-century West, while few historians would now wish to conclude western history at 1890 or 1920. Again the separation of historians (seeking verifiable truths) from the writers (seeking to explain, extol, and extend the myth) is very sharp.

Besides the geographical and cultural definitions, a few others appeared. Thirty historians (but only two editors and two writers) found the West distinctive as the place of greatest ethnic and racial mixing, the most varied multicultural region. Seventeen historians (but no editors or writers) found the presence of Indians a distinguishing feature. Twenty-eight historians (only two editors and two writers) noted the unusually extraction-oriented economy, and fourteen cited environmental attitudes and practices (reckless or careful) as western traits. Four historians believe the West is distinctive because slavery never flourished there. Nine historians said that the West cannot be defined; they see no distinguishing features that are not so riddled by exceptions as to make the regional concept useless.

A few replies could not easily be categorized. The West is defined, said one historian, by its lack of a distinct accent; another said it keeps shrinking; another said it is defined only by simple latitude and longitude; another by the use of six- and eight-man high school football teams. Among the writers, one said westerners are distinct because they *do* have a distinct accent; another cited "reading habits" (but didn't say what they are). One of the editors said the West simply has "fewer asses."

It seems clear that the idea of the West solely as place—where it now

is—has some way to go. The majority of WHA members, and larger proportions of western fiction writers and the editors and publishers of newspapers and magazines in the West, do not agree—not yet, anyway—that
the West is limited to the present western half of the country, or that
"frontier" is a dirty word, or that history began in 1850. The "new" and
"old" western histories each claim many adherents. To judge by the results
of this survey, they will be arguing the place-versus-process question for
a long time.

NOTES

1. Outstanding examples are Patricia Nelson Limerick, *The Legacy of Conquest:
The Unbroken Past of the American West* (New York: W. W. Norton. 1987); Patricia
Nelson Limerick, Clyde A. Milner II, and Charles E. Rankin, *Trails: Toward a New Western History* (Lawrence: University Press of Kansas, 1991); Richard White, *'It's Your Mis-
fortune and None of My Own': A New History of the American West* (Norman: University of Oklahoma Press, 1991); and William Cronon, George Miles, and Jay Gitlin, eds.,
Under an Open Sky: Rethinking America's Western Past (New York: W. W. Norton,
1992).

2. Limerick, *Legacy of Conquest,* 26–27.

3. Patricia Nelson Limerick, "Making the Most of Words: Verbal Activity and
Western America," in Cronon, Miles, and Gitlin, eds., *Under an Open Sky: Rethinking
America's Western Past,* 167.

4. Rodney Geaney and Dorothy East of the Social Science Training Laboratory in
the University of Notre Dame counseled me on survey design and carried out mailing
and tabulation of data sheets.

5. Early in 1990 I obtained the WHA mailing list, which consisted of connected
strips of mailing labels arranged by zip codes, beginning with Maine and ending with
Alaska. On each strip were a dozen names. Ignoring institutional members I chose two
or three names from each strip. This method seemed to assure randomness about as well
as any other.

6. The journalists' names are from a standard 1986 reference work giving names,
addresses, circulation, and other data about newspapers and magazines. The age of the
issue seriously reduced the journalists' responses—my fault and not theirs.

7. This response rate, especially the WHA response, is unusually high. In any survey some mailings are undeliverable.

8. Of the WHA group, replies came from 68 percent of 230 males, and 41 percent of 75 females, who were sent questionnaires. I cannot explain the gender difference,
which carried through every occupational and geographic subgroup. Occupationally,
two-thirds were college and university faculty, and the rest were public historians,
writers, and "buffs." Closely reflecting geographic distribution of WHA membership, 58
questionnaires went to Californians, 22 to Texans, 21 to Coloradians, and the rest to
people in all but four states. People who belong to both WHA and WWA received two
questionnaires.

9. The survey responses may be of use to students of regionalism; this report does
not exhaust their contents. I hope to deposit them at a later time in an accessible place,
probably the Huntington Library.

10. By "large" cities I mean here 500,000 and up; "medium" meaning 100,000 to
500,000; "small" meaning under 100,000; "rural" meaning anywhere under 25,000.

11. One specifically named the Dallas-Fort Worth airport, but failed to state which
concourse.

12. I have lived in Topeka and would not call it western, but I would certainly agree
with four respondents who find themselves in the West when they drive about forty

miles west of Topeka into the Flint Hills of Kansas. But some would say the Flint Hills are only a preview. After them, going west, one has to pass through the corn and wheat fields from Abilene to near Hays before finding "the West" again.

13. On average, regardless of group (WHA, journalists, WWA), each respondent gave just under two definitions—some giving only one, others several.

2 THE AMERICAN WEST: FROM FRONTIER TO REGION

Martin Ridge

Is the American West a frontier, or a region? Or both? Do the terms "West," "frontier," and "region" mean different things, or do they overlap so much that they mean different aspects of the same thing? Here the author explains how these terms have developed different meanings since the Wisconsin historian Frederick Jackson Turner first explained "the significance of the frontier in American history" in a famous essay by that name in 1893, when (like others) he thought the frontier period in American history was over. The frontier, Turner wrote, explains why Americans are different, indeed unique. His explanation has been criticized for leaving out Indians, other white and non-white groups, and frontier women, and for leaving unanswered the question of what happened to Americans and their culture after the frontier ended—a rather important question if it was truly what had shaped them.

In the twentieth century, the last frontier became what is now the West. How may we define the West as a region? What makes it different? Its open spaces? Despite them, the fact that it has been the most urban region throughout the twentieth century? That it is home to most Native Americans? That it is ethnically and racially the most diverse region? Or its mountains, desert, and arid climate? The author suggests that it is all of these and more, and that ultimately the West as a region (and former frontier) must be defined culturally.

Do you agree? What principle best organizes the West as a region? What was or is, in American history, a frontier? Are there any left?— editors

WE ARE FAST approaching the centennial of the Bureau of the Census' 1890 declaration of the closing of the frontier. It would seem appropriate to mark that centennial by asking why and how American historians became interested in the history of the American frontier, and why and how, in recent years, there has been increasing attention paid to the West as a region. And why studying the West as a region poses special problems. The history of the frontier and the regional West are not the

same, but there is a significant intellectual overlay that warrants examination.

A little more than a century ago the scholarly discipline of American
history was in its formative stages. The tradition of gifted authors—men
like Francis Parkman, Brooks Adams, Theodore Roosevelt, John Fiske, and
James Ford Rhodes—who wrote romantic narratives, philosophical tracts,
and often partisan political history—was well entrenched. They were separated from the handful of academically trained historians in several ways.
They wrote engrossing books on large subjects that were intended for a
general audience while the professional historians selected arcane subjects and wrote for themselves. More important, the popular writers, even
the very best of them, often overlooked the institutional dynamics of
American society because they tended to focus on dramatic episodes and
personalities; while professionally trained academic historians who studied American history, especially those influenced by the modern German scientific school, embraced a structural approach to their subject—
they were less interested in dramatic events and personalities and more
concerned with seeking the origins of American institutions. The popular
writers often offered explicit interpretations of the past or philosophies of
history; the academic historians, fascinated by the techniques for proving
the validity of the facts, were intrigued with formal, especially legal, documents because they were easily subjected to scientific tests. The academi-
cians boasted that they not only built their work on the "true facts" but
also that they were scientific, dispassionate, and objective in their analyses, albeit many admitted that the final products of their labors were rather
ponderous and dull studies. Nor were the scientific historians immune
from turning to the philosophy of history. Many of them sought general
laws to explain all of the past, and, as Brooks Adams once observed, every
historian's inkstand held a potential theory or universal law of history.

Despite its scholarly strengths, the primary shortcoming of this burgeoning scientific school was not its literary inadequacies, great as some
of them were—people are willing to read a lot of almost deadly stuff if it
is meaningful—or its inability to draft general laws, but its failure to provide an organizing principle with the intellectual power necessary to explain American history. Moreover, almost by consensus, the quest for origins of American institutions was predetermined. Since the major colonies
in North America had been English, the historians searched for the origin
or germs of American institutions deep in the Anglo-Saxon and Germanic
past. The "germ theory," which so strongly stressed the continuity of institutions, minimized change and deemphasized the significance of the
American experience. Almost invariably its American focus was on colonial New England and Virginia or the early national period of the Republic.
Of course, the division between the gifted writers and the scientific professionals was sometimes blurred, as in the case of Henry Adams, but one
point is clear—there was no accepted explanatory hypothesis around

which to organize many important aspects of the American past. For that reason, much American historical scholarship was narrow, parochial, and filiopietistic.

This state of historical development could not persist. American scholars—especially those who were born in the Middle West, the Deep South, or the Far West and those who came of age toward the close of the nineteenth century, when the rise of nationalistic historical writing profoundly influenced many Western European intellectuals from the Black Sea to the North Sea—were dissatisfied when they confronted an American history that denied their own experience as citizens of an emerging world power and democratic nation. Whether of old-line American stock or of new immigrant extraction, they were acutely aware that they matured in a continental rather than a coastal nation. They looked for American historical explanations that turned on an axis of the more recent past—explanations more area specific to their own experience than to the forests of medieval Europe, the fens of England, or even the English colonial plantations. They wanted an American history that spoke to all Americans, that addressed recent problems in the nation's internal development, that explained the process of Americanization which created a nation out of diverse peoples and geographic fragments, and that set forth the meaning or ethos of America in terms equal to those propounded by Europe's national historians.

Such a theory was first offered to the historical profession at an international historical conference held during the Chicago World's Columbian Exposition of 1893 by a young professor from the University of Wisconsin named Frederick Jackson Turner. Turner's conference paper—"The Significance of the Frontier in American History"—suggested that the process and experience of settling the continent was so unique that it profoundly influenced virtually every aspect of national life and character. It was an organizing principle for a history of the United States that addressed the questions of its internal development and escaped both the "germ theory" and the colonial and Atlantic coastal emphasis.

When Turner published his essay on the significance of the frontier, there was a sense of immediacy about his work because parts of the United States had not yet achieved statehood. In fact, Turner fastened on the idea of the importance of the closing of the frontier after the Bureau of the Census reported in 1890 that it was no longer possible, as it had been in the past, to draw an unbroken frontier line on an American census map. This was the beginning of the formal study of the frontier in the United States.

Turner sometimes defined the frontier as the point of contact between civilization and savagery. The experience of white men and women—both native and foreign born—as they seized the opportunity to wrench land from the Indian and exploit it with the active support of the government, or with only a minimum of governmental restraint, highlighted the idea that the contact points of white society and the virtually limitless ex-

2. Frederick Jackson Turner, author of the "frontier thesis," at the bronze doors of the Henry E. Huntington Library, San Marino, California. *Courtesy of the Huntington Library, San Marino, California.*

ploitable natural resources on the edges of, or in advance of, settled areas, offered a wholly new way to look at the American past. This was a history that began on the borders of the colonial world and extended across a continent, looking as much for examples of American exceptionalism as for evidence of historical continuities.

It is important to understand that many of the ideas that Turner expressed about the characteristics of the frontier and its impact—even the word frontier—had been used earlier by scholars and writers so diverse as the political economist William Graham Sumner, the social gospel preacher Josiah Strong, the publicist Edwin L. Godkin, and that moody New England Brahmin, Brooks Adams. Whatever the sources of Turner's thought (and it has been traced to innumerable historical writings, including the Italian political economist Achille Loria), it is Turner's idea of the frontier that is transcendent. It differs significantly from that of any other single individual (for example, read carefully and compare Turner with Brooks Adams), and it emerged eventually as the most evocative explanatory hypothesis for American historians for almost half a century. Turner purported to explain why the United States and its people were unique. Unlike earlier American authors who had expressed similar notions about the character of America, Turner's was a secular doctrine to be demonstrated by inductive research rather than, for example, an act of faith, as was Walt Whitman's expression of the same idea.

Although Turner expressed himself with the imagery of a poet and speculated about the past with the language of a seer, he was at heart a scientific historian who believed in economic and political history. But he also realized that by studying the behavior of masses of the people, as distinct from the actions of the articulate elite, he could explain the larger aspects of American human history as clearly as evolutionary geologists or Darwinian biologists could interpret its natural history. This quest drove him and his followers to seek evidence from a variety of sources—maps, census records, climatic studies, congressional records, diaries, and election data, to name only a few—and to endeavor to draw correlations from among them. They borrowed ideas and models from other social sciences, too. Their methods by today's standards were primitive, but they did yield insights that no one had before suggested; and they pointed up the importance of studying change over time as well as structure if the historian wanted to achieve a deeper understanding of the past.

Even more important than Turner's own research, which was concentrated on the Middle West and the Old Southwest, was the new kind of American historian that followed him and the new type of neopositivistic evolutionary American history they wrote. If, as Turner speculated, for example, American institutions underwent a series of rebirths each time white men and women encountered a new frontier and passed through the stages of social evolution from primitivism to civilization, his ideas required testing in various settings—among miners, farmers, and cattlemen as well as in different physical and climatic areas such as the near-rain forests of the Northwest, the arid regions of Nevada and Utah, or the semi-arid Great Plains. If, for example, eastern and foreign institutions—like churches—were changed when they became part of the steady march of the moving frontier, each must be studied in a new context. And how did immigrants become Americanized, for Turner postulated the idea that the frontier played a significant role in the process. Congressional votes on such issues as the tariff, road construction, land prices, and declarations of war were correlated with the home state and place of birth of each congressman as well as party to see the influence of region on political behavior. Institutions, too, such as the army and the Bureau of Indian Affairs, now warranted a quite different analysis. New fields of historical research, such as agricultural history, were born of frontier study and assumed major importance. Thus, the story of the establishment of even the smallest community, in fact of every human activity on the frontier, became part of a large and significant narrative—the making of the American national character and the formation and function of a democratic society.

Turner's variety of history demanded that American historians write analytical studies of institutions and give them meaning and significance by placing them in the widest national and even international context. He raised the level of the study of the pioneer period of local and regional history—whether in Indiana, Iowa, Texas, California, or the Great Basin—from a parochial or antiquarian exercise to make it part of the national pageant. The legislative and constitutional history of the United States as well as the story of the nation's wars and diplomacy were depicted in terms of their interrelationship with the struggle to acquire and settle western lands. Moreover, neither Turner nor some of his followers hesitated to employ statistical methods.

Although Turner was interested in the broadest implications of the westward movement of masses of people, he often wrote in terms of archetypes and applied them in an evolutionary context. Thus, for him, not only did communities and regions pass through various stages of development until they attained levels of civilization comparable to those of the East or Europe but also his archetypes passed in evolutionary order over the natural landscape. Here was an American history as clear as evolutionary science. "Stand at the Cumberland Gap," he wrote, "and watch the procession of civilization, marching in single file—the buffalo following the trail to the salt springs, the Indian, the fur trader and hunter, the cattle-raiser, the pioneer farmer—and the frontier has passed by. Stand at South Pass in the Rockies a century later and see the same procession with wider intervals between. The unequal rate of advance compels us to distinguish the frontier into the trader's frontier, the rancher's frontier, or the miner's frontier, and the farmer's frontier."

This kind of archetypical generalization opened the way for the mythologizing and romanticizing of the American pioneering experience that captured the imagination of the general public. For example, even after research proved that the evolutionary historical model was flawed—that people of all economic and social groups appeared almost simultaneously in virtually every frontier setting—Turner's evolutionary model remains, larger than life, especially in fiction and the movies. Serious scholarship about western archetypes has never been able to displace the myths and romantic images conjured in the public mind by publicists, even those contemporaries most familiar with the frontier experience. Whether cowboy, investment banker, Indian, homesteader, hunter, farm laborer, soldier, hurdy-gurdy girl, or gambler, they are all fair game for the author of fiction. Nothing, for example, is further from the truth than the depiction of the American farmer as a sort of virtuous yeoman living happily in nature's garden, gathering her fruits in a life devoid of the stresses and constraints of the urban world and the market economy. Farmers were the linchpin of the Turner evolutionary scheme because they were the last frontier stage, but they enjoyed anything but the generous bounty of nature's garden: they were re-makers of the natural landscape who struggled to overcome the hardships of the configuration of the land as well as the uncertainties of the weather and the economy. They were in reality anything but autonomous and independent.

Romantic myths aside, the study of frontier periods in American history proved immensely popular among serious historians from the outset and has continued to be so, not only because it is a convenient and informed way to look at how a laissez-faire society exploited an underdeveloped country in the nineteenth century but also because so many historians lived in regions of the country which had, within the memory of living man, recently emerged from, or were still part of, such a society. Therefore, they could write the history of their own communities or regions. It was no longer necessary to travel to a distant archive to write about an important subject.

But even more germane, for a later generation of regional historians, whether in New Mexico, Utah, or California, the frontier paradigm called for the study of the interrelationship of local and national institutions over time, for comparative analysis, and for a plethora of demographic work that could be correlated to a host of other variables. It challenged historians to avoid simplistic chronological political narratives and narrow institutional studies, and to substitute, at least at the outset, geographic, cultural, and economic contexts in which to write. It called for measurement of the extent of universality over particularity as an area emerged from partial to complete integration within the national economy and social culture.

By no means have all of the questions raised by the study of the frontier been exhausted. The analysis of the internal migration of peoples and institutions within the United States continues to attract serious attention, albeit historians may be more interested in social institutions, such as the family or the family farm. All kinds of issues, including religion, urbanization, native peoples, the environment, and politics, are still far from settled.

The idea of the frontier, however, has achieved so celebrated a status in American society that the very word frontier in itself has become a metaphor, encompassing public feeling about both the national character and the national past. As a metaphor frontier has come to describe a people whose national character was formed in an environment of economic opportunity based on vast areas of readily available underdeveloped land, rich mineral resources, individualism, pragmatism, political democracy, equality, an unrestrained society, courage, wastefulness of natural resources, geographic migration and rapid social mobility, personal and communal regeneration, personal violence, and vigilantism as well as a host of other factors, especially the greatest personal liberty.

Even Europeans accept the metaphor and see Americans in this way, accustomed as they are, and we are not, to believing that individuals demonstrate national character traits. In addition, so far as Europeans and we ourselves employ the word regarding the nation's past, the metaphor also includes the near genocide of the Indians, the repression of racial and ethnic minorities, the intimidation of, or wars on, neighboring nations in the name of manifest destiny, the opening of virgin lands, and the ruthless, if not mindless, assault on the natural environment for personal gain without consideration of the consequences for future generations.

Metaphors, assert anthropologists, have a way of becoming self-fulfilling prophecies. This is certainly true of the frontier for both the American people and their leaders. From Thomas Jefferson to Ronald Reagan, presidents have not only spoken of the nation in terms of frontier values but also of national and personal traits of citizens in the same way. Franklin Delano Roosevelt, for example, acknowledged the existence of this tradition and urged its abandonment in a 1935 radio address advocating the need for governmental planning. "Today," he declared, "we can no longer escape into virgin territory: we must master our environment. . . . We have been compelled by stark necessity [of the depression] to unlearn the too uncomfortable superstition that the American soil was mystically blessed with every kind of immunity to grave economic maladjustments, and that the American spirit of individualism—all alone and unhelped by the co-operative efforts of government—could withstand and repel every form of economic disarrangement or crisis."

The more traditional example of the metaphor's self-fulfilling quality—always evident among frontier politicians—is the so-called Sage Brush Rebellion, which recently swept the Rocky Mountain and high country states. When the 1973 oil shortage held out the promise for the rapid exploitation of coal and shale oil, western political and economic conservatives, who have long sought control over ranch lands, demanded that the federal government release into the hands of western states control over petroleum resources so they could be developed without current federal environmental and other governmental restraints. The power of the frontier as a metaphor is such that it compels continued serious study of the actual past lest the metaphorical interpretation overwhelm or distort reality.

Regardless of its current power as a metaphor, and attractive and valuable as the idea of the frontier was during the first quarter of the twentieth century for historians who were studying both the frontier and the history of the United States, it had many limitations. The most important limitation on the frontier as an organizing principle is that it offered little or no guidance for understanding the internal history of the United States in the post-frontier period or the twentieth-century West. In fact, scholars were quick to realize that, by accepting the passing of the frontier line in 1890 as a paradigm, they really defined much of post-frontier trans-Mississippi and twentieth-century West as a separate historical problem that was not directly part of their basic organizing principle. This did not, however, affect historians who tried to organize the frontier in the context of the Hispanic advance into the West.

What had struck Turner and his colleagues, however, as extremely significant as they studied the advance of the frontier was little more than a Bureau of the Census statistical curiosity. The idea of the frontier is still important as an organizing principle for studying the internal history of the United States in the nineteenth century, but the passing of the frontier, in the context of the Bureau of Census map, has a quite different meaning than Turner and his immediate disciples attached to it. There is no doubt that it was a national historical, psychological, and demographic watershed, and the fact that it occurred on the eve of the greatest depression the nation had yet known certainly appeared to enhance its importance.

This was especially so because many intellectuals of Turner's generation associated landed proprietorship with personal political independence. But it never represented a genuine discontinuity. All problems and opportunities that existed in the areas of sparse settlement of the western United States before 1890 existed after 1890 as well. The rise of Populism, for example, more closely correlates with national demographic trends and the world economy than with the disappearance of the frontier line. And the vast amounts of land alienated under the Homestead Law did not diminish after 1890.

Turner wondered what would nurture a democratic society when the free or cheap arable lands in the nation were all taken up. The idea, deeply rooted in the seventeenth-century republican concept, that personal political freedom and independence were inseparable from landed proprietorship, was of greater importance to Turner and his critics than to historians of the frontier or scholars interested in the post-frontier and twentieth-century West. It became part of an argument about the heritage or legacy of the frontier that interested primarily intellectual historians and students of American nationality and national character.

The material and social consequences of the frontier experience loomed far larger for most regional historians. From the point of view of studying parts of the country where frontier conditions no longer existed, Turner's initial questions, archetypes, and typologies were of limited value, since they pertained to periods only before or during settlement. Oddly enough, Turner himself stumbled early on the same basic problem. To understand the role of frontier political and economic issues in national affairs, he decided to analyze the development of the American states during the years 1830 to 1850. These were years when frontier conditions gradually ceased to exist in the Middle West and the South. He required a new principle of historical organization, and he found it in what he called sectionalism. He divided the nation into several parts, which he called sections: Northeast, Southeast, Old Northwest, and Old Southwest—the latter two were in the process of transition from frontier to settled areas during those two decades.

For scholarly purposes Turner was compelled to define his sections when he began to analyze their institutions over time. His definitions, partly based on physical geography, partly on a variety of socio-economic factors, centered primarily on how the people in each area responded to a set of political and economic variables. Sectional interests, he came to believe, would eventually become so strong that American public policy would demonstrate sectional compromises on national issues. The Congress, he felt, would be a brokering agency for competing geographical entities. Since Turner was interested in the expansion of political democracy and economic equality, his initial concern was how the sections interacted to create an increasingly egalitarian national policy. Terminology aside, geographers recognized Turner's sections were socio-physiographic provinces or regions.

As a scientific and Progressive historian for whom American history was a study of the growth of freedom and equality through conflict and resolution, Turner looked to institutions within regions that addressed those questions—mostly but not entirely political parties. Thus, Turner explained his interest in sections as a natural outgrowth of studying the frontier. In fact, there is a very charming exchange of letters in the Huntington Library between Turner and his brilliant student, Carl Becker—a leading scholar of the eighteenth century who taught at Cornell University and who chided Turner for abandoning frontier studies to look at sectionalism—in which Turner explains that the frontier cannot be studied except by various forms of regional analyses and that the post-frontier period must be part of this work if historians are to understand critical relationships.

Historians of the trans-Mississippi West as a region confronted a similar problem because virtually all of their history is that of a modernizing society in the post-frontier era. Like the generation to which Turner belonged, they wanted an American history that addressed their concerns and was area specific rather than vaguely national. They pointed out that the post-frontier internal history of the United States deserved as much attention today as the frontier warranted a century ago. They realized that, except for the South, with its legacy of slavery, the modernization of America has not meant its homogenization. One should never confuse the existence of trans-local or inter-regional institutions, they insisted, with the absence of local and regional differences.

There is a distinct regional history of the United States, and it is seldom masked by national organizations and institutions. Anyone familiar with American folk music, folklore, language, material culture, religious customs, food, marketing, governmental planning, census study, or ethnic and racial identity will readily attest to regional differences. These regional distinctions have been in the making since the years of early settlement and the heavy in-migration of diverse peoples into physically different geographic settings. In fact, the United States is virtually a blanket of regional divisions, even if one ignores the way governmental agencies have carved it up.

Most scholars of the West as a region, except for being interdisciplinary, are little like the early followers of Turner. They do not assert that any specific regional history is in itself a valid organizing principle for understanding the whole of twentieth-century American history. They are far less likely to be seen as geographic or economic determinists. Nor would they assert that our national character or democratic institutions hinge on the political or economic nature of the region. But they do point out that the post-frontier development of the eleven western states—the area stretching from Texas and the High Plains to the Pacific Ocean—affords a unit for study that covers almost a century in time and that this unit, because of its size and complexity, is unique.

They have as good or better a case than scholars of other regions because of the West's nature and rate of change. The nation has seen an accelerated westward tilt in population distribution since 1900. Because of the nature of its industry and agriculture, the West, throughout the past century, has been the most urbanized portion of the country. More new large cities have grown up in the West than anywhere else. It is hard for people in the Midwest and East to believe that places named San Jose, Phoenix, Dallas, Houston, Los Angeles, and San Diego are listed among the ten largest cities in the nation.

The West contains the area with the largest amount of federally owned land. Today, most of the American Indian population lives in the West. The West is also the region that has spawned the environmental movement perhaps because westerners were among the first to recognize the fragility of ecosystems. Some portions of western states are the most water deficient in the nation; others are surfeited.

The West in the last half century has been the portal for a whole new immigrant population, and there has been an obvious social impact. Under the current state law requiring bilingual education, for example, the City of Los Angeles must provide teachers in eighty languages and dialects— only one of which, Spanish, is a major European tongue. Los Angeles' multicultural character is a microcosm of what has happened from San Antonio to Seattle, and makes what historians once called the new immigration—people from Southern and Eastern Europe—pale by comparison. American Roman Catholicism may soon find its basis in western rather than eastern population centers. Los Angeles is already the largest diocese in the nation.

Meanwhile, because of changes in technology, mining, resource depletion, erosion, and new industries, the population in some western states has plummeted, while in others it has soared, gaining more rapidly than ever in the past. Los Angeles County's population, for example, has increased by more than eight hundred thousand people since the 1980 census. And because all of this is so recent, a scholar has available the best records and data for studying the structure, persistence, and change of political, economic, and social institutions—from criminal justice to family structure. It also allows for a renewed look at the complex relationships that exist between the West and the nation's political and financial centers in the East.

All of this sounds like a bonanza for a new group of regionalists or the less traditional scholars of the Turner school, who have moved to incorporate the regional history of the post-frontier West into their research. But the study of the regional West is a field with significant pitfalls. Perhaps the most obvious is also the most critical—how to define the West and around what principle can it be organized for study. This has proven far from an easy task.

The complexity of the issue was recognized years ago by the followers of Herbert Eugene Bolton—the leader in the study of Latin American

Borderlands—who conceived of the history of the trans-Mississippi West within the context of Spanish expansion and then attempted to continue it in terms of Anglo-American penetration, state-making, and economic development. So long as the Boltonians worked on the Southwest and the Pacific Rim prior to the American war on Mexico their scheme had viability, but when they moved forward chronologically into the American period, the result was a disjointed narrative and an analysis without a thesis. Bolton hinted at the idea of a spiritual dissension between the Spanish Borderlands and the areas where Spain had not conquered, but this insight was never fully examined. Oddly enough, militant Chicano intellectuals in the 1960s took it up in the battle cry Aztlan—by which they meant the lands of the bronze people or where the Spanish had settled—which is essentially a Boltonian Borderlands concept. They want to reclaim the Southwest from the English-speaking population whom they see as foreign oppressors. This idea, however dramatic, has never spread widely even within the Hispanic community.

At present there are a host of competing approaches to the study of the West as a region, some quite simplistic, others very sophisticated. One of the most popular is the assertion that the West is a desert, and what exists there is an oasis culture. The difficulty with the oasis theory is that it does not fit the whole West, parts of which are well watered. The most imaginative presentation of this organizing principle remains Walter Prescott Webb's magisterial *The Great Plains*, which attempts to correlate western culture exclusively with water. Although much that Webb said was true, the theory was highly vulnerable. As one sharp, but facetious, critic of this idea once observed: "If the shortage of water is the key to understanding western culture, why is the total immersion Baptist church so strong in Texas?"

Actually, scholars who think exclusively of water often fall into the trap of viewing the West from the perspective that defines the norm as the amount of water necessary for the production of corn. Certainly the location, amount, and distribution of water remain significant factors in western life and culture, but water cannot be the single organizing principle, unless one is concerned with its quality.

An equally popular thesis regarding the West is that it is a province exploited by eastern interests within a capitalist system. This idea is associated with a theory of internal colonialism. This is a neo-Turnerian concept stemming from the economic conflicts between frontier people and the metropolitan centers on which they were often dependant. Today, it is freighted with an ethnic and racial component that sees non-whites as the laboring class within an exploitative system. Although intriguing as a hypothesis, it often breaks down into an argument not over whether there should be exploitation of the West but who should exploit it, and how, and for whose benefit. It is the familiar story of the world we lost—a make-believe time and place in the past when local communities presumably controlled their own resources and developed them for the common good. This is an angry history because it emphasizes the misuse of resources and the struggle for the recapture of the control of the West by groups that feel alienated from the system. It is a history where ideology is too often substituted for evidence. Much more useful are suggestions that environmental factors and cultural patterns can be correlated to provide unique insight. Such work allows for the incorporation of a variety of significant variables that have influenced life in the West but do not fit into the simple oasis context or the exploitative developmental model. It also affords an opportunity to study space, social structure, and change over time. Cultural geographers have pioneered this approach. This approach tends to break the West down into smaller, more coherent, and more manageable units of study. This is the kind of study that D. W. Meinig has done so well. It also provides the basis for comparative work.

Another organizing principle emphasizes modernization, and may call for the study of institutions and organizations with or without regard to the environment but highly sensitive to larger and often technological changes in society as a whole. The primary stress is on the gradual integration of regional organizations or institutions into their national counterpart, and how an institution or organization functions during periods of transformation. The simplest example of this is the impact of containerization on transportation, which was developed by the Southern Pacific Railway and has now become part of the nation's railroad systems.

These examples are merely illustrative of the dynamic character of the field. Paradigms based on the environment, demographic analysis, and even politics could also be mentioned. Historians, geographers, and sociologists have offered a spate of constructs with which to study the West and about which they still debate. There is no clear consensus among them. In fact, today there is almost as much chaos among historians in quest of a synthesis as there was when Turner wrote. And if every historian lacks Brooks Adams' inkstand holding a potential theory of historical explanation, he or she has a computer with comparable capabilities.

I am an intolerant pluralist so far as an interpretative basis of the twentieth-century West is concerned. I want every hypothesis given a fair hearing. I am willing to listen attentively to anyone who suggests how we can better recognize, interpret, and study what the westerners themselves have defined as the region.

It is ironic, at least to me, that the boundaries of the West seem best defined not by academics studying it but by the people who live there. A delineation exists in the minds of women and men, and it is strangely physiographic. There is a location on the plains of the West where, for some undetermined reason, people think of themselves as being westerners and not middle westerners or southerners. It would be convenient if it were at the one-hundredth meridian—the so-called line of semi-aridity—but it is not. There is a psychological and not a physiographic fault line that separates regions. As these people see it, they are not from the South but from the Southwest; not from the Middle West but from the West; not from the prairies but from the High Plains; and they think of St. Louis, not Denver, as being in the East. They may or may not be part of the nation's middle-class dominant cultural group, but they do have a sense of identity, which is regionally specific and even evokes a kind of pride and loyalty. The West retains a sense of particularity despite the enormous power of the forces working to create a universal national culture.

This prompts me to suggest—but not insist upon—my own organizing principle. Since I have come to the study of the West from the Turnerian tradition—with an interest in national character and American exceptionalism—it is the sense of identity—the western ethos—that intrigues me and that I employ in defining the West. Unlike the nation, the West does not have a shared purpose, but it does have the advantages of shared special experiences. The West is a cultural phenomenon. It involves, "all the things that a group of people inhabiting a common geographical area do, the way they do things . . . and their values and symbols." And this culture serves a profoundly conservative function. This gives the post-frontier West some of the metaphoric power of the term frontier but opens the way for the broadest basis of analysis. The cultural West permits, as well as subsumes within it, almost any approach to the subject. This is evident in historical work so diverse as the changing attitudes of western women toward the cult of domesticity when their labor was no longer needed in the field or on the range on the one hand and the social basis for the California State Supreme Court's significant modifications of tort law on the other. Webb found it in the mentalité of the man with a six-gun. I confess that as an organizing principle culture may say virtually everything and yet nothing. But it does urge the thesis that there is a culturally defined public entity with geographic boundaries that is part of the larger national whole to which it contributes and with which it interacts in a significant fashion.

How do you write this kind of history? Frederick Jackson Turner each year asked his seminar students to write two papers—the first on a narrow frontier subject and the second on why it was important in the nation's history. His theory is valid today: there is no western history without a national context. We no longer need two essays, but we must always keep in mind the two ideas. Any other kind of writing will doom the field to a parochialism from which it was rescued a century ago.

Turner made the history of the frontier so vital a part of American history that it virtually became our national narrative. After Turner there was a rise of other perspectives that gave the study of American history its depth and richness. The frontier became a sub-field within the history of the nation. But it also provided the basis for a western regional history to explain the internal history of a large portion of the nation in the post-frontier period. Unlike the study of the frontier, which offers both an explanation of national character and the internal history of early settlement, the study of the regional West is in a more fluid state with no consensus as yet regarding its boundaries or means to organize material within them. A cultural basis not only for fixing boundaries of the West but also for giving it meaning and significance may well prove to be that organizing principle.

3 FRONTIERS AND EMPIRES IN THE LATE NINETEENTH CENTURY

Walter Nugent

During the late nineteenth and early twentieth centuries, steam-powered ships and railroads made the movement of people and goods (and armaments) into remote regions much more feasible. Europeans settled some of these regions, and simply brought others under European political and military control. Were the underlying motivations of settlement and control much different? In both situations, people of European stock took over places that had been home to native-stock people. Settlement of frontiers displaced "Indians" in the United States, Canada, Brazil, and Argentina, Maoris in New Zealand, aborigines in Australia, and (less successfully) Bantu peoples in southern Africa. Empire-building put European or American governments in control of India, Indochina, parts of the coast of China, many Pacific islands, and much of Africa. Today, a century later, the European empires have virtually disappeared (Hong Kong's restoration to China in 1997 is the last major example), while the frontiers of that time remain firmly European-stock. Why did empires disappear, but frontiers last?

The essay also distinguishes "type I" and "type II" frontiers in the American West (and the distinction applies elsewhere too). What were these differences and in what ways were they significant? Which of these types of frontiers more closely resembled empire-building?—editors

IN THE LATE nineteenth century, Europeans and their colonial descendants around the world pushed into new regions on a scale they had never before managed, and with an assuredness they would never again possess after 1914. Sometimes they expanded into frontiers, and sometimes into empires. The purpose of this essay is to suggest ways in which frontier-building and empire-building were similar, and ways in which they were different.[1]

Europeans began sailing around southern Africa to South and East Asia, and westward to the Americas, just before 1500. They established the Spanish and Portuguese seaborne empires in the sixteenth century, and the French, Dutch, and English in the seventeenth. The eighteenth century became, from the European standpoint, a "second age of discov-

ery" with the exploration of the Pacific. There were new varieties of European expansion: demographic, with the rise of population in modern Britain, Europe, and North America; economic, with the beginning of industrialization; political, with the independence of the United States in 1776
and of Latin America during and just after the Napoleonic Wars (1810–
1822); and diplomatic-imperial, in the form of contacts and conquests involving North Africa and the Middle East, China (1839–1842), and Japan
(1853). Up to this point the "rise of the West" or "expansion of Europe"
is a familiar story. It principally involved political or military elites. But
during the nineteenth century, Europe's population began to move across
borders and even across the Atlantic. The population of the United States,
without much help from Europe and without significant Malthusian
checks, multiplied by one-third every decade up to 1860. The arrival of
steam-powered industry and transportation in the third quarter of the
century transformed European expansiveness into a mass movement. Ad-
vances in technology also created a North Atlantic nexus of political and
economic energy that drove much of the world until 1914, and in some
places until after 1945. In the four hundred years since Vasco da Gama
and Columbus, Europe's expansive power and self-confidence were never
greater than in the forty-odd years before 1914, and in the 1880s it was
probably greatest of all.

The thesis here is that in the 1870–1914 period, the frontier impulse
and the imperial impulse were related in source and performance; that
frontiers may be distinguished and a typology of frontiers developed; and
that empire-building (imperialism), in context, appears to be a special type
of frontier. The key to the typology, though not its only ingredient, is demography. Demographic stability, or the lack of it, provided firmness or
transiency for frontiers and empires. In general, empires proved transient
and frontiers evolved into permanent societies.

A few more words, however, should be said about why the late nineteenth century—especially the 1880s—was special. Why might Europeans
and Americans of that time have thought their achievements unique and
their ballooning self-confidence justified? In the 1880s several factors—
economic, technological, cultural-nationalistic, and political—converged
to produce an exuberant proliferation of expansionist episodes. The
slightly longer period of 1873 to 1896 was once regarded, especially in Britain, as a "Great Depression," largely because British growth lost ground
compared to earlier Victorian times and because the long-term trend in
money supply was deflationary. But "Great Depression" does not fit the
larger transatlantic context.[2] Even a neoclassical historical economist who
retains the term and rightly points to the severity of the 1873–1878 and
1893–1897 depressions in the United States properly calls the 1880s "a
decade of buoyant growth" in the United States as well as Britain.[3] From
the economic standpoint, in fact, expansion lasted in the United States
from the recovery in late 1878 until the panic of mid-1893, and in Britain,
France, and Germany from late 1879 to 1891. Industrial production rose

20 to 25 percent in France and Britain in those years, and about 50 percent in Germany.[4] This robust material climate was a necessary part of the expansionism of the period.

Economic growth and technological innovation were legion during the 1880s. Steel output doubled in France, tripled in Britain, and quintupled in Germany and the United States.[5] Not so different in population size at that time, Germany and the United States led Europe and the Americas in demographic and industrial expansion. The basic railway networks of Europe and North America were mostly in place by the early 1890s. In the 1880s alone, four new transcontinental lines were added to the Union Pacific/Central Pacific line of 1869, while John A. Macdonald's National Policy bore fruit (if often bitter for early prairie farmers) in the completion of the Canadian Pacific in 1885. Elsewhere, the trans-Siberian railroad began in 1891, while other railroad-building, less dramatic than those immense efforts yet critical for their regions, flung lines across the Argentine pampas and the São Paulo plateau, as well as throughout eastern Germany, divided Poland, Austria-Hungary, and Romania.

Sudden, effective improvements in public health and sanitation lowered mortality and disease rates after 1880, dramatically in European and American cities.[6] Public authorities and physicians began to accept the germ theory and the grim costs of bad sanitation. The *Scientific American* advised its readers that "of the cases of disease now current in civilized communities, about *one-third* could have been prevented by intelligent sanitation, personal or general." Microorganisms were everywhere, people learned.[7] Sanitation regulations also improved the safety of migrant embarkation and debarkation ports such as Hamburg, New York, Santos, and Buenos Aires, as well as the steamships cruising between them.

The period saw not only great economic and technological change but also an unprecedented churning of people. Eight million Europeans migrated between 1880 and 1890 alone, across provincial and national boundaries within Europe and among New World countries. They used the newly-built networks of railroads within Europe, steamships to cross the Atlantic, and railroads again to travel to inland cities, coffee plantations, mines, or wheatfields.[8] Millions ventured out of Hamburg, Bremen, Antwerp, Naples, Trieste, and Odessa, to North and South America—and, often, back again. As late as the 1920s, Ukrainians and other East Europeans completed the settlement of the Canadian prairie frontier. They also ended a farm-seeking migration process that, in its basic shape, began around 1720 when Germans from the Rheinpfalz and Scots-Irish from Ulster started migrating to farmsteads in eastern Pennsylvania and northern Virginia. In the early nineteenth century Germans and Italians similarly colonized Brazil's Rio Grande do Sul. From about 1850 through the 1880s British, German, and Scandinavian farm families peopled the upper Mississippi Valley and Great Plains while other Europeans migrated to newly available farmland in New Zealand, Australia, and South Africa. In this traditional transatlantic migration, a family traded in, so to speak,

3. Gregory's Farm, Modbury, South Australia, 1906: an antipodal settlement frontier. *The Mortlock Library of South Australiana, State Library of South Australia; SSL:B24-304.*

4. Frontier farm village in Alberta, Canada, about 1905. *Glenbow Archives, Calgary, Canada; #NA-1709-4.*

5. Nucleo Bandeirante, a settlement village in central
Brazil, not far from Brasilia, 1958. *Arquivo Publico do
Distrito Federal [Public Archive of the Federal District],
Brasilia, Brazil; photo by Mario Fontenelle; nov.d 04.04
B.01, ficha 0131.*

a small, no longer competitive farm in northern Europe for a larger, efficient, potentially productive one in the United States, Canada, or southern Brazil. Repatriation was uncommon in this farmseeking, family migration.

Increasingly after 1880, however, transatlantic steamships carried temporary migrants, sometimes called "golondrinas" or "birds of passage." Most
of them were young men seeking marginal wage advantage somewhere
in the Americas, putting aside or sending home cash, returning to Europe
after a season or two, and migrating again when opportunity appeared.
Labor-seeking, temporary migration within Europe, was an old practice;
examples can be found in the seventeenth century or even earlier without stretching definitions of "labor-seeking" too far. With steam-powered
transportation in place, the range of opportunities expanded from trans-
Alpine or trans-Elbian to transatlantic, creating a migrant labor pool involving hundreds of thousands of persons every year, traveling thousands
instead of hundreds of miles, out of Europe, mainly to Canada, the United
States, Brazil, and Argentina, and often back again.

Nearly two and one-half times as many people left Europe in the 1880s
than in the 1870s. After a dip in the 1890s the number of migrants reached

11.4 million from 1901 to 1910, the all-time high for one decade.[9] The new element in the 1880s was the labor-seeking, temporary migration, adding to the continuing farm-family migration. Most of the 800,000 people who went to Argentina in the 1880s were labor-seekers, and so, with certain differences, were the 500,000 who went to Brazil, the 900,000 who went to Canada, and the nearly 5,000,000 who went to the United States—the destination of half to two-thirds of all European emigrants throughout the whole period of mass emigration from the 1840s to World War I. Borders were more open than they were before or later, government policies generally encouraged migration rather than restricted it, and the means of travel were safer and more accessible. The Atlantic became a two-way boulevard, and the demographic character of both Europe and the Americas changed irrevocably.

So did their frontiers, the lands within the New World countries previously unoccupied by people of European stock. Elsewhere in the world, the migration of European population could also mean farm settlement or wage-seeking, as it did in Australia and New Zealand. It could also represent empire-building. The availability of "free" land in the United States and Canada (both with attractive homestead policies), the tenant contracts on the Argentine pampas and São Paulo's coffee plantations (both areas opening to development and settlement at about the same rate as the North American Great Plains), as well as the wages to be earned in factories and mines in the United States and elsewhere, attracted Europeans irresistibly to the New World's many frontiers. The newly founded African and Asian colonies of the Great Powers were far less enticing. Unless one counts Canada and Australia, or North Africa, as sites of empire—and they were very different from Rhodesia or India, Indochina or the Philippines—it becomes clear that empire-building was not in the same demographic class with frontier-settling or labor-seeking migration.

An important similarity between frontiers and empires lies in the fact that no "new" (to Europeans) region was truly empty. No region of the world, tropical or temperate, to which people of European stock migrated in the 1870–1914 period, lacked indigenous people. The permanence or transience of the European approach depended greatly on what those indigenous people were like and how successfully they could resist or absorb the Europeans. Some of the indigenes were weak militarily, loosely organized socially, or technologically simple. Others were strong, old, highly developed civilizations that did not share the European and European American's sense of racial superiority toward them. Some indigenes lived in areas recognized in international law to be within the limits of sovereign territory of the European-stock nation, as was true of Native Americans from Patagonia to the Arctic, or aboriginal Australians. Others lived in places sometimes far distant from the intruding European-stock nation, as was the case with Africans or Indians. Frontiers, in other words, were within territorial boundaries; empires were outside them. This difference bore consequences, to be sure, but it should not obscure the fact that both were targets of European-stock migration.

In the frontier group were the largest of the New World nations, territorially and in population (except Mexico): Canada, the United States, Brazil, and Argentina.[10] All four confronted relatively weak native peoples and, therefore, contained extensive "free" lands within their own borders. The second group included the most powerful European states: Germany, France, and Britain. Creating or adding to far-flung empires, they superimposed themselves upon peoples and civilizations older than their own, as in South and East Asia, or at least radically different from theirs, as in Africa and Oceania. The frontierspeople and the empire-builders—all Europeans or European Americans sharing the same transatlantic economy, technology, and migration pool, all migrants, all in some way expanders—differed less in who they themselves were than in whom they met.[11]

Between the New World frontier societies and the Old World empire-builders, and within each group, national peculiarities strongly nuanced the expansionist drive. In the case of the four Euro-American countries, the task was to colonize the interior: the Great Plains of Canada and the United States, the potentially coffee-bearing plateau of São Paulo state and adjacent areas, and the pampas of central and northern Argentina. The three European imperial powers, on the other hand, thrust into the African interior from all points of the compass, into Indonesia and other Pacific islands, into Malaysia and Indochina, and to the limited degree possible, into the Chinese empire.

Sometimes the Europeans made permanent inroads, sometimes not. In places where political control was already consolidated in western-style, formally liberal political systems, the frontier area was assimilated in every functional way. Familiar cases are the United States and Canada: Despite lingering western-state or prairie–province resentment toward Washington or Ottawa, no one could possibly argue that today the American and Canadian Wests are anything but secure parts of those countries. But in places where political control was newly imposed from Europe, and kept in place by an authority more military than moral and more physical than cultural, such control seldom survived long after 1945. In the German case (though for intra-European, not intrinsically colonial reasons) it endured only until 1918.

These different results can be explained by differences in culture, technology, and military strength, or in other ways. I would like to point out demographic considerations (among them the relative sizes of the indigenous populations) that, together with social and cultural factors, help explain their success or failure vis-à-vis the Europeans. In North America, native peoples offered fierce but sporadic and ineffective resistance. The Comanche and Apache of Texas and the desert Southwest brought the Spanish to a stalemate for two centuries on the thinly populated northern border of New Spain, but gave way to the overwhelming mass of incoming Anglo-Americans in the 1870s and 1880s.[12] A high cultural level was of no help. The civilized tribes of the southeastern United States were removed with ease (not to themselves) in the 1830s to a place hundreds of miles westward. In Brazil, the indigenes consisted chiefly of jungle peoples, pushed out of the central plateaus in the eighteenth century.[13] In Argentina, the army drove the Araucanians off the pampas and largely exterminated them in the "Conquest of the Desert" ending in 1880, in an effort "even more effective than the Indian wars of the [U.S.] Mid-west."[14] Several writers have pointed out that European-stock frontierspeople defeated the Sioux, the Araucanians, and the Zulu, all in or about 1879, and the *mètis* and their Indian allies in western Canada in 1885.[15] No conveniently coincidental date marks native–white contact in Australia and New Zealand, because the Europeans had already taken over.[16]

The native peoples of the Western Hemisphere, though at times formidable, did not present to Europeans the intractable resistance of the Hindi, the Annamese, the Thai, or the Javanese. Nor were Zulu, Abyssinians, or Sudanese easy marks. Thus, in the Western Hemisphere, the willingness of the United States and Canadian peoples to settle and not simply exploit their hinterlands and the relative powerlessness of the native peoples to prevent it, meant firm and permanent control over the frontier. Their control was inhibited only by lack of caution in dealing with unfamiliar and delicate environments such as the High Plains and Great Basin of the United States or the northern prairies of Canada. In late-nineteenth-century Brazil, the unoccupied area was so utterly vast that even the headlong thrusts of coffee culture three hundred to five hundred miles inland got the Europeans less than halfway to the Andes. Fortunately for Brazil, no powerful enemy with expansionist designs lurked on the Pacific coast, threatening to cross the mountains into the Brazilian Far West. (None threatened the United States either.) The New World frontier countries did not compete with each other, having enough to do within their own boundaries.

In Africa, however, competition among the European powers weakened the grip of all of them, though they did not seem weak to the native peoples. Occasionally the European transplant took root, at least for a time, as was the case with the Danish coffee farmer (and writer) Isak Dinesen in Kenya.[17] The French in West Africa mingled well enough to leave more than just a residue of language, culture, and even genes, more than did the British. But then the French enjoyed much better relations with native peoples in North America in the seventeenth and eighteenth centuries than the British did, and they got along better than the British did in nineteenth-century Africa too. Since 1945, however, the European presence everywhere in Africa, though often dogged, has been retreating. The sole remaining European-stock regime, South Africa, holds itself in control of a large indigenous majority by force, so far preventing a takeover by native peoples, such as happened in Zimbabwe in 1979.[18]

Frontiers differed from each other, not just geographically, but demographically and culturally. Within the United States, many frontiers appeared and disappeared over time and space. They have been classified in various ways. One simple typology, resting on gross demographic contrasts, separates frontiers within the United States. It may also assist in comparing them with frontiers in other New World countries and with empire-building in Africa and Asia. This typology includes two categories, which may be labeled, neutrally, I and II. Type I consists of farming frontiers. They appeared in the Virginia Piedmont and western New England early in the eighteenth century. They kept reappearing across the Appalachians, the Mississippi, and the Missouri, until all the land that was truly cheap and arable had been occupied on the High Plains and the Canadian prairies early in the twentieth century. The people of the farming frontiers were the colorless many. Type II includes mining camps and cattle towns, as far back as the tobacco plantations of the seventeenth-century Chesapeake, before its population became self-sustaining. Its people were the colorful few: cowboys, forty-niners, prostitutes, gunfighters, and mountain men. They were transients on the make, most of them male. Type I frontiers included women and children; Type II frontiers rarely did. The myths and symbols of frontiers and the West in American culture derive largely from events that happened on Type II frontiers. Farm frontiers-people were too busy trying to raise families and eke out a living to become legendary. Yet the settlement of the interior of the United States (and Ontario and western Canada), i.e. the transformation of millions of acres from wilderness to farmland, resulted from the Type I frontier repeating itself for several generations in new settings. The major differences are as follows:

Type I	Type II
farming, farm-building	mining, cattle, other extraction
families, usually nuclear	individuals
balanced sex distribution	80% to 90% (or more) male
many children	absence of children
a few over 45	almost none over 45
high birth rate	low birth rate
relatively permanent	transient
peaceful	violent
colonizing	imperialist, exploitative

The Overland Trail illustrates both types. In the 1840s and 1850s, over three hundred thousand people trekked from settled areas and closing frontiers east of the Mississippi to points on the Missouri River, at or beyond the edge of farm settlement, and followed the Overland Trail across future Nebraska and Wyoming toward destinations to the west. Until the late 1840s, virtually all overlanders headed for Oregon's Willamette Valley. But beginning in 1847, Mormons followed the trail for much of its length until crossing the continental divide. Then, instead of proceeding north-westward toward Oregon, they turned southwest until they reached the land between the Great Salt Lake and the western slope of the Wasatch Range. A third group of overlanders, quite distinct from either the Oregon settlers or the Mormons, and much larger than either, followed the trail in the four summers from 1849 through 1852, passing through Mormon country and on west to the Sierras and the gold fields of California. By 1850 the Overland Trail thus could lead to Oregon, Utah, or California—three very different frontiers.

The United States Census counted heads in all three areas for the first time in 1850. The age and sex structures of the areas were not the same:[19]

Area [18]	Population	Male	Age: 0–14	15–44	Over 44
Oregon	13,000	62%	38%	54%	8%
Utah	11,000	55%	45%	55%	neglig.
California	93,000	92%	6%	91%	3%

Oregon shows sex and age distributions normal for farming (Type I) frontiers in their early stages. The male proportion declines in later years, gradually approaching parity with females, first when young men who had arrived in Oregon by themselves found places and then sent for brides, and later as children and grandchildren replaced the pioneers. Utah exhibits an unusually balanced sex ratio for a frontier, and more children than usual: evidence that the Mormons emigrated as families, and that they continued their procreative duty. California, in contrast to both, was a classic Type II frontier.

A similar contrast appeared in the 1860 census in two neighboring territories farther east. By 1860 the western line of agricultural settlement, the "frontier line" (really the "Type I frontier line"), had penetrated eastern Kansas. At the same time the Front Range of the Rockies, from Pike's Peak to Denver, was the target of a gold rush, with the usual Type II characteristics:[20]

Area [19]	Population	Male	Age: 0–14	15–44	Over 44
Kansas	107,000	55%	42%	57%	1%
Colorado	34,000	97%	3%	94%	3%

In the Type I cases (Oregon and Utah in 1850, Kansas in 1860), the males were in the majority, but only slightly, and children accounted for a large part of the population. Most of the rest were women and men in their twenties and thirties. The Type I frontier, in short, was a land of young people, forming families simultaneously with farms—the demographic and economic sides of the same coin. The Type II frontiers of 1850 California and 1860 Colorado were very different, lands of young men in their late teens, twenties, or thirties. Women were absent and, therefore, so were children.

The social consequences of these demographic differences have never been quantified, but they seem incontestable. Vigilantes, shootouts, homicides, rapes, fights over mining claims and grazing rights, prostitution, and other social ills for which the early American West is so famous (overly so) were the products of the relatively few, the young males, who populated Type II frontiers. The Type I majority of frontierspeople were occupied more productively, and the female component made substantive contributions to community building and stability. One final difference needs to be noted. Type II frontiers were notoriously unstable; they could disappear as quickly as they formed. If the silver or gold played out or if a closer railhead opened for shipping the cattle east, the young men moved on. Type I frontiers were by no means perfectly stable. People climbing the agricultural ladder moved fairly often. But landowning, once achieved, usually meant roots.

This simple typology is about frontiers, i.e. areas in their initial years of white settlement. It has much less to offer about most of the twentieth-century West, where farm-family frontiers have disappeared or never existed in the first place, yet where sex ratios have become normal and the age distribution much broader. Furthermore, some agricultural frontiers, in the United States and in Latin America, do not easily fit Type I, and fit Type II only with strain. For the period before 1920, however, Types I and II appear to encompass most of the frontier activity, farm and otherwise, within the United States.

So too with Canada.[21] From the 1830s until cheap land was gone in the 1860s, Ontario was a Type I farm frontier quite similar to the area of the United States from Lake Ontario westward to the Mississippi. But the Canadian search for farmland was diverted to the United States for the next thirty years by the Canadian Shield, that vast unplowable land of granite and muskeg between central Ontario and Winnipeg. Because of that barrier, Canada lost more people than it gained from migration between 1870 and 1900. After 1901, however, thanks to the Canadian Pacific Railroad, active recruitment of farm families by the railroad and by governments, an enlightened homestead policy, and favorable grain prices, the prairie provinces joined adjacent parts of the United States in becoming the last great Type I frontier. Canadian development, in other words, included expansive Type I frontier activity for about a century prior to the 1920s, except for 1870–1900. Canada also had Type II frontiers, in fact predominantly so if one classifies the fur trade as such. Certainly the 1859 Fraser River gold rush and the Yukon rush of the late 1890s qualify. Because of the early presence of governmental authority (especially the Mounted Police), Canadian frontiers escaped the violence that marred some of the American ones. The Canadian experience shows that the social pathologies of the United States's Type II frontiers were not an inevitable consequence of the demography.[22]

In Brazil and Argentina, the typology has to be revised considerably. In both countries, the lines of settlement moved rapidly westward or northwestward from the 1870s or 1880s to 1914 or beyond. European immigrants arrived in large numbers. Both countries earned prominent places in world agricultural markets—Brazil with coffee, Argentina with beef and wheat. Vast areas were opened to productive settlement, indeed settlement (by Europeans) of any kind, prodded by railroad building. Brazil's frontier tradition, however, had included sugar plantations in the Northeast, and more recently coffee plantations in the Southeast, together with mining for gold and precious metals in Minas Gerais. Sugar and coffee production depended on African slaves as their labor source until slavery was abolished in a series of steps completed in 1888. At that point the coffee planters, backed by the state of São Paulo, which they controlled politically, recruited families of immigrants (chiefly northern Italians) as a new labor force. Evaluations of the situation of these *colonos* vary. Some say their lot was miserable, others that it was "enviable" compared to slaves or Mexican peons. Nearly all scholars agree, however, that unless the family of *colonos* arrived with some wherewithal, they were not likely to become landowners in their own generation. It was possible to climb the agricultural ladder, but very difficult. The distinctive feature of most migration from southern Europe to Brazil was its family character. Yet those families able to step into independent landholding were a small minority, with the rest functioning in some kind of sharecropping or tenant contract.[23]

In Argentina new arrivals on the pampas after 1880 were also likely to be northern Italians, but in the early years at least, single men who migrated back and forth seasonally, rather than families. From farm laborers they rose in many cases—with families by that point—to tenants, owning their implements, but not their land. The Argentine ladder to independent family farm ownership was easier to climb than the Brazilian, harder than the North American. From the standpoint of the small farmer, neither Argentina nor Brazil had much of a Type I frontier. Neither country enacted effective homestead legislation or conducted a land survey to provide secure title. Independent landowning, though possible, was the exception. The moving frontier line of young, large families, so common in the United States and Canada, was just not there. Land was available in Argentina and Brazil, indeed an almost endless supply; but not 'free' land.[24]

In the *bandeirante*, Brazil had a frontier tradition. As the Brazilian writer Vianna Moog describes him, the original *bandeirante* of colonial Brazil was an "emigrant . . . [who] came to Brazil without his wife, without his children, without his possessions, in search of wealth and adventure," and with "the intention of getting rich quickly and returning even more quickly." The *bandeirantes* "were initially conquistadors, not colonizers." Clearly Type II men. The North American archetype, Moog says, contrasted greatly. He was the "pioneer," the "colonizer, not conqueror," the man who with wife and children built a farm out of virgin soil.[25]

Clearly Type I. The large coffee planters in Brazil resemble antebellum southern planters more closely than either Type I or II frontierspeople, and the *estancieros* of the pampas with their horses, cattle, and thousands of hectares of land resemble the great ranchers of Texas and the northern plains. Overlooking many qualifications and local variants, then, it can be said that the opening of the pampas and the coffee region after 1870 did not involve smallholders as in the United States and Canada's Type I frontier. Instead, one finds large landowners using a heavily immigrant labor force under various tenancy contracts. One could wedge some of these immigrants under the umbrella of Type I, since some did achieve the equivalent of homesteads. But not many did.

The landowner–tenant arrangement so common in Brazil and Argentina does have a parallel in the United States. It is not exact, but is suggestive. Large-scale irrigated agriculture, typical of California's Central Valley in the twentieth century, and also present in Washington, Arizona, Colorado, and other western states, involves ownership by a family or a corporation of substantial acreage, using migrant wage laborers to work it. This is not Type I homesteading, although it could be considered Type II entrepreneuring. The migrant farm workers of late-nineteenth- or early twentieth-century California (Chinese, Japanese, Filipino, Punjabi) exhibited the skewed age and sex distributions of Type II frontiers, while later migrants (Okie-Arkie, Black, Mexican) did not. Large-scale agriculture using migrant labor goes on. Either at some yet unspecified point the frontier gave way to modern capitalism (as applied to agriculture), or the frontier still continues.[26] More likely, the Type I frontier concluded with the end of cheap arable land, while the Type II frontier still continues, without the demographic distinctiveness it once had. In the transatlantic context, among the four major frontier nations of 1870–1914, the Type I homesteading frontier becomes the anomaly—a great attraction as long as it lasted. Without it, and it never was really present in Argentina or Brazil, migrant wage labor became the norm in pan-American agriculture as it had been for centuries in European. To simplify even further: In Type I frontiers the farmer owned the land, the means of production; in Type II, some tenants (in Argentina, occasionally Brazil) owned implements, which were also means of production; in Type II, past and present migrant wage laborers own(ed) essentially no means of production. This last group includes not only farm workers, but also hard-rock miners, lumber workers, and other migrants, single or not.

What, finally, of empires? In an extended sense they too are Type II frontiers. They combined the demographic weaknesses and the economic exploitativeness of older Type II frontiers, as well as the landlord–tenant, capitalist–worker relationships, which are continuing versions. Demographic examples include the British Raj, Rhodesia, South Africa, the Belgian Congo, Francophone West Africa, and Indochina. In these important Asian and African cases a small European population, disproportionately male (partly because much of it was military) superimposed itself on an indigenous population that had existed for centuries or longer and had possessed every quality of a self-replenishing population, including normal sex and age distributions.[27]

Europeans had been colonists earlier, of course, creating the nations of the New World during the nearly four hundred years since Columbus. The apparent success of frontier-making, especially by the United States, in fact encouraged European empire-building.[28] With obvious exceptions such as Puritans and Mennonites, the initial motives for that older colonization—by the Spanish in Mexico and Peru, the Portuguese in Brazil, the English in Virginia—had been largely economic. In the 1870s and 1880s, with few exceptions (such as the German colonies in East and West Africa, the result more of nationalistic policy than of any population pressure), European empire-building was exploitative.[29]

It was also frequent. When the 1880s opened, as indigenes were suppressed on the pampas and the Great Plains and as railroads and settlers quickly appropriated the land they vacated, the British were at war in Afghanistan, France annexed Tahiti, and the Boers defeated a British force at Majuba Hill (February 1881). In 1882 the British defeated Arabs at Tel-el-Kebir and occupied Egypt and the Sudan. In 1883 the French began "protecting" Annam and Tonkin. Germany occupied Southwest Africa, Togo, and Kamerun in 1884, while Britain established protectorates in Basutoland, the Somali Coast, Nigeria, and New Guinea. In 1885 the Mahdi overran "Chinese" Gordon at Khartoum, but Germany annexed Tanganyika and Zanzibar, while Leopold II of Belgium became proprietor of the Congo. From then until 1890, Burma, Zululand, Baluchistan, much of Borneo, Uganda, and Sikkim went to the British; meanwhile Germany occupied parts of Oceania, including the Bismarck Archipelago, reaffirmed its treaty rights in Samoa, and stepped toward a base at Kiaochow in north China. France began ruling Dahomey in 1892. From a late-twentieth-century standpoint the outward thrust of Europe is astonishing for its reach, as well as its rapidity—and the completeness of its reversal. Of all these places, only Tahiti remains connected politically to Europe.

New World frontier-making, in contrast, involved many more people and, consequently, remained a reality. The Type I frontier ended, often painfully, with the over-farming of the High Plains in the Dakotas, the Front Range states, Oregon, Saskatchewan, and Alberta. Tens of thousands of homesteaders poured into those areas from 1901 to about 1915 (and into northwestern Alberta and Saskatchewan into the 1920s), and tens of thousands withdrew from many parts of the Great Plains and Great Basin after 1920, defeated by low crop prices, drought, and other problems. The cultural momentum of two hundred years of Type I frontiering, it seems, carried many would-be settlers farther than they should have gone. Miserable and tragic as homestead failures were, however, they pale in comparison to the carnage involved in the creation of the European empires and in their later collapse.

And they pale in comparison to the permanent harm done to indigenous peoples, as all such cross-cultural contact had done since 1492. If the cultures coming into contact were different in substance but about equally complex, as was true of the British–Hindu or French–Annamese contacts and if they shared the same diseases and immunities, then the European incursion did not last beyond about 1950. If the Europeans carried more diseases and the indigenous culture lacked immunities, then the indigenes were usually destroyed or, at best, made permanently dependent. According to William H. McNeill, land was "free" or "open" because culture combined with biology to the great disadvantage of the indigenes: "The 'empty' frontier Turner spoke of arose from the destruction of Amerindian populations by infections imported from the Old World, sporadically reinforced by resort to armed force,"[30] as well as superior skills in agriculture, warfare, administration or something else. In South and North America, much of this destruction took place on Type II frontiers.

The years from 1870 to 1914 were especially marked by the expansion of European empires and of European-stock frontiers. Except for the numbers of Europeans involved—few with the empires, many with the frontiers—the lines between the two thrusts cannot be drawn sharply. Both resulted from similar impulses including gain, self-improvement, conquest, greed, *missions civilisatrices*, and others—and without much consideration for the indigenous people and culture, primitive or advanced. Such was the world of a century ago. Perhaps one of its lessons is that enduring conquests (or defenses) are demographic.

NOTES

1. This is a revised version of an essay which appeared in Michael Heyd et al., eds., *Religion, Ideology and Nationalism in Europe and America: Essays in Honor of Yehoshua Arieli* (Jerusalem, 1986). The author thanks Professor Arieli for graciously consenting to its republication. He also thanks Charles S. Peterson for encouragement and for incisive questions that brought about clarification of many points.

2. S. B. Saul, *The Myth of the Great Depression in England* (London, 1969); Dan S. White, "Political Loyalties and Economic Depression in Britain, France, and Germany, 1873–1896," unpublished paper delivered at the American Historical Association meeting, December 1979.

3. Jeffrey G. Williamson, *Late Nineteenth-Century American Development: A General Equilibrium Theory* (New York, 1974), 93, chp. 5.

4. B. R. Mitchell, *European Historical Statistics 1750–1970* (New York, 1976), 335.

5. Ibid., 399.

6. Edward Meeker, "The Improving Health of the United States, 1850–1915," *Explorations in Economic History*, 9 (Summer 1972), 353–73.

7. From the "50 and 100 Years Ago" columns, *Scientific American*, (April 1984, November 1984).

8. B. R. Mitchell, *International Historical Statistics: The Americas and Australasia* (Detroit, 1983), 657–58, 661–62. For railway lines in operation, see Mitchell, *European Historical Statistics*, 583–84.

9. Mitchell, *European Historical Statistics*, 135. The per-decade totals of migrants leaving Europe are (in millions): 1851–1860, 2.2; 1861–70, 2.8; 1871–1880, 3.2; 1881–1890, 7.8; 1891–1900, 6.8; 1901–1910, 11.4; 1911–1920, 6.8; 1931–1940, 1.2.

10. Mexico, impoverished by the free-trade policies of the Porfirio Diaz regime (1874–1911), and racked for the decade after that by revolution, was in no position to develop whatever frontier it had left, much of which had been swallowed by the United States in the war of 1846–1848 anyway. Like the South of the United States, Mexico already had an oversupply of poor people and an undersupply of jobs. Europeans had no reason to migrate there, either for farms or for wages.

11. Comparative frontiers have received many enlightening discussions in recent years. Two that have helped me most are William H. McNeill, *The Great Frontier: Freedom and Hierarchy in Modern Times* (Princeton, 1983), and Alistair Hennessy, *The Frontier in Latin American History* (Albuquerque, 1978).

12. As Mexico gave way politically in Texas in 1836.

13. Hennessy, *The Frontier*, 66–67.

14. Hennessy, *The Frontier*, 65. Also, James R. Scobie, *Revolution on the Pampas: A Social History of Argentine Wheat, 1860–1910* (Austin, 1964), 39.

15. See, for example, James Gump, "The Subjugation of the Zulus and Sioux: A Comparative Study," *Western Historical Quarterly*, 19 (January 1988), 21–36.

16. On New Zealand and the reduction of the Maori, see Alfred W. Crosby, *Ecological Imperialism: The Biological Expansion of Europe, 900–1900* (Cambridge, 1986), 172–73, 265–66.

17. Isak Dinesen, *Out of Africa*, repr. ed. (New York, 1952).

18. This was so in 1989, when this essay first appeared, but ceased to be so when apartheid ended in the early 1990s and Nelson Mandela became president in 1994.

19. U.S. Bureau of the Census, *Historical Statistics of the United States, Colonial Times to 1970* (Washington, D.C., 1975), Series A195–209, I:25–36.

20. Ibid.

21. French Canada excepted; whatever "frontier" it had was filled before 1850, and as was true of settled, rural New England, its excess population migrated not to western farms, but to nearby cities, often ones in the United States.

22. Helpful studies of Canadian population, migration, and frontiers include Yolande Lavoie, *L'Émigration des Canadiens aux États-Unis avant 1930. Mésure du Phénomene* (Montreal, 1972); Warren E. Kalbach and Wayne W. McVey, *The Demographic Bases of Canadian Society*, 2d. ed. (Toronto, 1979); R. H. Coats and M. C. Maclean, *The American-Born in Canada: A Statistical Interpretation* (Toronto, 1943); Leon E. Truesdell, *The Canadian Born in the United States: An Analysis of the Statistics of the Canadian Element in the Population of the United States 1850 to 1930* (New Haven, 1943); Chester Martin, *'Dominion Lands' Policy* (Toronto, 1973); Gerald Friesen, *The Canadian Prairies: A History* (Lincoln, 1984). Martin's book does for Canada what Paul W. Gates's *History of Public Land Law Development* (Washington, D.C., 1968) does for the United States public domain. Friesen's book is a finely crafted, readable, comprehensive history of the prairie provinces.

23. Useful works on Brazilian demography, migration, and frontiers include Paul Hugon, *Demografia Brasileira Ensaio de Demoeconômia Brasileira* (São Paulo, 1977); Lucy Maffei Hutter, *Imigração Italiana em São Paulo (1880–1889): Os Primeiros Contactos do Imigrante com o Brasil* (São Paulo, 1972); Thomas Lynn Smith, *Brazil, People and Institutions*, 4th ed. (Baton Rouge, 1972); Thomas William Merrick and Douglas H. Graham, *Population and Economic Development in Brazil: 1800 to the Present* (Baltimore, 1979); Warren Dean, *Rio Claro. A Brazilian Plantation System, 1820–1920* (Stanford, 1976); Thomas H. Holloway, *Immigrants on the Land: Coffee and Society in São Paulo, 1886–1934* (Chapel Hill, 1980); Manual Diegues Junior, *População e Propriedade da Terra no Brasil* (Washington, D.C., 1959).

24. For Argentine migration and frontiers, some of the best works are Ezequiel Gallo, *La Pampa Gringa: La Colonización Agrícola en Santa Fe (1870–1895)* (Buenos Aires, 1982); Roberto Cortes Conde, *El Progreso Argentino 1880–1914* (Buenos Aires, 1979); James R. Scobie, *Revolution on the Pampas: A Social History of Argentine Wheat, 1860–1910* (Austin, 1964); and—excellent for explicit comparisons—Carl E. Solberg, *The

Prairies and the Pampas: Agrarian Policy in Canada and Argentina, 1880–1930 (Stanford, 1987).

25. Clodomir Vianna Moog, *Bandeirantes and Pioneers* (New York, 1964), 92, 103.

26. In his excellent comparative history of white settlement in six Southern Hemisphere countries, Donald Denoon defines capitalism in a way that covers agriculture, as well as mining and manufacturing: "Here it is taken as a mode of production in which the means of production are privately owned, and labour is performed by workers who sell their labour for wages." Donald Denoon, *Settler Capitalism: The Dynamics of Dependent Development in the Southern Hemisphere* (New York, 1983), 8.

27. Though birth and death rates were very high compared to a late twentieth-century industrialized society. On the male-skewedness of French West Africa, see William B. Cohen, *Rulers of Empire: The French Colonial Service in Africa* (Stanford, 1971), 23: "Because of the deplorable health conditions the administrators could not bring their families with them and few men were willing to accept a career involving nearly lifetime separation from their families."

28. Raymond F. Betts, "Immense Dimensions: The Impact of the American West on Late Nineteenth-Century European Thought about Expansion," *Western Historical Quarterly*, 10 (April 1979), 149–66, esp. 150, 152, 154.

29. For a recent discussion of German policy, see Klaus J. Bade, "Imperial Germany and West Africa: Colonial Movement, Business Interests, and Bismarck's 'Colonial Policies,'" in *Bismarck, Europe and Africa: The Berlin Conference 1884–1885 and the Onset of Partition*, ed. by Stig Foerster, Wolfgang J. Mommsen, and Ronald Robinson (London, 1988), 121–47. For a summary of motives for imperialism, see Winfried Baumgart, *Imperialism: The Idea and Reality of British and French Colonial Expansion, 1880–1914* (New York, 1982), 39–46. A typology of imperialism with examples from the nineteenth century and also the very recent past is Tony Smith, *The Pattern of Imperialism: The United States, Great Britain and the Late-Industrializing World since 1815* (New York, 1981). V. G. Kiernan, *From Conquest to Collapse: European Empires from 1815–1960* (New York, 1982), is a handy narrative survey of European conquests.

30. McNeill, pp. 11, 17.

PART II

THE
EIGHTEENTH
CENTURY

4   RANCHERAS AND THE LAND: WOMEN AND PROPERTY RIGHTS IN HISPANIC CALIFORNIA

Gloria Ricci Lothrop

Here the author examines the law and practice of property hold-ing by women in California during the Spanish and Mexican peri-ods before the American takeover. She shows that women had many rights under Spanish and Mexican law that they did not have under English law, which operated in the thirteen Atlantic colonies and later, without much change, in the United States until quite recently. The 1848 treaty which ended the Mexican–American War and legalized the acquisition of California by the United States theoretically preserved women's rights, but in practice those rights proved to be very difficult to maintain, as Anglo-American law became the norm. What were these rights that Spanish-heritage women enjoyed and then found threatened?

After 1848, Lothrop explains, female landowners and operators of businesses defended their properties in American courts only with difficulty. Anglo-American squatters invaded some properties and claimed that because they "developed" that land, they should get title to it. Should they, in fact? Court defenses by Hispanic women were costly even when successful. Gradually Spanish law gave way to En-glish; how were married women viewed in each type of law? In which system did women enjoy fewer independent rights, and why? Although the early constitution and legislation of American California recog-nized some rights of women in property, a "growing inequity" devel-oped, in Lothrop's phrase, until women won more equal rights in the twentieth century. Explain the development of this inequity.—editors

O NE FACET of Spanish colonial policy directly affecting California women was the equitable legal status enjoyed by wives. It allowed them to remain as economically autonomous as unmarried women. Under Spanish law a married woman retained her property, wages, legal rights, and even her maiden name, after marriage. Unlike the laws of England, the laws of Spain recognized the rights of married women to independently inherit, own, mortgage, convey, even pawn property they acquired before or during marriage. The legal system also recognized an equal partnership between the husband and wife regarding property acquired during marriage. As under English law, it was stipulated that, under normal circumstances, the husband administered the property of the conjugal relationship. But unlike English law, Spanish law did not preclude married women from being sole traders. As holders of property they could meet their own contractual obligations and operate as independent businesswomen.

Given the unique position of married women under Spanish law, it would be useful to examine the implications of this favorable legal status in terms of rancho ownership in Alta California. This presentation will also note the appeals made by several land-owning Californians before the Board of Land Commissioners, and highlight the changing legal status of married women in the state after the ratification of the Treaty of Guadalupe Hidalgo at the conclusion of the war with Mexico.

In the distant provincial outpost of California, where the developing culture responded to the challenges of an isolated colonial settlement, Spanish, and later Mexican, law was sometimes interpreted in a unique manner. But the favored position of married women under the law remained unchanged. It continued to benefit female colonial settlers, especially those nearly three score which became recipients of California land grants.

Women settlers were integral to the California colonization plan. To relieve the plight of California soldiers, who in the estimation of officer Miguel Costansó, would otherwise be "condemned to a perpetual and involuntary celibacy," Juan Bautista de Anza included twenty-nine wives among the contingent of soldiers and settlers he brought to California in 1775.[1] One gave birth to a fine son, Salvador Linares, on Christmas Day, and the next day continued with the other settlers on the arduous 400-mile trek from Culiacan in Sinaloa to California. Another died in childbirth the day of departure from Tubac, the only loss by death of the entire eight-month journey. A third, Dona Feliciana Arballo y Gutíerrez, a young widow with two small daughters, sang saucy songs along the way, much to the distress of Father Pedro Font. When Dona Feliciana finally arrived at Mission San Gabriel, riding her horse like an experienced *vaquerita*, she caught the eye of a young soldier of the guard, Juan Francisco Lopez. She and Lopez soon celebrated their nuptial, highlighted by a weeklong fiesta, and the expedition traveled on toward northern California without her. Among the descendants of that union were Pío and Andrés Pico, both governors of California, as well as the late actor Leo Carrillo.[2]

As part of the Spanish colonial plan to send women to help establish and propagate civilization in the distant territories, the 1781 expedition of *pobladores* destined to settle the pueblo of Los Angeles included a contingent of women and children. Somewhat later, three wives joined a group of artisans who sailed to California in 1797.[3] In an effort to expand the child-bearing population, two years later, the viceregal authorities sent twelve female orphans between the ages of six and ten, along with nine males, to be placed in private homes in California.[4] They were to be known as

Lorenzanas in honor of their benefactor, the Archbishop of Toledo. The funds he made available were used to provide clothing, linen, blankets, food, refreshments and other supplies, including "tobacco for seven young women whom, officials reported, smoked cigars excessively." By supplying tobacco the authorities hoped that "the women would not have to ask the soldiers, coachmen, and peons for cigars."[5]

Other women came as a result of formal requests made to authorities to allow their families' settlement in the distant province of California in lieu of their husbands' serving prison sentences in Mexico. Some petitioners, in an effort to assure a favorable decision, added information about the number of marriageable females in the household.[6]

As a result of various settlement efforts, by 1830 the 264 women outnumbered the 258 male residents in Los Angeles, the largest pueblo in Alta California.[7] Their presence was augmented by prolific childbearing. Between 1769 and 1850 two thousand two hundred and eighty births were recorded among Spanish-Mexican families of California. The average family size was 8.84 children. The largest, however, was a family of nineteen children.[8] An early nineteenth-century visitor noted:

> Childbirth in Nueva California seems to be very easy among the Spanish women. Senora Arguello, who had given birth to fifteen children, of whom thirteen are still living, assured us that she did not remember ever hearing of the death of a woman in childbirth.[9]

Casilda Sinoba, wife of Miguel Pico, provides an example of other exponential population growth in early California. When she died at the age of seventy-four, her descendants included fifteen children, one hundred and sixteen grandchildren and ninety-seven great-grandchildren.[10]

Another statistic which contributed to the historical profile of California's early female colonizers indicates that by 1844 more than 13 percent of all households in the pueblo of Los Angeles were headed by women. In the census of 1850 the percentage rose to 25 percent.[11] In a letter to Thomas Oliver Larkin, Florencio Serrano noted that seven of the twenty-six boys enrolled in the Monterey Public School in September 1846 came from households headed by women.[12]

Not only were women a significant presence in California, they also enjoyed a degree of autonomy and authority. Nowhere was this more evident than in the area of land ownership. By 1850 the average landholding of California colonists was valued at $2,100.[13] Holdings included lots owned by both men and women in the pueblos of San Jose, Los Angeles and Branciforte, and others near the presidios of Monterey and Santa Barbara. They also claimed much larger pastoral holdings conferred by the Spanish colonial administration, and much more extensively, by the Mexican government after the secularization of mission lands in 1834.[14] The number of grants increased gradually, reaching a peak of 67 in 1844. In part this reflected the growing population, which between 1840 and

1846, grew twenty percent. Furthermore, by the mid-1840s many grants were awarded to close associates of the territorial administration in anticipation of the expected rise in land values following American occupation. The total number of named and unnamed ranches granted by the Spanish and Mexican government reached approximately eight hundred and ranged in size from one to eleven leagues, a league being 4,426 acres.[15]

It is worthy of note that fifty-five of these grants were made to women or were conveyed by gift or bequest to women, many of whom were married.[16] Rancho Rodeo de las Aguas, also known as Beverly Hills, was granted to Vicente Villa and María Rita Valdez de Villa around 1821. Testimony before the Board of Land Commission indicated that the couple retired to the land after he left military service.[17]

Upon Villa's death the widow assumed proprietary control. In 1828 María Rita Valdez de Villa and her eleven children continued to occupy the land of "the gathering of the waters." In 1831 Los Angeles Alcalde Vicente Sanchez officially granted the 4,500-acre rancho to María Rita and kinsman Luciano Valdez. Her development of the rancho with the assistance of 89 retainers and tenants was described by Francisco Villa:

> When I first knew it [Rancho Rodeo de las Aguas] in 1833, it was occupied by María Rita Valdez and a relative of hers . . . She had cattle on the land but not one hundred and fifty head of cattle, which was necessary at that time to entitle her to a grant of land and have a brand for cattle. This mission of San Gabriel of which I was majordomo, lent her sufficient to make up that number. She also had horses. She built a house on the land the same year, in which she lived and still continues living there. She has two small houses on the land. . . . She has cultivated a small garden.[18]

In 1834 Valdez complained to Governor José Figueroa that her partner was "intolerable." She claimed that he drove off her cattle, appropriated a *cañada* she had spent three months clearing, interfered with her planting, and had constructed a dwelling which blocked access to her home. As a result, in 1840 Governor Juan Alvarado gave María Rita sole title to the rancho. The Los Angeles *ayuntamiento* to whom the matter had been referred ordered Valdez to vacate the property in return for reimbursement for improvements amounting to $17.50, which María Rita paid on August 11, 1844.

The Mexican government granted the 12.6-acre Rancho Huerta de Cuati to Victoria Reid, the Indian wife of Scots businessman Hugo Reid.[19] It was this opportunity to own land independently, and by inference, to trade, invest and enter into contractual agreement which may have led scholars to observe that, "Mexican women prior to 1848 were probably freer than women elsewhere in the world."[20]

William Heath Davis, reflecting upon his six decades in California, wrote:

During my long and intimate acquaintance with Californians, I have found the women as a class much brighter, much quicker in their perceptions, and generally smarter than the men. Their husbands oftentimes look to them for advice and direction in their general business affairs. As a rule they were not much educated; but they had abundant instinct and native talent, and the women were full of natural dignity and self-possession; they talked well and intelligently, and appeared to much better advantage than might have been supposed from their meagre educational facilities.[21]

Clearly, these able women were equal to the opportunities assured them under Spanish and later Mexican law. Spanish law carefully delineated the legal equality of the spouses, resulting in the ownership of more than 13 percent of all Spanish-Mexican land grants in California by married, as well as single women. Spanish colonial courts administered a wide-ranging body of formal law, drawn from long tradition, the earliest provision being the Fuero Juzgo promulgated in 693 A.D. The most famous was the *Recoplacion de leyes do los reynos de las Indias* of 1680, which codified into 6,400 laws the nearly half million royal orders issued for the colonies in the preceding two centuries. In 1805 this nine-volume legal compendium was supplemented by the *Novisima recopilacion*.[22]

The first section of Spanish civil law addressed domestic relations. Articles 41 through 69 outlined the relationship of spouses' property acquired before or during marriage. For example, Article 41 permitted a wife to accept all inheritances without the permission of her husband. Article 42 permitted the granting of authority to the wife to administer her property, enter into contracts, appear in court, accept or reject inheritances, and alienate property, if a husband improperly withheld his consent, or his absence represented some jeopardy to the holdings. Article 43 recognized the partnership of the couple to property acquired during marriage. Such community property was defined as including the fruits of their joint labor, the income from their separate property, but not property acquired by the individuals through inheritance, donation or bequest. Community property was further defined in Section 49 as an equal share of the community, even if one of them at the time of marriage might have been without means.[23]

An aspect of *brenes parafernales* or marital law deriving directly from the Spanish *Siete Partidas*, addressed paraphernal property, that which the wife owned independently of her husband. This property, whether movable or immovable, was to be administered by the wife, unless she expressly conferred administration upon the husband. Where there was doubt, it was assumed the wife retained administrative rights. While she could not alienate her property, nor represent her property interests in court without the permission of the husband, a protocol often honored in the breech, the paraphernal property, along with its increase or deterioration, belonged to the wife.[24] In one case argued before a Mexican court the wife of José Sandoval brought suit against her husband for "gambling away her burro to another man." The court ordered the burro returned to the wife and fined the men two pesos each for gambling.[25]

In another case where a husband's gambling debts had exhausted all of the income and part of the wife's principal, under threat of death to the wife, on the recommendation of the court the governor ordered "the husband jailed and the property put in the hands of a trustee." Faced with this sentence, the husband agreed to pay his wife all that he owed her.[26] In an earlier case, also illustrating a married woman's right to separate property, María de las Rivas brought suit against her son-in-law to prevent his removing his wife's dowry from the town of Tulancingo, since Dona María would be "the rightful heir should her daughter die childless."[27]

The right of women to be property holders was underscored in a Royal Cedula regarding the governance of the province of California, issued March 21, 1775. It noted that buildings, lots, and fields should be granted to settlers, retiring soldiers or their widows, adding that these properties should be "entailed in perpetuity on their sons and their descendants or on their daughters who marry useful settlers . . . "[28]

Sections of Spanish law also underscored the authority of mothers as well as fathers over their children. Emancipation from maternal and paternal rule, in most cases, occurred with the lawful marriage of the child. In California, however, it was observed, "A son or daughter, although married, was under orders of the parents who retained the right to punish them."[29] Women's authority over their children, and their rights to both community and paraphernal property provide some explanation of the fact cited earlier that in Los Angeles in 1844 women headed 13 percent of all households.[30]

Despite a married woman's right to property, and hence the ability to enter into business contracts, records provide slim evidence of California women as independent traders. Perhaps this is a reflection of the fact that California's was a pastoral economy resting largely on a system of barter. Richard Henry Dana claimed to have seen only two shops run by *Californios*, although a resident observed that "women had shoe shops in their homes where they made their footwear."[31]

The few references to businesswomen include Bancroft's mention of a woman who was much admired for the quality of the artificial flowers she made. The historian also records that Tia Boronda kept a little shop in Monterey from 1811 to 1836. Several accounts refer to the boarding house in San Francisco operated by Juana Briones to which deserting sailors sometimes fled.[32] In Los Angeles the forty-one-year-old widow Ignacia Sepulveda relied upon her earnings as a seamstress to support her five young children.[33]

Census records in New Mexico, another territory administered under Hispanic law, reveal that women were self-employed in a variety of fields, as gold-panners, healers, midwives, and bakers. In the capital of that southwest colony "women were often in the town plaza selling products of domestic animals or gardens, or vending whiskey and traders' goods in stalls along the main streets, or dealing cards in gambling games." A sister of the governor dispensed whiskey from an old coffee pot, and the widow of yet another governor who owned the only pool table in Santa Fe rented it to gamblers for a few *pesos* a week.[34]

In California, entrepreneurial enterprise, such as there was, was nurtured by a handful of Boston traders, many of whom entered into advantageous marriages with California women. Richard Henry Dana observed: "In Monterey there are a number of English and Americans (English or *Ingles* all are called who speak the English language) who have married Californians, become united to the Roman Church, and acquired considerable property. Having more industry, frugality and enterprise than the natives, they soon get nearly all the trade into their hands. They usually keep shops."[35]

California wives experienced few changes in laws governing married women as power shifted from Spain to Mexico. Very little changed in the law as a result of Mexico's independence from Spain in 1821. While procedural law was modified, substantive law, defining duties, rights and liabilities, continued to be based on Spanish precedent.[36] As a result, married women joined in applying for grants to vast grazing lands made available after Mexican secularization of mission lands in 1834, which opened the way for full implementation of the Colonization Act of 1824 and the Supplemental Regulations of 1828.[37] These land concessions ranged in size from 9 to 48,000 acres, although some earlier Spanish grants had been up to 158,000 acres. To qualify for the final approval of the grant, the recipient agreed to build a stone house on each claim and to stock the claim with at least two thousand head of cattle.

Approximately thirty such concessions were made during the period of Spanish rule.[38] But California's rancho economy developed far more during the period after Mexican independence. Eighty ranchos were granted between 1825 and 1835. The trend was hastened by the decree of 1828, which authorized the granting of vacant lands to settlers who met the same conditions as had been stipulated under Spanish law. "Any Mexican of good character, or any foreigner willing to become a permanent resident of Mexico could petition for up to one square league of irrigable land, four of non-irrigable land, and six of grazing land—a total of 11 square leagues."[39]

The conditions to be met were much the same as during the Spanish period, involving a petition, a description, *diseño* or map, and proof of occupation and cultivation. The actual survey of the grant was carried out with an amiable disregard for accuracy. For example, the location of the Rancho Sespe in the Santa Clara Valley was described as being between the lands of Mission San Buenaventura and those of Mission San Fernando, and between the "mountains to the north and the high hills on the south."[40]

The secularization of lands held by the twenty-one missions administered by the Franciscan Friars, which was authorized by the Mexican Con-

6. Juan Bandini, a major
Californio landowner, and
his daughter, about 1840.
*Courtesy of the Hunting-
ton Library, San Marino,
California.*

gress on August 17, 1833, and implemented by Governor José Figueroa the
following year, was to result in the creation of approximately seven hundred vast cattle ranches. While the regulations stipulated that half the mission lands would be reserved for the neophytes as common grazing lands
and for Indian villages—Indian families were to receive land, neither less
than 100 varas nor more than 400 varas square along with agricultural supplies—the most fertile tracts were claimed by Californios.[41]

Among the married women who carried their claims from petition
through patent was Josefa Romero de Castro, who acquired Rancho
Animas or Sitio de la Brea in 1835. The four-square-league Rancho Laguna
Seca in Santa Clara County, the Rancho San Francisquito in Santa Clara
County, and Rancho Vicente in Monterey County were all granted to the
enterprising Catalina Manzaneli de Munras, a married woman, in 1833
and in 1834–35. In 1845 joint ownership of Rancho Valle de las Palmas in
Santa Barbara County was granted to two married women, María Josefa
Carrillo de Fitch and Guadalupe Estudillo de Argüello. In 1839 María
de Los Angeles Castro and Candida Castro were awarded Canada de
Raimunda in San Mateo County. In 1839 Antonia Chaboyo (also spelled
Chabollo) was the grantee of the Rancho Yerba Buena located near the present Evergreen district in Santa Clara County. Rancho Guajome in San
Diego County was presented by Abel Stearns as a wedding gift to Isadora
Bandini at the time of her marriage to Cave Couts.[42] Subsequent corre-
spondence between Stearns and Mrs. Couts indicates her active participation in the administration of the ranch.

Women's involvement in land acquisition during the rancho period has been largely unexamined because the records have often been obscured. For example, in Cowan's respected *Ranchos of California* the names of seven female grantees are given male endings, although in the original *Index of Expedientes* the grantees are all listed as women.[43] According to Shumate, Antonia, not Antonio, Olivera was claimant of Casmalia Ranch.[44] Encarnacio is listed in the Jimeno and Hartness Index as Dona Encarnacion Sepulveda, who was granted Ojo de Agua Rancho in 1840.[45] Antonio originally appears as Antonia Caceras, the grantee of Rancho Canada de Pogolomi in 1844.[46] Basilio in contemporary records appears as Dona Basilia Bernal, the grantee of Rancho Embarcadero de Santa Clara in 1845 and 1846.[47] Similarly, Hilario Sánchez in present records was originally entered as Ylaria Sánchez, grantee of Tamalpais, a ranch covering two leagues in Marin County.[48]

In some cases there is complete disagreement. Cowan claims Rancho Santa Manuela in San Luis Obispo County was granted to Francis X. Branch, but the Index of Land Concessions assigns the rancho to Manuela Carlon, who was made grantee of record on April 7, 1837.[49] Rancho Boca de la Canada de Pinole is attributed to Manuel Valencia. But the official record of land concessions compiled by Jimeno and Hartnell cites the grantee as being Dona María Manuela Valencia.[50]

Of the approximately 700 ranch grants recorded during the Spanish and Mexican periods, fifty-five were awarded to women grantees, representing nearly 13 percent of the total. An additional number of ranchos were inherited by widows and their children.

Confusion surrounds the claim of Eulalia Perez de Guillon to Rancho El Rincon de San Pasqual.[51] It is probable that Fr. Sánchez made the grant of mission lands as a reward for Eulalia Perez's long and faithful service to the mission as *llavera* or "keeper of the keys." But the actual grantee of record was her second husband, Juan Marine. The elderly Eulalia personally believed that Sánchez had given her the land, often saying: "When the land was given to me I was already married to Juan Marine and afterwards he only gave me half."[52]

Titles to existing ranchos were sometimes transmitted as bequests to married daughters.

As her share following the division of Rancho le Zanja, Manuela Nieto de Cota received from her father Rancho Los Cerritos, which covered the future townsites of Lakewood, North Long Beach, Paramount, Bellflower, and Signal Hill. She and her husband had eleven children who shared in her estate when she died about 1840.[53]

In 1882 four daughters and their husbands were heirs to the more than twenty-thousand-acre Dominguez Ranch, including Rattle Snake Island in San Pedro Bay.[54] After years of litigation Martina Castro Alvarado acquired, as a result of a bequest by her mother, a 15/22 claim to the four-league San Pablo Ranch in Contra Costa County.[55] The failure of Luis Peralta to convey any part of the large Peralta grant in Alameda County to his daughters resulted in lengthy litigation, the neglected heirs contending that such action indicated that Peralta was not in his right mind at the time of his death at age ninety-seven in 1841.

It is true that in some cases the awarding of land to wives represented a legal fiction by which husbands tried to exempt their land from debts they might have incurred. After reviewing the claims to the De Haro Ranch to which the husband asserted that he had no interest, the Board of Land Commissioners expressed skepticism. Ultimately, it found against Dona de Haro's claim of ownership.[56]

In many cases, however, Californians were far more than titular recipients of ranchos. It was not unusual for women to assume active roles in ranch management. Pío Pico recalled that during the harvest everyone worked, "throwing grain into baskets hanging from their backs," and added that "During the seasonal rodeos women worked alongside men preparing hides for market."[57]

From the one-and-a-half-story Garfias hacienda on Rancho San Pascual, Dona Encarnacion Sepulveda de Avila administered the entire operation for her son-in-law, who preferred politics, and served as Los Angeles County Treasurer in 1850–51. She not only made sure that the fine board floors were scrubbed and the green shutters brightly painted, but also oversaw the work of the mayordomo and negotiated the price of hides.[58] Near San Leandro Dona Soledad Ortega, widow of Luis Argüello, formerly governor of California, supervised the operation of El Rancho de las Pulgas, while caring for her four children.[59]

In testimony on behalf of land claimant Isabel Yorba before the Board of Land Commissioners, Andrés Pico provided specific information about the work of women rancheras. He observed that in 1836 Isabel Yorba had first run horses and grazed cattle, necessitating seasonal rodeos, on her Rancho Guadalasca, which extended over five leagues. By 1840 she had constructed a stone house as required under Mexican law.[60]

Another Yorba, the widow of Tómas, after his death in 1845, administered Rancho Santa Ana Vieja. In addition to overseeing four children and maintaining an eighteen-room house, Vicenta Sepulveda de Yorba administered a ranch having "2000 head of cattle, 900 ewes and their males, three herds of 100 mares and their stallions and 19 mules, also . . . 2 vineyards with some wooden fence and some fruit trees."[61] Respected merchant William Heath Davis described Dona Vicenta as a fine customer, who would personally come to his ship in San Pedro. There, the practical, as well as beautiful, ranchera would inspect all the merchandise before making her purchases.[62]

Enterprising Californianas were found in the north as well as the south. In 1843 W. H. Thomas, a sailor, reported buying milk for his crewmates from Juana Briones, whose adobe faced what is now Washington

Square in San Francisco. Having obtained an official separation from her husband Apolinario Miranda, the "widow" Briones supported her eight children with profits from her dairy, often "milking a dozen stubborn cows by putting the calf first at the teats, after which the lady . . . milked the unruly creatures with perfect composure. . . . "[63] In 1847 Briones moved her family to a 4,400-acre ranch she purchased in what is today Palo Alto and the Los Altos Hills.

Sometimes the enterprise of the rancheras extended beyond pastoral economy. In the 1870s the new town of Soledad became the bustling southern terminus of the Southern Pacific Coast Railroad. Its route and the town's establishment were actively supported by Dona Catalina Munras, who granted the railroad the right-of-way over San Vicente, one of her three ranches.[64]

Munras and other rancheras were inevitably affected by the changes which occurred as California passed from Mexican to American rule at the conclusion of the Mexican War in 1848. As landowners they were to be profoundly affected by the reaction of the United States Senate to the provisions negotiated in the Treaty of Guadalupe Hidalgo at the conclusion of the hostilities. A majority of the Senate rejected Article X, relating to land titles in the Mexican Cession territories, and modified Article IX, relating to the rights of Mexican residents in the transferred territories.[65]

At the urging of Mexican officials, an effort to compensate for the deleted Article X was attempted in the Protocol of Queretero, which proposed adoption of provisions in the Treaty of Louisiana, affirming that, "all the privileges and guarantees, civil, political and religious, which would have been possessed by the inhabitants of the ceded territories will be enjoyed under the substitute article."[66]

The Protocol was never ratified by the United States, whose officials argued that the wording and spirit of the agreement was contained in Article VIII of the Treaty which stated: "In the said territories, property of every kind, now belonging to the Mexicans now established there, shall be inviolably respected."[67]

Unfortunately, Article VIII did not solve the ambiguities surrounding the property rights of Mexican residents. The issue was referred to the courts and subsequently, to the Board of Land Commissioners. In 1851 the California Land Act provided for a three-person board to review the documentary evidence and hear testimony of all land holders, even those with perfect claims. The act permitted subsequent appeal to the board's decision through the courts.[68]

Not infrequently, the thirty-three steps required to place a grantee in juridical possession of land or title grant, as outlined in the Colonization Act of 1824 and the Supplemental Regulations of 1828, had not been completed. Most often the petition and survey notes were not submitted to the territorial legislature, "and the rancho's validity rested solely on the governor's signature."[69] Such oversights were scrutinized by the Board of Land Commissioners.

María de la Soledad was among the first to appear before the land board to defend her land title.[70] Other rancheras who appeared, like Joaquina Sepulveda, were at a disadvantage because of the imprecision of the official description of the grants, submitted as part of the original *expediente*. A partial description of her boundaries follows:

> Being a part of the Rancho called Paso de Bartolo and situated a little below the willows whose position determines the line from North to South along the edge of the aquaduct [sic] that runs to the land of Don Tomas Sanchez, one thousand and one hundred varas which terminates at the corner of the fence of the garden of said Tomas Sanchez, and from said corner course from East to West to the line of the large sycamore (aliso) which is the boundary of said rancho and that of Dona Josera Cota . . . [71]

In another case, the attorney's attempt to justify the claim of María de Jésus Garcia to the original boundaries of Rancho Nogales underscores the challenges presented by the simply sketched *diseños*, as well as the imprecise surveys. The confusion surrounding the claims and the counterclaims is reflected in the following passage:

> The lines, landmarks and distances named in the record of the pretended juridical measurement are absolutely repugnant and inconsistent . . . The starting point is not the same. In the record the official starts at the foot of the hill, in the canada; in his testimony he begins at the nogal tree, nearly three miles distant therefrom—while in the Reynolds map a sycamore tree is made the initial point . . . [72]

The attorney's argument was successful. A new survey was ordered by the court. But that decision was appealed nine years later. On appeal it was determined that the lower court had used an incorrect translation of the original grant to determine the metes and bounds. Furthermore, it had ignored the official act of concession, the traditional description of extent, the designation by name, and the correct *diseño*.[73] Needless to say, María García retained her claim.

In another drawn-out case the land board rejected the claims to Rancho Paso de Bartolo advanced by Pío Pico and Juan Perez. The decision was sustained on appeal, recognizing the legitimate land claims of Joaquina Sepulveda and her partner, Bernardino Guirado, to whom parcels had been bequeathed by the original grantee, Juan Crispin Perez.[74]

Given the complexity and the length of many of these land cases, it is not surprising that attorney's fees mounted. An informal inventory of cases represented by the law firm of Halleck, Peachy and Billings reveals that in 1852 in the Northern Judicial District the firm represented Juana Briones and a Mrs. Read, a claimant to Tamalpais Ranch. In the south the firm represented four other women grantees. The titles had been lost, however, to both Los Huertas and El Alamo Pintado grants. In light of only the faint hope the firm could offer the claimant, Dona Maria Antonio de la Guerra de Lataillade, she was charged a mere $50. But for Ysabel Yorba's claim to Rancho Guadalasca, which the firm felt had merits and would settle successfully four years later, the fee was $500.[75]

In the course of defending the claims of the widow Dona Josefa Cota de Nieto and Ramon Yorba to portions of Rancho Santa Gertrudis, Abel Stearns lent them the Land Commission fee of fifty young cows. He also lent money to members of the family at the rate of 5 percent compounded monthly, a fairly common practice. As a result, the debt doubled within a year. In 1861 Rancho Los Bolsas was sold at auction to satisfy the $28,043 note Stearns held. He acquired the ranch land for a bid of $15,000.[76]

María Rita Valdez de Villa was one of those who was forced to justify her land claim without the benefit of title papers. Her records, she explained, had been removed from a trunk in her Los Angeles townhouse during the American occupation in 1846. Her proof of ownership, therefore, had to be provided by witness. A son, Manano, testified that she had cultivated the ranch land since 1832, with the exception of two years when his brother-in-law was in charge. General José Castro recounted that Governor Juan Alvarado had transmitted to him the official title granting María Rita one league of land.

The board confirmed the title in September 1855, and it was affirmed on appeal by the United States District Court in June of 1857. By then María Rita had sold her ranch, the future site of Beverly Hills, to Henry Hancock and Benjamin D. Wilson for $1,300.[77]

Despite the lost titles, the ambiguity of evidence claims, in its first five years of hearings the board reviewed 813 claims, confirming 603 and rejecting 190. Ten of the latter had been advanced by female claimants.[78]

As grantees, the Californianas endured equally the cataclysm which beset the ranchos in the 1860s. In addition to litigation cost and expensive land title examinations, the years brought epidemic disease, attacks by cattle rustlers, infestations by grasshoppers, drought, and floods. During the severe rains in January 1868, the Los Angeles *News* reported that, as a result of the flooding in San Francisquito Canyon, "Dona Neviu's ranch was washed away."[79]

Challenges facing California land holders also included the blatant disregard of their claims by the increasing number of American settlers. Not accustomed to such vast holdings, the newcomers' interest in the land soon extended beyond usufructuary rights (the right to enjoy profits from another's land or property) and riparian rights (the rights of an owner of land bordering a watercourse). Many of them became squatters, exercising, they declared, preemptive rights to the land. Having thus established their claim, they sometimes even sold it to others.

Such a sequence of events caused the widow Ampara Burton and her two children to be evicted in 1871 from their Rancho Jamul, which her late husband General Henry Stanton Burton had acquired from Pío Pico.

After three years of litigation, the Supreme Court of California recognized Burton's legal claim, set forth in her own concisely logical briefs, to the land as confirmed by the Board of Land Commissioners, the U.S. District Court and the U.S. Supreme Court. The court, therefore, ordered a payment to Mrs. Burton of $10,000 in damages by W. N. Robinson, although he argued that he had purchased the land in good faith from William Cant, who had presented the claim as public land, which he was acquiring by preemption.[80] The dispute, which extended over 23 years, led Burton to write a veiled autobiographical novel entitled *The Squatter and the Don*.

Espiritu Leonis also fell victim to land grabbers. Fortunately she was represented by the very able Stephen M. White, who, first of all, secured for Espiritu a fair share of her husband's estate. Ultimately, he was forced to represent her three more times, once before the California Supreme Court. It was not until 1905 that he ultimately succeeded in protecting her inheritance. The unwitting widow had been the victim of a number of dishonest schemes.

> She gave power of attorney to Laurent Etchepare, who a few months later claimed she owed him $5000. Another man, using a paper she had signed, sold cattle belonging to her and then kept the money. Two others who owed the Leonis estate about $12,000 used her signature on a paper as proof they had paid her $8000. As a climax, Etchepare maneuvered so that all her property was conveyed to him.[81]

Fortunately, the capable Stephen White assisted her in each instance.

Not all were as fortunate as Espiritu in finding able champions. Dona Merced Williams Rains, widow of the murdered John Rains, who left no will, was persuaded to surrender her power of attorney and convey the lands of Rancho Cucamonga to her children. During an all-day session March 14, 1863, in her drawing room the young widow was pressured to take these actions by six male relatives and so-called family advisors. Three of them were lawyers—one from Yale and another from Harvard. Finally, her ambitious brother-in-law, Robert Carlisle, secured her power of attorney. Of that day a friend later said, "There was placed an iron chain around the necks of all concerned and it ruled their lives for years."[82]

New California residents, not unlike those who had gathered at Rancho Cucamonga, convened at Monterey in September 1849 to draft a state constitution. The majority came from a culture grounded in the Anglo-Saxon legal tradition. For them, the law which governed their essentially male world was adversarial in style. To them, the Spanish tradition of conciliatory dispute resolution was characterized, at best, as the absence of law. Equally alien to them was the idea of a married woman having a separate identity before the law.[83]

In contrast with Spanish law, English and American law designated husbands as the legal representatives of their wives. Indeed, according to that legal tradition, marriage represented civil death for the wife, commonly referred to as coverture, or by its traditional description, "the law of *baron et feme*," or lord and woman. As legal justification for this interpretation, nineteenth-century lawyers on both sides of the Atlantic consistently cited Blackstone's *Commentaries on the Laws of England*, which stated:

> By marriage, the husband and the wife are one person in law . . .
> that is, the very being as legal existence of the woman is suspended
> during the marriage, or, at least, is incorporated and consolidated
> into that of the husband; under whose wing, protection and cover,
> she performed everything.[84]

Single women could function on an equal basis with men in the area of property ownership, but wives suffered a mediated claim to their property. As a result, married women under English law were denied the right to buy, sell, or lease property. Nor could they use their property as collateral, alter, build upon, nor devise it to heirs. As long as a woman was married, English law contended, even her interest in property acquired before marriage remained dormant, to be controlled along with its profits by the husband. English law defined a married woman as chattel of her husband, who controlled her property, her earnings and even her children.[85]

Control of property differed by class, however. The wealthy in England and the colonies established trusts for daughters, or required future spouses to sign prenuptial agreements. In England these separate estates were administered by the courts of equity, rather than the courts of law. Unfortunately, although the Chancery Courts concerned with equity law adjudicated marriage settlements and defined and enhanced married women's property rights the courts of common law often failed to enforce these judgments. Furthermore, the laws of equity were rarely defined in statute. Consequently, they were not codified in Blackstone's *Commentaries*, which provided the basis for American jurisprudence.[86]

In America the interpretation of English law differed from colony to colony. For example, New Englanders accorded husbands even more control than in the other colonies over family property, including what wives earned or inherited. In Connecticut the land brought to a marriage by a wife became the husband's absolutely, and upon his death the wife was entitled to only a share of the property, with no influence over the mortgage or sale of the holdings. In light of such practices, it is interesting that researchers have found only a few examples of agreements protecting the separate estates of married women in colonial America.

The failure in the colonies, and later in United States law, to protect a married woman's dower and inheritance resulted from the colonists' aggressive elimination of the courts of chancery. This facet of the English judicial system, which dispenses equity law so crucial for married women, was opposed by colonists as being too time consuming, since it was required that all records submitted to Chancery courts be in written form. Chancery courts were also criticized as being dependent upon the subjective judgment of the chancellor, often referred to as "the keeper of the king's conscience." As a result, the Courts of Chancery were closely identified with the abhorrent royal prerogative.[87]

Such were the legal traditions and the juridical frame of reference shared by the young American delegates to California's first constitutional convention. During the deliberations in Colton Hall, Monterey, the drafting committee submitted, as Section 13 of the "Miscellaneous Provision," a statement using the exact language found in the Texas constitution, addressing the issue of women's rights. Not surprisingly, the ensuing debate expressed the common sentiment that woman was neither the physical nor the mental equal to man, and hence she could not be man's social, business, or legal peer.[88]

Despite this unfavorable assessment of women, the California Constitution of 1849 continued to recognize the principles of community property traditionally respected under Spanish law and thus assumed in Article VIII of the Treaty of Guadalupe Hidalgo. It directed that:

> All property, both real and personal of the wife, owned or claimed
> by [before] marriage, and that acquired afterwards by gift, devise, or
> descent, shall be her separate property; and laws shall be passed
> more clearly defining the rights of the wife, in relation as well to
> her separate property, as to that held in common with the husband.[89]

This departure from the Anglo-Saxon legal principle of the civil death of the wife after marriage and the adoption, instead, of a recognition of a husband's and wife's community property, as held under Spanish law, is particularly significant since on April 13, 1850, the Legislature declared that "the Common Law of England shall be the rule of decision in all courts of this state."[90]

Some historians contend that the endorsement of the concept of community property reflected the growing sense of democracy and egalitarianism found along the western frontier, as well as a practical response to the need to attract women settlers. It is true that the Oregon Donation Act of 1850 granted land ownership to women, as did the Homestead Acts of 1860 and 1890.[91] But the recognition of community property rights in the states which had been part of the Mexican Cession is more clearly derivative of the Spanish tradition, in which community property was incorporated into substantive law in order to strengthen the economic control by a wife and her relatives.[92]

The favorable disposition for the United States to accept such foreign precedent in acquired territories had been established as early as 1828 when the Supreme Court addressed the governing policies to be employed in the Territory of Florida. It determined then that although political allegiance may be changed, laws regulating the general conduct of individuals should remain in place. Californios cited the decision as being applicable in California and thus existing law, not in conflict with United States laws, should remain in place.

Consistent with this position, the first legislature of California, meeting at San Jose in 1851, acknowledged the principle of community property in Section I of "An Act Defining the Rights of Husband and Wife."[93] The failure of the legislators to either understand or embrace the principle of the equality of marital partners was clearly evident, however, in Section 13. It stipulated that any sale of the wife's property for the benefit of the husband would be deemed gift. There was no provision made for examination of the wife's testimony, nor request for her written consent.

Other acts approved in the first legislative session prohibited a married woman from altering her will without the written consent of her husband annexed to the will.[94] Another statute regulating conveyances stipulated that marriage would extinguish the right of a woman to continue to serve as an administratrix.[95]

Additional statutes and court decisions invoking common law precedent continued to undermine the traditional legal status of California women as defined under Hispanic law, and the principle of community property. In 1861 a law was passed allowing the estate of a deceased wife to revert to the husband rather than to her children. It became Civil Code Section 1401.

By the latter part of the century the status a married woman had enjoyed under Spanish law was effectively undermined. Section 172 of the Civil Code allowed a husband absolute power to sell, mortgage, or exchange the community property.[96]

The growing inequity, rather than parity and quality vaunted along the democratic western frontier, inspired the following rhymed complaint about California's community property laws.

> When back we turn the leaves of time
> And note the world's advance
> We see its progress founded in
> Advantage, might and chance
> Final justice and equality
> Have not an influence large
> That they who access have to power
> Hold ruling force and charge.[97]

Evidence of the weakening of community property by statute and judicial precedent, and the diminished rights of married women generally, prompted the passage in California of the Married Woman's Property Act. In a community property state it was a seeming redundancy that had, in fact, been made necessary by the erosion of rights assured under Hispanic law.[98]

Ironically, despite legal obstructions, the tradition of married women independently owning land continued in this increasingly inhospitable environment. The 1886 State Surveyor General's Report of Spanish and Mexican Land Grants included among existing owners the names of twenty-four rancheras who had received patents to their lands before the American occupation, and subsequently had proven successfully the validity of their claims before the Board of Land Commissioners.[99]

These rancheras represented a continuing tradition of independent land ownership by women which was eroded over the passage of time. Only with the passing decades and with indomitable struggle would ranks of California's feminist reformers recapture, through the courts and the ballot box, their long-lost rights, as only now women begin to successfully recapture their long-lost history.

NOTES

1. Salome Hernandez, "No Settlement Without Women: Three Spanish California Settlement Schemes, 1790-1800," *Southern California Quarterly*, 72 (Fall 1990): 204.

2. Susanna Bryant Dakin, *Rose or Rose Thorn* (Berkeley: Friends of the Bancroft Library, University of California, Berkeley, 1963), pp. 1-12. See also Frances R. Conley, "Martina Didn't Have a Covered Wagon: A Speculative Reconstruction," *The Californians*, 7 (March/August 1989): 48-54.

3. Hernandez, "No Settlement Without Women," pp. 205-212.

4. Ibid., pp. 210-212.

5. Ibid., p. 215.

6. Ibid., pp. 220-222.

7. Richard Griswold del Castillo, *The Los Angeles Barrio, 1850-1890: A Social History* (Berkeley: University of California Press, 1979), p. 8.

8. Data derived from Marie E. Northrop, *Spanish-Mexican Families of Early California: 1769-1850* (2 vols., Burbank, Calif.: Southern California Genealogical Society, 1984).

9. *Langsdorf's Narrative of the Resanov Voyage to Nueva California in 1806*, translated by T. C. Russell (San Francisco: Howell-North Books, 1927), quoted by W. Turrentine Jackson, *Readings on California in the Spanish–Mexican Period* (Davis, 1978), p. 95.

10. Hubert H. Bancroft, *Register of Pioneer Inhabitants of California, 1542 to 1848* (Los Angeles: Dawson's Book Shop, 1964), p. 778.

11. Griswold del Castillo, *Los Angeles Barrio*, pp. 65-66. See also Barbara Laslett, "Household Structure on the American Frontier: Los Angeles, California in 1850," *American Journal of Sociology*, 10 (July 1975), and Marie Northrop, "Los Angeles Padron of 1844," *Southern California Quarterly*, 42 (December 1960): 360-422.

12. George P. Hammond, ed., *The Larkin Papers: Personal, Business, and Correspondence of Thomas Oliver Larkin* (10 vols., Berkeley and Los Angeles: University of California Press, 1951-1967), V:239.

13. Griswold del Castillo, *Los Angeles Barrio*, p. 46.

14. David Hornbeck, "Land Tenure and Rancho Expansion in Alta California, 1784-1846," *Journal of Historical Geography*, 4 (Winter 1978): 371-390.

15. Robert G. Cowan, *Ranchos of California: A List of Spanish Concessions, 1775-1822 and Mexican Grants 1822-1846* (Los Angeles: Historical Society of Southern California, 1977); William Cary Jones, "Report on Land Titles in California," *Senate Executive Document No. 17*, 31st Congress, 2nd Session, 1850; rancho title papers and maps are available in Record Group 49, Records of the General Land Office, California Pri-

vate Land Claims, National Archives, Washington, D.C.; Warren A. Beck and Ynez D. Haase, *Historical Atlas of California* (Norman, Oklahoma: University of Oklahoma Press, 1969), pp. 24–39.

16. Data derived from analysis of Cowan, *Ranchos of California*; Hubert H. Bancroft, *Pioneer Register*, and Eugene B. Drake, comp., *Jimeno's and Hartnell's Index to Land Concessions from 1830 to 1846, Including Toma de Razon or Registry of Titles for 1844–45* (San Francisco: Kenny and Alexander, 1861).

17. W. W. Robinson, *Land in California* (Berkeley and Los Angeles: University of California Press, 1948), p. 57.

18. Doyce B. Nunis Jr., ed. *Southern California Local History: A Gathering of the Writing of W. W. Robinson* (Los Angeles: Historical Society of Southern California, 1993), p. 5.

19. Susanna Bryant Dakin, *A Scotch Paisano in Old Los Angeles* (Berkeley and Los Angeles: University of California Press, 1939), pp. 51–52. Dakin may be incorrect in also attributing Rancho Santa Anita to Dona Victoria. Cowan notes that Hugo Reid purchased it from Henry Dalton for $2,700. See also Robinson, *Land in California*, p. 71.

20. Richard Griswold del Castillo, *La Familia: Chicano Families in the Urban Southwest, 1848 to the Present* (Notre Dame, Indiana: University of Notre Dame Press, 1984), p. 129.

21. William Heath Davis, *Seventy-Five Years in California*, Harold A. Small, ed. (San Francisco, 1967), p. 45.

22. David J. Langum, *Law and Community on the Mexican California Frontier* (Norman: University of Oklahoma, Press, 1987), pp. 30–31. Additional bodies of Spanish law included in the Fuero Real (1255), Siete Partidas (1263), Nueva recopilacion (1567), Cedulas from the Council of the Indies, and decrees of the Spanish Cortes (1820 to September 23, 1821), as well as the Partidas and the Laws of Toro.

23. Gustavus Schmidt, *The Civil Laws of Spain and Mexico: Arranged on the Principles of the Modern Codes With Notes and References* (New Orleans: Printed for the Author by Rea, 1851).

24. Schmidt, *Civil Laws of Spain and Mexico*, p. 81.

25. Janet Lecompte, "The Independent Women of Hispanic New Mexico, 1821–1846," *Western Historical Quarterly*, 12 (January 1981): 26.

26. Ibid., p. 27.

27. María de las Rivas, "Informacion" (Tolancingo, Mexico, 1562). File in Bancroft Library, University of California, Berkeley.

28. John E. Johnson, trans., *Regulations for Governing the Provinces of the Californias Approved By His Majesty by Royal Order Dated October 24, 1781* (San Francisco: Grabhorn Press, 1929), p. 44.

29. Antonio Coronel, "Cosas de California," p. 229, Bancroft Library.

30. Griswold del Castillo, *Los Angeles Barrio*, p. 65.

31. Hernandez, "No Settlement Without Women," p. 209.

32. Hubert H. Bancroft, *History of California* (7 vols., San Francisco: History Company, 1886–1890), II: 420, 614; III: 719.

33. Leonard Pitt, *Decline of the Californios* (Berkeley: University of California Press, 1970), p. 264. Neither the first census of the Los Angeles District in 1834, nor La Padron, the Census of 1844, lists employed women. See J. Gregg Layne, comp., "The First Great Census of the Los Angeles District," *Historical Society of Southern California Quarterly*, 18 (September/December 1936): 81–114, and Marie Northrop, "Padron of 1844," *Historical Society of Southern California Quarterly*, 42 (December 1960): 360–422.

34. Lecompte, "Independent Women of New Mexico," p. 21.

35. Jackson, *Readings on California in the Spanish-Mexican Period*, p. 105.

36. David Langum, "Mexican California's Legal System," *The Californians*, 5 (May/June 1987): 46–47.

37. The provisions of these laws are fully discussed in H. W. Hallock, "Report on California Land Claims," *House Executive Document No. 17*, 31st Congress, 1st Session, 1850, pp. 118–182.

38. Estimates of land concessions made during the Spanish period range from less than twenty in Robert G. Cleland, *Cattle on a Thousand Hills* (San Marino, Calif.: Henry E. Huntington Library, 1951), p. 19, to about thirty, according to Robinson, *Land in California*, p. 57.

39. Iris H. W. Engstrand, "An Enduring Legacy: California Ranchos in Historical Perspective," *Journal of the West*, 27 (July 1988): 10.

40. Cleland, *Cattle on a Thousand Hills*, p. 26.

41. Manuel P. Servin, "The Secularization of the California Mission," *Southern California Quarterly*, 47 (June 1965): 133–150; Iris H. W. Engstrand, "California Ranchos: Their Hispanic Heritage," *Southern California Quarterly*, 67 (Fall 1985): 281–290; Cleland, *Cattle on a Thousand Hills*, pp. 20–23.

42. Cowan, *Ranchos of California*, wherein various ranchos are listed alphabetically.

43. Ibid.

44. Albert Shumate, *Boyhood Days* (San Francisco: California Historical Society, 1983), p. 93.

45. Jimeno and Hartnell, *Index to Land Concessions*, No. 122, p. 14.

46. Bancroft, *History of California*, 4: 672.

47. Jimeno and Hartnell, *Index of Land Concessions*, No. 275, p. 15.

48. Ibid., No. 441, p. 11.

49. Ibid., p. 7.

50. Jimeno and Hartnell, *Index to Land Concessions*, No. 284, p. 17.

51. After Merine's death the grant was denounced for lack of improvements and Juan Perez, Enrique Sepulveda and Manuel Garfias paid her for the stone house which had been built on the property. See W. W. Robinson, "Pasadena's First Owner as Disclosed in the Expediente for the Rancho San Pascual," *Quarterly of the Historical Society of Southern California*, 19 (September/December 1937): 132–140.

52. Nunis, ed., *Southern California Local History*, p. 110.

53. Orange County, California Genealogical Society, *Saddleback Ancestors: Rancho Families of Orange County, California* (Orange County, Calif., n.p., 1969), pp. 123–124.

54. Harris Newmark, *Sixty Years in Southern California* (Los Angeles: Zeitlin and Ver Brugge, 1970), p. 174.

55. Bancroft, *Pioneer Register*, p. 750.

56. U.S. Commission on Land Claims in California, "Title papers. Briefs of Counsel Opinion of the Board and Decree of Confirmation in Case N. 81, J. R. Bolton vs. the United States for the Lands of ex-Mission Dolores" (San Francisco: John A. Lewis, 1855), pp. 72–73.

57. Pío Pico, "Narracion Historica," Bancroft Library, quoted in Griswold del Castillo, *Los Angeles Barrio*, p. 70.

58. W. W. Robinson, *Land in California*, p. 86.

59. Alfred Robinson, *Life in California*, p. 41.

60. U.S. Land Commission, Case No. 117, Dona Isabel Yorba (Maitorena) vs. The United States (San Francisco: n.d.).

61. Orange County, California Genealogical Society, *Saddleback Ancestors*, pp. 72–73.

62. Davis, *Seventy-Five Years in California*, p. 223.

63. Jeanne McDonnell, "Juana Briones de Miranda, 1802–1889," Unpublished manuscript. Women's Heritage Museum, Palo Alto, California.

64. Shumate, *Boyhood Days*, p. 10.

65. Richard Griswold del Castillo, *The Treaty of Guadalupe Hidalgo: A Legacy of Conflict* (Norman: University of Oklahoma Press, 1990), pp. 89–91.

66. George P. Hammond, ed., *The Treaty of Guadalupe Hidalgo: February Second,

1848 (Berkeley: University of California Press, 1949), p. 67. See also John Curry, *Treaty of Guadalupe Hidalgo and Private Land Claims and Titles Existing in California at the Date of the Treaty* (n.p., 1891).

67. Geoffrey P. Mawn, "A Land-Grant Guarantee: The Treaty of Guadalupe Hidalgo or the Protocol of Queretaro," *Journal of the West*, 4 (October 1975): 61.

68. Commission For Settling Private Land Claims in California. *Instructions of the Department of the Interior to the Commission* (San Francisco, 1852). See also Paul Wallace Gates, "The California Land Act of 1851," *California Historical Society Quarterly*, 50 (December 1971); William W. Morrow, *Spanish and Mexican Private Land Grants* (San Francisco, 1923).

69. Hornbeck, "Land Tenure," p. 380. See also Jacob Bowman, *Index to Spanish–Mexican private land grant cases and records of California* (Berkeley: Bancroft Library, 1958).

70. Robinson, *Land in California*, p. 102.

71. Peachy and Billings, "Brief [in California Lands Case 31, S.D. 127] for Rancho Guadalasca, Isabel Yorba Maitorena, Claimant" (1856), Halleck, Peachy and Billings Papers, Huntington Library, San Marino.

72. Glassell, Chapman and Smith, "The United States vs. Maria de Jesus Green," p. 16, Glassell, Chapman and Smith Papers, Huntington Library.

73. Glassell, Chapman and Smith, "U.S. Appellee vs. Maria de Jesus Garcia, *et al.* Appellants: Reply to Brief for the United States" (Los Angeles: n.p.). Ibid.

74. "Confirmation and Title and Patent for Part of Paso de Bartolo Granted to Bernardino Guirado" (Washington, D.C.: September 27, 1867). Ibid.

75. Halleck, Peachy and Billings, [Lists of California and Claims] Cases to Be Submitted to Northern and Southern California District [Courts], (1852), Halleck, Peachy and Billings Papers.

76. *Saddleback Ancestors*, p. 128.

77. Nunis, ed., *Southern California Local History*, pp. 10–12.

78. Cowan, *Ranchos of California*, p. 14, passim.

79. Thompson and West, *History of Los Angeles County, California* (Reprint ed., Berkeley: Howell-North Books, 1959), p. 54.

80. Supreme Court of the State of California, Maria Burton, *et al.*, Plaintiffs and Respondents, vs. W. N. Robinson. Appellant and Defendant" (San Diego, 1874). For a discussion of preemption as a fundamental American land policy, see Paul Wallace Gates, "California's Embattled Settlers" *Quarterly of the California Historical Society*, 41 (June 1962): 99–130. See also the letters of Maria Amparo Burton to Don Mariano Guadalupe, Henry E. Huntington Library.

81. Lynn Bowman, *Los Angeles: Epic of a City* (Berkeley: Howell-North Books, 1974), pp. 207–208.

82. Esther B. Black, *Rancho Cucamonga and Dona Merced* (Redlands, California: San Bernardino County Museum Association, 1975), pp. 83–85.

83. Langum, "Mexican California's Legal System," p. 144. "In most cases plaintiff and defendant appeared before the alcalde called *Juez* in his official capacity, for an attempt at conciliation. If the juez could not reconcile the parties, each named an arbitrator, or *hombre bueno* whose opinion the juez considered before pronouncing his judgment. If plaintiff and defendant did not agree with the judgment, the case was dropped, or the plaintiff made a formal charge whereupon witnesses were called, testimony taken, and the proceedings sent to the governor for a verdict. Appeal from the governor's verdict was to the superior tribunal in Guadalajara (later Chihuahua), a slow and costly process." Lecompte, "Independent Women of Hispanic New Mexico," p. 24.

84. Edward Blackstone, *Commentaries on the Laws of England* (19th ed., Philadelphia: Lippincott and Co., 1891), p. 355.

85. Linda K. Kerber, "The Paradox of Women's Citizenship in the Early Republic: The Case of Martin vs. Massachusetts, 1805," *American Historical Review*, 97 (April 1992): 349–378.

86. Mari J. Matsuda, "The Western Legal Status of Women: Explanation of Frontier Feminism," *Law in the West*, David Langum, ed. (Manhattan, Kansas: Sunflower Press, 1985), pp. 4–55.

87. Marilyn Salmon, *Women and the Law of Property in the United States* (Chapel Hill: University of North Carolina Press, 1986), pp. 81–119. See also Joan Hoff Wilson, *Unequal Before the Law: A Legal History of United States Women* (New York: Simon and Schuster, 1991).

88. Donald E. Hargis, "Women's Rights: California 1849," *Historical Society of Southern California Quarterly* 37 (December 1955): 333.

89. Richard R. Powell, *Compromises of Conflicting Claims: A Century of California Law, 1760 to 1860* (Dobbs Ferry, N.Y.: Oceana Publisher, 1977), p. 199. See also Susan Praeger, "The Persistence of Separate Property Concepts in California's Community Property System, 1849–1975," *UCLA Law Review*, 24 (1976): 1–2; Marion R. Kirkwood, "Historical Background and Objectives of the Law of Community Property in the Pacific Coast States," *Washington Law Review* 11 (1936): 1–4; Orrin K. McMurray, "The Beginning of the Community Property System in California and the Adoption of the Common Law," *California Law Review* 3 (1915): 359; Ray August, "The Spread of Community Property Law to the Far West," *Western Legal History*, 3 (Winter/Spring 1990): 35–66.

90. Powell, *Compromises of Conflicting Claims*, p. 199. For a fuller explanation, see Edwin W. Young, "California and the Common Law," *Historical Society of Southern California Quarterly* XLIX (December 1960), 318–324.

91. Matsuda, "The West and the Legal Status of Women," p. 42. See also Gordon Bakken, *Development of Law on the Rocky Mountain Frontier: Civil Law and Society, 1850–1912* (Westport, Conn.: Greenwood Press, 1983), pp. 21–40.

92. Barbara A. Armstrong, *California Family Law* (2 vols., San Francisco, 1953), I: 431; Matsuda, "Western Legal Status of Women," pp. 51–55.

93. "An Act Defining the Rights of Husband and Wife," *Acts of the First California Legislature* (San Jose, 1851), pp. 1–4.

94. "An Act Concerning Wills," *Acts of the First California Legislature*, Section 2, p. 164.

95. "An Act Concerning Conveyances," *Acts of the First California Legislature*, Section 58, p. 628.

96. Mrs. Willoughby Rodman, *Laws of California Relating to Women and Children* (Los Angeles: n.p., n.d.), pp. 36–39. See also Mrs. J. W. Stowe, *Probate Codification and the Unjust Laws which Govern Women* (n.p., 1876), pp. 5–7; J. M. Days, J. N. Turner and C. G. Freeman, "Report of Special Committee in Relation to Granting Women Political Equality," *Appendix to Journal of the Senate and Assembly of the Nineteenth Session of the Legislature of California* (Sacramento: State Printer, 1872), III: 4.

97. Martin J. Boutelle, *Community and Separate in California: The Laws of Property in Form Unique* (Pasadena: Calif.: n.p., 1914).

98. Peggy Rabkin, "The Origin of Social Reform: The Significance of the Passage of the Early Married Woman's Property Act," *Buffalo Law Review*, 24 (1975): 683.

99. State Surveyor General, *Corrected Report of Spanish and Mexican Land Grants in California Complete to February 25, 1886* (Sacramento, 1886).

PART III

THE NINETEENTH CENTURY

5 MOUNTAIN MAN AS JACKSONIAN MAN

William H. Goetzmann

The "Mountain Men" of the early-nineteenth-century Far West are, as Professor William Goetzmann of the University of Texas notes here, among "the most studied and least understood figures in American history." Beyond all the mythology, archetypes, and stereotypes, who were they really? What were their motives in living what Goetzmann discovers to have been an extremely risky and low-paying life, far from civilization? What were they trying to do for themselves, and what (mostly unintentionally) did they do to promote American development and territorial acquisition?

This essay recounts the leading myths about the Mountain Men and ties them to another stereotype of the early nineteenth century, "Jacksonian Man"—the acquisitive, ambitious, materialistic, and ideologically conservative American of that time, whether or not he actually voted for Andrew Jackson ("he" because, of course, women did not vote in those days). Goetzmann then analyzes all the evidence that is reliable on several hundred known Mountain Men, especially as to what they did and how successful they were. The results often belie the stereotype.

Finally, the essay sets forth three ways in which the combination of the Mountain Man and Jacksonian Man personalities influenced western and American development: by helping make the West commercial and not just agrarian; by exploring and mapping the West, thus greatly aiding settlers in finding their way to it; and by making sure that the West, as a geographical region, would become American—not Spanish, French, or British—in politics and culture. They were agents of "manifest destiny." Do you agree? Should they have been?—editors

ONE OF THE most often studied and least understood figures in American history has been the Mountain Man. Remote, so it would seem, as Neanderthal, and according to some almost as inarticulate, the Mountain Man exists as a figure of American mythology rather than history. As such he has presented at least two vivid stereotypes to the public imagination. From the first he has been the very symbol for the romantic banditti of the forest, freed of the artificial restrictions of civilization—a picturesque wanderer in the wilderness whose very life is a constant and direct association with Nature.

> "There is perhaps, no class of men on the face of the earth," said Captain Bonneville [and through him Washington Irving], "who lead life of more continued exertion, peril, and excitement, and who are more enamoured of their occupations, than the free trappers of the west. No toil, no danger, no privation can turn the trapper from his pursuit. His passionate excitement at times resembles a mania. In vain may the most vigilant and cruel savages beset his path; in vain may rocks, and precipices, and wintry torrents oppose his progress; let but a single track of a beaver meet his eye, and he forgets all dangers and defies all difficulties. At times, he may be seen with his traps on his shoulder, buffeting his way across rapid streams amidst floating blocks of ice: at other times, he is to be found with his traps on his back clambering the most rugged mountains, scaling or descending the most frightening precipices, searching by routes inaccessible to the horse, and never before trodden by white man, for springs and lakes unknown to his comrades, and where he may meet with his favorite game. Such is the mountaineer, the hardy trapper of the west; and such as we have slightly sketched it, is the wild, Robin Hood kind of life, with all its strange and motley populace, now existing in full vigor among the Rocky mountains."[1]

To Irving in the nineteenth century the Mountain Man was Robin Hood, a European literary convention. By the twentieth century the image was still literary and romantic but somewhat less precise. According to Bernard De Voto, "For a few years Odysseus Jed Smith and Siegfried Carson and the wing-shod Fitzpatrick actually drew breath in this province of fable," and Jim Beckwourth "went among the Rockies as Theseus dared the wine-dark seas. Skirting the rise of a hill, he saw the willows stirring; he charged down upon them, while despairing Blackfeet sang the death-song—and lo, to the clear music of a horn, Roland had met the pagan hordes. . . ."[2]

On the other hand, to perhaps more discerning eyes in his own day and down through the years, the Mountain Man presented another image—one that was far less exalted. Set off from the ordinary man by his costume of greasy buckskins, coonskin cap and Indian finery, not to mention the distinctive odor that went with bear grease and the habitual failure to bathe between one yearly rendezvous and the next, the Mountain Man seemed a forlorn and pathetic primitive out of the past. "They are stared at as though they were bears," wrote Rudolph F. Kurz, a Swiss artist who traveled the Upper Missouri.[3]

The Mountain Man, so it was said, was out of touch with conventional civilization and hence not quite acceptable.[4] Instead in his own time and

THE TRAPPER'S LAST SHOT.

7. A mounted man with his rifle, on the lookout. *The Denver Public Library, Western History Collection.*

even more today he has been viewed as a purely hedonistic character who lived for the year's end rendezvous where he got gloriously drunk on diluted rot-gut company alcohol, gave his beaver away for wildly inflated company trade goods and crawled off into the underbrush for a delirious orgy with some unenthusiastic Indian squaw. In this view the romantic rendezvous was nothing more than a modern company picnic, the object of which was to keep the employees docile, happy and ready for the coming year's task. Pacified, satisfied, cheated, impoverished and probably mortified the next day, the Mountain Man, be he free trapper or not, went back to his dangerous work when the rendezvous was over. He was thus to many shrewd observers not a hero at all but a docile and obedient slave of the company. By a stretch of the imagination he might have seemed heroic but because of the contrast between his daring deeds and his degraded status he seemed one of the saddest heroes in all history. Out of date before his time was up, he was a wild free spirit who after all was not free. He was instead an adventurer who was bringing about his own destruction even as he succeeded in his quest to search out the beaver in all of the secret places of the mountain West. A dependent of the London dandy and his foppish taste in hats, the Mountain Man was Caliban. He was a member of a picturesque lower class fast vanishing from the face of America. Like the Mohican Indian and quaint old Leatherstocking he was a vanishing breed, forlorn and permanently class-bound in spite of all his heroics.[5]

Both of these stereotypes embody, as do most effective stereotypes,

more than a measure of reality. The Mountain Man traveled far out ahead
of the march of conventional civilization, and the job he did required him
to be as tough, primitive and close to nature as an Indian. Moreover, it was
an out-of-doors life of the hunt and the chase that he often grew to like.
By the same token because he spent much of his time in primitive isolation in the mountains, he very often proved to be a poor businessman ig-
norant of current prices and sharp company practices. Even if aware of his
disadvantageous position he could do nothing to free himself until he had
made his stake.

The fact is, however, that many Mountain Men lived for the chance to
exchange their dangerous mountain careers for an advantageous start in
civilized life. If one examines their lives and their stated aspirations one
discovers that the Mountain Men, for all their apparent eccentricities, were
astonishingly similar to the common men of their time—plain republican
citizens of the Jacksonian era.

Jacksonian Man, according to Richard Hofstadter, "was an expectant
capitalist, a hardworking ambitious person for whom enterprise was a
kind of religion."[6] He was "the master mechanic who aspired to open his
own shop, the planter, or farmer who speculated in land, the lawyer who
hoped to be a judge, the local politician who wanted to go to Congress, the
grocer who would be a merchant. . . . "[7] To this list one might well add the
trapper who hoped some day, if he hit it lucky and avoided the scalping
knife, to be one or all of these, or perhaps better still, a landed gentleman
of wealth and prestige.

"Everywhere," writes Hofstadter, the Jacksonian expectant capitalist
"found conditions that encouraged him to extend himself."[8] And there
were many like William Ashley or Thomas James who out of encouragement or desperation looked away to the Rocky Mountains, teeming with
beaver and other hidden resources, and saw a path to economic success
and rapid upward mobility. In short, when he went out West and became
Mountain Man the Jacksonian Man did so as a prospector. He too was an
expectant capitalist.

Marvin Meyers has added a further characterization of Jacksonian
Man. He was, according to Meyers, the "venturous conservative,"[9] the
man who desired relative freedom from restraint so that he might risk his
life and his fortune, if not his sacred honor, on what appeared to be a long-
term, continent-wide boom. Yet at the same time he wished to pyramid his
fortune within the limits of the familiar American social and economic
system, and likewise to derive his status therefrom. Wherever he went, and
especially on the frontier, Jacksonian Man did not wish to change the system. He merely wished to throw it open as much as possible to opportunity, with the hope that by so doing he could place himself at the top instead of at the bottom of the conventional social and economic ladder.
"They love change," wrote Tocqueville, "but they dread revolutions."[10] Instead of a new world the Jacksonian Man wished to restore the old where
the greatest man was the independent man—yeoman or mechanic, trader

or ranchero—the man who basked in comfort and sturdy security under his own "vine and fig tree."

The structure of the Rocky Mountain fur trade itself, the life stories of the trappers and on rare occasions their stated or implied aspirations all make it clear that if he was not precisely the Meyers—Hofstadter Jacksonian Man, the Mountain Man was most certainly his cousin once removed, and a clearly recognizable member of the family.

It is a truism, of course, to state that the Rocky Mountain fur trade was a business, though writers in the Mountain Man's day and since have sometimes made it seem more like a sporting event. The Mountain Man himself often put such an ambiguous face on what he was doing.

> "Westward! Ho!" wrote Warren Ferris, an American Fur Company
> trapper. "It is the sixteenth of the second month A.D. 1830, and I
> have joined a trapping, trading, hunting expedition to the Rocky
> Mountains. Why, I scarcely know, for the motives that induced me
> to this were of a mixed complexion,—something like the pepper
> and salt population of this city of St. Louis. Curiosity, a love of
> wild adventure, and perhaps also a hope of profit,—for times *are*
> hard, and my best coat has a sort of sheepish hang-dog hesitation to
> encounter fashionable folk—combined to make me look upon the
> project with an eye of favor. The party consists of some thirty men,
> mostly Canadian; but a few there are, like myself, from various
> parts of the Union. Each has some plausible excuse for joining, and
> the aggregate of disinterestedness would delight the most ghostly
> saint in the Roman calendar. Engage for money! no, not they;—
> health, and the strong desire of seeing strange lands, of beholding
> nature in the savage grandeur of her primeval state,—these are the
> only arguments that *could* have persuaded such independent and
> high-minded young fellows to adventure with the American Fur
> Company in a trip to the mountain wilds of the great west"[11]

Ambiguous though the Mountain Man's approach to it may have been, it is abundantly clear that the Rocky Mountain fur trade was indeed a *business*, and not an invariably individualistic enterprise at that. The unit of operation was the company, usually a partnership for the sake of capital, risk and year-round efficiency. Examples of the company are the Missouri Fur Company, Gantt and Blackwell, Stone and Bostwick, Bean and Sinclair, and most famous of all, the Rocky Mountain Fur Company and its successors, Smith, Jackson, and Sublette, Sublette & Campbell, and Sublette, Fitzpatrick, Bridger, Gervais and Fraeb. These were the average company units in the Rocky Mountain trade and much of the story of their existence is analogous to Jackson's war on the "Monster Bank" for they were all forced to contend against John Jacob Astor's "Monster Monopoly," the American Fur Co., which was controlled and financed by eastern capitalists.

Perhaps the most interesting aspect of the independent fur companies was their fluid structure of leadership. There was indeed, "a baton in every knapsack" or more accurately, perhaps, in every "possibles" bag. William Ashley, owner of a gun powder factory, and Andrew Henry, a former Lisa lieutenant, and lead miner, founded the Rocky Mountain Fur Company.[12] After a few years of overwhelming success, first Henry, and then Ashley, retired, and they were succeeded by their lieutenants, Jedediah Smith, David Jackson and William Sublette, three of the "enterprising young men" who had answered Ashley's advertisement in the St. Louis *Gazette and Public Advertiser* in 1823. When Smith and Jackson moved on to more attractive endeavors first William Sublette and Robert Campbell, then Tom "Broken Hand" Fitzpatrick, James "Old Gabe" Bridger, Henry Fraeb, Milton "Thunderbolt" Sublette and Jean Baptiste Gervais moved up to fill their entrepreneurial role.

In another example Etienne Provost was successively an employee of Auguste Chouteau, partner with LeClair and leader of his own Green River brigade, and servant of American Fur.[13] Sylvestre Pattie became a Santa Fe trader, then an independent trapper, then manager of the Santa Rita (New Mexico) Copper Mines and ultimately leader of an independent trapping venture into the Gila River country of the far Southwest—a venture that ended in disaster when he was thrown into a Mexican prison in California and there left to die.[14] Most significant is the fact that few of the trappers declined the responsibility of entrepreneurial leadership when it was offered them. On the contrary, the usual practice was to indenture oneself to an established company for a period of time, during which it was possible to acquire the limited capital in the way of traps, rifle, trade goods, etc., that was needed to become independent and a potential brigade leader. Referring to his arrangement with the old Missouri Fur Company in 1809, Thomas James wrote,

> We Americans were all private adventurers, each on his own hook, and were led into the enterprise by the promises of the Company, who agreed to subsist us to the trapping grounds, we helping to navigate the boats, and on our arrival there they were to furnish us each with a rifle and sufficient ammunition, six good beaver traps and also four men of their hired French, to be under our individual commands for a period of three years.

> By the terms of the contract each of us was to divide one-fourth of the profits of our joint labor with the four men thus to be appointed to us.[15]

James himself retired when he could from the upper Missouri trade and eventually became an unsuccessful storekeeper in Harrisonville, Illinois.[16]

In addition to the fact of rapid entrepreneurial succession within the structure of the independent fur companies, a study of 446 Mountain Men (perhaps 45 percent of the total engaged in this pursuit between 1805 and 1845) indicates that their life patterns could be extremely varied. One hundred seventeen Mountain Men definitely turned to occupations other than trapping subsequent to their entering the mountain trade. Of this number, 39 followed more than one pursuit. As such they often worked at as many as four or five different callings.[17]

Moreover, beyond the 117 definite cases of alternative callings, 32 others were found to have indeterminate occupations that were almost certainly not connected with the fur trade,[18] making a total of 149 out of 154 men for whom some occupational data exists who had turned away from the trapping fraternity before 1845. Of the remaining men in the study, 110 men yielded nothing to investigation beyond the fact that they had once been trappers, 182 can be listed as killed in the line of duty and only five men out of the total stayed with the great out-of-doors life of the free trapper that according to the myth they were all supposed to love.

Table 5.1

Total Number of Cases	446
Persons whose other occupations are known	117
Persons whose other occupations are probable	32
Persons with more than one other occupation	39
Persons who stayed on as trappers	5
Persons whose status is unknown	110
Persons killed in the fur trade	182

The list of alternative callings pursued by the trappers is also revealing. Twenty-one became ranchers, fifteen farmers, seventeen traders (at stationary trading posts), eight miners, seven politicians, six distillers, five each storekeepers and army scouts, four United States Indian agents, three carpenters, two each bankers, drovers and hatters and at least one pursued each of the following occupations: sheepherder, postman, miller, medium, ice dealer, vintner, fancy fruit grower, baker, saloon keeper, clockmaker, cattle buyer, real estate speculator, newspaper editor, lawyer, lumberman, superintendent of schools, tailor, blacksmith, and supercargo of a trading schooner. Moreover many of these same individuals pursued secondary occupations such as that of hotel keeper, gambler, soldier, health resort proprietor, coal mine owner, tanner, sea captain, horse thief and opera house impresario.

From this it seems clear that statistically at least the Mountain Man was hardly the simple-minded primitive that mythology has made him out to be. Indeed it appears that whenever he had the chance, he exchanged the joys of the rendezvous and the wilderness life for the more civilized excitement of "getting ahead." In many cases he achieved this aim, and on a frontier where able men were scarce he very often became a pillar of the community, and even of the nation. From the beginning, as Ashley's

Table 5.2
List of Occupations

A. *Primary*

1. Farmer	15	17. Blacksmith	1
2. Rancher	21	18. Tailor	1
3. Politician	7	19. Supercargo	1
4. Sheepherder	1	20. Superintendent of Schools	1
5. Scout [For Govt.]	5	21. Lumberman	2
6. Trader	17	22. Newspaper Editor	1
7. Miner	8	23. Carpenter	3
8. Postman	1	24. Cattle Buyer	1
9. Distiller	6	25. Clockmaker	1
10. Miller	1	26. Saloon Keeper	1
11. Storekeeper	5	27. Baker	1
12. Medium	1	28. Fruit Grower	1
13. Banker	2	29. Vintner	1
14. Drover	2	30. Ice Dealer	1
15. Hatter	2	31. Real Estate Speculator	1
16. Indian Agent	4	32. Lawyer	1

B. *Secondary*

1. Trader	4	12. Lumberman	2
2. Transportation	2	13. Gambler	3
3. Scout	5	14. Blacksmith	1
4. Hotel Keeper	1	15. Soldier	1
5. Miner	2	16. Spa Keeper	1
6. Farmer	5	17. Coal Mine Operator	1
7. Politician	3	18. Tanner	1
8. Rancher	5	19. Opera House Impresario	1
9. Storekeeper	4	20. Sea Captain	1
10. Miller	3	21. Carpenter	1
11. Real Estate	3	22. Horse Thief	1

famous advertisement implied, the Mountain Men were men of "enterprise" who risked their lives for something more than pure romance and a misanthropic desire to evade civilization. The picturesqueness and the quaintness were largely the creation of what was the literary mentality of an age of artistic romanticism. For every "Cannibal Phil" or Robert Meldrum or "Peg-Leg" Smith there was a Sarchel Wolfskill (vintner), a George Yount (rancher) and a William Sublette (banker-politician).

Two further facts emerge in part from this data. First, it is clear that though the Jeffersonian agrarian dream of "Arcadia" bulked large in the Mountain Man's choice of occupations, it by no means obscured the whole range of "mechanical" or mercantile pursuits that offered the chance for success on the frontier. Indeed, if it suggests anything, a statistical view of the Mountain Man's "other life" suggests that almost from the beginning the Far Western frontier took on the decided aspect of an urban or semi-urban "industrial" civilization. Secondly, though it is not immediately apparent from the above statistics, a closer look indicates that a surprising number of the Mountain Men succeeded at their "other" tasks to the extent that they became regionally and even nationally prominent.

William H. Ashley became Congressman from Missouri and a spokesman for the West, Charles Bent an ill-fated though famed governor of New Mexico. "Doc" Newell was a prominent figure in the organization of Oregon Territory. Elbridge Gerry, William McGaa and John Simpson Smith were the founders and incorporators of Denver. Lucien Maxwell held the largest land grant in the whole history of the United States.

Joshua Pilcher was a famous superintendent of Indian Affairs. William Sublette, pursuing a hard money policy, saved the Bank of Missouri in the panic of 1837 and went on to be a Democratic elector for "young hickory" James K. Polk in 1844. Benjamin Wilson was elected first mayor of Los Angeles. James Clyman and his Napa Valley estate were famous in California as were the ranches of George Yount and J. J. Warner, while Sarchel Wolfskill was a co-founder of the modern California wine industry. James Waters built the first opera house in Southern California, and Kit Carson, in his later years a silver miner, received the supreme tribute of finding a dime novel dedicated to his exploits in plunder captured from marauding Apache Indians who had recently attacked and massacred a wagon train.[19]

Many of the Mountain Men achieved fame and national status through works that they published themselves, or, as in the case of Carson, through works that immortalized correctly, or as was more usual, incorrectly, their exploits. Here one need only mention Kit Carson's *Autobiography* and his favorable treatment at the hands of Jessie Benton Frémont, T. D. Bonner's *Life and Adventures of James Beckwourth*, Francis Fuller Victor's *River of the West* (about Joe Meek), James Ohio Pattie's *Personal Narrative*, Thomas James' *Three Years among the Indians and Mexicans*, H. L. Conard's *Uncle Dick Wooton*, David Coyner's *The Lost Trappers* (about Ezekial Williams), Irving's portrait of Joseph Reddeford Walker in *The Adventures of Captain Bonneville*, Zenas Leonard's *Narrative*, Peg-Leg Smith's "as told to" exploits in *Hutchings' California Magazine*, Stephen Meek's *Autobiography*, Warren Ferris' letters to the Buffalo, New York, *Western Literary Messenger*, John Hatcher's yarns in Lewis H. Garrard's *Wah To Yah and The Taos Trail* and perhaps most interesting of all, trapper John Brown's pseudo-scientific *Mediumistic Experiences*, to realize the extent and range of the Mountain Man's communication with the outside world in his own day. Not only was he a typical man of his time, he was often a conspicuous success and not bashful about communicating the fact in somewhat exaggerated terms to his fellow countrymen.

Direct evidence of the Mountain Men's motives is scarce, but it is clear their intentions were complex.

"Tell them that I have no heirs and that I hope to make a fortune," wrote Louis Vasquez ("Old Vaskiss" to Bernard De Voto) in 1834 from "Fort Convenience" somewhere in the Rockies.[20] Later, as he set out on one last expedition in 1842 he added somewhat melodramatically, "I leave to make money or die."[21] And finally Colonel A. G. Brackett, who visited Fort Bridger (jointly owned by Bridger and Vasquez), described him as "a Mexican, who put on a great deal of style, and used to ride about the country in a coach and four."[22]

"It is, that I may be able to help those who stand in need, that I face every danger," wrote Jedediah Smith from the Wind River Mountains in 1829, "most of all, it is for this, that I deprive myself of the privilege of Society and the satisfaction of the Converse of My Friends! but I shall count all this pleasure, if I am allowed by the Alwise Ruler the privilege of Joining my Friends. . . . " And he added "let it be the greatest pleasure that we can enjoy, the height of our ambition, now, when our Parents are in the decline of Life, to smooth the Pillow of their age, and as much as in us lies, take from them all cause of Trouble."[23] So spoke Jedediah Smith of his hopes and ambitions upon pursuing the fur trade. No sooner had he left the mountains, however, than he was killed by Plains Indians before he could settle down in business with his brothers as he had intended.[24] Noble and ignoble were the motives of the Mountain Men. Colonel John Shaw, starting across the southern plains and into the Rockies in search of gold; Thomas James, desperate to recoup his failing fortunes; the Little Rock *Gazette* of 1829 "confidently" believing "that this enterprise affords a prospect of great profit to all who may engage in it"; the St. Louis *Enquirer* in 1822 labeling the Rocky Mountains "the Shining Mountains," and innocently declaring, "A hunter pursuing his game found the silver mines of Potosi, and many others have been discovered by the like accidents, and there is no reason to suppose that other valuable discoveries may not be made";[25] Ashley calling clearly and unmistakably for men of "enterprise," all added up to the fact that the Mountain Man when he went West was a complex character. But in his complexity was a clearly discernible pattern—the pattern of Jacksonian Man in search of respectability and success in terms recognized by the society he had left behind. His goal was, of course, the pursuit of happiness. But happiness, contrary to Rousseauistic expectations, was not found in the wilderness; it was an integral product of society and civilization.

If the Mountain Man was indeed Jacksonian Man, then there are at least three senses in which this concept has importance. First, more clearly than anything else, a statistical and occupational view of the various callings of the Mountain Man tentatively indicates the incredible rate and the surprising nature of social and economic change in the West. In little more than two decades, most of the surviving enterprising men had left the fur trade for more lucrative and presumably more useful occupations. And by their choice of occupations it is clear that in the Far West a whole step in the settlement process had been virtually skipped. They may have dreamed of "Arcadia," but when they turned to the task of settling the West as fast as possible, the former Mountain Men and perhaps others like them brought with them all the aspects of an "industrial," mercantile and quasi-urban society. The opera house went up almost simultaneously with the ranch, and the Bank of Missouri was secured before the land was properly put into hay.

Secondly, as explorers—men who searched out the hidden places in the western wilderness—the Mountain Men as Jacksonian Men looked with a flexible eye upon the new land. Unlike the Hudson's Bay explorer who looked only for beaver and immediate profit, the Mountain Man looked to the future and the development of the West, not as a vast game preserve, but as a land like the one he had known back home.

"Much of this vast waste of territory belongs to the Republic of the United States," wrote Zenas Leonard from San Francisco Bay in 1833. "What a theme to contemplate its settlement and civilization. Will the jurisdiction of the federal government ever succeed in civilizing the thousands of savages now roaming over these plains, and her hardy freeborn population here plant their homes, build their towns and cities, and say here shall the arts and sciences of civilization take root and flourish? Yes, here, even in this remote part of the Great West before many years will these hills and valleys be greeted with the enlivening sound of the workman's hammer, and the merry whistle of the ploughboy . . . we have good reason to suppose that the territory west of the mountains will some day be equally as important to the nation as that on the east."[26]

In 1830 in a famous letter to John H. Eaton, the Secretary of War, Jedediah S. Smith, David E. Jackson and William L. Sublette aired their views on the possibilities of the West. Smith made clear that a wagon road route suitable for settlers existed all the way to Oregon, and Sublette dramatized the point when he brought ten wagons and two dearborns and even a milch cow over the mountains as far as the Wind River rendezvous. Their report made abundantly clear that in their opinion the future of the West lay with settlers rather than trappers. Indeed they were worried that the English at Fort Vancouver might grasp this fact before the American government.[27] In short, as explorers and trappers theirs was a broad-ranging, flexible, settler-oriented, public view of the Far West.

Tied in with this and of the greatest significance is a third and final point. Not only did they *see* a settler's future in the West, but at least some of the Mountain Men were most eager to see to it that such a future was *guaranteed* by the institutions of the United States government which must be brought West and extended over all the wild new land to protect the settler in the enjoyment of his own "vine and fig tree." The Mexican government, unstable, and blown by whim or caprice, could not secure the future, and the British government, at least in North America, was under the heel of monopoly. France was frivolous and decadent. Russia was a sinister and backward despotism. Only the free institutions of Jacksonian America would make the West safe for enterprise. So strongly did he feel about this that in 1841 the Mountain Man Moses "Black" Harris sent a letter to one Thornton Grimsley offering him the command of 700 men, of which he was one, who were eager to "join the standard of their country, and make a clean sweep of what is called the Origon [sic] Territory; that is clear it of British and Indians." Outraged not only at British encroachments, he was also prepared to "march through to California" as well.[28] It may well have been this spirit that settled the Oregon question and brought on the Mexican War.[29]

Settlement, security, stability, enterprise, free enterprise, a government of laws which, in the words of Jackson himself, confines "itself to equal protection, and as Heaven does its rains, showers its favors alike on the high and the low, the rich and the poor,"[30] all of these shaped the Mountain Man's vision of the West and his role in its development. It was called Manifest Destiny. But long before John L. O'Sullivan nicely turned the phrase in the *Democratic Review*,[31] the Mountain Man as Jacksonian Man—a "venturous conservative"—was out in the West doing his utmost to lend the Almighty a helping hand. James Clyman perhaps put it most simply:

> *Here lies the bones of old Black Harris*
> *who often traveled beyond the far west*
> *and for the freedom of Equal rights*
> *He crossed the snowy mountain Hights*
> *was free and easy kind of soul*
> *Especially with a Belly full.*[32]

NOTES

The term "Jacksonian Man" is used throughout this essay in a general rather than a particular sense. It is intended to describe a fictional composite, the average man of the period under consideration regardless of whether or not he was a follower of Andrew Jackson and his party. Those qualities which I take to be general enough to characterize the average man are defined in my quotations from Richard Hofstadter, Marvin Meyers and Alexis de Tocqueville. It should not be inferred from this that I seek to portray the Mountain Men as members of Andrew Jackson's political party nor that I mean to suggest that the particular objectives of the Democratic Party were necessarily those described by Hofstadter, Meyers and Tocqueville. Rather their terms seem to characterize to some extent men of all political persuasions in this period. Lee Benson in his recent book, *The Concept of Jacksonian Democracy*, has shown that in New York State, at least, the Jackson party had no particular monopoly on such terms as "egalitarianism" and "democracy," and that indeed most parties in the state including the Whigs actually preceded the Jackson men in their advocacy of these views. He thus demonstrates that there were certain values and goals common to all men of the day. Benson then concludes that instead of calling the period "The Age of Jackson," it should properly be called "The Age of Egalitarianism." His evidence indicates to me, however, that a still more precise term for the period might well be "The Age of Expectant Capitalism," and following Hofstadter and Meyers, and before them Frederick Jackson Turner, I have seen this as the most generally applicable descriptive concept for the period. Thus it forms the basis for my definition of "Jacksonian Man," or *Genus Homo Americanus* during the years of the presidency of Andrew Jackson and his successor Martin Van Buren.

1. Washington Irving, *The Rocky Mountains: or, Scenes, Incidents, and Adventurers in the Far West* (2 vols.; Philadelphia, 1837), I, 27.

2. Bernard De Voto, "Introduction," *The Life and Adventures of James P. Beckwourth*, ed. T. D. Bonner (New York, 1931), p. xxvii.

3. Quoted in Dorothy O. Johansen, "Introduction," *Robert Newell's Memoranda* (Portland, Ore., 1959), p. 2.

4. Ibid., pp. 2–3; see also Ray A. Billington, *The Far Western Frontier* (New York, 1956), p. 44.

5. Billington, pp. 46–47; Robert Glass Cleland, *This Reckless Breed of Man* (New York, 1952), pp. 24–25; Bernard De Voto, *Across the Wide Missouri* (Boston, 1947), pp. 96–104. See also Henry Nash Smith, *Virgin Land* (Boston, 1950), pp. 59–70, 81–89. My portrait is a composite derived, but not quoted, from the above sources.

6. Richard Hofstadter, *The American Political Tradition* (New York, 1955), p. 57.

7. Ibid., p. 59.

8. Ibid., p. 57.

9. Marvin Meyers, *The Jacksonian Persuasion* (New York, 1960), pp. 33–56.

10. Quoted in ibid., p. 43.

11. W. A. Ferris, *Life in the Rocky Mountains*, ed. Paul C. Phillips (Denver, Colo., 1940), p. 1.

12. Harrison C. Dale, *The Ashley-Smith Explorations and the Discovery of a Central Route to the Pacific, 1822–1829*, rev. ed. (Glendale, Calif. 1941), pp. 57–61.

13. Dale L. Morgan, *Jedediah Smith* (Indianapolis and New York, 1953), pp. 145–48; Ferris, pp. 150, 156, 158.

14. James Ohio Pattie, *Personal Narrative*, ed. Timothy Flint (Cincinnati, 1831), passim.

15. Thomas James, *Three Years Among the Indians and Mexicans*, ed. Milo M. Quaife (Chicago, 1953), pp. 9–10.

16. Ibid., p. 100. When his store failed, Thomas James set out in May 1821 on a trading venture to Santa Fe. By July of 1822 he had returned to his home in Illinois.

17. This study is based upon the lives of the Mountain Men whose entrance into the Rocky Mountain fur trade during the period 1805–45 can be proven, and who fit the criteria listed below. As anyone who has worked in the field will undoubtedly understand, the estimated one-thousand-man total given for those who would possibly qualify for consideration under these criteria represents merely an informed guess, since it is impossible with present-day evidence to determine with accuracy *all* of the Mountain Men who entered the West during this period. The data upon which this study is based is the sum total of men and careers that the extensive investigation described below has yielded. The author believes this to be the most extensive such investigation undertaken to date and also the largest number of such Mountain Men and careers located as of the time. However, in presenting this statistical analysis, the author wishes to stress the tentativeness of the conclusions herein reached. Further study of those whose "other occupations were indeterminable," and those "whose other occupations are probable" quite obviously might alter the present statistical results to a significant degree, and though the attempt was made to determine the occupations of as many men as possible, the author wishes specifically to acknowledge this possibility.

The basic sources for this sample study were: (1) general histories of the western states (in this respect the pioneer register in H. H. Bancroft's *History of California* proved to be particularly useful); (2) original and modern editions of the relevant fur trade classics listed in Henry Raup Wagner and Charles Camp, *Plains and Rockies*; (3) the many available monographs and biographies relating to the fur trade, such as those by Hiram M. Chittenden, Paul C. Phillips, Dale L. Morgan, and John E. Sunder; (4) the files of historical journals containing materials on the fur trade of the Far West; (5) reports submitted to the United States Government and published in the House and Senate document series; and (6) newspapers and periodicals for the fur trade period. In this category the author's research was by no means complete, nor was it possible to carry out the research project to the extent of consulting the multitude of local and county histories that almost certainly would have yielded further information. Enough research was conducted in these latter two categories of materials, however, to indicate the probable extent of their utility, which the author deemed insufficient for the present purposes.

The criteria for selecting the men to be included in the study are relatively simple: (1) They must have been associated with the fur trapping enterprise during the period 1805–45. (2) They must have pursued their trapping activities in the Rocky Mountains, northern or southern; hence the term Mountain Man. (3) They could not be employees of the American Fur Company, nor engagées at any of the Missouri River trading posts. The American Fur Company men are excluded from this study for two reasons: first, because the majority of them were river traders, not Mountain Men, and they have never been classified under the old stereotyped images; secondly, of those few American Fur men who did go into the mountains in this period a large percentage were killed. Further study of the survivors, however, indicates that they too changed occupations much as did the Mountain Men. (See for example the career of Warren A. Ferris.)

18. This conclusion is deduced by the author primarily upon the basis of their residence during this period in places far removed from fur trapping or trading activities.

19. Kit Carson, *Autobiography*, ed. Milo M. Quaife (Chicago, 1935), p. 135.

20. Quoted in Leroy Hafen, "Louis Vasquez," *The Colorado Magazine*, 10 (1933), 17. De Voto's nickname for Vasquez appears in *Across the Wide Missouri*, p. xxvi.

21. Ibid., p. 19.

22. Ibid., p. 20.

23. Jedediah Smith to Ralph Smith, Wind River, East Side of the Rocky Mountains, December 24, 1829. MS. Kansas State Historical Society. Also reproduced in Morgan, *Jedediah Smith*, pp. 351–54.

24. Jedediah S. Smith to Ralph Smith, Blue River, fork of Kansas, 30 miles from the Ponnee Villages, September 10, 1830. MS. Kansas State Historical Society. Also reproduced in Morgan, *Jedediah Smith*, pp. 355–56.

25. St. Louis *Enquirer* quoted in Donald McKay Frost, *Notes on General Ashley* (Barre, Mass., 1960), p. 67. Little Rock *Gazette* quoted in Leroy R. Hafen, "The Bean–Sinclair Party of Rocky Mountain Trappers, 1830–32," *The Colorado Magazine*, 31 (1954), 165.

26. Zenas Leonard, *Narrative of the Adventures of Zenas Leonard*, ed. John C. Ewers (Norman, Okla., 1959), pp. 94–95.

27. Reproduced in Morgan, *Jedediah Smith*, pp. 343–48.

28. Quoted in Charles L. Camp, ed. *James Clyman Frontiersman* (Portland, Ore., 1960), pp. 61–62.

29. Ray Allen Billington, *The Far Western Frontier*, pp. 154–73. See also Frederick Merk, *Manifest Destiny and Mission in American History* (New York, 1963).

30. James D. Richardson, ed., *A Compilation of the Messages and Papers of the Presidents 1789–1897* (1900), II, 590–91. Italics mine.

31. John L. O'Sullivan, "Annexation," unsigned article, *United States Magazine and Democratic Review*, 17 (July–August 1845), 797–98. See also his more popular statement in the *New York Morning News*, December 27, 1845.

32. Camp, *James Clyman Frontiersman*, p. 64.

6

BISON ECOLOGY AND BISON DIPLOMACY: THE SOUTHERN PLAINS FROM 1800 TO 1850

Dan Flores

 Did white Americans defeat the Indians of the Great Plains by wiping out the buffalo, which supplied the Indians with food and many other necessities? No doubt that helped, especially against the Sioux and Cheyenne on the northern Plains. But here, Dan Flores argues that the Indian–buffalo relationship was already in trouble on the southern Plains by 1850, before white conquest took place.

Flores raises the question of why, if the Comanches and their Kiowa allies were so dominant on the southern Plains, and the buffalo herds as huge as most people have thought, were the Indians complaining by 1850 that they were starving? Why did buffalo hunters in the 1870s, the decade of the most thorough massacres of the buffalo, bring in only 3.5 million hides from the southern Plains instead of the much larger number everyone expected?

Flores' explanation begins with the arrival of the Comanches on the southern Plains by the early 1700s, their conversion to "horse culture" after the Spanish re-introduced horses from Europe, and the consequences of that cultural change. By ingenious methods, he estimates not only the Indian population but also the number of buffalo. (What are these methods? Explain.) Did the Comanches truly achieve an "ecological equilibrium" with the buffalo, or were they, contrary to widely held opinion about Indians, not in ecological balance? What factors— he discusses several—combined to lead both animals and Indians to the precarious edge of physical starvation and cultural confusion between 1800 and 1850? These go far to explain the Comanches' furious and legendary resistance to white incursion, as well as their failure to prevent it.

The essay combines western and environmental history. What does it say about the myth that the Plains were a kind of Garden of Eden before whites arrived, a tranquil place where humans, animals, and plants lived together in timeless balance? When all is said and done, was the horse a blessing or a curse for the Plains Indians?—editors

IN BRIGHT spring light on the Great Plains of two centuries ago, governor Juan Bautista de Anza failed in the last of the three crucial tasks

that his superiors had set him as part of their effort to reform New Mexico's
Comanche policy. Over half a decade, Anza had followed one success with
another. He had brilliantly defeated the formidable Comanche *nomnekaht*
(war leader) Cuerno Verde in 1779, and as a consequence in 1786, he had
personally fashioned the long-sought peace between New Mexico and the
swelling Comanche population of the Southern Plains. His third task was
to persuade the Comanches to settle in permanent villages and to farm.[1]

But the New Mexico governor found the third undertaking impossible.
Observers of Plains Indian life for 250 years and committed to encouraging agriculture over hunting, the Spaniards were certain that the culture
of the horse Indians was ephemeral, that the bison on which they depended
were an exhaustible resource. Thus Anza pleaded with the tribes to give
up the chase. The Comanches thought him unconvincing. Recently liber-
ated by horse culture and by the teeming wildlife of the High Plains, their
bands found the Arkansas River pueblo the governor built for them unen-
durable. They returned to the hunt with the evident expectation that their
life as buffalo hunters was an endless cycle. And yet Anza proved to be a
prophet. Within little more than half a century, the Comanches and other
tribes of the Southern Plains were routinely suffering from starvation and
complaining of shortages of bison. What had happened?[2]

Environmental historians and ethnohistorians whose interests have
been environmental topics have in the two past decades been responsible
for many of our most valuable recent insights into the history of native
Americans since their contact with Euro-Americans.[3] Thus far, however,
modern scholarship has not reevaluated the most visible historic interaction, the set piece, if you will, of native American environmental history.[4]
On the Great Plains of the American West during the two centuries from
1680 to 1880, almost three dozen native American groups adopted horse-
propelled, bison-hunting cultures that defined "Indianness" for white
Americans and most of the world. It is the end of this process that has
most captured the popular imagination: the military campaigns against
and the brutal incarceration of the horse Indians, accompanied by the
astonishingly rapid elimination of bison, and of an old ecology that dated
back ten thousand years, at the hands of commercial hide hunters. That
dramatic end, which occurred in less than fifteen years following the end
of the Civil War, has by now entered American mythology. Yet our focus
on the finale has obscured an examination of earlier phases that might
shed new light on the historical and environmental interaction of the horse
Indians and bison herds on the Plains.

In the nineteenth-century history of the Central and Southern Plains,
there have long been perplexing questions that environmental history
seems well suited to answer. Why were the Comanches able to replace
the Apaches on the bison-rich Southern Plains? Why did the Kiowas, Cheyennes, and Arapahoes gradually shift southward into the Southern Plains
between 1800 and 1825? And why, after fighting each other for two decades, did these Southern Plains peoples effect a rapprochement and alli-

ance in the 1840s? What factors brought on such an escalation of Indian raids into Mexico and Texas in the late 1840s that the subject assumed critical importance in the Treaty of Guadalupe–Hidalgo? If the bison herds were so vast in the years before the commercial hide hunters, why were there so many reports of starving Indians on the Plains by 1850? And finally, given our standard estimates of bison numbers, why is it that the hide hunters are credited with bringing to market only some 10 million hides, including no more than 3.5 million from the Southern Plains, in the 1870s?

Apposite to all of these questions is a central issue: How successful were the horse Indians in creating a dynamic ecological equilibrium between themselves and the vast bison herds that grazed the Plains? That is, had they developed sustainable hunting practices that would maintain the herds and so permit future generations of hunters to follow the same way of life? This is not to pose the "anachronistic question" (the term is Richard White's) of whether Indians were ecologists.[5] But how a society or a group of peoples with a shared culture makes adjustments to live within the carrying capacity of its habitat is not only a valid historical question, it may be one of the most salient questions to ask about any culture. Historians of the Plains have differed about the long-term ecological sustainability of the Indians' use of bison, particularly after the Euro-American fur trade reached the West and the tribes began hunting bison under the influence of the market economy. The standard work, Frank Roe's *The North American Buffalo*, has generally carried the debate with the argument that there is "not a shred of evidence" to indicate that the horse Indians were out of balance with the bison herds.[6] Using the new insights and methods of environmental history, it now appears possible systematically to analyze and revise our understanding of nineteenth-century history on the Great Plains. Such an approach promises to resolve some of the major questions. It can advance our understanding of when bison declined in numbers and of the intertwining roles that Indian policies—migrations, diplomacy, trade, and use of natural resources—and the growing pressures of external stimuli played in that decline. The answers are complex and offer a revision of both Plains history and western Indian ecological history.

Working our way through to them requires some digression into the large historical forces that shaped the Southern Plains over the last hundred centuries. The perspective of the *longue durée* is essential to environmental history. What transpired on the Great Plains from 1800 to 1850 is not comprehensible without taking into account the effect of the Pleistocene extinctions of ten thousand years ago, or the cycle of droughts that determined the carrying capacity for animals on the grasslands. Shallower in time than these forces but just as important to the problem are factors that stemmed from the arrival of Europeans in the New World. Trade was an ancient part of the cultural landscape of America, but the Europeans altered the patterns, the goods, and the intensity of trade. And the introduction of horses and horse culture accomplished a technological revolution for the Great Plains. The horse was the chief catalyst of an ongoing remaking of the tribal map of western America, as native American groups moved onto the Plains and incessantly shifted their ranges and alliances in response to a world where accelerating change seemed almost the only constant.

At the beginning of the nineteenth century, the dominant groups on the Southern Plains were the two major divisions of the Comanches: the Texas Comanches, primarily Kotsotekas, and the great New Mexico division, spread across the country from the Llano Estacado Escarpment west to the foothills of the Sangre de Cristo Mountains, and composed of Yamparika and Jupe bands that only recently had replaced the Apaches on the High Plains. The Comanches' drive to the south from their original homelands in what is now southwestern Wyoming and northwestern Colorado was a part of the original tribal adjustments to the coming of horse technology to the Great Plains. There is reason to believe that the Eastern Shoshones, from whom the Comanches were derived before achieving a different identity on the Southern Plains, were one of the first intermountain tribes of historic times to push onto the Plains. Perhaps as early as 1500 the proto-Comanches were hunting bison and using dog power to haul their mountain-adapted four-pole tipis east of the Laramie Mountains. Evidently they moved in response to a wetter time on the Central Plains and the larger bison concentrations there.[7]

These early Shoshonean hunters may not have spent more than three or four generations among the thronging Plains bison herds, for by the late seventeenth century they had been pushed back into the mountains and the sagebrush deserts by tribes newly armed with European guns moving westward from the region around the Great Lakes. If so, they were among a complex of tribes southwest of the lakes that over the next two centuries would be displaced by a massive Siouan drive to the west, an imperial expansion for domination of the prize buffalo range of the Northern Plains, and a wedge that sent ripples of tribal displacement across the Plains.[8]

Among the historic tribes, the people who became Comanches thus may have shared with the Apaches and, if linguistic arguments are correct, probably with the Kiowas, the longest familiarity with a bison-hunting life-style. Pressed back toward the mountains as Shoshones, they thus turned in a different direction and emerged from the passes through the Front Range as the same people but bearing a new name given them by the Utes: Komantcia. They still lacked guns but now began their intimate association with the one animal, aside from the bison, inextricably linked with Plains life. The Comanches began acquiring horses from the Utes within a decade or so after the Pueblo Revolt of 1680 sent horses and horse culture diffusing in all directions from New Mexico. Thus were born the "hyper-Indians," as William Brandon has called the Plains people.[9]

The Comanches became, along with the Sioux, the most populous and widespread of all the peoples who now began to ride onto the vast sweep of grassland to participate in the hunters' life. They began to take possession of the Southern Plains by the early 1700s. By 1800 they were in full control of all the country east of the Southern Rocky Mountains and south of the Arkansas River clear to the Texas Hill Country. Their new culture, long regarded as an ethnographic anomaly on the Plains because of its western and archaic origins, may not be unique, as older scholars had supposed it to be—at least if we believe the new Comanche revisionists. Irrespective of their degree of tribal unity, however, when they began to move onto the Southern Plains with their new horse herds, their culture was adapting in interesting ways to the wealth of resources now available to them.[10]

To the Comanches, the Southern Plains must have seemed an earthly paradise. The Pleistocene extinctions ten thousand years earlier had left dozens of grazing niches vacant on the American Great Plains. A dwarf species of bison with a higher reproductive capability than any of its ancestors evolved to flood most of those vacant niches with an enormous biomass of one grazer. In an ecological sense, bison were a weed species that had proliferated as a result of a major disturbance.[11] That disturbance still reverberated, making it easy for Spanish horses, for example, to reoccupy their old niche and rapidly spread across the Plains. Those reverberations made the horse Indians thrive on an environmental situation that has had few parallels in world history.

The dimensions of the wild bison resource on the Southern Plains, and the Great Plains in general, have been much overstated in popular literature. For one thing, pollen analysis and archaeological data indicate that for the Southern Plains there were intervals, some spanning centuries, others decades, when bison must have been almost absent. Two major times of absence occurred between 5000 and 2500 B.C. and between A.D. 500 and 1300. The archaeological levels that lack bison bones correspond to pollen data indicating droughts. The severe southwestern drought that ended early in the fourteenth century was replaced by a five-hundred-year cycle of wetter and cooler conditions, and a return of bison in large numbers to the Southern Plains from their drought refugia to the east and west. This long-term pattern in the archaeological record seems to have prevailed on a smaller scale within historic times. During the nineteenth century, for example, droughts of more than five years' duration struck the Great Plains four times at roughly twenty-year intervals, in a long-term dendrochronological pattern that seems to show a drying cycle (shorter drought-free intervals) beginning in the 1850s.[12]

More important, our popular perception of bison numbers—based on the estimates of awed nineteenth-century observers—probably sets them too high. There very likely were never 100 million or even 60 million bison on the Plains during the present climate regime because the carrying capacity of the grasslands was not so high. The best technique for determining bison carrying capacity on the Southern Plains is to extrapolate from United States census data for livestock, and the best census for the extrapolation is that of 1910, after the beef industry crashes of the 1880s had reduced animal numbers, but before the breakup of ranches and the Enlarged Homestead Act of 1909 resulted in considerable sections of the Southern Plains being broken out by farmers. Additionally, dendrochronological data seem to show that at the turn of the century rainfall on the Southern Plains was at median, between-droughts levels, rendering the census of 1910 particularly suitable as a base line for carrying capacity and animal populations.[13]

The 1910 agricultural census indicates that in the 201 counties on the Southern Plains (which covered 240,000 square miles), the nineteenth-century carrying capacity during periods of median rainfall was about 7,000,000 cattle-equivalent grazers—specifically for 1910, about 5,150,000 cattle and 1,890,000 horses and mules.[14] The bison population was almost certainly larger, since migratory grazing patterns and coevolution with the native grasses made bison as a wild species about 18 percent more efficient on the Great Plains than domestic cattle. And varying climate conditions during the nineteenth century, as I will demonstrate, noticeably affected grassland carrying capacity. The ecological reality was a dynamic cycle in which carrying capacity could swing considerably from decade to decade.[15] But if the Great Plains bovine carrying capacity of 1910 expresses a median reality, then during prehorse times the Southern Plains might have supported an average of about 8.2 million bison, the entire Great Plains perhaps 28–30 million.[16]

Although 8 million bison on the Southern Plains may not be so many as historians used to believe, to the Comanches the herds probably seemed limitless. Bison availability through horse culture caused a specialization that resulted in the loss of two-thirds of the Comanches' former plant lore and in a consequent loss of status for their women, an intriguing development that seems to have occurred to some extent among all the tribes that moved onto the Plains during the horse period.[17] As full-time bison hunters, the Comanches appear to have abandoned all the old Shoshonean mechanisms, such as infanticide and polyandry, that had kept their population in line with available resources. These were replaced with such cultural mechanisms as widespread adoption of captured children and polygyny, adaptations to the Plains that were designed to keep Comanche numbers high and growing.[18] That these changes seem to have been conscious and deliberate argues, perhaps, both Comanche environmental insight and some centralized leadership and planning.

Comanche success at seizing the Southern Plains from the native groups that had held it for several hundred years was likewise the result of a conscious choice: their decision to shape their lives around bison and horses. Unlike the Comanches, many of the Apache bands had heeded the Spaniards' advice and had begun to build streamside gardening villages that became deathtraps once the Comanches located them. The Apaches' vulnerability, then, ironically stemmed from their willingness to diversify their economy. Given the overwhelming dominance of grasslands as opposed to cultivable river lands on the Plains, the specialized horse and bison culture of the Comanches exploited a greater volume of the thermodynamic energy streaming from sunlight into plants and the economies of any of their competitors—until they encountered Cheyennes and Arapahoes with a similar culture.[19] The horse-mounted Plains Indians, in other words, made very efficient use of the available energy on the Great Plains, something they seem instinctively to have recognized and exulted in. From the frequency with which the Comanches applied some version of the name "wolf" to their leaders, I suspect that they may have recognized their role as human predators and their ecological kinship with the wolf packs that like them lived off the bison herds.[20]

The Comanches were not the only people on the Southern Plains during the horse period. The New Mexicans, both Pueblo and Hispanic, continued to hunt on the wide-open Llanos, as did the prairie Caddoans, although the numbers of the latter were dwindling rapidly by 1825. The New Mexican peoples and the Caddoans of the middle Red and Brazos rivers played major trade roles for hunters on the Southern Plains, and the Comanches in particular. Although the Comanches engaged in the archetypal Plains exchange of bison products for horticultural produce and European trade goods and traded horses and mules with Anglo-American traders from Missouri, Arkansas, and Louisiana, they were not a high-volume trading people until relatively late in their history. Early experiences with American traders and disease led them to distrust trade with Euro-Americans, and only once or twice did they allow short-lived posts to be established in their country. Instead, peace with the prairie Caddoans by the 1730s and with New Mexico in 1786 sent Comanche trade both east and west, but often through Indian middlemen.[21]

In the classic, paradigmatic period between 1800 and 1850, the most interesting Southern Plains development was the cultural interaction between the Comanches and surrounding Plains Indians to the north. The Kiowas were the one of those groups most closely identified with the Comanches.

The Kiowas are and have long been an enigma. Scholars are interested in their origins because Kiowa oral tradition is at odds with the scientific evidence. The Kiowas believe that they started their journey to Rainy Mountain on the Oklahoma Plains from the north. And indeed, in the eighteenth century we had them on the Northern Plains, near the Black Hills, as one of the groups being displaced southwestward by the Siouan drive toward the buffalo range. Linguistically, however, the Kiowas are southern Indians. Their language belongs to the Tanoan group of Pueblo languages in New Mexico, and some scholars believe that the Kiowas of later history are the same people as the Plains Jumanos of early New Mexico history, whose rancherias were associated during the 1600s and early 1700s with the headwaters of the Colorado and Concho rivers of Texas. How the Kiowas got so far north is not certainly known, but in historical times they were consummate traders, especially of horses, and since the Black Hills region was a major trade citadel they may have begun to frequent the region as traders and teachers of horse lore.[22]

Displaced by the wars for the buffalo ranges in the north, the Kiowas began to drift southward again—or perhaps, since the supply of horses was in the Southwest, simply began to stay longer on the Southern Plains. Between 1790 and 1806, they developed a rapprochement with the Comanches. Thereafter they were so closely associated with the northern Comanches that they were regarded by some as merely a Comanche band, although in many cultural details the two groups were dissimilar. Spanish and American traders and explorers of the 1820s found them camped along the two forks of the Canadian River and on the various headwater streams of the Red River.[23]

The other groups that increasingly began to interact with the Comanches during the 1820s and thereafter had also originated on the Northern Plains. These were the Arapahoes and the Cheyennes, who by 1825 were beginning to establish themselves on the Colorado buffalo plains from the North Platte River all the way down to the Arkansas River.

The Algonkian-speaking Arapahoes and Cheyennes had once been farmers living in earth lodges on the upper Mississippi. By the early 1700s both groups were in present North Dakota, occupying villages along the Red and Sheyenne rivers, where they first began to acquire horses, possibly from the Kiowas. Fur wars instigated by the Europeans drove them farther southwest and more and more into a Plains, bison-hunting culture, one that the women of these farming tribes probably resisted as long as possible.[24] But by the second decade of the nineteenth century the Teton Sioux wedge had made nomads and hunters of the Arapahoes and Cheyennes.

Their search for prime buffalo grounds and for ever-larger horse herds, critical since both tribes had emerged as middlemen traders between the villagers of the Missouri and the horse reservoir to the south, first led the Cheyennes and Arapahoes west of the Black Hills, into Crow lands, and then increasingly southward along the mountain front. By 1815 the Arapahoes were becoming fixed in the minds of American traders as their own analogue on the Southern Plains; the famous trading expedition of August Pierre Chouteau and Jules De Mun that decade was designed to exploit the horse and robe trade of the Arapahoes on the Arkansas. By the 1820s, when Stephen Long's expedition and the trading party including Jacob Fowler penetrated the Southern Plains, the Arapahoes and Cheyennes were camping with the Kiowas and Comanches on the Arkansas. The Hairy Rope band of the Cheyennes, renowned for their ability to catch wild horses, was then known to be mustanging along the Cimarron River.[25]

Three factors seem to have drawn the Arapahoes and Cheyennes so far south. Unquestionably, one factor was the vast horse herds of the Comanches and Kiowas, an unending supply of horses for the trade, which by 1825 the Colorado tribes were seizing in daring raids. Another was the milder winters south of the Arkansas, which made horse pastoralism much easier. The third factor was the abnormally bountiful game of the early-nineteenth-century Southern Plains, evidently the direct result of an extraordinary series of years between 1815 and 1846 when, with the exception of a minor drought in the late 1820s, rainfall south of the Arkansas was considerably above average. So lucrative was the hunting and raiding that in 1833 Charles Bent located the first of his adobe trading posts along the Arkansas, expressly to control the winter robe and summer horse trade of the Arapahoes and Cheyennes. Bent's marketing contacts were in St. Louis. Horses that Bent's travelers drove to St. Louis commonly started as stock in the New Mexican Spanish settlements (and sometimes those were California horses stolen by Indians who traded them to the New Mexicans) that were stolen by the Comanches, then stolen again by Cheyenne raiders, and finally traded at Bent's or Ceran St. Vrain's posts, whence they were driven to Westport, Missouri, and sold to outfit American emigrants going to the West Coast! Unless you saw it from the wrong end, as the New Mexicans (or the horses) seem to have, it was both a profitable and a culturally stimulating economy.[26]

Thus, around 1825, the Comanches and Kiowas found themselves at war with Cheyennes, Arapahoes, and other tribes on the north. Meanwhile, the Colorado tribes opened another front in a naked effort to seize the rich buffalo range of the upper Kansas and Republican rivers from the Pawnees. These wars produced an interesting type of ecological development that appeared repeatedly across most of the continent. At the boundaries where warring tribes met, they left buffer zones occupied by neither side and only lightly hunted. One such buffer zone on the Southern Plains was along the region's northern perimeter, between the Arkansas and North Canadian rivers. Another was in present-day western Kansas, between the Pawnees and the main range of the Colorado tribes, and a third seems to have stretched from the forks of the Platte to the mountains. The buffer zones were important because game within them was left relatively undisturbed; they allowed the buildup of herds that might later be exploited when tribal boundaries or agreements changed.[27]

The appearance of American traders such as Bent and St. Vrain marked the Southern Plains tribes' growing immersion in a market economy increasingly tied to worldwide trade networks dominated by Euro-Americans. Like all humans, Indians had always altered their environments. But as most modern historians of Plains Indians and the western fur trade have realized, during the nineteenth century not only had the western tribes become technologically capable of pressuring their resources, but year by year they were becoming less "ecosystem people," dependent on the products of their local regions for subsistence, and increasingly tied to biospheric trade networks. Despite some speculation that the Plains tribes were experiencing ecological problems, previous scholars have not ascertained what role market hunting played in this dilemma, what combination of other factors was involved, or what the tribes attempted to do about it.[28]

The crux of the problem in studying Southern Plains Indian ecology and bison is to determine whether the Plains tribes had established a society in ecological equilibrium, one whose population did not exceed the carrying capacity of its habitat and so maintained a healthy, functioning ecology that could be sustained over the long term.[29] Answering that question involves an effort to come to grips with the factors affecting bison populations, the factors affecting Indian populations, and the cultural aspects of Plains Indians' utilization of bison. Each of the three aspects of the question presents puzzles difficult to resolve.

In modern, protected herds on the Plains, bison are a prolific species whose numbers increase by an average of 18 percent a year, assuming a normal sex ratio (51 males to 49 females) with breeding cows amounting to 35 percent of the total.[30] In other words, if the Southern Plains supported 8.2 million bison in years of median rainfall, the herds would have produced about 1.4 million calves a year. To maintain an ecological equilibrium with the grasses, the Plains bison's natural mortality rate also had to approach 18 percent.

Today the several protected bison herds in the western United States have a natural mortality rate, without predation, ranging between 3 and 9 percent. The Wichita Mountains herd, the only large herd left on the Southern Plains, falls midway with a 6 percent mortality rate. Despite a search for it, no inherent naturally regulating mechanism has yet been found in bison populations; thus active culling programs are needed at all the Plains bison refuges. The starvation-induced population crashes that affect ungulates such as deer were seemingly mitigated on the wild, unfenced Plains by the bison's tendency—barring any major impediments—to shift their range great distances to better pasture.[31]

Determining precisely how the remaining annual mortality in the wild herds was affected is not easy, because the wolf/bison relationship on the Plains has never been studied. Judging from dozens of historical documents attesting to wolf predation of bison calves, including accounts by the Indians, wolves apparently played a critical role in Plains bison population dynamics, and not just as culling agents of diseased and old animals.[32]

Human hunters were the other source of mortality. For nine thousand years native Americans had hunted bison without exterminating them, perhaps building into their gene pool an adjustment to human predation (dwarfed size, earlier sexual maturity, and shorter gestation times, all serving to keep populations up). But there is archaeological evidence that beginning about A.D. 1450, with the advent of "mutualistic" trade between Puebloan communities recently forced by drought to relocate on the Rio Grande and a new wave of Plains hunters (probably the Athapaskan-speaking Apacheans), human pressures on the southern bison herd accelerated, evidently dramatically if the archaeological record in New Mexico is an accurate indication. That pressure would have been a function of both the size of the Indian population and the use of bison in Indian cultures. Because Plains Indians traded bison-derived goods for the produce of the horticultural villages fringing the Plains, bison would be affected by changes in human population peripheral to the Great Plains as well as on them.[33]

One attempt to estimate maximum human population size on the Southern Plains, that of Jerold Levy, fixed the upper limit at about 10,500 people. Levy argued that water would have been a more critical resource than bison in fixing a limit for Indian populations. Levy's population figures are demonstrably too low, and he lacked familiarity with the aquifer-derived drought-resistant sources of water on the Southern Plains. But his argument that water was the more critical limiting resource introduces an important element into the Plains equation.[34]

The cultural utilization of bison by horse Indians has been studied by Bill Brown. Adapting a sophisticated formula worked out first for caribou hunters in the Yukon, Brown has estimated Indian subsistence (caloric requirements plus the number of robes and hides required for domestic use) at about 47 animals per lodge per year. At an average of 8 people per lodge, that works out to almost 6 bison per person over a year's time. Brown's article is not only highly useful in getting us closer to a historic Plains equation than ever before; it is also borne out by at least one historic account. In 1821 the trader Jacob Fowler camped for several weeks with 700 lodges of Southern Plains tribes on the Arkansas River. Fowler was no ecologist; in fact, he could hardly spell. But he was a careful observer, and he wrote that the big camp was using up 100 bison a day. In other words, 700 lodges were using bison at a rate of about 52 per lodge per year, or 6.5 animals per person. These are important figures. Not only do they give us some idea of the mortality percentage that can be assigned to human hunters; by extension they help us fix a quadruped predation percentage as well.[35]

Estimates of the number of Indians on the Southern Plains during historic times are not difficult to find, but they tend to vary widely, and for good reason, as will be seen when we look closely at the historical events of the first half of the nineteenth century. Although observers' population estimates for the Comanches go as high as 30,000, six of the seven population figures for the Comanches estimated between 1786 and 1854 fall into a narrow range between 19,200 and 21,600.[36] Taken together, the number of Kiowas, Cheyennes, Arapahoes, Plains Apaches, Kiowa-Apaches, and Wichitas probably did not exceed 12,000 during that same period. Contemporaries estimated the combined number of Cheyennes and Arapahoes, for example, as 4,400 in 1838, 5,000 in 1843, and 5,200 in 1846.[37] If the historic Southern Plains hunting population reached 30,000, then human hunters would have accounted for only 195,000 bison per year if we use the estimate of 6.5 animals per person.

But another factor must have played a significant role. While quadruped predators concentrated on calves and injured or feeble animals, human hunters had different criteria. Historical documents attest to the horse Indians' preference for and success in killing two- to five-year-old bison cows, which were preferred for their meat and for their thinner, more easily processed hides and the luxurious robes made from their pelts. Studies done on other large American ungulates indicate that removal of breeding females at a level that exceeds 7 percent of the total herd will initiate population decline. With 8.2 million bison on the Southern Plains, the critical upper figure for cow selectivity would have been about 574,000 animals. Reduce the total bison number to 6 million and the yearly calf crop to 1.08 million, probably more realistic median figures for the first half of the nineteenth century, and the critical mortality for breeding cows would still have been 420,000 animals. As mentioned, a horse-mounted, bison-hunting population of 30,000 would have harvested bison at a yearly rate of less than 200,000. Hence I would argue that, theoretically, on the Southern Plains the huge biomass of bison left from the Pleistocene extinctions would have supported the subsistence needs of more than 60,000 Plains hunters.[38]

All of this raises some serious questions when we look at the historical evidence from the first half of the nineteenth century. By the end of that period, despite an effort at population growth by many Plains tribes, the population estimates for most of the Southern Plains tribes were down. And many of the bands seemed to be starving. Thomas Fitzpatrick, the Cheyennes' and Arapahoes' first agent, reported in 1853 that the tribes in his district spent half the year in a state of starvation. The Comanches were reported to be eating their horses in great numbers by 1850, and their raids into Mexico increased all through the 1840s, as if a resource depletion in their home range was driving them to compensate with stolen stock.[39] In the painted robe calendars of the Kiowas, the notation for "few or no bison" appears for four years in a row between 1849 and 1852.[40] Bison were becoming less reliable, and the evolution toward an economy based on raiding and true horse pastoralism was well under way. Clearly, by 1850 something had altered the situation on the Southern Plains.

The "something" was, in fact, a whole host of ecological alterations that historians with a wide range of data at their disposal are only now, more than a century later, beginning to understand.

As early as 1850 the bison herds had been weakened in a number of ways. The effect of the horse on Indian culture has been much studied, but in working out a Southern Plains ecological model, it is important to note that horses also had a direct effect on bison numbers. By the second quarter of the nineteenth century the domesticated horse herds of the Southern Plains tribes must have ranged between .25 and .50 million animals (at an average of 10 to 15 horses per person).[41] In addition, an estimated 2 million wild mustangs overspread the country between south Texas and the Arkansas River. That many animals of a species with an 80 percent dietary overlap with bovines and, perhaps more critically, with similar water requirements, must have had an adverse impact on bison carrying capacity, especially since Indian horse herds concentrated the tribes in the moist canyons and river valleys that bison also used for watering.[42] Judging from the 1910 agricultural census, 2 million or more horses would have reduced the median grassland carrying capacity for the southern bison herd to under 6 million animals.

Another factor that may have started to diminish overall bison numbers was the effect of exotic bovine diseases. Anthrax, introduced into the herds from Louisiana around 1800, tuberculosis, and brucellosis, the latter brought to the Plains by feral and stolen Texas cattle and by stock on the overland trails, probably had considerable impact on the bison herds. All the bison that were saved in the late nineteenth century had high rates of infection with these diseases. Brucellosis plays havoc with reproduction in domestic cattle, causing cows to abort; it may have done so in wild bison, and butchering them probably infected Indian women with the disease.[43]

Earlier I mentioned modern natural mortality figures for bison of 3 percent to 9 percent of herd totals. On the wilderness Plains, fires, floods, drownings, droughts, and strange die-offs may have upped this percentage considerably. But if we hold to the higher figure, then mortality might have taken an average of 50 percent of the annual bison increase of 18 percent. Thirty thousand subsistence hunters would have killed off only 18 percent of the bison's yearly increase (if the herd was 6 million). The long-wondered-at wolf predation was perhaps the most important of all the factors regulating bison populations, with a predation percentage of around 32 percent of the annual bison increase. (Interestingly, this dovetails closely with the Pawnee estimate that wolves got 3 to 4 of every 10 calves born.) Wolves and other canids are able to adjust their litter sizes to factors like mortality and resource abundance. Thus, mountain men and traders who poisoned wolves for their pelts may not have significantly reduced wolf populations. They may have inadvertently killed thousands of bison, however, for poisoned wolves drooled and vomited strychnine over the grass in their convulsions. Many Indians lost horses that ate such poisoned grass.[44]

The climate cycle, strongly correlated with bison populations in the archaeological data for earlier periods, must have interacted with these other factors to produce a decline in bison numbers between 1840 and 1850. Except for a dry period in the mid- to late 1820s, the first four decades of the nineteenth century had been a time of above-normal rainfall on the Southern Plains. With the carrying capacity for bison and horses high, the country south of the Arkansas sucked tribes to it as into a vortex. But beginning in 1846, rainfall plunged as much as 30 percent below the median for nine of the next ten years. On the Central Plains, six years of that decade were dry.[45] The growth of human populations and settlements in Texas, New Mexico, and the Indian Territory blocked the bison herds from migrating to their traditional drought refugia on the periphery of their range. Thus, a normal climate swing combined with unprecedented external pressures to produce an effect unusual in bison history—a core population, significantly reduced by competition with horses and by drought, that was quite susceptible to human hunting pressure.

Finally, alterations in the historical circumstances of the Southern Plains tribes from 1825 to 1850 had serious repercussions for Plains ecology. Some of those circumstances were indirect and beyond the tribes' ability to influence. Traders along the Santa Fe Trail shot into, chased, and disturbed the southern herds. New Mexican *Ciboleros* (bison hunters) continued to take fifteen to twenty-five thousand bison a year from the Llano Estacado. And the United States government's removal of almost fifty thousand eastern Indians into Oklahoma increased the pressure on the bison herds to a level impossible to estimate. The Southern Plains tribes evidently considered it a threat and refused to abide by the Treaty of Fort Holmes (1835) when they discovered it gave the eastern tribes hunting rights on the prairies.[46]

Insofar as the Southern Plains tribes had an environmental policy, then, it was to protect the bison herds from being hunted by outsiders. The Comanches could not afford to emulate their Shoshonean ancestors and limit their own population. Beset by enemies and disease, they had to try to keep their numbers high, even as their resource base diminished. For the historic Plains tribes, warfare and stock raids addressed ecological needs created by diminishing resources as well as the cultural impulse to enhance men's status, and they must have seemed far more logical solutions than consciously reducing their own populations as the bison herds became less reliable.

For those very reasons, after more than a decade of warfare among the buffalo tribes, in 1840 the Comanches and Kiowas adopted a strategy of seeking peace and an alliance with the Cheyennes, Arapahoes, and Kiowa-Apaches. From the Comanches' point of view, it brought them allies against Texans and eastern Indians who were trespassing on the Plains. The Cheyennes and Arapahoes got what they most wanted: the chance to hunt the grass- and bison-rich Southern Plains, horses and mules for trading, and access to the Spanish settlements via Comanche lands. But the peace meant something else in ecological terms. Now all the tribes could freely exploit the Arkansas Valley bison herds. This new exploitation of a large, prime bison habitat that had been a boundary zone skirted by Indian hunters may have been critical. In the Kiowa Calendar the notation for "many bison" appears in 1841, the year following the peace. The notation appears only once more during the next thirty-five years.[47]

One other advantage the Comanches and Kiowas derived from the peace of 1840 was freedom to trade at Bent's Fort. Although the data to prove it are fragmentary, this conversion of the largest body of Indians on the Southern Plains from subsistence/ecosystem hunters to a people intertwined in the European market system probably added critical stress to a bison herd already being eaten away. How serious the market incentive could be is indicated by John Whitfield, agent at William Bent's second Arkansas River fort in 1855, who wrote that 3,150 Cheyennes were killing 40,000 bison a year.[48] That is about twice the number the Cheyennes would have harvested through subsistence hunting alone. (It also means that on the average every Cheyenne warrior was killing 44 bison a year and every Cheyenne woman was processing robes at the rate of almost one a week.) With the core bison population seriously affected by the drought of the late 1840s, the additional, growing robe trade of the Comanches probably brought the Southern Plains tribes to a critical level in their utilization of bison. Drought, Indian market hunting, and cow selectivity must stand as the critical elements—albeit augmented by minor factors such as white disturbance, new bovine diseases, and increasing grazing competition from horses—that brought on the bison crisis of the midcentury Southern Plains. That explanation may also illuminate the experience of the Canadian Plains, where bison disappeared without the advent of white hide hunting.[49]

Perhaps that would have happened on the American Plains if the tribes had held or continued to augment their populations. But the Comanches and other tribes fought a losing battle against their own attrition. While new institutions such as male polygamy and adoption of captured children worked to build up the Comanches' numbers, the disease epidemics of the nineteenth century repeatedly decimated them. In the 1820s, the Comanches were rebuilding their population after the smallpox epidemic of 1816 had carried away a fourth of them. But smallpox ran like a brush fire through the Plains villages again in 1837–1838, wiping whole peoples off the continent. And the forty-niners brought cholera, which so devastated the Arkansas Valley Indians that William Bent burned his fort and temporarily left the trade that year. John C. Ewers, in fact, has estimated that the nineteenth-century Comanches lost 75 percent of their population to disease.[50]

Did the Southern Plains Indians successfully work out a dynamic, ecological equilibrium with the bison herds? I would argue that the answer remains ultimately elusive because the relationship was never allowed to play itself out. The trends, however, suggest that a satisfactory solution was improbable. One factor that worked against the horse tribes was their short tenure. It may be that two centuries provided too brief a time for them to create a workable system around horses, the swelling demand for bison robes generated by the Euro-American market, and the expansion of their own populations to hold their territories. Some of those forces, such as the tribes' need to expand their numbers and the advantages of participating in the robe trade, worked against their need to conserve the bison herds. Too, many of the forces that shaped their world were beyond the power of the Plains tribes to influence. And it is very clear that the ecology of the Southern Plains had become so complicated by the mid-nineteenth century that neither the Indians nor the Euro-Americans of those years could have grasped how it all worked.

Finally and ironically, it seems that the Indian religions, so effective at calling forth awe and reverence for the natural world, may have inhibited the Plains Indians' understanding of bison ecology and their role in it. True, native leaders such as Yellow Wolf, the Cheyenne whom James W. Abert interviewed and sketched at Bent's Fort in 1845–1846, surmised the implications of market hunting. As he watched the bison disappearing from the Arkansas Valley, Yellow Wolf asked the whites to teach the Cheyenne hunters how to farm, never realizing that he was reprising a Plains Indian/Euro-American conversation that had taken place sixty years earlier in that same country.[51] But Yellow Wolf was marching to his own drummer, for it remained a widespread tenet of faith among most Plains Indians through the 1880s that bison were supernatural in origin. A firsthand observer and close student of the nineteenth-century Plains reported,

> Every Plains Indian firmly believed that the buffalo were produced in countless numbers in a country under the ground, that every spring the surplus swarmed like bees from a hive, out of great cave-like openings to this country, which were situated somewhere in the great 'Llano Estacado' or Staked Plain of Texas.

This religious conception of the infinity of nature's abundance was poetic. On one level it was also empirical: Bison overwintered in large numbers in the protected canyons scored into the eastern escarpment of the Llano Estacado, and Indians had no doubt many times witnessed the herds emerging to overspread the high Plains in springtime. But such a conception did not aid the tribes in their efforts to work out an ecological balance amid the complexities of the nineteenth-century Plains.[52]

In a real sense, then, the more familiar events of the 1870s only delivered the *coup de grace* to the free Indian life on the Great Plains. The slaughterhouse effects of European diseases and wars with the encroaching whites caused Indian numbers to dwindle after 1850 (no more than fourteen hundred Comanches were enrolled to receive federal benefits at Fort Sill, in present-day Oklahoma, in the 1880s). This combined with bison resiliency to preserve a good core of animals until the arrival of the white hide hunters, who nonetheless can be documented as taking only about 3.5 million animals from the Southern Plains.[53]

But the great days of the Plains Indians, the primal poetry of humans and horses, bison and grass, sunlight and blue skies, and the sensuous satisfactions of a hunting life on the sweeping grasslands defined a meteoric time indeed. And the meteor was already fading in the sky a quarter century before the Big Fifties began to boom.

NOTES

1. See Jacobo Loyola y Ugarte to Juan Bautista de Anza, Oct. 5, 1786, roll 10, series 11, Spanish Archives of New Mexico, microfilm (New Mexico State Archives, Santa Fe).

2. Ibid. One line reads: "use all your sagacity and efficiency, making evident to the [Comanche] Captains . . . that the animals they hunt with such effort at sustenance are not at base inexhaustible." See also Alfred B. Thomas, ed., *Forgotten Frontiers: A Study of the Spanish Indian Policy of Don Juan Bautista de Anza, Governor of New Mexico, 1777–1787* (Norman, 1932). 69–72, 82.

3. See Alfred W. Crosby, Jr., *The Columbian Exchange: Biological Consequences of 1492* (Westport, 1972); Alfred W. Crosby, Jr., *Ecological Imperialism: The Biological Expansion of Europe, 900–1900* (New York, 1986); Henry Dobyns, *Native American Historical Demography* (Bloomington, 1976); Henry Dobyns, *Their Number Become Thinned: Native American Population Dynamics in Eastern North America* (Knoxville, 1983); Calvin Martin, *Keepers of the Game: Indian-Animal Relations and the Fur Trade* (Berkeley, 1979); Richard White, *Roots of Dependency* (Lincoln, 1983); William Cronon, *Changes in the Land: Indians, Colonists, and the Ecology of New England* (New York, 1983); Paul Martin and Henry Wright, Jr., eds., *Pleistocene Extinctions: The Search for a Cause* (New Haven, 1967); and Paul Martin and Richard Klein, eds., *Quarternary Extinctions* (Tucson, 1985).

4. See Richard White, "American Indians and the Environment," *Environmental Review*, 9 (Summer 1985), 101–3; Richard White, "Native Americans and the Environment," in *Scholars and the Indian Experience: Critical Reviews of Recent Writings in the Social Sciences*, ed. W. R. Swagerty (Bloomington, 1984), 179–204; Christopher T. Vecsey and Robert W. Venables, eds., *American Indian Environments: Ecological Issues in Native American History* (Syracuse, 1980); Richard White and William Cronon, "Ecological Change and Indian–White Relations," in *Handbook of North American Indians*, ed. William C. Sturtevant (20 vols., Washington, D.C., 1978–1989), IV, 417–29; and Donald J. Hughes, *American Indian Ecology* (El Paso, 1983).

5. See White, "American Indians and the Environment," 101; and White and Cronon, "Ecological Change and Indian–White Relations."

6. Several earlier scholars have addressed this question. For an early argument that the horse Indians overhunted bison, see William T. Hornaday, "The Extermination of the American Bison, with a Sketch of its Discovery and Life History," *Smithsonian Report*, 1887, pp. 480–90, 506. For statements of this position that offer nothing beyond anecdotal evidence, see James Malin, *History and Ecology*, ed. Robert Swierenga (Lincoln, 1984), 9, 31–54; George Hyde, *Spotted Tail's Folk* (Norman, 1961), 24; and Preston Holder, *The Hoe and the Horse on the Plains* (Lincoln, 1970), 111, 118. For the contrary view, see Frank Roe, *The North American Buffalo: A Critical Study of the Species in its Wild State* (Toronto, 1951), 500–505, 655–70; and Frank Roe, *The Indian and the Horse* (Norman, 1955), 190–91. The breadth and authority of Roe's books have given him priority in the field.

7. Since it utilizes long-ignored Spanish documents, on the Comanches' migration I follow Thomas Kavanagh, "Political Power and Political Organization: Comanche Politics, 1786–1875," (Ph.D. diss., University of New Mexico, 1986), rather than Ernest Wallace and E. Adamson Hoebel, *The Comanches: Lords of the South Plains* (Norman, 1951). Dimitri Boris Shimkin, *Wind River Shoshone Ethnography* (Berkeley, 1947); James A. Goss, "Basin-Plateau Shoshonean Ecological Model," in *Great Basin Cultural Ecology: A Symposium*, ed. Don D. Fowler (Reno, 1972), 123–27.

8. Richard White, "The Winning of the West: The Expansion of the Western Sioux in the Eighteenth and Nineteenth Centuries," *Journal of American History*, 65 (Sept. 1978), 319–43.

9. Kiowa origin myths set on the Northern Plains are at variance with the linguistic evidence, which ties them to the Tanoan speakers of the Rio Grande pueblos. Scholars are coming to believe that there is a connection between the mysterious Jumano peoples of the seventeenth- and eighteenth-century New Mexico documents and the later Kiowas. See Nancy Hickerson, "The Jumano and Trade in the Arid Southwest, 1580–1700," 1989 (in Dan Flores's possession). I am indebted to Ms. Hickerson for allowing me to examine her work. William Brandon, *Indians* (Boston, 1987), 340.

10. Ernest Wallace, "The Habitat and Range of the Kiowa, Comanche and Apache Indians Before 1867," prepared for the United States Department of Justice for Case No. 257 before the Indian Claims Commission, 1959 (Southwest Collection, Texas Tech University, Lubbock). See Thomas Kavanagh, "The Comanche: Paradigmatic Anomaly or Ethnographic Fiction," *Haliksa'i*, 4 (1985), 109-28; Melburn D. Thurman, "A New Interpretation of Comanche Social Organization," *Current Anthropology*, 23 (Oct. 1982), 578-79; Daniel J. Gelo, "On a New Interpretation of Comanche Social Organization," ibid., 28 (Aug.-Oct. 1987), 551-52; Melburn D. Thurman, "Reply," ibid., 552-55. For the earlier position that the Comanches are atypical on the Plains, see Symmes Oliver, *Ecology and Cultural Continuity as Contributing Factors in the Social Organization of the Plain Indians* (Berkeley, 1972), 69-80.

11. Jerry McDonald, *North American Bison: Their Classification and Evolution* (Berkeley, 1981), 250-63.

12. Tom Dillehay, "Late Quaternary Bison Population Changes on the Southern Plains," *Plains Anthropologist*, 19 (Aug. 1974), 180-96; Darrell Creel et al., "A Faunal Record from West-Central Texas and Its Bearing on Late Holocene Bison Population Changes in the Southern Plains," ibid., 35 (April 1990), 55-69. For Great Plains dendrochronology, see Harry Weakly, "A Tree-Ring Record of Precipitation in Western Nebraska," *Journal of Forestry*, 41 (Nov. 1943), 816-19; and Edmund Schulman, *Dendroclimactic Data from Arid America* (Tucson, 1956), 86-88. For use of meteorological data to argue that climate variability was exponentially greater on the Southern Plains than farther north, see Douglas Barnforth, *Ecology and Human Organization on the Great Plains* (New York, 1988), 74.

13. Weakly, "Tree-Ring Record of Precipitation in Western Nebraska," 819.

14. U.S. Department of Commerce, Bureau of the Census, *Thirteenth Census of the United States, Taken in the Year 1910*, vols. VI and VII: *Agriculture, 1909 and 1910* (Washington, 1913). My method has been to compile 1910 cattle, horse, and mule figures for the then-existing Plains counties of Texas (119), western Oklahoma (45), New Mexico (10), counties below the Arkansas River in Colorado (8), and counties in southwestern Kansas (19). The carrying capacity for a biome such as the Great Plains ought to be measured by the use of the county figures. The principal problem with this technique in the past has been overgeneralization of stock numbers through reliance on state totals. It was first used by Ernest Thompson Seton, *Life Histories of Northern Animals* (2 vols., New York, 1909), I, 259-63; and more recently by Bill Brown, "Comancheria Demography, 1805-1830," *Panhandle—Plains Historical Review*, 59 (1986), 8-12. Range management commonly assigns cows a grazing quotient of 1.0, bulls a quotient of 1.30, and horses and mules 1.25.

15. Joseph Chapman and George Feldhamer, eds., *Wild Mammals of North America: Biology, Management and Economics* (Baltimore, 1982) 978, 986, 1001-2. Modern bison ranchers claim that bison achieve greater land-use efficiency and larger herd size on native grass compared to cattle. The editors of the above work call for more research into this question. See also Charles Rehr, "Buffalo Population and Other Deterministic Factors in a Model of Adaptive Process on the Shortgrass Plains," *Plains Anthropologist*, 23 (Nov. 1978), 25-27.

16. For the use of a different formula (mean potential bovine carrying capacity per acre) to arrive at similar totals see Tom McHugh, *The Time of the Buffalo* (New York, 1972), 16-17. For the reasonably convincing argument that because of climate variability and less nutritious grasses, population densities of Great Plains bison were lowest on the Southern Plains, see Bamforth, *Ecology and Human Organization on the Great Plains*, 74, 78.

17. The figure for loss of plant lore is based on a comparison of remembered ethnobotanies for the Shoshones (172 species) and the Comanches (67 species). See Brian Spykerman, "Shoshoni Conceptualizations of Plant Relationships" (M.S. thesis, Utah State University, 1977); and Gustav Carlson and Volney Jones, "Some Notes on the Uses of Plants by the Comanche Indians," *Papers of the Michigan Academy of Science, Arts,*

and Letters, 25 (1939), 517–42. On women's loss of status, see Holder, *Hoe and the Horse on the Plains*.

18. Wallace and Hoebel, *Comanches*, 142. On the loss of Shoshone birth control mechanisms among Comanche women, see Abram Kardiner, "Analysis of Comanche Culture," in *The Psychological Frontiers of Society*, ed. Abram Kardiner et al. (New York, 1945). For a report of 500 adopted captives in a decade, see Jean Louis Berlandier, *The Indians of Texas in 1830*, ed. John C. Ewers (Washington, 1969), 119. Estimates on the Euro-American constituency of nineteenth-century Comanche bands as approaching 75 percent are probably too high, but 30 percent may not be. On Comanche adoption and captives trade, see Carl C. Rister, *Border Captives: The Traffic in Prisoners by Southern Plains Indians, 1835–1875* (Norman, 1940); and Russell Magnaghi, "The Indian Slave Trader: The Comanche, a Case Study" (Ph.D. diss., St. Louis University, 1970). Indian Agent Thomas Fitzpatrick was adamant that Comanche raids were for children, "to keep up the numbers of the tribe." See Kardiner, "Analysis of Comanche Culture," 89. On hunter-gatherer carrying capacity, see Marvin Harris and Eric Ross, *Death, Sex, and Fertility: Population Regulation in Preindustrial and Developing Societies* (New York, 1987), 23–26; and Ezra Zubrow, *Prehistoric Carrying Capacity: A Model* (Menlo Park, 1975).

19. David Kaplan, "The Law of Cultural Dominance," in *Evolution and Culture*, ed. Marshall Sahlins and Elman Service (Ann Arbor, 1960), 75–82. On Apache vulnerability, see George E. Hyde, *Indians of the High Plains: From the Prehistoric Period to the Coming of Europeans* (Norman, 1975), 65, 70, 91. Other explanations include the Spanish refusal to trade guns to the Apaches and Comanche superiority at horse care. For less monocausal interpretations, see Frederick W. Rathjen, *The Texas Panhandle Frontier* (Austin, 1973), 47–48.

20. For references to Comanche names containing the word *wolf* (rendered by Euro-Americans as *isa, ysa, esa*, or sometimes with an *sh* second syllable), see George Catlin, *Letters and Notes on the Manners, Customs, and Conditions of the North American Indians* (2 vols., New York, 1973), II, 67–69; Noel Loomis and Abraham Nasatir, eds., *Pedro Vial and the Roads to Santa Fe* (Norman, 1967), 488n22a; and Thomas, *Forgotten Frontiers*, 325–27.

21. On Comanche trade with Anglo-Americans, see Dan Flores, ed., *Journal of an Indian Trader: Anthony Glass and the Texas Trading Frontier, 1790–1810* (College Station, 1985), esp. 3–33; and Thomas James, *Three Years among the Indians and Mexicans*, ed. Walter Douglas (St. Louis, 1916), 191–235. For the argument that the Comanches were among the earliest Plains traders, and that Comanche leadership evolved in a trade/market situation, see Kavanagh, "Political Power and Political Organization." See Charles Kenner, *A History of New Mexican–Plains Indian Relations* (Norman, 1969); and William Swagerty, "Indian Trade in the Trans-Mississippi West to 1870," in *Handbook of North American Indians*, ed. Sturtevant, IV, 351–74.

22. See Hickerson, "Jumano and Trade in the Arid Southwest." On Kiowa origins, see also Maurice Boyd, *Kiowa Voices: Ceremonial Dance, Ritual, and Songs* (2 vols., Fort Worth, 1981); and John Wunder, *The Kiowas* (New York, 1989).

23. Elizabeth A. H. John, "An Earlier Chapter of Kiowa History," *New Mexico Historical Review*, 60 (no. 4, 1985), 379–97. On traders' contacts with the Kiowas, see, particularly, Maxine Benson, ed., *From Pittsburgh to the Rocky Mountains: Major Stephen Long's Expedition, 1819–1820* (Golden, 1988), 327–36.

24. Holder, *Hoe and the Horse on the Plains*. See also Bea Medicine and Pat Albers, *The Hidden Half: Studies of Plains Indian Women* (Lanham, 1983); and Katherine Weist, "Plains Indian Women: An Assessment," in *Anthropology on the Great Plains*, ed. Raymond Wood and Margot Liberty (Lincoln, 1980), 255–71.

25. Joseph Jablow, *The Cheyenne in Plains Indian Trade Relations, 1795–1840* (Seattle, 1950); Donald Berthrong, *The Southern Cheyennes* (Norman, 1963), 4–21; Loomis and Nasatir, eds., *Pedro Vial and the Roads to Santa Fe*, 256–58.

26. Alan Osburn, "Ecological Aspects of Equestrian Adaptations in Aboriginal

North America," *American Anthropologist*, 85 (Sept. 1983), 563–91; Berthrong, *Southern Cheyenne*, 25–26; Jablow, *Cheyenne in Plains Indian Trade Relations*, 67; David Lavender, *Bent's Fort* (Lincoln, 1954), 141–54; George Phillips, *Chiefs and Challengers: Indian Resistance and Cooperation in Southern California* (Berkeley, 1975), 42–43; Eleanor Lawrence, "The Old Spanish Trail from Santa Fe to California" (M.A. thesis, University of California, Berkeley, 1930).

27. On the intertribal buffer zones, see Berthrong, *Southern Cheyennes*, 76, 93. On their function in preserving wildlife in other ecosystems, see Harold Hickerson, "The Virginia Deer and Intertribal Buffer Zones in the Upper Mississippi Valley," *Man, Culture, and Animals*, ed. Anthony Leeds and Andrew Vayda (Washington, 1965), 43–66.

28. Raymond Dasmann, "Future Primitive," *CoEvolution Quarterly*, 11 (1976), 26–31; David Wishart, *The Fur Trade of the American West, 1807–1840* (Lincoln, 1979); Arthur Ray, *The Fur Trade and the Indian* (Toronto, 1974); White, *Roots of Dependency*, 147–211.

29. Zubrow, *Prehistoric Carrying Capacity*, 8–9.

30. Chapman and Feldhamer, eds., *Wild Mammals of North America*, 980–83; Arthur Halloran, "Bison (Bovidae) Productivity on the Wichita Mountains Wildlife Refuge, Oklahoma," *Southwestern Naturalist*, 13 (May 1968), 23–26; Alisa Shull and Alan Tipton, "Effective Population Size of Bison on the Wichita Mountains Wildlife Refuge," *Conservation Biology*, 1 (May 1987), 35–41.

31. Data on the modern bison herds on the Great Plains are from the refuge managers and superintendents of the Wichita Mountains Wildlife Refuge, Theodore Roosevelt National Memorial Park, and Wind Cave National Park. The National Bison Refuge in Montana did not respond to my inquiries. Robert Karges to Dan Flores, March 18, 1988 (in Flores's possession); Robert Powell to Flores, Feb. 10, 1988, ibid.; Ernest Ortega to Flores, Feb. 11, 1988, ibid. See Graeme Caughley, "Eruption of Ungulate Populations, with Emphasis on Himalayan Thar in New Zealand," *Ecology*, 51 (Winter 1970), 53–72. This study has been widely cited in wildlife ecology as evidence that starvation rather than predation is often the key to regulating natural population eruptions. The only documentary evidence I have seen for starvation of bison on the Southern Plains is Charles Goodnight's account of seeing "millions" of starved bison along a front 25 by 100 miles between the Concho and Brazos rivers in 1867, after bison migration patterns had been disrupted by settlements. J. Evetts Haley, *Charles Goodnight, Cowman and Plainsman* (Norman, 1949), 161.

32. The nineteenth-century documentary evidence assigns wolves roles as scavengers of bison killed by other agents; as cullers of weak, sick, and old animals; and as predators of bison calves. The last, I believe, best expresses the regulatory effect of wolves on Plains bison population dynamics. See Gary E. Moulton. ed., *The Journals of Lewis and Clark Expedition* (5 vols, Lincoln, 1987), IV, 62–63; Donald Jackson and Mary Lee Spence, eds., *The Expeditions of John Charles Fremont* (5 vols., Urbana, 1970–1984), I, 190–91; Henry Boller, *Among the Indians: Four Years on the Upper Missouri, 1858–1862*, ed. Milo Milton Quaife (Lincoln, 1972), 270–71; Maria Audubon and Elliott Coues, eds., *Audubon and His Journals* (2 vols., New York, 1986), I, 49; and W. Eugene Hollon, ed., *William Bollaert's Texas* (Norman, 1989), 255. For other descriptions, see Stanley P. Young and Edward A. Goldman, *The Wolves of North America* (2 vols., New York, 1944), I, 50, 218, 224–31.

33. Katherine Spielman, "Late Prehistoric Exchange between the Southwest and Southern Plains," *Plains Anthropologist*, 28 (Nov. 1983), 257–79. For the argument that essential plant resources from this trade ended a nutrition "bottleneck" and therefore allowed the buildup of much larger human populations on the Southern Plains, see Bamforth, *Ecology and Human Organization on the Great Plains*, 8.

34. Jerold Levy, "Ecology of the South Plains," in *Symposium: Patterns of Land Use and Other Papers*, ed. Viola Garfield (Seattle, 1961), 18–25.

35. Brown, "Comancheria Demography," 10–11; H. Paul Thompson, "A Technique Using Anthropological and Biological Data," *Current Anthropology*, 7 (Oct. 1966), 417–

24; Jacob Fowler, *The Journal of Jacob Fowler: Narrating an Adventure from Arkansas through the Indian Territory, Oklahoma, Kansas, Colorado, and New Mexico, to the Sources of the Rio Grande del Norte*, ed. Elliott Coues (New York, 1898), 61, 63.

36. Wallace and Hoebel, *Comanches*, 31–32. The anthropological literature tends to set Comanche population much more conservatively, often at no more than 7,000. See, for example, Bamforth, *Ecology and Human Organizations on the Great Plains*, 104–14. Such low figures ignore eyewitness accounts of localized Comanche aggregations of several thousand. I have a historian's bias in favor of documentary evidence for estimating human populations; Plains observers computed village sizes relatively easily by counting the number of tents.

37. Berthrong, *Southern Cheyennes*, 78, 92, 107. The Kiowas and Kiowa-Apaches seem to have averaged about 2,500 to 3,000 from 1825 to 1850, and the Prairie Caddoans perhaps 2,000, shrinking to 1,000 by midcentury. *Report, Commissioner of Indians Affairs, 1842*, cited in Josiah Gregg, *Commerce of the Prairies*, ed. Max Moorhead (Norman, 1961), 431–32n3.

38. Because of the tough meat and the thick hides that made soft tanning difficult, Indians (and whites hunting for meat) rarely killed bison bulls. See Roe, *North American Buffalo*, 650–70; and Larry Barsness, *Heads, Hides, and Horns: The Compleat Buffalo Book* (Fort Worth, 1974), 69–72, 96–98. Dean E. Medin and Allen E. Anderson, *Modeling the Dynamics of a Colorado Mule Deer Population* (Fort Collins, 1979). Whether 60,000 hunters ever worked the Southern Plains in precontact times is now unknowable, but Coronado's chronicler, Castaneda, wrote that there were more people on the Plains in 1542 than in the Rio Grande pueblos. Pedro de Castaneda, "The Narrative of the Expedition of Coronado," in *Spanish Explorers in the Southern United States, 1528–1543*, ed. Frederick W. Hodge and Theodore H. Lewis (Austin, 1984), 362. For a seventeenth-century population estimate in the Rio Grande pueblos of about 30,500, see Marc Simmons, "History of Pueblo-Spanish Relations to 1821," in *Handbook of North American Indians*, ed. Sturtevant, IX, 185 (table 1).

39. For Thomas Fitzpatrick's report, see Berthrong, *Southern Cheyennes*, 124. The English traveler William Bollaert mentions that the Texas Comanches supposedly ate 20,000 mustangs in the late 1840s. See Hollon ed., *William Bollaert's Texas*, 361. On the escalating stock raids and trade to New Mexico beginning in the 1840s, see J. Evetts Haley, "The Comanchero Trade," *Southwestern Historical Quarterly*, 38 (Jan. 1935), 157–76. Haley generally ascribes the situation to Comanche barbarity and Hispanic lack of respect for Lockean private property rights. See also Kenner, *History of New Mexican–Plains Indian Relations*, 78–97, 155–200.

40. See James Mooney, *Calendar History of the Kiowa Indians* (Washington, 1979), 287–95; Levy, "Ecology of the South Plains," 19. The decline in the number of bison was becoming noticeable as early as 1844, two years before the 1846–1857 drought. See Solomon Sublette to William Sublette, Feb. 2, May 5, 1844, William Sublette Papers (Archives, Missouri Historical Society, St. Louis, Mo.). In 1845 the trader James Webb and his party traveled from Bent's Fort to Missouri without killing a bison. "Memoirs of James J. Webb, Merchant in Santa Fe, N.M., 1844," typescript, p. 69, James Webb Papers, ibid.

41. John C. Ewers, *The Horse in Blackfoot Culture* (Washington, 1955). For systematic assessment of the effects of horses on seasonal band size, camps, and resources, see John Moore, *The Cheyenne Nation: A Social and Demographic History* (Lincoln, 1987), 127–75. For a dynamic rather than a static horse ecology, see James Sherow, "Pieces to a Puzzle: High Plains Indians and Their Horses in the Region of the Arkansas River Valley 1800–1860," paper presented at the Ethnohistory Conference, Chicago, 1989 (in Flores's possession). Clyde Wilson, "An Inquiry into the Nature of Plains Indian Cultural Development," *American Anthropologist*, 65 (April 1963), 355–69.

42. J. Frank Dobie, *The Mustangs* (New York, 1934), 108–9. Dobie's estimate, as he pointed out, was a guess, but my work in the agricultural censuses indicates that it was a good guess. On horse/bovine dietary overlap see L. J. Krysl et al., "Horses and Cattle

Grazing in the Wyoming Red Desert, I. Food Habits and Dietary Overlap," *Journal of Range Management*, 37 (Jan. 1984), 72–76. On the drier climate on the Plains between 1848 and 1874, see Weakly, "Tree-Ring Record of Precipitation in Western Nebraska," 817, 819; and Levy, "Ecology of the South Plains," 19.

43. I follow Chapman and Feldhamer, eds., *Wild Mammals of North America*, 991–94.

44. McHugh, *Time of the Buffalo*, 226–27. For scientific discussion of predation by wolves on large ungulates, see David Mech, *The Wolf* (New York, 1970); see also Chapman and Feldhamer, eds., *Wild Mammals of North America*, 994–96. For estimates that the reintroduction of wolves to Yellowstone would reduce the bison herd there between 5 percent and 20 percent, see Barbara Koth, David Lime, and Jonathan Vlaming, "Effects of Restoring Wolves on Yellowstone Area Big Game and Grizzly Bears: Opinions of Fifteen North American Experts," in Yellowstone National Park, *Wolves for Yellowstone?* (n.p., 1990), 4–71, 4–72, and the computer simulation, 3–31. Young and Goldman, *Wolves of North America*, II, 327–33.

45. Schulman, *Dendroclimatic Data from Arid America*, fig. 22; Weakly, "Tree-Ring Record of Precipitation in Western Nebraska," 817, 819.

46. For emphasis on disruption by whites, see Douglas Bamforth, "Historical Document and Bison Ecology on the Great Plains," *Plains Anthropologist*, 32 (Feb. 1987), 1–16. On the *Ciboleros*, see Kenner, *History of New Mexican–Plains Indian Relations*, 115–17. Jablow, *Cheyenne in Plains Indian Trade Relations*, 72.

47. My interpretation of the great 1840 alliance of the Southern Plains tribes has been much influenced by Jablow, *Cheyenne in Plains Indian Trade Relations*, 72–73; Levy, "Ecology of the South Plains," 19; Mooney, *Calendar History of the Kiowa Indians*, 276–346.

48. John Whitfield, "Census of the Cheyenne, Comanche, Arapaho, Plains Apache, and the Kiowa of the Upper Arkansas Agency," Aug. 15, 1855, Letters Received, Records of the Office of Indian Affairs, RG 75, microfilm M234, reel 878 (National Archives). Letters between the principals at Bent's Fort make it clear that the Comanche trade in robes was Bent and St. Vrain's chief hope for economic solvency in the early 1840s. See W. D. Hodgkiss to Andrew Drips, March 25, 1843, Andrew Drips Papers (Archives, Missouri Historical Society).

49. Records on the robe trade are fragmentary and frequently at odds with one another; see T. Lindsay Baker, "The Buffalo Robe Trade in the 19th-Century West," paper presented at the Center of the American Indian, Oklahoma City, April 1989 (in T. Lindsay Baker's possession). John Jacob Astor's American Fur Company was taking in 25,000 to 30,000 robes a year from the Missouri River from 1828 to 1830, and St. Louis was receiving 85,000 to 100,000 cow robes a year by the end of the 1840s. Baker cannot yet estimate how many of those came from the Southern Plains, but the trend toward a larger harvest seems apparent. On the Canadian experience, see Ray, *Fur Trade and the Indian*, 228.

50. Berlandier, *Indians of Texas in 1830*, ed. Ewers, 84–85. Thirteen epidemics and pandemics would have affected the Comanches between 1750 and 1864; see Dobyns, *Their Number Become Thinned*, 15–20. On the abandonment of Bent's first Arkansas River post, see Lavender, *Bent's Fort*, 338–39. John C. Ewers, "The Influence of Epidemics on the Indian Populations and Cultures of Texas," *Plains Anthropologist*, 18 (May 1973), 106. Ewers bases his decline on an estimated early nineteenth-century Comanche population of only 7,000. If my larger estimate is accepted, the Comanche population decline was more than 90 percent. A falloff in the birthrate as Indian women contracted Bang's disease from brucellosis-infected bison may have contributed importantly to Indian population decline.

51. James W. Abert, *The Journal of Lieutenant J. W. Abert from Bent's Fort to St. Louis in 1845*, ed. H. Bailey Carroll (Canyon, 1941), 15–16; U.S. Congress, Senate, *Report of the Secretary of War, Communicating in Answer to a Resolution of the Senate, a*

Report and Map of the Examination of New Mexico, Made by Lieutenant J. W. Abert, of the Topographical Corps, 30 cong., 1 sess., Feb. 10, 1848.

52. Richard I. Dodge, *Our Wild Indians* (Hartford, 1882), 286. The idea has lingered in the preserved mythologies of the Southern Plains tribes. In 1881 representatives of many of those tribes assembled on the North Fork of the Red for the Kiowa Sun Dance, where a Kiowa shaman, Buffalo Coming Out, vowed to call on the herds to reemerge from the ground. The Kiowas believed the bison had gone into hiding in the earth, and they still call a peak in the Wichita Mountains Hiding Mountain. Alice Mariott and Carol Rechlin, *Plains Indian Mythology* (New York, 1975), 140; Peter Powell, *Sweet Medicine* (2 vols., Norman, 1969), I, 281–82. There is no mention of this idea in the major work on Comanche mythology, but it is far from a complete compilation: Elliott Canonge, *Comanche Texts* (Norman, 1958). On the bison's wintering in protected canyons, see Randolph Marcy, *A Report on the Exploration of the Red River, in Louisiana* (Washington, 1854), 125–31.

53. Wallace and Hoebel, *Comanches*, 32; Richard I. Dodge in *The Plains of North America and Their Inhabitants*, ed. Wayne Kime (Newark, 1989), 155–57. On these figures for bison, see Roe, *North American Buffalo*, 440–41.

7 MEXICAN OPINION, AMERICAN RACISM, AND THE WAR OF 1846

Gene M. Brack

In *1821*, *Anglo-Americans began accepting land grants in Texas from the Mexican government. Mexico's purpose was to populate, and thereby fortify, its far northern frontier against possible encroachment from the United States, just as Spain had tried to fortify the same area against France in the eighteenth century. The conditions of the land grants were that the new settlers become Mexican citizens, become Catholic (Mexico's official religion, as it had been Spain's), and bring no slaves into Texas. By 1830 the Anglo-Americans—and the slaves they illegally brought with them—outnumbered Spanish-speakers by two or three to one. In 1836, the Americans declared and successfully defended their independence from Mexico.*

Nine years later, in 1845, the United States annexed Texas by mutual agreement with the Texans. Mexico had never recognized Texan independence and now regarded the United States as complicit in this alienation of Mexican territory. As Gene Brack shows, opinion in Mexico ran high against the United States in 1845–46; an American army force under Zachary Taylor was camped on the Rio Grande, 150 miles farther into Mexico than the traditional border at the Nueces River, and an American naval force was anchored off Monterey, California, seemingly awaiting the moment to capture it. Mexican presidents José Joaquín Herrera (to December 1845) and Mariano Paredes y Arrillaga both resented these intrusions, but both also realized that Mexico was not prepared to offer effective resistance. Yet, writes Brack, Mexican public opinion permitted them no other course. When Mexicans fired on Taylor's troops in April 1846, and U.S. President James K. Polk chose to construe that as an act of war, Mexico had no choice but to resist. The disastrous war ensued in which Mexico lost not only Texas but New Mexico, California, and the rest of its territory north of the Rio Grande and Gila River.

Why, asks Brack, did Mexican public opinion so deeply fear American encroachment that it prevented Mexico's leaders from avoiding that result? The basic answer was the American track record with regard to Indians and slaves, and the oft-repeated and well-known contempt that Americans had for Mexico and Mexicans. In this essay, Brack lays out the dilemma faced by Mexican leadership, and provides evidence for the Mexican popular opinion that created one horn of the dilemma—the other being the actions of the United States.—editors

WHEN MEXICAN forces attacked a detachment of General Zachary Taylor's army on the east bank of the Rio Grande in April 1846, President James K. Polk justified a declaration of war against Mexico with the charge that "American blood" had been shed upon "American soil." The clash culminated two decades of abrasive relations between the United States and Mexico. By 1846 the most palpable cause of contention was the rapid expansion of the United States toward the borderlands of Mexico. The Polk administration appeared determined to carry forward a program of expansion which would ultimately embrace much of northern Mexico. The Mexican government seemed equally determined to avoid losing any part of her national domain. For nine years Mexico had refused to recognize Texas independence and more recently had rejected Polk's offer to purchase upper California. Failing to gain concessions by peaceful means, Polk then made a show of force: it did not fit the purpose of the president's war message to acknowledge that the boundary between the United States and Mexico was undetermined, the area between the Nueces and Rio Grande rivers being disputed territory rather than "American soil"; that for weeks the mouth of the Rio Grande had lain under an American blockade; that an American squadron hovered near Vera Cruz; or that an American "exploratory" expedition had entered upper California.[1]

Merely to cite American provocations does not wholly explain Mexico's reaction. Her decision to fight rather than surrender territory by any means was a momentous one for both countries, yet since the publication in 1919 of Justin H. Smith's *The War With Mexico*, American writers have given scant attention to the factors that may have influenced Mexico's course of action. Smith explained that the decision was in large measure based upon Mexican confidence in their military superiority; believing their army larger and more powerful, Mexicans also remembered that the United States had demonstrated martial ineptitude during the War of 1812. Thus, according to Smith, Mexicans sought war, for, "vain and superficial, they did not realize their weakness."[2]

But for years Mexico had vowed to respond to American annexation of Texas with an immediate declaration of war against the United States. Therefore, if she sought war, why did Mexico not launch it in 1845 when Texas joined the American Union? It was the administration of José Joaquín de Herrera, who had become president in December 1844, that determined Mexico's response to annexation. Herrera's alternatives were to preserve peace by simply recognizing the irrevocable loss of Texas, or to act upon the threats of previous administrations and to declare war. The president appeared obligated to pursue the latter course, not only because

8. Antonio Lopez de Santa Anna, several times President of Mexico, leader of Mexican forces in the Mexican-American War of 1846–48.

of Mexico's previously announced position, but also because the revolution that brought Herrera to power had as an important purpose the creation of a government that would take a firm stand against the United States.[3]

Herrera nevertheless wished to avoid war. He explained his position in a pamphlet which declared that it served the true interests of the country to preserve peace, that there was no longer any hope of recovering Texas, and that war, in Mexico's present circumstances, would lead to disaster.[4] In accordance with Herrera's conciliatory policy, the government agreed in October of 1845 to admit an American envoy. Such a measure required support from outside the administration, however, and in November 1845 the foreign secretary sent a circular letter to local officials throughout Mexico soliciting their cooperation. The secretary agreed that Mexico had ample justification for declaring war, but he realized also that the country lacked the means to support an army hundreds of miles away on the distant frontier. The northern divisions could scarcely maintain their garrisons, let alone take the offensive. The secretary informed the local officials that Mexico could depend upon neither military nor financial support from other nations, and that in such circumstances the administration believed it expedient to avoid disaster by peacefully ceding an underpopulated part of Mexico's immense territory.[5]

Thwarted by the combined opposition of the press, an aroused public, and rival political factions, Herrera's appeals went unheeded. When the American envoy arrived late in 1845 he was refused recognition, nominally because his credentials were improper, actually because Herrera could not afford further to offend public opinion by negotiating with a representative of the United States. The concession failed to save Herrera. He had assumed a moderate position when Mexicans would accept no course but a militant one.[6] In December 1845 he was overthrown by General Mariano Paredes y Arrillaga. But the new president was also unable to breathe energy into a bankrupt and divided people.[7]

When Paredes seized power he was aware of the nation's impotence. During the summer of 1845, while commanding a large body of the Mexican army at San Luis Potosi, Paredes himself had predicted that a clash with the United States would disgrace his nation before the eyes of the world.[8] And correspondents from the capital had informed Paredes that, for lack of funds, the army could not be strengthened.[9]

During the summer and fall of 1845 Paredes had received frequent communications from General Mariano Arista, commanding Mexican forces on the northern frontier, informing him of Mexican weakness along the Rio Grande. In July Arista wrote that the army was in a state of "dreadful misery"; an advance upon Texas was out of the question, because the army lacked the means of bare subsistence.[10] To Arista the frontier appeared threatened, and he wrote that he would do what he could to protect it, but that it was impossible to defend the nation with "hungry and naked" troops. He felt that he would weaken his army even more by sending a brigade to protect the department of Coahuila; to guard the entire line of the Rio Grande appeared impossible.[11] Arista informed Paredes that he was convinced that the United States intended to attack and that Mexico would be defeated and then "dominated by Americans."[12]

In October Arista wrote that he was desperate, his troops were hungry and that "the situation was very sad."[13] Apparently preparing to advance upon Matamoros, the gringos had seized all of the passages across the Nueces, and Arista could do nothing to prevent it. The autumn weather was frigid, his men had neither coats nor blankets. They were perishing from cold and hunger, and yet the "public writers" had declared war.[14]

Thus Arista, who would be ordered in the spring of 1846 to initiate hostilities, appeared more apprehensive than bellicose. And Paredes, regardless of his intentions when he entered the presidency, knew that Mexico was vulnerable and did not order an attack until seriously provoked by the United States. Arista's lament that the public writers had declared war clearly underscores the role of the press and of public opinion in creating the paradoxical situation confronted successively by the administrations of Herrera and Paredes. And within the tangled web of events that led to war it is particularly significant that American officials were aware of the paradox.

Prior to the termination of official diplomatic relations in the spring of 1845, the American minister at Mexico had informed his government that Mexican opinion was so decidedly hostile to the United States that Mexican leaders were considered traitorous unless they appeared to cater to that opinion.[15] In one of his last despatches from Mexico, the American minister reported that the Mexicans who realized war would be "ruinous" and "disastrous" were compelled "to join the public clamor, in order to maintain their positions."[16]

When formal relations were terminated, the Polk administration continued to receive despatches from its consul and from William Parrott, its "confidential agent" in Mexico City. Both repeatedly informed their government that Mexican opinion favored war, but that Mexican officials, realizing their army was weak and the treasury empty, would stop short of fighting. In the summer of 1845 the American consul reported that the present Mexican government had no intention of declaring war. Nor did he think the opposition, should it come to power, would "ever seriously think of entering into a war (in earnest) with the United States."[17] Parrott informed the Polk administration of Arista's weakness when he reported in September that the Mexican general had no more than three thousand men to defend a line of "about 140 leagues," and thus could have no hope of success even if he did intend to launch an attack.[18]

From such reports the Polk administration must have known that Mexican officials sought to avoid war if possible; it also must have known that public opinion in Mexico limited the options of Mexican leaders. But by ordering General Taylor to the Rio Grande and by taking other hostile measures during the winter and spring of 1845–1846, was not the Polk administration further inflaming Mexican opinion and restricting the freedom of action of the Mexican government? It might be argued that the Slidell mission offered peace to Mexico, but Paredes logically defended his dismissal of Slidell by stating that the presence of an American army on the Rio Grande and of an American fleet in Mexican waters prohibited negotiations. To the Mexican president it appeared that by intimidating Mexico the United States hoped to acquire territory for the asking.[19] Paredes was trapped by forces beyond his control: his countrymen demanded war, and the actions of the United States apparently left him no room for maneuvering. The only alternative was to surrender territory to the Americans, and that was clearly unacceptable.

The historian must approach public opinion with great care. Modern devices measure it none too accurately, and when one is dealing with scattered fragments of the past, the difficulties are enormously increased. But if the foregoing is a reasonably accurate reconstruction of the circumstances leading to the Mexican War, it becomes important to devote more than passing attention to the factors that created a climate of opinion so rigidly hostile toward the United States that it led Mexico into a war for which she was dubiously prepared. In other words, it becomes important to know why the alternative—ceding territory to the United States—was so abhorrent to Mexicans.

At least a partial explanation may be that some Mexicans, like many Americans of that period, discerned a relationship between American expansion and racist elements within the United States. They were aware

that many Americans looked upon Mexicans as inferior beings; the implications, when combined with the American desire for Mexican soil, were
frightening. Americans apparently had no respect for the culture of those
whom they considered inferior. They had been merciless in their treatment of the Indian. The Negro, also deemed inferior, had been reduced to
a brutal form of servitude. Similar treatment probably awaited Mexicans
should their northern departments fall under American control. The
American failed to respect his agreements with the Indian; he could hardly
be relied upon to be trustworthy when dealing with Mexicans. Perhaps
this is what many Mexicans had in mind when they insisted that should
Texas and California be lost, other Mexican territory would soon follow.

During the two decades prior to the war, Mexicans often criticized the
United States for proclaiming humanitarian principles while driving the
Indian from his land and condoning slavery. The degree to which the
United States was prepared officially to defend slavery became apparent to
Mexicans in the 1820s when Joel Poinsett, the first American minister to
Mexico, introduced the subject while negotiating a treaty of limits between the two countries. Mexicans questioned a clause in the treaty providing for the detention of escaped slaves. They maintained that public opinion in Mexico would be outraged by the proposed clause. Poinsett
reasoned that the border ought to be settled by a law-abiding population
and suggested that slave owners were an especially orderly and desirable
class. The treaty was eventually ratified without the offending clause, but
Poinsett's arguments in its defense revealed to Mexico the ardor with
which the United States would support the rights of its citizens to own
human property.[20]

Accounts of Poinsett's activities, as well as of other matters pertaining to the United States, were disseminated in newspapers throughout
Mexico. Each important faction in Mexican politics usually had one or
more newspapers to articulate its position, and these newspapers were
widely distributed. In tertulias—informal discussions, often held in tav-
erns—a literate Mexican might read aloud to his non-reading friends; all
would then discuss the topics of the day.[21] The United States was among
the topics. Much of the information in Mexican newspapers was likely to
be doctored and misleading, but they did place the subject of the United
States frequently before the public.[22]

Typical of the kind of information that began appearing in the Mexican press during the 1820s was an anecdote describing a tyrannical Virginia slaveholder who ordered an old black man to hit a recaptured slave
three hundred times, whereupon the old man fatally stabbed first the
owner and then himself.[23] At this time Mexicans also began to reveal an
interest in American treatment of the Indian. The important conservative
newspaper El Sol printed a letter written by John C. Calhoun in which the
American cabinet official recommended sending Indians to uninhabited
western regions. The Mexican editor urged his countrymen to take note
of the matter not only because it seemed to reflect the American attitude

toward Indians, but also because it portended future danger to the frontier of Mexico.[24] The same newspaper later printed a letter written by an unidentified American citizen who criticized his government's Indian policy for being too lenient. Making treaties and compensating Indians for their lost land, he thought, only created needless expense. Instead of negotiating with the Indian, the United States should simply force the Indian to submit. It was absurd to purchase land from those who failed to cultivate it, for in this way the savages became the "depositories of the wealth that resulted from the progress and industry of the white population." The Mexican editor declared the letter typical of the American attitude toward the Indians.[25] In 1840 El Mosquito Mexicano told its readers that Branch Archer of the Texas government favored the conquest of all Mexico and was known to have said that Mexicans, like the Indians, should give way to the energetic force of the Anglo-Americans.[26]

El Amigo del Pueblo was a liberal organ whose editors were friendly toward the United States, but it too expressed concern at the systematic demoralization of the Indian by Americans. It reported in 1828 that it was the objective of the United States to expand to the Pacific. The process would eventually threaten Mexican territory, but presently the chief victim was the Indian. He was first deprived of his lands by a combination of deceit and force, and then his institutions were shattered. In this way a noble, brave, fiercely independent soul was reduced to a state of utter degradation. And Spaniards also had been insulted, cheated and robbed by the United States in the course of acquiring Florida. Therefore Mexicans should be concerned at the rapid approach of Americans toward the frontier.[27]

Mexicans expressed alarm with increasing frequency at the threat of American expansion and at the growing realization that American condescension toward others included Mexicans. As early as 1822 the first Mexican minister at Washington warned his government that the Americans were an arrogant people who thought of Mexicans as inferiors.[28] El Sol reported in 1826 that John Randolph in a senate speech insisted that his countrymen ought not to associate as equals with the people of Latin America, some of whom had descended from Africans. The Mexican editor believed that Randolph's view was typical of the "fanatical intolerance" that prevailed in the United States.[29]

An article in La Aguila Mexicana stressed American contempt for the civilization and culture of Indians, who were called savages because their customs were different from those of the Anglo-Saxons. The writer was certain that Americans viewed Mexicans in the same way.[30] An anonymous Mexican who claimed to have resided for a time in New Orleans reported in the newspaper El Correo that Americans seemed totally disinterested in understanding Mexicans; the American press gave more attention to "Persians and to Asian Tartars" than to Mexicans, and any notice accorded their southern neighbors was invariably insulting.[31] Shortly before the Texas revolution El Mosquito Mexicano declared that the "refined egoism" of the white race caused Americans to treat persons of color with utter contempt and to assume the right to oppress them. The paper warned that Mexicans had much to fear from a people capable of such cruelty.[32]

Manuel Eduardo de Gorostiza, Mexican minister to the United States during the Texas revolution, was the leading man of letters in Mexico and an experienced diplomat. Arriving in Washington in 1836 he was shocked to hear widespread statements of hatred and contempt for Mexico. Treated rudely by the Jackson administration, Gorostiza returned to Mexico and published a pamphlet criticizing Americans for their complicity in the Texas revolution and for their condescending attitude toward Mexicans.[33] In 1840 Gorostiza urged the Mexican government not to surrender its claim to Texas. For Gorostiza there was a clear link between the expansionism of the United States and racism. He thought that Mexicans should make every sacrifice to retain Texas because they stood in danger of losing not only that territory, but also "sooner or later," their "nationality." The struggle to halt American expansion was a "war of race, of religion, of language, and of customs."[34]

José María Tornel y Mendivel, Mexico's secretary of war during the revolution in Texas, wrote in 1837 that the colossus of the north was obviously guilty of fomenting the revolt. He thought that it was the "roving spirit" of the Anglo-Saxon people that impelled them to sweep aside whatever stood in the way of their aggrandizement.[35] Like Gorostiza, Tornel was disturbed by American arrogance in their relations with Mexicans. In their treatment of Gorostiza, their encroachment upon Mexican territory, in statements by American officials and in the American press, there was ample evidence that many in the United States looked upon Mexicans as inferiors, possessing no rights that an American need respect.[36]

The church also seemed threatened. A pamphlet published in Puebla following the Texas revolution warned that when the United States acquired Mexican territory "the Catholic religion will disappear from Mexican soil." Mexicans, like the Indians in the United States, would be deprived of the last traces of their civilization.[37] *El Mosquito Mexicano* declared that the American advance toward Mexico involved more than the mere loss of Mexican territory; it threatened "the safety of the Catholic religion."[38] A newspaper published in northern Mexico stated that it was essential to prevent American encroachments because a new religion would be established upon Mexican soil. Mexican citizens would be "sold as beasts" since "their color was not as white as that of their conquerors."[39] *El Mosquito Mexicano* editors believed that the Catholic Church in Mexico faced the same danger from the United States as that of "the English under Henry VIII, the Irish under William, and Quebec under Wolfe."[40]

Mexican editors often supported their allegations of American condescension with evidence drawn from newspapers published in the United States. The official gazette of the department of Tamaulipas reported in 1836 that a New Orleans newspaper had declared the Texas revolution to be one of the most notable events of modern times. The American paper had gone on to say that greater events would follow because "the superiority of the Anglo-American over the primitive inhabitants" of Mexico was so clearly manifest that it "presaged the conquest of Mexico itself."[41] *El Diario* alleged that certain American newspapers had proclaimed that within ten years an "Anglo-Saxon" would be president of Mexico because Mexicans were incapable of governing themselves.[42] A New York newspaper had said that fighting Mexicans was similar to "coon hunting."[43] *El Siglo Diez y Nueve* expressed shock at the patronizing attitude of American journalists who believed that Mexico deserved to be conquered by those who were more industrious and efficient than her present inhabitants.[44] Both *El Diario* and *El Mosquito Mexicano* reprinted an unidentified Texan's speech that encouraged his fellow Texans to support the conquest of Mexico. He was reported to have said cowardly Mexican troops would abandon the population and "immense wealth" might be seized from Mexican churches and from contributions imposed upon a "vagrant, corrupt, and lascivious clergy"; that such a conquest would undoubtedly expand the limits of slavery was said to be an additional advantage.[45]

If any Mexican newspaper could be termed pro-American during these years, it would be the influential *El Siglo Diez y Nueve*, but in analyzing the differences separating the two countries, *El Siglo* also recognized the element of racism. The new world, it said, was divided between two distinct races, the Spanish and the English. Each had won its independence from colonial powers and had established almost identical institutions, but the two peoples had become strangers, if not enemies. Their laws, ideas, religion and customs were different: one was Catholic, generous, warlike and impetuous; the other Protestant, calculating, businesslike, astute. That the two should struggle when they made contact, as in Texas, was not strange.[46] *El Siglo* found it particularly annoying that Americans should judge Mexico so unsympathetically. Mexico's history made it difficult for her to advance as rapidly as the United States, yet Americans assumed that her slow progress was a mark of inferiority. American newspapers spoke of Mexicans as "savage, barbaric, immoral and corrupt." These words might describe an individual criminal but not an entire community. *El Siglo* hoped that Americans would recognize that the generality of Mexicans was no more lawless than the people of New York, for example, which though highly civilized also harbored immoral and corrupt individuals.[47]

Despite their moderation the editors of *El Siglo* nonetheless felt that Mexico must not surrender its claim to Texas. The fact that Americans in Texas owned slaves and professed opinions about the inferiority of all men "not of their race" made their defeat necessary.[48] And by 1844 *El Siglo* had lent its voice to those who warned that the United States threatened the very existence of Mexico. Lacking respect for other civilizations, the United States, according to *El Siglo*, conquered only to acquire land, giving no thought to improving the condition of the conquered. Some American politicians had declared themselves in favor of exterminating the "odious Spanish race" along with their religion. These Americans shared eccentric beliefs and professed the most contradictory doctrines. They could be terrorized by the predictions of insane religious fanatics, and they proclaimed liberty for all and yet had virtually annihilated the Indian. Given the chance, they would do the same to Mexicans.[49] Americans would not be content with merely acquiring Mexican territory; they would only be satisfied when they had destroyed the "Mexican Race."[50]

Until 1844 Mexicans did not exhibit a significant interest in American elections. The annexation of Texas was, of course, a leading issue in the presidential campaign of that year, and Mexicans, realizing that forces were at work in the United States which affected their vital interests, followed the campaign with much foreboding. To *El Siglo* the threat of Texas annexation was the most serious question to confront Mexico since independence. The loss of Texas would be a "mortal blow," indicating that Mexicans were incapable of preserving the nation bequested to them by an earlier generation. Instead of passing as it should into the hands of those who shared the same "memories and language," Texas would be controlled by a "rival and enemy" race. To lose Texas would mean not only losing the value of the land, it would also mean establishing upon Mexican soil the "superiority of the Anglo-Saxon race."[51] *El Diario* declared that the outcome of the election mattered little because all Americans, regardless of party, viewed Mexicans as vile, inept, degraded creatures. Regardless of who their president might be, Americans were determined to expand their dominion to include Mexico. The question before Mexico was obvious: "To be or not to be?" Americans recognized neither the rights of the Indians they had destroyed, nor of the Negroes, nor of Mexicans, whose territory they clearly intended to seize.[52] Every action taken by the United States in relation to Texas was covered in the Mexican press. Readers were persistently reminded that the loss of Texas would lead to even greater losses in the future. Much of the diplomatic correspondence between the two nations was printed, and in almost every instance the Mexican editors pointed to the apparent relationship between American slavery and expansionism.[53]

A pamphlet of 1845, urging Mexicans to fight for Texas, declared that Americans were energetic and ruthless in pursuing their objectives. They had displayed remarkable efficiency in eradicating their Indians and could be relied upon to treat Mexicans in the same way.[54] *El Estandarte Nacional* perhaps best summarized the Mexican attitude in April of 1845: to make territorial concessions would open the door to the "triumph of the Anglo-Saxon race," the enslavement of the Mexican people, the destruction of their language and customs, to the loss of what was most "dear and precious, their nationality."[55]

The cumulative effect of these and similar observations contributed to the creation of a public opinion that by the spring of 1846 was so rigidly opposed to American expansion that it forced Mexico into a war that she was not likely to win. Many of the pronouncements demanding war in order to "defend the national honor" (pronouncements often quoted by American writers who blame Mexico for the war) may be dismissed as chauvinistic appeals of demagogic politicians, ambitious soldiers, or irresponsible journalists, or as attempts to pursue private ends by exploiting anti-Americanism. But these demands struck a responsive chord among Mexicans who, rightly or wrongly, from their knowledge of the racist nature of American society, had come to fear the extinction of Mexican civilization should the United States acquire dominion in Mexico.

NOTES

1. The body of literature treating the origins of the Mexican War is somewhat sparse, and it tends to concentrate upon the motives and methods of the United States. The once fashionable theory that American policy toward Mexico was motivated by a southern conspiracy designed to expand slavery has been discredited. William Jay, *A Review of the Causes and Consequences of the Mexican War* (Boston 1849), and Hermann von Holst's treatment of the war in volume three of his *Constitutional and Political History of the United States* (Chicago 1881), typified the conspiracy thesis. Chauncey W. Boucher, "In Re That Agressive Slavocracy," *Mississippi Valley Historical Review*, 8 (June 1921), 13–79, effectively challenged its validity. Albert Weinberg, *Manifest Destiny* (Baltimore 1935), suggests that Americans believed themselves divinely willed to achieve continental dominion, a view expanded upon and somewhat modified by Frederick Merk's penetrating *Manifest Destiny and Mission in American History* (New York 1963). Norman Graebner, *Empire on the Pacific* (New York 1955), describes the importance of California's seaports in luring Americans westward. Richard R. Stenberg, "President Polk and the Annexation of Texas," *Southwestern Social Science Quarterly*, 14 (March 1934), 333–356, and Stenberg, "The Failure of Polk's Mexican War Intrigue of 1845," *Pacific Historical Review*, 4 (March 1935), 39–68, portray Polk as the person most directly responsible for the war. Glenn Price, *The Origins of the Mexican War: The Polk–Stockton Intrigue* (Austin 1967), takes a similar view of Polk's behavior. Polk's most recent biographer, Charles G. Sellers, is also critical of the president's actions in his *James K. Polk, Continentalist, 1843–1846* (Princeton 1966). Diplomatic relations between the two countries prior to the war are described in Jesse H. Reeves, *American Diplomacy under Tyler and Polk* (New York 1906), and George Lockhart Rives, *The United States and Mexico, 1821–1848* 2 vols. (New York 1913).

2. Justin H. Smith, *The War with Mexico* 2 vols. (New York 1919), I, 115. Although Smith's work is marred by an overzealous defense of the United States and indictment of Mexico, it remains useful because of the depth of his research. No subsequent treatment of the war has been based so extensively upon research in foreign archives and, possibly for that reason, his interpretation has been unduly influential. Mexican confidence on the eve of the war appears persistently in the pages of general accounts of the conflict. See, for instance, Robert S. Henry, *The Story of the Mexican War* (New York 1950), 36; Otis A. Singletary, *The Mexican War* (Chicago 1960), 20–21; and David Lavender, *Climax at Buena Vista* (New York 1966), 45. Smith's interpretation has reappeared in all its anti-Mexican zeal in a recent work by a Pulitzer Prize–winning historian, William H. Goetzmann's *When the Eagle Screamed* (New York 1966), chapter 4.

3. *Manifesto de Paredes y Arrillaga* (Mexico, November 1844).

4. *La guerra de Tejas sin máscara* (Mexico 1845).

5. *Comunicacion circular que el Exmo. Sr. Don Manuel Peña y Peña, estendió en año de 1845, como ministro de relaciónes, sobre de cuestión de paz o guerra, según el estado que quardaba en aquella época* (Querétaro, November 1845).

6. Thomas E. Cotner, Jr., *The Military and Political Career of José Joaqúin de Herrera, 1792–1854* (Austin 1949), 263–70.

7. Frank D. Robertson, "The Military and Political Career of Mariano Paredes y Arrillaga, 1797–1849" (Ph.D. dissertation, University of Texas 1955), 209–305.

8. Paredes to Mariano Riva Palacio, July 30, 1845, Paredes y Arrillaga Papers, University of Texas Library.

9. Luís Robles to Paredes, August 23, 1845; Miguel Arroyo to Paredes, September 5, 1845, Paredes Papers.

10. Arista to Paredes, July 13, 1845, Paredes Papers.

11. Arista to Paredes, July 16, 1845, Paredes Papers.

12. Arista to Paredes, September 5, 1845, Paredes Papers.

13. Arista to Paredes, October 5, 1845, Paredes Papers.

14. Arista to Paredes, October 24, 1845, Paredes Papers.

15. Wilson Shannon to John C. Calhoun, Secretary of State, October 28, 1844; Shannon to Secretary of State, March 27, 1845, William R. Manning, *Diplomatic Correspondence of the United States, InterAmerican Affairs, 1831–1860* (Washington 1937), 8, 650, 703.

16. Shannon to James Buchanan, Secretary of State, April 6, 1845, Manning, 8, 709.

17. John Black to Buchanan, June 21, 1845, Consular Despatches, Mexico City. Parrott, revealing the contradiction between public pronouncements and the apparently genuine intentions of Mexican officials, reported during the summer of 1845 that a recent editorial in the official newspaper was more "warlike" than usual. But another editorial in the newspaper *El Siglo Diez y Nueve*, which, because the paper was semiofficial and influential throughout the country, could be "taken as the *real* sentiments of the present administration," said that the nation must "rise above popular prejudice and establish peace." Parrott to Buchanan, July 15, 1845, Manning, 8, 738.

18. William Parrott to Buchanan, September 29, 1845, Manning, 8, 754. Earlier, Parrott had written Buchanan that "the cry now is war, war, war, but how they can make it is the question." July 30, 1845, Manning, 8, 744. In early September the Confidential Agent reported that Arista had called for reinforcements, but that he would not receive them because the government had no intention of increasing its forces on the frontier, even if it had the means of doing so, which it did not. Parrott to Buchanan, September 6, 1845, Manning, 8, 751.

19. *Ultimas comunicaciones entre el gobierno Mexicano y el enviado estradordinario y ministro plenipotenciario de los Estados Unidos, sobre la cuestíon de Texas* (Mexico, March 21, 1846).

20. William R. Manning, *Early Diplomatic Relations Between the United States and Mexico* (Baltimore 1916), chapters 7 and 9, provides the most detailed account of Poinsett's negotiations.

21. Hubert Howe Bancroft, *History of Mexico* 6 vols. (San Francisco 1883–1888), V, 35; José María Tornel y Mendivel, *Breve reseña histórica . . . de la nación Mexicana* (Mexico 1852), 80–81; Lorenzo de Zavala, *Ensayo histórico de las revoluciones de Mexico, desde 1808 hasta 1830* 2 vols. (Mexico 1836), I, 265.

22. Zavala, I, 288.

23. *La Aguila Mexicana*, June 6, 1825.

24. *El Sol*, April 9, 1825.

25. *El Sol*, July 12, 1825.

26. *El Mosquito Mexicano*, June 12, 1840.

27. *El Amigo del Pueblo*, February 13, 1828.

28. José de Onís, *The United States as Seen by Spanish American Writers, 1776–1890* (New York 1952), 135.

29. *El Sol*, April 15, 1826.

30. *La Aguila Mexicana*, August 30, 1827.

31. *Correro de la Federación Mexicano*, March 1, 1829.

32. *El Mosquito Mexicano*, January 1, 1836.

how can de Voto not be mentioned? [handwritten annotation]

33. Lota M. Spell, "Gorostiza and Texas," *Hispanic American Historical Review*, 37 (November 1957), 441–54.

34. Manuel Eduardo de Gorostiza, *Dictamen leido el 3 de junio de 1840 en el consejo de gobierno, sobre la cuestión de Tejas* (Mexico 1840).

35. José Maria Tornel y Mendivel, "Relaciones entre Texas, los Etados-Unidos, y Mexico" (Mexico 1837), in Carlos E. Castaneda, ed. and trans., *The Mexican Side of the Texas Revolution* (Dallas 1928), 287.

36. Castaneda, 295, 326.

37. *Ligeres indicaciones sobre la usurpación de Tejas* (Puebla, November 11, 1837).

38. *El Mosquito Mexicano*, July 23, 1839.

39. *La Luna* (Chihuahua), June 29, 1839.

40. *El Mosquito Mexicano*, January 31, 1843.

41. *Atalaya: periódico ofícíal del gobierno* (Victoria), December 17, 1836.

42. *Diario de la República Mexicana*, April 1, 1842.

43. *Diario de la República Mexicana*, February 18, 1843.

44. *El Siglo Diez y Nueve*, January 2, 1843.

45. *Diario de la República Mexicana*, August 13, 1843; *El Mosquito Mexicano*, August 22, 1843.

46. *El Siglo Diez y Nueve*, December 3, 1841.

47. *El Siglo Diez y Nueve*, March 5, 1843.

48. *El Siglo Diez y Nueve*, December 15, 1842.

49. *El Siglo Diez y Nueve*, May 13, 1844.

50. *El Siglo Diez y Nueve*, September 5, 1844.

51. *El Siglo Diez y Nueve*, May 16, 1844.

52. *Diario del Gobierno*, July 1, 1844.

53. *Diario del Gobierno*, May 21, 22, 25, June 17, 1844; *El Látigo de Texas* (Matamoros), May 30, June 17, 1844; *Gaceta de Gobierno de Tamaulipas* (Santa Anna), June 12, 26, 1844.

54. *Federación y Tejas, articulo publicada en la voz del pueblo, numero 29* (Mexico 1845).

55. *El Estandarte Nacionál*, April 5, 1845.

8 MORMON "DELIVERANCE" AND THE CLOSING OF THE FRONTIER

Martin Ridge

Mormonism has been called "a new religious tradition." It originated in the United States, and the Mormons have become a distinct ethnic group. Of the many religious utopias that have been
founded in America since the Puritans, it is the only one that has
lasted over 150 years and that continues to expand rapidly.

From the publication of the Book of Mormon in 1830, through their
arrival in Utah in 1847, until 1890, the Church of Jesus Christ of
Latter-day Saints, or Mormons, developed independently of the rest of
the United States. In many ways, in fact, they developed in opposition
to it. This essay traces that early history. The Mormons established several basic doctrines: "stewardship, polygamy, millennialism, and the
'gathering,'" as well as "a unique political entity—the kingdom of God—
which . . . was empowered to exercise control over the temporal Mormon
world." Together these beliefs contradicted the current American ideals
of separation of church and state, monogamy, manifest destiny, federal
authority, and individualism (because, to survive, the Mormons organized their economic life in cooperatives under church guidance).

In 1847, under Brigham Young's leadership, the Mormons isolated
themselves beyond the Rockies, eight hundred miles from the nearest
white settlements. Converts from within the United States and from
Europe continued to arrive, as part of the "gathering" of Saints. By the
1880s, too many had arrived, and had been born, for Utah to support.
The younger generations left to create new colonies from the Canadian
prairies to the Mexican mountains. Time thus modified the idea of the
"gathering," and it also modified other doctrines. The attack on polygamy, or plural marriage, was especially intense.

Why and in just what ways did the original Latter-day Saints' doctrines change by 1890? And how did those changes, which marked the
end of the first or apostolic phase in Mormon history, connect with the
closing of the American frontier, which according to the Census Bureau also ended in 1890 (although in fact both Mormonism and settlement continued well after that)?—editors

I FEEL HIGHLY honored to be invited to present the Tanner Lecture this
year. When the Tanner Lectureship was established, I was genuinely im-

pressed. The basic idea of this lectureship—to bring annually to the Mormon History Association an outsider—seemed to me both a mark of maturity and sophistication. No other learned society that I know of has the courage to do this. But when I began to think about what I would say today, I must confess that I came to feel this was essentially a shrewd Mormon plot to take a good, self-respecting gentile academic, and make him reread his old notes, look at new sources, and think far more deeply about Mormonism than he had in the past.

I also want to say a few things that do not fit into my formal presentation, although they may be annoying or perhaps even offensive to some of you. First, I remain completely astonished at how few historical landmarks exist in Utah that relate to some of the most significant and intimate aspects of Mormon history. For example, I could not find the site of the prison camp for cohabs in Salt Lake City without the help of a local historian, and he assured me that there were a score of other significant sites that remain equally hidden. What a pity! What a shame! Should not this organization make a case to the city of Salt Lake or to the state of Utah to act in this matter?

Second, in the clash of competing cultures that took place between Mormon and gentile societies, the fact that Mormonism, as it existed prior to 1890, lost out, is no sign of dishonor. That cultural conflict itself is an important part of the history of our evolving plural society. The sites and events of that struggle warrant as much recognition as Southern states give to the Confederate memorials of the Civil War.

Third, the record of what occurred during the first half century of Mormonism is not exclusively an LDS story; it belongs to our national history. In fact, from the point of view of civil liberties, it is one of our nation's darkest hours. If Jews throughout the world can point to the Holocaust and say: "Never again," surely American students of Mormonism should, if history has any meaning, be the strongest advocates of the First and Fifth amendments to the Constitution.

Fourth, half a decade ago, in commenting on recent books dealing with the Mormon experience, I wrote that

> Mormon historiography may not be a 'dark and bloody ground' for most American historians but it is virtually *terra incognita* for many of them. . . . Non-Mormons who have been willing to approach the field objectively have rarely had access to sources. At the same time, a past generation of Mormon historians were either entirely defensive or even more questioning of the Church than some outsiders. Contemporary non-Mormon historians, who have wanted to understand how the Mormons fit into both the American experience and a subset of American historiography, whether it be the American West or the history of religion, have come to rely on the new generation of Mormon scholars who demonstrate unusual sensitivity, tact, and honesty in dealing with their own past.[1]

As a non-Mormon who teaches the history of the Latter-day Saints, I have trusted to the validity of their work, even as they contend with one another about both the facts and the proper interpretations of Mormonism.

I must, however, take exception with Melvin T. Smith's view that non-Mormon scholars "rarely if ever, reveal and explicate those special and immediate qualities that made believing Mormons and Latter-day Saints what they were and what they still are today."[2] To agree with Smith would be to create a privileged history: something that I must emphatically reject. I do not believe that the history of any race, class, gender, or religion is privileged. I must also reject Mario S. De Pillis's assertion that "all non-Mormon historians are anti-Mormon in so far as they reject that truth."[3] There are many historical and anthropological methodologies that can resolve the problem of dealing with acts of faith in religions other than that of the scholar.

Now, let me turn to my paper.

In Hubert Howe Bancroft's *Book of the Fair*, published in 1893 to commemorate the Chicago World's Columbian Exposition, he points out that the Territory of Utah was represented by a fine pavilion with white pillars. It also boasted an Eagle Gate, replica of that in Salt Lake City, and a statue of Brigham Young. Bancroft notes that the funds for the Utah exhibition came from Mormon sources, stating that they did not come from the territorial government.[4] Although he does not mention it, the Mormon Tabernacle Choir also performed splendidly at the fair.

The Chicago Fair was also the site of the World's Congress of Historians and Historical Students, a rather immodest title for a small meeting of professional and amateur historians who presented scholarly papers, most of which are fortunately now forgotten. I do not know if any Saints attended these historical meetings; but if they did, they were probably shocked at a paper given by a young historian from the University of Wisconsin named Frederick Jackson Turner.[5] The primary thrust and theme of his essay—that American democracy was born on the frontier—would have brought a taste of gall and wormwood to the palate of any Mormon during the 1890s.

Moreover, if any older Saints were in the audience that evening, Turner must have caught their attention when he paraded a litany of circumstances and behavioral characteristics of the Americans as a frontier people. On Turner's frontier, men and women were few, and arable land was abundant; pragmatism was the dominant philosophy of life; innovation and experimentation were common practices; attachment to place was unimportant if not insignificant; wasting natural resources was an acceptable credo; culture and tradition were abandoned in the process of making a living; materialism was the prevailing creed; hard work was a persistent habit; and skill rather than anything else was the critical factor in defining an individual's status. The frontier, too, was a powerful force for assimilation. Turner's Mormon audience would surely have seen how thoroughly the Saints were Turner's true American frontier people and yet how different was their overall experience.

Turner's paper, "The Significance of the Frontier in American History," is a landmark in American scholarship,[6] but it should have a special relationship to Mormon history, because Turner predicated his essay on what he saw as a major disjunction in the history of the United States. He quoted from the Superintendent of the Census for 1890, who observed in a bulletin "that there can hardly be said to be a frontier line." "This brief official statement," Turner added, "marks the closing of a great historic movement."[7]

The closing date of the frontier has a unique meaning to Latter-day Saints because by 1890 eastern America had steadily closed in around them and compelled such drastic changes in Mormon thought and action that the Church would never be the same again. Without a new frontier to which to retreat, Mormons had no place to move. They found themselves defenseless. The only deliverance seemed to be statehood, in the hope that it would give them enough self-government to protect their institutions.

There is a strange irony in this because the Saints, who lived an indigenous American religion, had previously escaped persecution by living outside the mainstream of American life. Protestant America had dictated that they do this; but by 1890, isolation was neither possible nor acceptable; the government now demanded a virtual revolution in Mormonism before it could be incorporated within the nation state. How did this come to pass?

As a Mormon missionary would say: "It all began in the year 1820 when a young man named Joseph Smith, Jr., went into a wooded grove to pray."[8] What followed during the next quarter century is a story of the founding, growth, and persecution of the Church and its members. The Saints found little support in New York, where the Smith family lived; but after they started their celebrated move westward into Ohio, the Church grew rapidly. Neither upstate New York nor Ohio may have been frontier regions, depending on your definition of a frontier, but they were certainly primitive, underdeveloped rural areas marked by social disorientation, where the rapidly changing social status of many fortunate individuals created a fluid society.[9]

Traditional religious and social organizations suffered in this environment, as they did everywhere on the frontier. This was a fertile field for seers, evangelical revivalists, mystical gold hunters, visionary seekers, and founders of religions, new sects, and new communities. As Gordon Wood has observed, "The remains of eighteenth-century hierarchies fell away, and hundreds of thousands of common people were cut loose from all sorts of traditional bonds."[10] Many people sought something that would bring meaning and order to their lives. This was a setting well suited to the Mormon style as well as the Mormon message. Discipline, emotion, reason, self-interest, and a unique egalitarianism were some of the weapons in the arsenal of conversion.[11] Mormonism successfully gathered followers not only in the agrarian West and South but also among the disenchanted of the urban East.

From the inception of Mormonism, Joseph Smith propounded the idea of "continuous revelation," an element that proved essential to the Church's vitality and success because its doctrines could be dynamic.[12] Therefore, during the years of migration from upstate New York to Kirtland, Ohio, to Far West, Missouri, and back to Nauvoo, Illinois, the Church gradually came to embrace a body of essential doctrines that ultimately defined its identity: stewardship, polygamy, millennialism, and the "gathering." It also accepted the idea of a unique political entity—the kingdom of God—which, although quasi-independent, was empowered to exercise control over the temporal Mormon world.

Whether the concept of plural marriage had its origin in Ohio is not so important as what it meant to the Church. No doctrine was more controversial, even to our day, unless it is the Book of Mormon itself.[13] The fact that plural marriage was only one aspect of Joseph Smith's concern for the family, for extended kinship ties, and for social solidarity—after all, he wanted to establish a tribe in the Old Testament sense—was not lost on both his contemporaries and later generations.[14] Plural marriage created a deep moral chasm between Mormons and non-Mormons that could not be bridged and that led to repeated episodes of persecution.

The idea of the kingdom of God, a theocratic structure intimately tied to millennialism, was not a heavy hand within the Mormon community, but it was significant to Mormon thought and subject to easy misunderstanding in the gentile world.[15] Joseph Smith sought to establish a cohesive new order in which the Mormon spiritual and temporal worlds were united. If it had a democratic dimension, it could only be described as a "guided democracy." Thus, although Mormonism seemed in many ways quintessentially American, it stood "in radical opposition to the prevailing American religious and social pluralism."[16] It rejected the American ideal of the separation of church and state.

Moreover, it stood in opposition to the emerging spirit of manifest destiny that dominated mid-nineteenth-century America. Mormons never recognized the gentile concept of a great political democracy extending from pole to pole in the western hemisphere. Theirs was a different Zion. The Saints never expected more than a small fraction of gentiles to heed their millennial call. "The gathering" would be for those who could accept and live in the truth. Almost by definition, then, Mormons perceived all non-Mormons as anti-Mormon. As the United States struggled toward a variety of pluralism, the Mormon community increasingly moved in the opposite direction toward homogeneity. It was a counter-cultural force.[17] Those who were not with them were against them; and those who were against them constituted Babylon, even if they spoke for an enlarged and tolerant American republic.

In Mormonism the ordinary American saw custom, kinship, and law replaced in their entirety. Americans not only saw the Saints as cult followers with a different view of the future; they also recognized the Saints as a people with a new revelation, scripture, and priesthood, who rejected orthodox capitalism and federal authority. Little wonder then that even

9. Brigham Young (1801–
1877), Mormon leader.
*Courtesy of the Hunting-
ton Library, San Marino,
California.*

without Mormon economic success or increased political influence, the
Church drew the wrath of the Protestant evangelical community, which
viewed the Church as a serious threat.[18] Unable at the outset to manipu-
late effectively the tools of government to attack Mormonism, this community resorted to mob violence. This came as no surprise to the Saints,
who believed that the greater their effectiveness, the harder Satan would
fight against them. In this context, the martyrdom of the Prophet and
other leaders seems to have been inevitable.

The Mormon trek from Nauvoo to the Salt Lake Valley came to sym-
bolize both a religious and a temporal triumph in Mormon history and
mythology. This flight to the Great Basin frontier proved a trial of faith.
It may not have proven so arduous as has been sometimes stated; but for
the participants, it was as much deliverance under God's hand as was depicted in the book of Exodus. It also led to the development of a spirit of
identity and territoriality that differentiates Mormons from other religious
groups.[19] It reinforced the significance of the West as the place of "the gathering." Moreover, it was a continuing and revitalizing process, as each year
another group of Saints entered Zion, having shared with their brethren
and sisters the cross-plains journey. Richard Jensen captured the spirit of
joy associated with the overland trail's end and the integrating of the old
and the new settlers when he wrote, "The wagons coming out to meet the
immigrants with fruit and baked goods, and the throngs that met them as
they arrived in Salt Lake City . . . [were] a welcome part of the process of
assimilation."[20] They had arrived at the "place prepared."[21]

There is little reason to doubt Mormon assertions that for more than a decade prior to their departure from Nauvoo the LDS leadership already held a deep religious conviction that the Saints were destined to find a refuge and sanctuary outside of the United States in the Rocky Mountains.[22] Since Brigham Young, like Moses, believed that God would guide him in his quest for the prepared place, his decisions were based as much on spiritual as practical detailed information. Even after reaching the Salt Lake Valley, despite what cynics might argue, Young waited for a divine confirmation that this was indeed the place.

The Mormons had leap-frogged the frontier line in 1847, and they were for the first time free from the restraints of gentile society. They had entered Zion and were now virtually responsible for their own actions. Therefore, Brigham Young and the Mormon host had no pangs of conscience in taking Indian land because the Church believed that it was "both God's will and a positive virtue" to do so.[23] The leadership, under Brigham Young, instituted a theo-democratic legal system of ecclesiastical courts and a scheme of government that combined the temporal and the spiritual to create an orderly community where polygamy, the kingdom of God, the communal goal, and "the gathering" could be emphasized.

The Mormons struggled to implement communal goals that had been established in Nauvoo. For example, they based their use of the region's natural resources on stewardship and mutual benefit instead of on individual gain; they planned their economy around cooperation and sought to achieve self-sufficiency.[24] They confronted an entirely new physical environment, however, in which Mormonism could not survive without adaptation and innovation. Indicative of innovation and the commingling of spiritual and temporal power, the Mormons laid out their irrigation system by linking it to religious directives. In any less cohesive community, this would have diluted the sacred; but in early impoverished Utah, where no one knew how to farm successfully in the desert, spiritual control of temporal power made sound economic sense.[25]

There were other changes. The Latter-day Saints' strongly patriarchal system was restructured under frontier conditions. The pressing need for labor in an underdeveloped economy overcame quickly Mormonism's fundamental belief that women were primarily the guardians of the home and the family. This meant more than merely sharing the family farm workload. Despite the fact that the priesthood remained entirely in male hands, women were ultimately encouraged to enter professions and even assume large responsibilities of leadership within the female sphere. They were also among the first women to be enfranchised in the United States.

Even LDS doctrine regarding redeeming the Indians had to yield in the face of frontier reality. The Indians refused to be what Mormon theology said they were. Despite their brightest hopes, Mormon missionaries found Indians living in conditions loathsome yet difficult to change. When efforts to convert them resulted in open and protracted resistance, Brigham Young conceded that it was almost pointless to send missionaries among them because that generation of Indians would never be converted. He remained optimistic, but he found his policy of food not fight taxing.[26]

Jan Shipps, drawing an analogy between the Israelites and the Mormons on the Utah frontier, has posited that, for a brief period in their history, Mormons had escaped secular time.[27] This may be correct in a spiritual sense; but in a physical sense, the gentile world intruded early and harshly into Zion. Gold-seeking adventurers on their way to California were soon followed by pioneers from the very Mississippi Valley states from which the Mormons had been driven. The United States Army was not far behind, nor were a string of journalists, curious about Mormonism's "peculiar institution."

There is no need to catalogue all the hostility and recrimination that the encounters between Saints and gentiles produced during this time. One incident is so graphic and so problematic as to suffice. Even stripped of questionable evidence and disputed interpretations, the Mountain Meadows massacre is a monstrous example of frontier violence and retribution. Levi Peterson, who feels it represents a Mormon loss of innocence, and Maureen Beecher, who disagrees with him, may debate over this dark and bloody ground on how the Saints want to explain themselves to themselves and perhaps to others; but in terms of the frontier experience, no one has ever believed that the frontier was a peaceable kingdom.[28] The English, the French, and the Spanish all used Indians as allies when they waged war against each other. White men killed each other throughout the history of the frontier when cultures clashed. Only a naive romantic can deny that brutality was commonplace on the frontier.

The Utah War of 1857–58 should have served as a timely warning to the Mormons that the United States government had the power to reach deep into the frontier, especially after the Mexican War and the annexation of the Oregon country. It demonstrated that Utah's isolation was more a matter of convenience than reality. The United States could at any time exercise full authority and impose its national institutions and customs. But as long as transportation and communication remained difficult and as long as other parts of the frontier offered greater opportunity, expediency prevailed and the Mormon kingdom was left basically to its own devices.

The Utah War demonstrated the internal cohesion and discipline of the Saints, but it also disclosed critical economic weaknesses. Although official Church policy called for almost total economic self-sufficiency, Brigham Young and other Church leaders realized that it was impossible. Thus, they sought, as far as possible, to limit Mormon commercial ties to the outside world to prevent endangering the essentially communal character of their economy and to prevent making it dependent on the outside world by tying it marginally to the emerging capitalist society of the East. They remained, however, under steadily increasing pressures during the decade of the 1860s. The United States Army post at Camp Floyd provided a market for Mormon products, and the opening of the mining frontier in

Colorado, Nevada, and Idaho gradually turned Salt Lake City into a frontier commercial and business entrepot. Furthermore, individual enterprise, even if Mormon-controlled, was on the rise.

The arrival of the railroad at Ogden in 1869 was the final blow to Mormon frontier isolation. The railroad's operations meant the introduction of a society of non-Mormon working-class males; and it also resulted in the arrival of business leaders who advocated competitive capitalism, sought to gain access to the territory's economy, and intended to develop the region's resources. The railroad encouraged Methodists and Episcopalians to settle in Ogden and opened its depots for denominational services.[29] When gentiles opened schools to attract Mormon children, they set the stage for a controversy over control of the public schools.[30] For those Saints who still hoped to preserve Utah, or at least Ogden and Salt Lake City, as Mormon bastions or parts of the kingdom of God, the railroad locomotive engine's bell sounded a warning—perhaps even a death knell—to Mormon culture as it had existed. For along with the railroad came a slow but steady end to the self-sufficient, homogeneous, and relatively egalitarian Mormon economy. Shrewdly aware of the implications of the coming of the railroad, Church leaders sought to profit as much as possible from it, and they did their best to stave off its direst portents through collective action.

The completion of the railroad also revolutionized the emigration patterns of Mormon converts. As Mormons spread over the valleys of Utah in search of more arable land, Saints proselytized vigorously abroad. An all-steam company was organized in 1869 that brought converts from Liverpool to Ogden in twenty-four days, a far cry from the era of the three- to five-month trip. The story of the Mormon immigrant changed from that of the overland covered wagon to that of the modern voyager.[31]

Mormon converts differed from other immigrants in that, during the process of conversion, they had turned their backs not only on their former churches but also on their past cultures. In Utah the Church's process of integration meant the creation of a whole new English-speaking American way of life. A new Saint's mother tongue was rejected along with other vestiges of Babylon.[32] It was the avowed aim of the LDS Church to assimilate immigrants and resettle them as rapidly as possible.[33]

Persistently high migration rates to Utah led to the progressive undermining of the Mormon social structure. By the 1880s the Church had virtually given up trying to establish cooperative communities. Utah was filling up. Young Mormon men were being forced to move elsewhere if they wanted to farm for a living. There was an increase in individual or sibling-based migrations, and after 1875 the emphasis in migration was on economic advantages rather than building the Mormon kingdom. Although the Church still attempted to supervise and assist new communities, its aid came after rather than prior to the establishment of a town.[34] By 1890 the growth of the Church came primarily from within existing areas of settlement as colonization, both domestic and foreign, slowed.[35]

Equally indicative of the change in the Mormon community was a shift in attitude when John Taylor succeeded Brigham Young to the presidency of the LDS Church in 1877. Young was a firm adherent of self-sufficient communitarianism as the best form of human association. Taylor favored individualism and looked to legal incorporation and personal liberty. Under Taylor the Church did not turn to unrestrained laissez-faire, but it did encourage greater individual enterprise among the faithful.[36] The ease of this transition from staunch communitarianism to modified individualism suggests that the frontier had begun to break down romanticized communalism, at least in Mormon cities.

As gentiles joined Mormons in Salt Lake City, as the shift from cooperation to individualism persisted, and as attacks on polygamy increased in the 1880s, two types of Mormon community emerged. Charles Peterson put it aptly: "As Salt Lake City Mormons resisted the federal government they entered into a variety of interactions with their 'foes,' adopting many of the enemies' ways as they, in effect fought fire with fire. . . . Like it or not, the City of the Saints had become a 'city of two peoples,' its history more the story of an American conflict than an escape from society."[37] Traditional LDS ideals were preserved in the outlying Mormon villages, where the ward and the village were one unit and where temporal and ecclesiastical affairs were intermingled.[38]

Leonard Arrington is doubtless in some measure correct in asserting that by 1884 the Church's well-directed program of protecting the Mormon way against the changes wrought by the railroad achieved a good deal of success. A great deal of economic autonomy and spiritual integrity was preserved. The boycotting of gentiles, severe financial retrenchment, social investment in domestic capital programs like railroads, and Church cooperative efforts did, after all, produce results. "The joining of efforts through the United Orders, temple construction, and Zion's Central Board of Trade," Arrington wisely observes, "left the Mormons . . . nearer the realization of their ancient goal than when the ox-cart was outmoded in 1869."[39] Even more important, the Mormons had managed to retain the quasi-religious nature of large-scale private enterprise by keeping decision-making power in the hands of the Church's official family. Eighteen eighty-four, however, may have been some kind of watershed, as Arrington notes.[40] By 1890 there had been significant change. Private enterprise was profit seeking and not necessarily concerned with the religious community's goals.

Modern Mormons like to think that where they live is not so important as how they live, but this was scarcely true in the earliest days and is strictly the result of the closing of the frontier. Zion was a specific place more than a style of life.[41] Then the cry was, "Let all who can procure a loaf of bread, and one garment on their back, be assured there is water and pure by the way, doubt no longer, but come next year to the place of the gathering, even in flock, as doves fly to their windows before a storm."[42] Mass immigration, however, had made that impossible. In 1887 the Perpetual Emigrating Company was disincorporated. The elders were now told to explain that migration was an individual calling. Zion now meant the pure in heart and where the people and condition of the pure in heart live—a far cry from "redeem the faithful and bring them singing into Zion."[43] By the 1890s the original Mormon meaning of "the gathering" was no longer being preached.

By 1890, also, the failure of the Council of Fifty—the temporal-religious arm of the community—to restrain the federal government's attack on the LDS Church and its members because of plural marriage led to the ultimate weakening of the idea of the kingdom of God.[44] In 1890 the First Presidency of the Church could truthfully state that it did not claim that it controlled a temporal kingdom of God, and it reaffirmed that the Church and civil governments were distinct and separate bodies. An inevitable corollary of the decline of the idea of the temporal kingdom of God was a decline in millennial enthusiasm. It meant that the Saints were in transition from believers in the immediacy of divine deliverance to adherents of a creed not unlike those of other American religious groups.

The great struggle in the 1880s to defend polygamy was in a sense the armageddon of frontier Mormonism. Only the salvation of the ideal of plural marriage offered hope for retaining the Mormons' special view of a temporal and spiritual kingdom of God on earth. In the balance, too, probably hung that powerful millennial drive that had nurtured the Church from its inception. Hope of "the gathering" at a "place prepared" had already been virtually abandoned. The communal order was in increasing measure giving way to a more individualistic society, except perhaps in the Mormon villages where near-frontier conditions still prevailed. But even in villages, in many instances tithes were being paid in cash.

Plural marriage was the linchpin of what remained of the old order, except for the vestiges of the cooperative spirit and civic virtue. It was the most controversial aspect of the Church, as well as the source of continuing persecution of all the Saints, even those who were monogamous. For both Mormons and non-Mormons, it came to identify what the Church was. The defense of plural marriage, therefore, was critical. The desperate hope that Saints could escape the power of the federal government, if the Utah Territory could become a state and retain polygamy, prompted the Church leadership to engage in political lobbying activities on an unprecedented scale. Although many Eastern politicians seemed receptive to the idea, neither the Republican nor Democratic party when in power was willing to award the Saints statehood despite the Church's promises of future support.[45]

Instead, beginning in the early 1880s, the full might of the federal government was gradually unleashed against both the LDS Church and its members. The Edmunds Act and the Edmunds–Tucker Act plus the Supreme Court's decision in *Davis v. Beason* (which, appropriately enough, was decided in 1890) were disastrous assaults on the First Amendment as well as the Fifth. The results were catastrophic. The federal government was empowered to seize the assets and property of the Church. The Morrill Act of 1862 had already made polygamy illegal in the territories. Now, the Saints were disfranchised and forbidden to hold office or serve on juries, unless they took an oath to repudiate polygamy. Polygamous Saints fled into exile, suffered imprisonment, and accepted fugitive status rather than give up a sacred principle.

Never was the leadership more troubled or divided or in need of guidance. On 25 September 1890, President Wilford Woodruff issued a Manifesto that advised Latter-day Saints to refrain from contracting any marriage forbidden by the laws of the land. On 6 October 1890, the Manifesto was sustained by the Church's general conference. For the many Saints who refused to yield on the question of polygamy, the Manifesto of 1890 was and is "deliverance unto Babylon."

The Manifesto no more marked the end of polygamy than did the Superintendent of the Census's statement mark an end to available free land, to economic opportunity, and to the growth of the democratic spirit in America. The Manifesto served its purpose in paving the way for statehood and political deliverance. This was yet another yielding to governmental power, since the Church leadership had earlier expressly stated that Saints were free to join the political party of their choice. It also called for the disbanding of the old People's party, which had been the Mormon party in the territory.

These actions were to have serious broader and perhaps unanticipated consequences for the Church. Without "the gathering," without a compelling millennialism, without an overly intrusive temporal kingdom, and especially without polygamy, the Church stood at a threshold of a new century without much that it had developed during its frontier era. Of course, much remained—the tradition of the exodus of the overland trek, the repudiation of Babylon in individual conversion, the martyrdom of Joseph and Hyrum Smith, the Book of Mormon, the village—but it was not the Mormonism of the people of the "peculiar institution" who had arrived in the Salt Lake Valley under the guidance of Brigham Young and who had felt that they were carrying out the divine mandate of their prophet Joseph Smith. The Church, like the nation itself, would confront an urban plural society on a new footing after 1890. But that is another story.

If there were Mormons sitting in the audience when Frederick Jackson Turner remarked that 1890 witnessed the "closing of great historic movement," they could certainly appreciate his words in more ways than one. They could wonder how their church would now endure. It had, after the immediate migration to the Salt Lake Valley, enjoyed the benefits of frontier isolation. The time had been used well and the kingdom well established. But by 1890, that was over; the members of the Church were now not only in the world but also of the world. Mormons—who had found in the frontier a means to escape secular time and the secular world—had been recaptured by both.

In the frontier context, the secular historian must ask what Mormon "deliverance" actually meant after the closing of the frontier in 1890. The answer must first and in some way come from Mormons themselves before an historical assessment can be made. Perhaps, for the time being, it would be enough if Mormon historians were to recognize the inextricability of the Mormon "deliverance" and the closing of the American frontier.

NOTES

1. Ridge, "Joseph Smith, Brigham Young, and a Religious Tradition," *Reviews in American History* 14 (March 1986): 25.

2. Smith, "Faithful History: Hazards and Limitations," *Journal of Mormon History* 9 (1982): 61.

3. De Pillis, "Bearding Leone and Others in the Heartland of Mormon Historiography," *Journal of Mormon History* 8 (1981): 93.

4. Bancroft, *Book of the Fair* (Chicago: Bancroft Publishing, 1893), 2:831–32.

5. For a biography of Frederick Jackson Turner, see Ray Allen Billington, *Frederick Jackson Turner: Historian, Scholar, Teacher* (New York: Oxford University Press, 1973).

6. Martin Ridge, "The Life of an Idea: The Significance of Frederick Jackson Turner's Frontier Thesis," *Montana: The Magazine of Western History* 41 (Winter 1991): 2–13.

7. "The Significance of the Frontier in American History," *The Frontier in American History* (New York: Henry Holt and Company, 1920), 1.

8. Neal E. Lambert and Richard H. Cracroft, "Literary Form and Historical Understanding: Joseph Smith's First Vision," *Journal of Mormon History* 7 (1980): 31.

9. Marvin S. Hill, "The Rise of Mormonism in the Burned-over District: Another View," *New York History* 61 (October 1980): 417.

10. Gordon S. Wood, "Evangelical America and Early Mormonism," *New York History* 61 (October 1980): 361.

11. Thomas G. Alexander, "The Place of Joseph Smith in the Development of American Religion: A Historiographical Inquiry," *Journal of Mormon History* 5 (1978): 11.

12. Thomas F. O'Dea, *The Mormons* (Chicago: University of Chicago Press, 1957), 19–20; and Jan Shipps, "The Prophet Puzzle: Suggestions Leading toward a More Comprehensive Interpretation of Joseph Smith," *Journal of Mormon History* 1 (1974): 17.

13. Daniel W. Bachman, "New Light on an Old Hypothesis: The Ohio Origins of the Revelation on Eternal Marriage," *Journal of Mormon History* 5 (1978): 19.

14. Lawrence Foster, "From Frontier Activism to Neo-Victorian Domesticity: Mormon Women in the Nineteenth and Twentieth Centuries," *Journal of Mormon History* 6 (1979): 7.

15. Gustave O. Larson, *The Americanization of Utah for Statehood* (San Marino: The Huntington Library, 1971), 1.

16. Foster, "From Frontier Activism to Neo-Victorian Domesticity," 6; and Hill, "Quest for Refuge: An Hypothesis as to the Social Origins and Nature of the Mormon Political Kingdom," *Journal of Mormon History* 2 (1975): 14.

17. Timothy L. Smith, "The Book of Mormon in a Biblical Culture," *Journal of Mormon History* 7 (1980): 12.

18. Marvin S. Hill, "Comments," *Journal of Mormon History* 3 (1976): 103–4.

19. Dean May, "The Mormons," *Harvard Encyclopedia of American Ethnic Groups*, edited by Stephan Thernstrom (Cambridge: Harvard University Press, 1980), 720.

20. "Steaming Through: Arrangements for Mormon Emigration from Europe, 1869–1887," *Journal of Mormon History* 9 (1982): 22.

21. Ronald K. Esplin, "'A Place Prepared': Joseph, Brigham and the Quest for Promised Refuge in the West," *Journal of Mormon History* 9 (1983): 85–111.

22. Ibid., 88–92.

23. Charles S. Peterson, "Jacob Hamblin, Apostle to the Lamanites, and the Indian Mission," *Journal of Mormon History* 2 (1975): 29.

24. Charles S. Peterson, "The Mormon Village: One Man's West," *Journal of Mormon History* 3 (1976): 9.

25. De Pillis, "Bearding Leone and Others," 82.

26. Peterson, "Jacob Hamblin," 24–25.

27. Shipps, *Mormonism: The Story of a New Religious Tradition* (Urbana and Chicago: University of Illinois Press, 1985), 109–29.

28. Levi S. Peterson, "Juanita Brooks: Historian and Tragedian," *Journal of Mormon History* 3 (1976): 51–52; and Maureen Ursenbach Beecher, "Comment," ibid., 105–6.

29. Brian Q. Cannon, "Change Engulfs a Frontier Settlement: Ogden and Its Residents Respond to the Railroad," *Journal of Mormon History* 12 (1985): 23.

30. Charles S. Peterson, "The Limits of Learning in Pioneer Utah," *Journal of Mormon History* 10 (1983): 66.

31. Jensen, "Steaming Through," 21.

32. William Mulder, "Mormon Angles of Historical Vision: Some Maverick Reflections," *Journal of Mormon History* 3 (1976): 19–20.

33. May, "The Mormons," 723.

34. Richard Sherlock, "Mormon Migration and Settlement after 1875," *Journal of Mormon History* 2 (1975): 65–66; Jensen, "Steaming Through," 23.

35. Richard H. Jackson, "The Overland Journey to Zion," in *The Mormon Role in the Settlement of the West*, edited by Richard H. Jackson (Provo: Brigham Young University Press, 1978), xii.

36. Grant Underwood, "The New England Origins of Mormonism Revisited," *Journal of Mormon History* 15 (1989): 20.

37. Charles S. Peterson, "The Mormon Village," 10.

38. Douglas D. Alder, "The Mormon Ward: Congregation or Community," *Journal of Mormon History* 5 (1978): 67.

39. Arrington, *Great Basin Kingdom: An Economic History of Latter-day Saints, 1830–1900* (Lincoln: University of Nebraska Press, 1966), 234.

40. Ibid., 234.

41. Mulder, "The Mormon Gathering," in *Mormonism in American Culture*, edited by Marvin S. Hill and James B. Allen (New York: Harper & Row, 1972), 99; Underwood, "New England Origins," 50.

42. Mulder, "The Mormon Gathering," 100.

43. Ibid.

44. Klaus Hansen, "The Political Kingdom as a Source of Conflict," in Hill and Allen, *Mormonism in American Culture*, 126.

45. Leo Lyman, *Political Deliverance: The Mormon Quest for Statehood* (Urbana: University of Illinois Press, 1986).

9   SAND CREEK

Janet LeCompte

In the long and tawdry history of Indian–white relations in the United States, the Indian population declined sharply from the first contacts in the sixteenth century until about 1900, and has recovered in the twentieth century, very rapidly after 1960. Indian and white historians now agree that the most potent weapon the Europeans had was inadvertent: the diseases that they and their animals carried, against which the previously isolated native Americans had no immunities. Warfare caused much less population loss, and genocide—the purposeful extermination of Indians simply because they were of a different race—was rather rare.

Cases do exist, however, of exterminations that can only be called genocidal. One of these is the massacre of a village of Cheyennes and Arapahoes on the plains of eastern Colorado in 1864 by a United States Army detachment commanded by Col. John M. Chivington. In this essay, Janet LeCompte narrates this tragic episode. How can we explain Chivington's actions, so evil on their face? How can we explain the support he received for his action from the governor, the editor of the principal Denver newspaper, and much of the public—support which even in 1964, when LeCompte published her essay, was still widespread?

To their credit, other army officers on the scene attempted to carry out a policy of peace with these Indians, and some testified against Chivington in the subsequent investigations (one officer was murdered for doing so). The investigations squarely blamed Chivington, but he continued to be regarded as a defender of white settlers; a small town near the massacre site is named after him.

Have similar incidents taken place in American history? What about the killing of some five hundred civilians at My Lai, in Viet Nam, in March 1968?—editors

AT DAWN ON November 29, 1864, a regiment of cavalry under Colonel John M. Chivington charged a village of Cheyenne and Arapaho Indians on Sand Creek in eastern Colorado Territory, killing about a hundred and forty Indians.[1] Colonel Chivington claimed a great victory and expected to be rewarded with a brigadier-general's commission.[2] A month later, however, it was reported that the Sand Creek village had been a small and peaceful one under protection of Fort Lyon on the Arkansas. Furthermore, it was reported that Chivington's troops had misbehaved. They had not only killed but scalped and mutilated, and two-thirds of those slaughtered had been women and children. Eastern newspapers screamed "Massacre!" The War Department ordered a court-martial of Colonel Chivington. Both houses of Congress ordered investigations.

Testimony taken at the investigations showed that the troops were not altogether to blame. For one thing, they were not disciplined soldiers but citizens enlisted for a hundred days' service against Indians. As citizens, they had been assured by William Byers, editor of the *Rocky Mountain News*, that they were engaged in a desperate war with merciless savages. As citizens, they had been urged by Governor John Evans to "kill and destroy" hostile Indians and keep the booty. As citizens in uniform, they had been led by Colonel Chivington to the Indian village, reminded of Indian atrocities of the past summer, and sent whooping into the fray.

All this and more the investigations showed, but violent measures were taken to keep the testimony secret and the responsibility unassigned. On the whole these measures succeeded, and as a result the accounts of Sand Creek have suffered from lack of contemporary evidence. They have also suffered from the anger of the writers—understandably so, for Sand Creek's evil remains unpurged (the innocent have not yet received history's acquittal nor the guilty her full condemnation). The following account cannot claim to be free either of ignorance or of anger. It promises only an economical selection of facts, which in the opinion of the author indicate most directly the nature of the Sand Creek massacre.

When he ordered his last cavalry charge, John Milton Chivington was a huge man of forty-three with a rough, hearty manner and a thirst for glory. He had come to Denver in 1860 as a Methodist elder. When the war broke out, he put twenty years in the pulpit behind him and, declining the post of chaplain, signed up as major in the First Colorado Regiment.[3] In the spring of 1862, Chivington led two magnificently successful cavalry charges against Confederate invaders in New Mexico, and was rewarded with a colonelcy and the wild acclaim of the people of Colorado.[4] The triumph of his first battles sent the new colonel to Washington demanding that the Secretary of War make him a brigadier-general and attach his regiment to Pope's army. To his surprise, his demand was rebuffed, and he returned to Colorado humiliated but not humbled.[5]

For nearly two years afterwards, Colonel Chivington and his First Regiment sat out the war at Camp Weld near Denver, suffering from boredom, scurvy, damp barracks, and delayed mails. Denied a place in the great armies, the soldiers fretted and fumed, and in the spring of 1864 some of them hung their officers in effigy. The citizens of Colorado were equally discouraged. Business was dull, emigration slow. In the East the war was about to end (or so everyone thought), and still Colorado's people were not a part of the war's excitement and sacrifices. By April of 1864 soldiers and citizens alike were itching for a fight.[6]

Early in April, Colonel Chivington received a report that a band of Cheyennes had stolen one hundred seventy-five horses from a contractor's herd in eastern Colorado.[7] The report was never confirmed, never investigated; the theft was never acknowledged by the Indians nor the loss filed as an Indian depredation claim by the contractor.[8] Nevertheless the news was greeted with relief by nearly everybody. "It would be well to have the boys stirred up some," said a moderate newspaper carefully, as First Regiment soldiers galloped down the Platte to find the thieves.[9] When soldiers caught up with a party of Cheyennes, they attempted to disarm them and were fired upon—which was all that was needed to send more troops after more Indians.[10] "The Indian troubles have reached a climax," wrote Colonel Chivington's adjutant on April 16.[11] "The war is commenced in earnest," reported another officer in May, after he had surprised an Indian village, killing twenty-five men, women and children, "and must result in exterminating them," he added.[12]

So far it was a one-sided war. When troops approached, the Indians ran for their lives, leaving behind their ponies, buffalo robes, lodges, dried meat, buckskins, and cooking pots.[13] Afterwards the soldiers returned with their booty to camp and wrote up vainglorious reports that failed to fool even their most ardent supporter, the *Rocky Mountain News*. Declared the *News*: "We have always been of the opinion that this Indian war was 'a heap of talk for a little cider.' White men have undoubtedly been the aggressors."[14] By the end of May, the Indians had moved their villages out of the soldiers' way, and Colonel Chivington was obliged to report that the Indian war had "blown over for the present."[15]

Colorado's governor could not allow the Indian war to blow over so easily. John Evans was a kindly, dignified gentleman from the Midwest who had amassed a fortune in real estate and had achieved success in many other fields. Now, at the age of fifty, he had his heart set upon making Colorado a state and himself senator of that state.[16] Whether to further his political ambitions (as his enemies charged), or because of a terror of Indians, John Evans exaggerated the danger of an Indian war.[17] By the fall of 1863 he was convinced that the Indian war would begin in the spring of 1864.[18] After the reported theft of the contractor's horses, Evans wired Washington that his predictions about "an alliance among the various tribes of Indians on the plains for purposes of war on the settlements" had come true.[19] The day after Colonel Chivington declared that the Indian war had blown over, Governor Evans wrote General Curtis, department commander at St. Louis, that Colorado was "at war with a powerful combination of Indian tribes" which would "wipe out our sparse settlements."[20] Whatever his motives, Governor Evans' statements were not calculated to calm the populace, or to stay the trigger fingers of Colorado soldiers, who had no intention of returning to their muddy barracks without a fight.

For instance, on May 16 a young lieutenant and a hundred First Colorado men marched towards a Cheyenne village on the Smoky Hill River. As they approached, a head chief named Lean Bear rode out to greet them and was shot dead by the troops. Four soldiers and twenty-eight Indians died in the ensuing scrap.[21] If the Indian war were a contest to see how many of the enemy could be killed, the white soldiers were now ahead sixty-one to nine, by estimates in their own reports.[22]

In gaining publicity for their murders, however, the Indians soon took the lead. On June 11, a party of Roman Nose's Arapahoes on their way to their village on the North Platte, butchered four members of the Hungate family on a ranch thirty miles north of Denver.[23] "Extensive Indian murders," John Evans wired immediately, "the Indian war begun in earnest."[24] The mutilated bodies of the Hungates were displayed in Denver and the citizens went wild. Breaking into military warehouses, they stole arms and ammunition to fight off an approaching army of Indians.[25]

There was no army of Indians. In fact, for a month after the Hungate murders no Indian depredation was reported in Colorado. During this quiet time some Cheyennes managed to reach Governor Evans to tell him their side of the Indian war and convince him of their desire for peace.[26] On June 27, the Governor issued a proclamation "To The Friendly Indians of the Plains" telling them to bring their people into military posts where they could be fed and protected by the soldiers.[27] The Governor's gesture was humane but much worse than futile, for guards at the posts continued to shoot Indians on sight.[28]

After some "friendlies" had been fired on as they approached the posts, they ceased to be friendly. Between July 17 and July 20, a war party of Cheyennes galloped along the Platte a hundred miles below Denver, stealing stock and killing at least five and possibly eight herders and emigrants.[29] Platte valley ranchers abandoned their homes and the Denver militia was called out to repel an army of Indians.[30]

Again there was no army, but at last there was an Indian war—in Kansas, Nebraska, and the columns of the *Rocky Mountain News*. For the next three weeks no Indian depredations were reported in Colorado, but the jittery populace was fed a steady diet of attacks and atrocities by its leading newspaper.[31] A disgusted rival sheet pointed out that most of the incidents occurred east of Fort Kearny, over four hundred fifty miles from Denver, and that half the Indian deviltry below Kearny was "pure fabrication";[32] it implied, moreover, that some of the "fabrication" originated with the *News*'s editor, William N. Byers. Byers was a close friend of John Evans. Both were strong Methodists, strong Republicans, strongly for Colorado's immediate admission to statehood.[33] Their enemies even suggested that Byers, Evans, and Chivington cooked up the Indian war together, to prove that only as a state could Colorado get sufficient troops to control her Indians, and to show the people the necessity of voting for John Evans as senator and John Chivington as congressman on the state ticket in the coming election.[34] There is no evidence that such a collaboration existed, but evidence is abundant that Byers vigorously promoted the Indian war.

In August the Cheyennes and Arapahoes waged a war that was neither fabrication nor hundreds of miles away. On August 11 a party of friendly Cheyennes and Arapahoes tried to reach the commander of Fort Lyon, but were driven away by soldiers.[35] The result was that for the next few days the Indians raced up the Arkansas stealing horses, killing cattle, murdering five unfortunates they came across on the road—two near Fort Lyon, three near Pueblo—and capturing a woman.[36] For two more weeks the Indian war raged in Colorado. On Running Creek, thirty miles southeast of Denver, Indians killed a stockherder and a boy[37] and then ran off all the horses of soldiers camped at Jimmy Camp near Colorado City.[38] On the South Platte, Indians killed a man near Fort Lupton[39] and were reported to have driven off stock and killed a herder.[40] Elbridge Gerry, a gullible old-timer who lived on a ranch sixty-six miles northeast of Denver, was told by two Cheyenne Indians that a thousand savages were massing for an attack on the settlements. Gerry dashed off to warn Denver, and in his absence the Indians stole all his stock.[41]

For every real depredation there were scores of rumors and false reports. On the Platte and Arkansas, terrified ranchers abandoned their cattle and ripening crops and fled to towns or to improvised fortifications.[42] Hysteria reigned in Denver. Three women were said to have lost their minds from fright; the overland stage suspended operation; speculators bought up all the flour in hopes of a siege.[43]

Not to be out-panicked, Governor Evans wired the War and Interior departments that

> it will be the largest Indian War this country ever had, extending from Texas to the British line . . . the alliance of Indians on the plains reported last winter in my communication is now undoubted. A large force, say 10,000 troops, will be necessary to defend the lines and put down hostilities. Unless they can be sent at once we will be cut off and destroyed.[44]

A day later Evans issued a proclamation to the people of Colorado telling them to "kill and destroy" all hostile Indians (avoiding the friendly ones) and to "take captive, and hold to their own private use and benefit all the property of said hostile Indians."[45] Somehow the language of this proclamation lodged in the minds of those who became "hundred-daysers."

On August 11, Governor Evans received authority from Washington to raise a regiment of citizens to serve for a hundred days against Indians. Within a month the ranks were closed.[46] After a summer made hideous with reports of Indian atrocities, the Third Regiment of Colorado Volunteer

Cavalry was ready to go out and kill Indians with no more compassion than a posse of farmers out to shoot coyotes.

While the Third Regiment drilled at Camp Weld, news came from the Arkansas River that the Indian war was in danger of armistice. On September 24, Governor Evans received a letter from Major Edward Wynkoop, commander of Fort Lyon, saying that he had met some Cheyennes and Arapahoes in council on the Smoky Hill River and had received from them four white prisoners traded from the Sioux. In return, Major Wynkoop had promised to bring seven chiefs to Denver to hold a peace talk with the Governor.[47]

Colonel Chivington was not pleased. Immediately he wired General Curtis:

> I have been informed by E. W. Wynkoop, commanding Fort Lyon, that he is on his way here with Cheyenne and Arapahoe chiefs and four white prisoners they gave up. Winter approaches. Third Regiment is full, and they know they will be chastised for their outrages and now want peace. I hope the major-general will direct that they make full restitution and then go on their reserve and stay there. Would like to hear by telegraph.[48]

Governor Evans was not pleased, either. As soon as Major Wynkoop arrived in Denver the Governor went to see him at his hotel and told him that he could not make peace now, for (as Wynkoop remembered Evans' words a few months later) "it would be supposed at Washington that he had misrepresented matters in regard to the Indian difficulties in Colorado, and had put the Government to a useless expense in raising and equipping the regiment; that they had been raised to kill Indians and they must kill Indians." But, since Wynkoop had promised the chiefs a talk, the Governor agreed to see them.[49]

On September 28, Wynkoop marched his officers and Indian chiefs out to Camp Weld past hostile groups of Third Regiment men. In the stuffy office, John Evans presided over the meeting. "War has begun," he told the Indians, "and the power to make a treaty of peace has passed from me to the great war chief." To prove that war had begun, Evans spent the rest of the council questioning the chiefs about depredations of the past summer. Talk became desultory; the afternoon dragged on; the hope of reconciliation thinned out to nothing.[50]

Suddenly the council came to a surprising end. Colonel Chivington arose and spoke words that appeared to guarantee peace:

> I am not a big war chief, but all the soldiers in this country are at my command. My rule of fighting white men or Indians is, to fight them until they lay down their arms and submit to military authority. You are nearer Major Wynkoop than any one else, and you can go to him when you are ready to do that.[51]

10. Some of the major players at the Camp Weld conference, September, 1864. Seated in front, Maj. Edward
Wynkoop (*l*) and Capt. Silas Soule (*r*). At the center
among the five Indians is Black Kettle. *Courtesy of the
Colorado Historical Society, WPA-834.*

The Indians were ready to go to Major Wynkoop now—why else had
they come? Joyfully the Cheyenne chief Black Kettle embraced the governor and Major Wynkoop.[52] Enthusiastically Major Wynkoop told Colonel
Chivington and Governor Evans of his plans to bring the Indians close to
Fort Lyon where he could feed and protect them.[53]

After the council Colonel Chivington received a telegram from General Curtis:[54]

> I shall require the bad Indians delivered up; restoration of equal
> numbers of stock; also hostages to secure. I want no peace till the
> Indians suffer more. . . . It is better to chastise before giving any-
> thing but a little tobacco to talk over. No peace must be made with-
> out my directions.[55]

These were just the instructions Colonel Chivington had asked for,
and they were meant, obviously, to guide Major Wynkoop in his dealings
with the Indians. But Colonel Chivington did not show Wynkoop the telegram, either then or in the five days that Wynkoop remained in Denver.

Major Wynkoop did not hear of General Curtis' wishes until months later, when he was relieved of command and ordered east to explain why he had ignored them.[56]

On October 3, Major Wynkoop and his soldiers and chiefs started back to Fort Lyon through a countryside where farmers had returned to their farms and ranchers were collecting their scattered stock, assured by Wynkoop that the Indians would not molest them.[57] All the way to Fort Larned there was peace. The weekly mail came through without an escort; wagon trains relaxed their nervous vigilance and travelled in small numbers;[58] at Atchison, Kansas, a shipping official unloaded a wagon of revolvers intended for Colorado's Third Regiment and put on mining machinery instead, for the war was plainly over.[59]

On arrival at Fort Lyon, Major Wynkoop told Little Raven to move his Arapaho village close to the fort, and he sent Black Kettle and Left Hand out to collect their scattered people and bring them in.[60] On November 4, to the surprise of the garrison, Major Scott J. Anthony arrived from Kansas to relieve Major Wynkoop, and to "investigate and report upon the unofficial rumors that reach headquarters that certain officers have issued stores, goods, or supplies to hostile Indians, in direct violation of orders from the general commanding the department."[61] Major Anthony took over, but within a few days he saw that the Indians around Fort Lyon were peaceful and would have to be fed. After collecting their guns, he issued them rations.[62] When Black Kettle and eight other chiefs returned to Fort Lyon and announced that their villages were moving in towards the post, the harried commander, knowing that he did not have rations enough to feed them all, returned their arms and told the chiefs to take their villages out to the buffalo range where they could hunt game. His report of November 16 to the District Commander B. S. Henning stated that he told the Indians "no war would be waged against them until your pleasure was heard,"[63] but later he testified that "it was the understanding that I was not in favor of peace with them. They so understood me, I suppose; at least I intended they should."[64] But Anthony's vacillating intentions were not clear. The Indians understood, as did all the officers and civilians at Fort Lyon, that they were to be safe at their camp on Sand Creek, forty miles northeast.[65]

On November 26, a Cheyenne chief arrived at the fort and asked that a trader be sent out to the Sand Creek village, for the Indians now had a nice lot of buffalo robes to sell. Major Anthony sent three men to the Indians with a wagonload of sugar, coffee, bolts of dress goods, pins, needles, mirrors, and similar articles.[66] The next day, Major Wynkoop left for Fort Larned bearing two testimonials to the correctness of his dealings with the Indians, one signed by thirty-five grateful settlers of the Arkansas valley, and the other by all the officers at Fort Lyon, with a special endorsement by Major Anthony.[67]

On the morning of November 28, Colonel Chivington and six hundred men of the Third Regiment passed Fort Lyon and camped a mile below.

The Colonel ordered a guard surrounding the post, to prevent the Indians from being warned of his arrival. Told of Chivington's intent to attack the Indians on Sand Creek, Major Anthony rode out to greet him, saying that he was "damned glad" Chivington had come, and that he would have gone after the Indians himself if he'd had more men.[68]

Major Anthony issued orders to one hundred twenty-five First Colorado officers and men of the Fort Lyon garrison to prepare to march with the Third Regiment. During the day the officers of the fort came one by one to their commander to protest an attack on the Sand Creek village. Major Anthony answering them that Colonel Chivington had assured him the village would be surrounded, the stolen stock recovered, the friendly Indians spared and only the perpetrators of outrages killed. Then, said Major Anthony, the entire force would march thirty-five miles further and attack the two thousand Indians camped on the Smoky Hill River. It would be a long campaign—complete, vigorous warfare.[69]

Captain Silas Soule wanted to take his protest to Colonel Chivington in person, but, as he later testified, "I was warned by Major Anthony, Lieutenant Cramer, and some others not go to the camp where Colonel Chivington was; that he had made threats again me for language I had used that day against [his] command going out to kill those Indians on Sand Creek." Undaunted, Soule sent Chivington a strongly-worded note.[70] When Lieutenant Cramer boldly approached Chivington and insisted that Major Anthony had given his word the Indians would be safe on Sand Creek, Chivington shook his fist in Cramer's face shouting, "Damn any man who is in sympathy with Indians."[71]

The column left Fort Lyon at about eight that night. At dawn, in sight of one hundred twenty lodges of Black Kettle's sleeping village on Sand Creek, Chivington said to his men, "Now, boys, I shan't say who you shall kill, but remember our murdered women and children!"[72] And his troops, yelling like Comanches, galloped forward.

After destroying the village on Sand Creek, Colonel Chivington did not go on to attack the large camp of Indians on the Smoky Hill River. His horses, he reported, were exhausted. The next day the soldiers marched down Sand Creek to the Arkansas then east to the Kansas line, looking in vain for Little Raven's Arapahoes who had been camped near Fort Lyon. By that time the Third Regiment's term of enlistment had expired, and the soldiers returned to Fort Lyon.[73]

Three days before Christmas, the "bloody Thirdsters" as they called themselves, marched triumphantly into Denver. They were laden with booty—ponies, buffalo robes, Indian rings and earrings (some still attached to fingers and ears)—and government guns and horses. Indian scalps, some said a hundred, were displayed by the Third Regiment boys during intermission in Denver's two theaters, and strung across the tops of mirrors in Lawrence Street saloons.[74]

William Byers read the reports of Third Regiment officers and used them to write his editorials praising Colonel Chivington and his men.[75]

One report said the Indians had dug rifle pits in the bed of Sand Creek, in preparation for the battle. Another told of finding white men's effects in camp, and a fresh white scalp in a lodge. Somebody quoted Major Anthony's remark that he was "damned glad" Chivington had come. To William Byers and to all of Denver, these reports proved the hostility of the Indian village, and the justification for attacking it. Consequently, it was with surprise and indignation that Byers read a dispatch from the east on December 30, stating that an investigation would be made of the Sand Creek affair, because "high officials in Colorado say that the Indians were killed after surrendering and that a large proportion of them were women and children."[76] It was several days before Byers and his newspaper could summon the argument and invective to "checkmate" the "high officials."[77]

With expressions of horror the Sand Creek business was reported in eastern newspapers and on the floor of the Senate and House of Representatives. Before January was half over, two investigations had been ordered, one by the Senate Committee on the Conduct of the War, headed by radical Ben Wade,[78] and the other by Chief of Staff Halleck, who demanded a court-martial of Chivington but had to be content with a military investigation, since the Colonel had already resigned from the army.[79]

His actions fully vindicated, Major Wynkoop returned to command Fort Lyon in the middle of January, 1865.[80] At the same time, Captain Silas Soule left Fort Lyon to become Denver's provost marshal. Since the Indian war had really begun "in earnest," the district commander replacing Chivington had established an unpopular martial law, which Captain Soule was expected to enforce. Soule also had to relieve Third Regiment veterans of government property, an unpleasant and dangerous duty.[81] But far more dangerous was his assignment as first witness before the military commission called to "investigate the conduct" of John M. Chivington.

Captain Soule was called before the commission on February 15, 1865, and gave his evidence in a room at Camp Weld before the three commissioners, Colonel Chivington, and Colonel Chivington's attorney. His testimony was not singular; witness after witness would testify to the same things: No rifle pits but the doomed attempts of women and children to dig into the sand away from the bullets; no white scalps that Soule saw, but many, many Indian ones; few white effects that were not bought from the traders; and above all evidence that Colonel Chivington had been amply warned of the peaceful character of the Sand Creek village and of the protection Fort Lyon had offered it. In six days of questioning, Captain Soule established all these things in a terse and determined way,[82]—but the people of Colorado were not to know what he said. "No one can be benefitted by such publicity," the commissioners had declared before Soule took the stand, and the proceedings were closed to public and press.[83] Testimony of the investigation was not made public until two years later, and then only in the relatively inaccessible Senate documents. Had the people known at the time what the investigation uncovered, Sand Creek might have lost its controversial character a century ago. And Captain Silas Soule might have dandled grandchildren on his knee.

The week after Soule finished giving his testimony, he was fired at twice while making his nightly rounds as provost marshal.[84] At the end of March, Soule told another officer that he had been repeatedly threatened— how he did not say—and that he "fully expected to be killed" on account of his testimony.[85]

On Sunday evening, April 23, Captain Soule was shot dead on Lawrence Street as he went out to investigate (for the third night in a row) mysterious shots. His murderer was Charles W. Squires, an unassigned recruit of the Second Colorado Cavalry, and an adventurer who had been in Nicaragua with the filibuster, Walker. Squires promptly gave himself up and admitted shooting Soule, but before he could be questioned in detail, he vanished.[86] He was later recaptured and brought to Denver by a First Regiment officer who had testified against Colonel Chivington. The officer died the next day under questionable circumstances, and a few days later Squires again escaped, this time for good.[87] If either the officer's death or the murderer's escape were ever investigated, records of it have not come to light.

The military commission adjourned April 26 to attend Soule's funeral.[88] Colonel Chivington did not attend. He spent that day writing out the answers to nineteen questions sent him by Senator Ben Wade's Committee on the Conduct of the War. Chivington wrote (and swore to its truth) that there had been eleven or twelve hundred Indians in the Sand Creek village (six hundred is a better guess, based on the traditional average of five Indians to a lodge), mostly warriors "assembled there for some special purpose." Five to six hundred Indians were killed, said Chivington. He saw the bodies of only two women (one had hanged herself) and no children, and "from all I could learn . . . but few women or children had been slain." Chivington wrote further that "on my arrival at Fort Lyon, in all my conversations with Major Anthony, commanding the post, and Major Colley, Indian agent, I heard nothing of this recent statement that the Indians were under the protection of the government, &c." There, along with such justification as the Indian war provided, was Colonel Chivington's defense.[89] He stuck to it for the rest of his long life, even though some of his own witnesses before the military commission refuted it.

Who in Colorado was to know what the witnesses really said? The only glimpse Colorado people had of the testimony was a synopsis prepared by Colonel Chivington himself and published in the *Rocky Mountain News*. It was replete with fresh white scalps, rifle pits, and all the other accouterments of Chivington's defense, but it contained not a single word of the testimony of Soule and other commission witnesses.[90]

On May 30, the military commission adjourned.[91] The same day, the report of the Committee on the Conduct of the War, signed by Chairman Ben Wade, was published in the East, describing Sand Creek as "the scene of murder and barbarity," Chivington's actions as disgracing "the veriest savage," and Evans' testimony about the Indian war as characterized by "prevarication and shuffling." The report concluded that those responsible for the outrage should be removed from office.[92] Promptly President Johnson requested and received John Evans' resignation as Governor.[93] Ben Wade's report was not published in Colorado, and the people concluded that their Governor's removal was an inexplicable injustice—a conclusion supported by John Evans' long rebuttal of Wade's report, published in the *Rocky Mountain News*.[94]

William Byers leaped to his friend's defense with an attack on Ben Wade in the *News*, and he offered a cheery hope that a third group of investigators, three distinguished members of Congress now on their way to Denver, would "vindicate" Sand Creek. These men, said Byers, had been appointed to investigate Indian affairs all over the nation, and they were unprejudiced and fair.[95]

Byers was entirely too optimistic about his three congressmen, Messrs. Doolittle, Foster, and Ross, who were at this time with Major Wynkoop at the site of the Sand Creek village. Here, as Chairman Doolittle later wrote, they "picked up the skulls of infants whose milk teeth had not been shed, perforated with pistol and rifle shots, and [examined] the sworn accounts given of the scalping and mutilating of women and children by white men under Colonel Chivington." By the time the three congressmen reached Denver, they were hardly "unprejudiced." Determined, however, to have a "full and frank discussion of the Indian problem," they met with Governor Evans on the stage of the Denver Opera House and made their speeches to an overflow crowd[96]—an irritable crowd, for the dignitaries had kept it waiting an hour and a half.[97] Of his own speech, Senator Doolittle wrote:

> When I had referred in a cool and matter of fact way to the occasion of conflict between the whites and Indians, growing out of the decrease of the buffalo and the increase of the herds of cattle upon the plains of Kansas and Colorado and said: the question has arisen whether we should place the Indians upon reservations and teach them to raise cattle and corn and to support themselves or whether we should exterminate them, there suddenly arose such a shout as is never heard unless upon some battle field;—a shout almost loud enough to raise the roof of the Opera House—"Exterminate them! Exterminate them!"[98]

Senator Doolittle was as appalled by the demonstration as by the massacre itself. He returned to Washington convinced that "while it may be hard to make an Indian into a civilized white man, it is not so difficult a thing to make white men into Indian savages."[99]

Senator Doolittle blamed Colorado's troubles upon her people, but her leaders—Chivington, Evans, and Byers—were also at fault. Each of these leaders well knew the restless mood of the citizens and soldiers; by their acceptance and encouragement of this mood, the restlessness was heightened to hatred and fear and spread like a prairie fire out of control. The Indian war started as a First Regiment diversion and grew into an obsession that demented the whole territory.

But was the Indian war, regardless of how it started or progressed, a proper excuse for the massacre? Defenders of the attack on Sand Creek still use it as justification, as did Chivington, Evans, and Byers, but it does not serve to justify. If the Indians had been peaceful, or even if they had been hostile, the word of the commander of Fort Lyon that they would be safe on Sand Creek had to be honored by honorable soldiers. If the village had been hostile and not under protection of Fort Lyon, then was the attack justified? The attack, yes—but not the massacre.

What Chivington ordered and his men effected at Sand Creek violated all the rules of civilized warfare, all the tenets of Christianity, and the spirit of an enlightened democratic nation. Had Chivington or his soldiers made the slightest effort to spare women and children, had they foregone the brute pleasures of scalping and mutilating and the boastful show of their clotted trophies, they might have gotten away with their "glorious battle" for a while, because there were few people in Colorado who did not firmly believe in the hostility of Black Kettle's village and the propriety of Chivington's attack upon it.

There was no excuse, however, for the animal bloodlust displayed at Sand Creek, and Chivington's supporters did the only thing they could do, which was to suppress evidence of it. It is inconceivable that the controversy could have worried Colorado for a hundred years, had the testimony of the investigations been available to the people. But John Evans, William Byers, and hundreds of Sand Creek veterans lived out their long lives in Colorado and the evidence remained suppressed.

History has not yet finished her own investigation of Sand Creek. Her judgments are cool, her motives disinterested, and her values steady. It may take years or it may take centuries, but be assured that in time history will reach her inexorable conclusions about Sand Creek.

NOTES

1. Testimony of Samuel Colley, March 7, 1865, in U.S., Congress, Senate. *Condition of the Indian Tribes: Report of the Joint Special Committee Appointed under Joint Resolution of March 3, 1865*, 39th Cong., 2nd Sess., 1867 Report No. 165, p. 29 (referred to hereafter as *Condition of the Indian Tribes*), testimony of Edmond Guerrier, May 25, 1865, ibid., 66 (148 killed, 60 braves); Samuel F. Tappan, MS diary, library, State Historical Society of Colorado (144 dead, 35 braves).

2. Affidavit of Lt. Cossitt, Fort Lyon, 1865, *Condition of the Indian Tribes*, p. 74.

3. Isaac H. Beardsley, *Echoes from Peak and Plain* (Cincinnati: Curts & Jennings, 1898), pp. 341–53.

4. Ovando J. Hollister, *Boldly They Rode* (Lakewood, Colorado: Golden Press, 1949), pp. 61–66, 68–73, 89.

5. "The Pet Lambs: Colonel Chivington Tells About the Exploits of Colorado's Soldiers," *Denver Republican*, 1890, typescript copy in library, State Historical Society of Colorado.

6. Report of the District Inspector, March 20, 1864, *Official Records of the War of the Rebellion*, Series 1, Vol. 24, Part 2, pp. 670f (referred to hereafter as *OR*); *Daily Mining Journal* (Black Hawk), April 21, 1864, p. 2.

7. Col. Chivington, April 9, 1864, to A.A.A.G., Dept. of Kansas, *OR*, Series 1, Vol. 34, Part 3, p. 113.

8. U.S., Congress, House, *Indian Depredation Claims*, 43rd Cong., 2nd Sess., 1875, Doc. No. 65; George B. Grinnell, *The Fighting Cheyennes* (Norman: University of Oklahoma Press, 1956), p. 138.

9. *Daily Mining Journal* (Black Hawk), April 23, 1864, p. 3.

10. *OR*, Series 1, Vol. 34, Part 3, pp. 146, 166–67, *passim*.

11. Ibid., 190.

12. Report of Maj. Jacob Downing, May 3, 1864, ibid., 907–08.

13. Report of Maj. Downing, April 18, 1864, ibid., 218; report of Lt. Eayre, April 23, 1864, ibid., Part I, pp. 880f.; report of Maj. Downing, May 11, 1864, ibid., 916; *Rocky Mountain News* (W), April 27, 1864, p. 1.

14. *Rocky Mountain News* (W), May 4, 1864. p. 1.

15. *Daily Mining Journal* (Black Hawk), May 27, 1864, p. 3.

16. Edgar C. McMechen, *Life of Governor Evans* (Denver: Wahlgreen Pub. Co., 1924).

17. Frank Hall, *History of the State of Colorado* (Chicago: Blakely Printing Co., 1889). I, 325.

18. U.S., Congress, House, "Report of the Commissioner of Indian Affairs for 1864," *Report of the Secretary of Interior*, 38th Cong., 2nd Sess., 1865, Doc. No. 1. pp. 368f (referred to hereafter as *Indian Affairs, 1864*); testimony of John Evans, Washington, March 8, 1865, *Condition of the Indian Tribes*, pp. 45–46.

19. John Evans to Gen. Curtis, April 11, 1864, Indian Affairs Letter Book, John Evans Collection, State Historical Society of Colorado.

20. *OR*, Series 1, Vol. 34. Part 4, pp. 97–99.

21. Ibid., 402f; testimony of Maj. Wynkoop, U.S., Congress, Senate, *Report of the Secretary of War Communicating, in Compliance with a Resolution of the Senate of February 4, 1867, a Copy of the Evidence Taken at Denver and Fort Lyon, Colorado Territory, by a Military Commission Ordered to Inquire into the Sand Creek Massacre, November, 1864*, 39th Cong., 2nd Sess., 1867. Doc. No. 26, p. 85 (referred to hereafter as Military Commission Report); affidavit of Maj. Wynkoop, Fort Lyon, June 9, 1865, *Condition of the Indian Tribes*, p. 75.

22. See various reports in *OR*, Series 1, Vol. 34, Parts 1–4.

23. Notes of Simeon Whiteley of the Camp Weld Council, September 28, 1864, *Military Commission Report*, p. 216; *Daily Mining Journal* (Black Hawk), June 15, 1864, p. 2; report of the A.A.A.G., Camp Weld, June 13, 1864, *OR*, Series 1, Vol. 34, Part 4, pp. 354–55.

24. John Evans to W. P. Dole, June 14, 1864, Indian Affairs Letter Book, John Evans Collection, State Historical Society of Colorado.

25. Lt. Hawley, Denver, to Col. Chivington, Fort Lyon, June 18, 1864, *OR*, Series 1, Vol. 34, Part 4, p. 449.

26. John Evans to W. P. Dole, June 15, 1864, *Indian Affairs, 1864*, p. 384.

27. *OR*, Series 1, Vol. 41, Part I, pp. 963–64.

28. Notably Left Hand at Fort Larned. See affidavit of John Smith, *Military Commission Report*, p. 126; affidavit of Col. Ford, Fort Lyon, May 31, 1865, *Condition of the Indian Tribes*, p. 65; *Rocky Mountain News* (D), August 1, 1864, p. 2; testimony of William Bent, *Condition of the Indian Tribes*, p. 94.

29. *OR*, Series 1, Vol. 41, Part 1, pp. 73–74, and Part 2, pp. 256–57, 323; *Rocky*

Mountain News (D), July 18, 1864, p. 2; July 19, 1864, p. 2; *Rocky Mountain News* (W), July 27, 1864, p. 2.

30. *Rocky Mountain News* (D), July 18, 1864, p. 2.

31. Ibid., July 19, 1864, p. 2: July 20, 1864, pp. 2f.

32. *Daily Mining Journal* (Black Hawk), August 22, 1864, p. 3.

33. Robert L. Perkin, *The First Hundred Years* (Garden City, N.Y.: Doubleday & Co., 1959), pp. 257-58.

34. *Rocky Mountain News* (D), July 12, 1863, p. 2; *Daily Mining Journal*, December 3, 1864, p. 2.

35. *OR*, Series 1, Vol. 41, Part 1, pp. 238-39 Part 2, p. 673; testimony of Lt. Joseph A. Cramer, Denver, February 23, 1865, *Military Commission Report*, p. 33.

36. *OR*, Series 1, Vol. 41, Part 2, pp. 766-67 *Military Commission Report*, p. 33: *Rocky Mountain News* (D), August 25, 1864, p. 3; *Rocky Mountain News* (W), August 31, 1864, p. 4.

37. *Rocky Mountain News* (D), August 16, 1864, p. 2; August 17, 1864, p. 2; *Military Commission Report*, p. 216.

38. *OR*, Series 1, Vol. 41, Part 2, p. 810; *Military Commission Report*, p. 216.

39. *OR*, Series 1, Vol. 41, Part 2, pp. 843, 845.

40. *Rocky Mountain News* (W), August 31, 1864, p. 4.

41. *Indian Affairs, 1864*, p. 363: *Indian Depredation Claims*, p. 22.

42. *OR*, Series 1, Vol. 41, Part 2, pp. 766f; *Rocky Mountain News* (D), August 26, 1864, p. 2; Indian Affairs, 1864, p. 387, *Condition of the Indian Tribes*, p. 76.

43. Simeon Whiteley to John Evans, Denver, August 30, 1864, *Indian Affairs, 1864*, pp. 380f; Whiteley to Evans, September 13, 1864, ibid., 382.

44. *OR*, Series 1, Vol. 41, Part 2, p. 644.

45. *Rocky Mountain News* (D), August 12, 1864, p. 2.

46. Raymond G. Carey, "The 'Bloodless Third' Regiment, Colorado Volunteer Cavalry," *The Colorado Magazine*, 38 (October, 1961), 276-80.

47. *OR*, Series 1, Vol. 41, Part 3, pp. 242-43; *Rocky Mountain News* (D), September 24, 1864, p. 2.

48. September 26, 1864, *OR*, Series 1, Vol. 41, Part 3, p. 399.

49. Affidavit of Maj. Wynkoop, Fort Lyon, June 9, 1865, *Condition of the Indian Tribes*, p. 77: testimony of Maj. Wynkoop, *Military Commission Report*, p. 90.

50. Testimony of Amos Steck, *Military Commission Report*, p. 42; Whitley's notes on the Camp Weld council, ibid., 213-17.

51. Ibid., 217.

52. Testimony of Maj. Wynkoop, March 21, 1865, ibid., 91.

53. Ibid., 96.

54. Testimony of Lt. Cramer, March 3, 1865, ibid., 60.

55. Ibid., 173.

56. Affidavit of Maj. Wynkoop, Fort Lyon, June 9, 1865, *Condition of the Indian Tribes*, p. 76, in which he says, "I have never received any instructions in regard to the Indians and their treatment." He says it again in the *Military Commission Report*, p. 96.

57. Ibid., 91; *Rocky Mountain News* (D), October 3, 1864, p. 2.

58. N. P. Hill to his wife, Central City, October 3, 1864, "Nathaniel P. Hill Inspects Colorado: Letters Written in 1864," *The Colorado Magazine*, 34 (January, 1957), 41-45; Eugene P. Ware, *The Indian War of 1864* (Topeka: Crane and Co., 1911), pp. 340f.

59. Col. Chivington to Maj. Wynkoop, October 16, 1864, *OR*, Series 1, Vol. 41, Part 4, pp. 23f.

60. *Commission Report*, pp. 86-89, 91-92.

61. Special Order No. 4, HQ, Fort Riley, Kansas, October 17, 1864; *OR*, Series 1, Vol. 41, Part 4, p. 62; testimony of Major Wynkoop, *Military Commission Report*, p. 97.

62. Maj. Anthony, Fort Lyon, November 6, 1864, to A.A.A.G., Fort Riley, U.S. Congress, Senate, "Massacre of Cheyenne Indians." *Report of the Joint Committee on the*

Conduct of the War, 38th Cong., 2nd Sess. 1855. Report No. 142, p: 70 (referred to hereafter as *Massacre of Cheyenne Indians*); testimony of Maj. Anthony, March 14, 1865; ibid., 19.

63. *OR*, Series 1, Vol. 41, Part 1, p. 914.

64. *Massacre of the Cheyenne Indians*, p. 18.

65. Testimony of Capt. Soule, February 15, 1865, *Military Commission Report*, p. 14; testimony of Lt. Cramer, March 1, 1865, ibid., 48; testimony of Lt. Minton, April 3, 1865; ibid., 146; testimony of Maj. Wynkoop, March 30, 1865, ibid., 87; testimony of John Prowers, March 24, 1865, ibid., 104–06; and others.

66. Affidavit of John Smith, Fort Lyon, January 15, 1865, *Condition of the Indian Tribes*, p. 51; testimony of David Louderback, March 30, 1865, *Military Commission Report*, pp. 134–35; John Prowers testified March 25, 1865, that the Indians had been issued their annuities—"domestic, calico, Indian cloth, beads, knives, axes, sugar, coffee, bacon, flour, and numerous small articles, needles, thread, etc."—sometime in October. Ibid., 107.

67. Ibid., 93–95.

68. Testimony of Capt. Presley Talbot, May 11, 1865, ibid., 208; testimony of Lt. Harry Richmond, May 16, 1865, ibid., 212.

69. Testimony of Capt. Soule, February 16, 1865, ibid., 13; testimony of Lt. Cramer, February 28, 1865, ibid., 46–47; testimony of Lt. Cannon, March 22, 1865, ibid., 110; testimony of Lt. Winton, April 3, 1865, ibid., 146–49.

70. Testimony of Capt. Soule, February 18, 1865, ibid., 21.

71. Testimony of Lt. Minton, April 3, 1865, ibid., 147; testimony of Lt. Cannon, April 6, 1865, ibid., 153; testimony of Lt. Cramer, March 1, 1865, ibid., 147.

72. Testimony of Capt. A. J. Gill, February 3, 1885, ibid., 179; testimony of James P. Beckwith, March 6, 1885, ibid., 68; testimony of Lt. Cannon, March 27, 1885, ibid., 112; report of Lt. Col. Leavitt L. Bowen, Sandy Creek, November 30, 1864, *Massacre of Cheyenne Indians*, p. 52; testimony of Robert Bent, *Condition of the Indian Tribes*, p. 96; *Miners' Register* (Central City), January 7, 1865, p. 2.

73. Report of Col. Chivington, December 13, 1864, *Massacre of the Cheyenne Indians*, p. 49.

74. Affidavit of Simeon Whiteley, July 27, 1865, *Condition of the Indian Tribes*, p. 71; testimony of Corp. James Adams, *Military Commission Report*, p. 142; A. C. Hunt, Washington, March 15, 1865, *Massacre of the Cheyenne Indians*, p. 44; *Rocky Mountain News* (D), December 21, 1864, p. 3.

75. *Rocky Mountain News* (D), December 17, 1864, p. 2.

76. Ibid., December 30, 1864, p. 2.

77. Ibid., January 4, 1865, p. 1.

78. *Massacre of the Cheyenne Indians*, p. 1.

79. Gen. Halleck to Gen. Curtis, January 11, 1865, *OR*, Series 1, Vol. 48, Part I, p. 489; *Military Commission Report*, pp. 1–8.

80. Special Order No. 42, HQ, Fort Riley, Kansas, December 31, 1864, *OR*, Series 1, Vol. 41, Part 4, p. 971; Wynkoop's testimony, *Military Commission Report*, p. 95.

81. *Rocky Mountain News* (D), February 6, 1865, p. 2.

82. Testimony of Capt. Soule, February 15–21, 1865, *Military Commission Report*, pp. 8–29.

83. Ibid., 3.

84. *Daily Mining Journal* (Black Hawk), April 25, 1865, p. 2; *Rocky Mountain News* (D), May 1, 1865, p. 2.

85. Affidavit of Capt. George F. Price, May 3, 1865, *Military Commission Report*, p. 189.

86. *Rocky Mountain News* (D), April 24, 1865, p. 2; April 25, 1865, p. 2; April 26, 1865, p. 2; May 1, 1865, p. 2; *Daily Mining Journal* (Black Hawk), April 24, 1865, p. 2; April 25, 1865, p. 2; April 26, 1865, p. 2; May 2, 1865, p. 3.

87. *Rocky Mountain News* (D), July 12, 1865, p. 2; July 14, 1865, p. 4; July 15, 1865,

p. 1; July 18, 1865, p. 4; October 4, 1865, p. 4; October 6, 1865, p. 4; October 10, 1865, p. 4; *Daily Denver Gazette*, October 14, 1865, p. 2; *Rocky Mountain News* (D), November 3, 1865, p. 1; November 6, 1865, p. 1.

88. *Military Commission Report*, p. 161.

89. Affidavit of Col. Chivington, Denver, April 26, 1865, *Massacre of Cheyenne Indians*, pp. 101–08.

90. *Rocky Mountain News* (D), June 24, 1865, pp. 2–3.

91. *Military Commission Report*, p. 228.

92. *Massacre of Cheyenne Indians*, pp. i–vi.

93. McMechen, *Life of Governor Evans*, pp. 139f.

94. *Rocky Mountain News* (D), September 12, 1865, p. 2; September 13, 1865, p. 2; the rebuttal was dated Denver, August 6, 1865.

95. Ibid., July 19, 1865, p. 1; August 19, 1865, p. 1.

96. Letter of Senator Doolittle to Mrs. L. F. S. Foster, March 7, 1881, "Notes and Documents," *New Mexico Historical Review*, 26 (April, 1951), 156–57.

97. *Daily Denver Gazette*, July 21, 1865, p. 2.

98. Senator Doolittle to Mrs. Foster, *New Mexico Historical Review*, 26 (1951), 156–57.

99. Ibid.

10 COWBOY STRIKES AND UNIONS

David E. Lopez

The American cowboy is popularly regarded as the ultimate in macho individualism. The "Marlboro Man" represents this, as did John Wayne and other heroes of western films and videos, as well as the rough-hewn "a man's gotta do what he's gotta do" names of vehicles like Bronco and Wrangler. David Lopez demonstrates different truths about cowboys, how they worked, how subservient or independent they really were, and how much control they had over their hours, wages, and conditions of work. In a few cases, which Lopez describes, western cowboys organized, forming unions in attempts to exert collective pressure on rancher-employers. Were they an advance guard not just of western settlement, but of capitalist working conditions? How did they resemble, or differ from, miners and factory workers under industrial conditions of collective employment?

Lopez's essay is valuable because it throws the cold light of realism on an occupation that has been almost unrecognizably mythologized. The "long drives" of herds numbering from a few dozen to as many as 3,000 head of cattle from Texas to Kansas and the northern Plains lasted only a few years—just 1866 to 1873 to the railheads in Kansas, and from about 1879 to 1886 to Wyoming and Montana. The drives did not involve great numbers of cowhands; Lopez, in fact, puts the total number between 1870 and 1900 at no more than 20,000. (Other historians have pointed out that a good many were black—emancipated slaves in many cases—and Hispanic.) Who owned these cattle and who owned the ranches? Why did cowhands find working life difficult—so difficult that they formed unions several times in the 1880s to combat and change these conditions? Why did they strike? Why did their strikes fail? What became of the striking cowhands after that? —editors

CORPORATE CATTLE ranching developed during a time of considerable labor and small proprietor unrest in the United States, the West not excepted. In Texas and other western states the Grange and later the Farmers' Alliance demonstrated that small farmers could organize effectively. Railroad, telegraph and mine workers, often under the Knights of Labor, agitated and struck with varying degrees of success throughout the cattle country. By the early 1880s the western resentment towards "Eastern Capital" was being directed against the vast absentee owned ranches, to the point that the cattle barons could not get juries of townsmen to convict known rustlers. One rancher was obliged (and able) to found his own county to get around this problem. The rationalization of work that accompanied infusions of eastern and European capital meant increased regimentation of cowboys and the end of privileges that they had formerly taken for granted. Corporate ranches set and cut wages through the stock associations that they controlled.[1]

In this context it would be surprising if ranch workers had remained totally quiescent. There were no enduring cowboy unions and no concerted efforts by labor organizers to bring cowboys into the fold. But, contrary to the cowboy's place in American mythology, he did go on strike at times. The story of these strikes is a neglected chapter in the history of American labor. Perhaps more important, the reasons why he struck so rarely and with such little success have nothing to do with the imaginary cowboy as portrayed in fiction and so much western history.

Cowboys acting like workers ill fits the usual western image. Many standard works on cowboys and cattlemen do not mention such things at all.[2] Other authors devote only a parenthetical or inaccurate sentence to cowboy strikes.[3] The general absence of labor organization among cowboys has traditionally been ascribed to their independence and "rugged individualism."[4] But there is no need to resort to such dubious character causation. The difficulty of coordination across vast spaces combined with the unusual organization of work made striking problematic enough. But these technical aspects are secondary to socioeconomic structures inhibiting solidarity: the persistent excess of applicants over jobs, the dilemma of winter unemployment, and the consequent clientelistic subordination of cowboys.

Strikes and associations among herders were neither common nor often successful. Part of the difficulty lies in the organization of work. Herding requires a small and usually diffused labor force. When individual workers are given responsibility for a particular range or herd (the post system), and especially if this is combined with some sort of share arrangement, they have even less opportunity and motivation to organize around demands for better pay or working conditions. Instead they tend to regard their income as dependent on only their own individual luck and hard work.[5]

But shares and post systems were virtually unknown in North American plains cattle ranching between 1870 and 1900. Instead cowboys were divided up or combined into work gangs according to the task at hand. Herds, and later fences, were patrolled by small groups or individual cowboys. Roundups and trail drives required more concentrated work forces as

11. A few hardy men. *The Library of Congress.*

did the haying (the cutting and putting up of feed) that came to occupy an ever larger part of "cowboy" work. Strikes were possible only under these circumstances of greater concentration and in fact the two major cowboy strikes were "harvest" strikes at the beginning of spring roundups.[6]

Mounted herders have always been an elite among rural workers. But the privilege of being elevated above agricultural labor brings with it the dependence that is "loyalty" from the employer's point of view.[7] Cowboys were no exception. The work was hard, seasonal, and not particularly well-paid. But for at least a portion of the western work force it compared favorably to their realistic alternatives. This portion did not have to be very large to insure a steady excess of recruits. Even where ranching was a dominant industry, herding was always a minor occupation. Between 1870 and 1900 there were never many more than 20,000 cowboys in the entire United States. Only about half worked in the major range cattle states (Texas, New Mexico, Colorado, Montana, and Wyoming), where cowboys were outnumbered by various occupations of roughly equal status and skill requirements: farm labor, mining, hauling, sheep herding, and miscellaneous town labor.[8]

But young men went West to be cowboys, not laborers. The initial co-
hort of recruits were among the tens of thousands of Southerners unwilling or unable to return home after the war. These "Texas" cowboys predominated in the early years of ranching and trail driving. But by the early
1880s the bulk of new recruits were "eastern" cowboys from Kansas and
Nebraska. Their primary impulse was also necessity, the failing family
farms of the Eastern plains. But they were also influenced by the romanticized image of cowboy life presented by the dime novels that were so
widely disseminated by 1880. Cowboys were perhaps the first occupational group to suffer directly from mass media romanticization.[9]

Even at peak season unemployed cowboys and would-be cowboys were
not hard to find. But it was winter survival that provided the greatest inducement to loyalty. Over half of the summer crews were laid off half the
year or more. Where winters were more severe the proportion laid off and
the length of the lay-off were greater. A large ranch in Montana had only
three year-round hands, hiring twelve additional riders only for the summer months.[10]

How did cowboys survive the winter? Their first preference was year-
round employment, even if at reduced wages, which usually was the case.
But most of these positions went to the trusted top hands. Some ranches
fed and housed an additional portion of their regular riders, who in exchange did odd jobs and could be called on during an emergency. Another
possibility was "sundowning" (i.e., riding the "grubline" from ranch to
ranch and doing odd jobs in exchange for a few days of hospitality). As a
last resort cowboys could "hole up" (i.e., spend the winter with a few comrades in an abandoned mountain shack), subsisting on meager purchased
supplies and "slow elk" (poached cattle).[11]

Free room and board, sundowning, and holing up in the vicinity of
ranches were all opposed and gradually done away with by the corporate
ranches that dominated the range by the mid-1880s. Given the ease of
poaching and rustling and the opposition of cowboys to the new conditions, the least expensive alternative for the ranchers would probably have
been to feed and house most of the ranch workers over the winter. The
consequent gratitude would also probably have resulted in fewer "lost"
cattle during roundups. But any give-away was anathema to the cattle
barons, particularly those who remained in Britain or the East and did not
understand or care about conditions on the range.

The limited and declining number of winter subsistencies meant that
by 1885 most cowboys were not secure dependents. But it did set up rivalry for favored status, especially among the marginal workers: the Negro,
Mexican, and older cowboys who had little hope of attaining top hand
status. The general situation of unemployment, exacerbated by a constant
flow of farm boys who wanted to be cowboys, combined with the growing
problem of winter unemployment, made for competition rather than cooperation among cowboys. But their rugged individualism did not extend

to relations with employers, where stark material considerations made them loyal and untroublesome employees. To curry favor ranch workers turned over homestead claims to the boss and voted as he directed. They yielded to the ranchers' demands that they own neither homestead nor cattle, even though the ranch workers had as much right as the owner to graze cattle on the public domain. They also did his violent bidding in range wars and against farmers and smaller ranchers, one of the few points at which the cowboy legend is accurate.[12] All these extra-economic services are typical of clientelistic employment in which the terms of exchange are balanced in favor of the employer.

In this context the surprising thing is that cowboys ever struck at all. Only a handful of efforts are described in primary or reliable secondary sources, and most of these were brief and unsuccessful wildcat affairs. But two stand out for their scope and organization.[13] Both took place in the mid-1880s and, significantly, in the two areas where corporate ranching had advanced the furthest: the Texas Panhandle and Wyoming. The first was a large effort but a failure; the second was smaller and at least temporarily successful.

The Panhandle strike occurred in the spring of 1883, *before* the major mining strikes in the West. Texas and Colorado ranchers had moved into the Panhandle late in the 1870s and by purchases, leasing, intimidation, and brute force rapidly established large territorially-distinct ranches. By 1881 a handful of large operators acting through the Panhandle Stock Association had a firm grip on the better grazing land and newcomers, especially small stock raisers, were effectively excluded. Ranch hands were forbidden to own any cattle of their own and the Association enforced a twenty-five- or thirty-dollar standard wage. This compared favorably with herders' wages in central and especially southern Texas where Mexican and Negro cowboys predominated. But Panhandle cowboys compared themselves to ranch workers in Wyoming and Colorado, where wages were higher. This was not just white supremacy; the harsh Panhandle winters made the working season shorter than in most of Texas. In addition they felt that other terms and conditions of their employment were unsatisfactory, although these do not seem to have been any worse than elsewhere.[14]

The precise origins of the strike are not known, but it had been planned several months in advance and timed to take place before the spring roundup. Estimates of the number of cowboys involved varies from three hundred and twenty-five to "only forty to fifty." Two hundred is the figure given most often and there could not have been many more for in the area of the strike there were only a few hundred cowboys. It involved the majority of the hands from every large ranch in the region (the LS, LX, T-Anchor, LE, and LIT); but in no case did every hand on a ranch participate. On at least one, Mexican riders were prominent among the nonstrikers and apparently it was the brown, black, very young and very old hands—those for whom the job meant the most—who refrained from joining the strikers.[15]

Sources differ on the exact set of grievances put together by the cowboys; perhaps it was never all that uniform from ranch to ranch. In the apparently authentic "cowboy ultimatum" that survives only the wage issue is mentioned. The strikers demanded a minimum wage of fifty dollars a month for all cowboys regardless of their skill.[16] A rancher oriented newspaper decried the leveling egalitarianism of this demand. But the cowboys had no intention of abolishing status distinctions. Wagon bosses and other subforemen were to receive seventy-five dollars a month, which preserved the proportion of the previous pay differential. Several other issues are mentioned by various sources. The ranch hands demanded better food, in particular the addition of potatoes, onions, canned corn, and tomatoes to their flatulent diet of beans and sow-belly. In light of the hard work, exposure, and health problems suffered by cowboys, food was no minor issue. In addition they wanted the right to brand mavericks for themselves and the right to run small herds on the public domain range land "belonging" to their employers. These non-wage demands seem to have been tacked on *after* the initial ultimatum and consequent lockout. But they were hardly afterthoughts. The cattle ownership and mavericking issues were fundamental ones throughout the range country but they were challenges to the system and as such the cowboys hesitated to bring them forward. When their wage request met with opposition they were apparently prompted to include these more basic issues.[17]

The size of the wage demands was pointed to as proof of cowboy irresponsibility. Whether or not the cattlemen could have managed to pay is hard to say. According to an anti-rancher newspaper the strike was sparked by revelations of the vast profits the Panhandle stock companies were realizing.[18] In any case increased wages were clearly a bargaining demand, not an absolute one. The cowboys only wanted to negotiate, but the cattlemen would have none of it. Spokesmen presented the cowboy ultimatum and waited, the various crews acting in coordination but separately. The ranch owners appeared to act autonomously, but in fact they had met and agreed to not budge on any demand, as a point of principle. The strikers were obliged to leave the ranch centers and camp on the range. Ranchers threatened to evict them by force, with the aid of the Texas Rangers, if the dissidents did not leave the ranch lands. Since the ranches claimed all the public domain as well as land they actually owned outright this was tantamount to insisting that the strikers leave the region entirely, so for a few weeks at least the cowboys stood their ground.[19]

Some ranches pretended to negotiate. Others tried to bribe the leaders into bringing the boys back and were surprised and offended when they were rebuffed. One ranch fired its strikers outright, armed its few loyal hands, and waited. Another pretended to offer forty dollars and was refused. This so outraged the owner that he immediately fired all the strikers. Whatever front they put up, all the ranches were also busy recruiting scab crews. This included the ranch that offered forty dollars. It intended to get the roundup going and then fire the rebellious cowboys as soon as a new crew could be assembled. The obstinacy of this ranch owner is indicated by his unwillingness to offer more than forty dollars even in double-cross.[20]

Within a few weeks replacements had been recruited and the strikers were definitely fired and chased off the ranch lands. Word of the strike had spread quickly among cowboys, not as a blow for "Labor" but as an extraordinary spring employment opportunity. Cowboys from New Mexico, Kansas, and southern Texas began to arrive before the strike was over and in the end no more than a week or two was lost in getting the spring roundup started. Even at this time of peak seasonal employment the ranchers had no difficulty replacing intransigent strikers. A troop of Texas Rangers was called in to aid in this dispersal, but it is not clear that they ever went into action. The meager strike fund had been quickly dissipated and the errant range-knights of labor were forced to leave the area.[21]

The other major strike occurred three years later, at the beginning of the spring roundup in Wyoming. By 1885 Wyoming ranchers were having second thoughts about the profitability of cattle raising. Mismanagement and early skimming had resulted in returns far below the twenty to thirty percent investors had been promised. Under the coordination of the Wyoming Stock Growers' Association economy measures were initiated in 1885. The grubline was eliminated and a larger than usual proportion of the hands were laid off over the winter of 1885–1886. One newspaper noted that "cowboys are being compelled to leave ranches and seek other quarters for the winter" and warned that this hardship for the "boys" could backfire on the ranch owners. The winter eviction and rumors of worse to come produced apprehension among ranch workers and early the following spring a Laramie paper reported that a Cowboy Union was being formed in Cheyenne under the auspices of the Knights of Labor. A month later the same paper noted, without elaboration, that "There is said to be a strike of cowboys on the Sweetwater [River]." A Colorado newspaper described the same strike in more detail: it reported that the strike was for a five-dollar increase and seemed to be supported by all the cowboys. Actually the issue was a bit different. The standard summer wage in Wyoming had been forty dollars for several years, but the large owners decided to enforce a reduction to thirty-five dollars, and some even went down to thirty.[22]

The strike began in one roundup district, and spread only as far as the two adjoining ones. Its only demand was a restoration of the five-dollar cut and in the three districts where it was organized the strike was quickly successful. But in the fall, when most of the cowboys were laid off as usual, the active strikers were informed that they would never be rehired in Wyoming, or anyplace else if the ranchers had their way.[23]

Why was the Wyoming strike at least temporarily successful while the Panhandle strike failed? Part of the reason was timing. Not only was the roundup season shorter in the north, but the northern strikers took care not to play their hand until the roundup was actually under way. In addition fewer cowboys in the north remained unemployed during the peak spring roundup season; by the time idle workers from other regions could be brought in the season would have been half over. The Panhandle strike was called two weeks before the roundup was to begin, and there was abundant idle labor nearby.

Another factor in the northern success was the very organization of the work. The grazing land of the state, overwhelmingly public domain, was divided into roundup districts, each consisting of a few large ranches and several medium-sized ones. Herds intermingled on the range and companies pooled their cowboys who worked in large groups. The larger companies sent representatives to adjacent districts to look after any stock that might have wandered. So inter-ranch organization and inter-district communication were facilitated. With the hands of so many ranches collected together, far from towns or any ranch headquarters, the power of the ranch owners was greatly weakened, and authorities could not easily intervene. Even so the strike affected only a small portion of the roundup. In the Panhandle roundups were on individual ranches. The large ranchers could coordinate their anti-strike efforts through their Association but riders from different ranches could cooperate only with great difficulty. Strike organization was more problematic and the mass solidarity that imparts a feeling of invincibility was lacking. Since the strikes had to be carried out on individual ranches those hands most susceptible to the bosses' pressures were less likely to participate, and in fact the Panhandle strike was not unanimous on any ranch.

The only other cowboy strikes about which anything is known were brief and limited to single ranches. What appears to be the very first broke out at the Comanche Pool Ranch in Kansas in the fall of 1882. The story is sketchy; apparently it was simply a strike for higher wages. Most hands initially sympathized but the owner broke down this support by talking to the men individually, firing the few with the nerve to stand up to him.[24]

Another strike, in midsummer 1886, may well have been inspired by the spring roundup strike in Wyoming. It occurred during haying time, was limited to one ranch (the Milbrook), and was a distinct failure. The hands demanded a partial restoration of their wages, from thirty to thirty-five dollars, but the owner refused, arguing that he had no choice since the stock association set wages and violations brought a fine of five hundred dollars. Twelve of the twenty-nine summer hands quit and were set walking (to Laramie, a distance of eighteen miles) "carrying their beds and baggage on their shoulders" (cowboys rarely owned horses).[25]

A third and, apparently, final cowboy strike (at least in the nineteenth century) can be counted a dubious success. It took place on a drive from the Matador Ranch into Colorado in 1887. On the trail the eight herders demanded a substantial raise or they would quit on the spot and all the cattle would be lost. The quick-thinking trail boss summarily fired the two leaders, who were apparently obliged to walk to the nearest town, but granted the other six a five-dollar raise. As the trail boss pointed out in his report it was actually cheaper to pay six cowboys the additional sum than to keep all eight on at the original wage. The remaining six were pleased by the raise and shaken by seeing the two leaders fired, so they did the additional work imposed on them.[26]

A common element in all three of these strikes, and probably the Panhandle strike as well, was the personal pressure the ranch manager or owner could apply. This was not just interpersonal influence at work; it was also the most effective way to lay out the strikers' alternatives: to continue striking was to gain the sure enmity of the ranch, something that would be felt far beyond its boundaries. But capitulation would demonstrate "loyalty" and bring forgiveness and perhaps even a winter position.

The Panhandle and Wyoming strikes were the result of prior organization but neither these nor any other cowboy strikes produced any enduring cowboy unions. The connections between ranch workers and organized labor were slight and perhaps more wishful thinking than reality. That Cowboy Union supposedly formed under the tutelage of the Knights of Labor in Wyoming did not outlive the strike that occurred a few weeks later, and possibly was not connected with it at all. In the southwest the Knights may have been active among ranch workers before and after the Panhandle strike. A student of labor organization in Texas found that messages from cowboy locals were among the exhibits in the congressional investigation of the 1886 Southwest strikes and recalls, enthusiastically, that the "strike was active in the very heart of the ranch country."[27] But this was a railroad strike and there is no evidence that it spilled over to the ranches. Nor is there any reason to believe that these cowboy locals survived for more than a few weeks, if they existed at all. The only established cowboy participation in the 1886 railroad strikes was that of unemployed cowboys serving as scab labor. Three years later they did the same duty in the Minneapolis streetcar strike.[28]

Leading participants in the Wyoming and Panhandle strikes were blacklisted by the regional stock associations, who barred them from ranch employment and classed them with rustlers. The influence of these blacklists reached far beyond the official boundaries of the stock association. In 1892 a rancher in central Montana wrote to the Wyoming Stock Growers' Association for confirmation of a rumor that one of the men in his employ had been blacklisted by the Association.[29] Those blacklisted cowboys who could started up as independent small ranchers, but most probably moved into other areas and occupations. The prime movers of the two strikes (Tom Harris in the Panhandle and Jack Flagg in Wyoming) both became small ranchers and later were important leaders in the small ranchers' struggles against the large corporate ranches. Exactly how they set themselves up is a point of debate. A pro-cattleman author reports that the Panhandle strikers became rustlers to "get even" with the men who had defeated them. Another author states that "several of the cowboys started up on their own hook within the larger domains" as small ranchers. The two accounts are really saying the same thing for in the Panhandle, as in Wyoming a few years later, whether one was a rustler or a small rancher was only a question of point of view.[30]

Accounts of less militant cowboy organizations are as illuminating as the spotty history of strikes. In the spring of 1886 in northern New Mexico a meeting of about eighty small cattlemen and ranch workers (mostly the latter) decided to form the Northern New Mexico Small Cattleman and Cowboy's Union, to be open to all cowboys and to owners employing no more than two hands. The Union's organic resolution is careful to state that their interests and those of the existing Northern New Mexico Stock Growers' Association "should not conflict, our interests being mutual." They proposed a plan whereby ordinary hands would receive either thirty dollars a month year-round, or forty dollars for only six months, novices receiving slightly less and top hands, slightly more. Their major concern was year-round sustenance, not actual wage levels, and certainly not being forced to do work cowboys supposedly disdained, as can be seen in the following resolution:

> Resolved that the working season of the average cowboy is only about five months, and we think it is nothing but justice that the cowmen should give us living wages the year round. Realizing the fact that they cannot keep us all the year in idleness, we are therefore willing, when the cow work is over, to do any honest work that may be needed by our employers, that they may get full value received.[31]

I have not been able to determine if such a resolution was ever actually presented to the ranch owners and if so what ever came of it. Little could have come of it since this resolution was passed just before the devastating winter of 1886–1887 and subsequent depression in the cattle industry. In fact all of these strikes and organizational programs date from 1887 or before. After 1887 unemployment and wages became considerably worse, in part because of the poor state of the industry, but also because the corporate ranches were able to solidify their grasp on the range when the 1887 disaster wiped out smaller operations.[32]

But even earlier cowboys had recognized the growing weakness of their bargaining position, as another Northern New Mexican Union resolution reveals:

> Resolved that recognizing the fact that they [the owners] can import cheap labor, but after making the cow business our profession we deem it nothing but right that we should be recognized first, and get what we are worth after many years' experience. You cannot do

without us, and we are dependent on you, and we expect to be treated like men by men.[33]

The first part of this resolution indicates they realized that the second part was only wishful thinking. In this and the resolution quoted previously they were arguing from a non-market, particularistic basis; but notions of justice and right meant little to the owners of ranch businesses.

A different sort of cowboy organization was the mythical Cowboy's Cattle Company. In the spring of 1884 several newspapers reported that

the cowboys in the vicinity of Deer Trail, Colorado are agitating the subject of starting a company to be called the Cowboy's Cattle Company. Any cowboy on the range can invest his earnings at so much per share, hard earned dollars which are now thrown away or worse, can be saved to the country as a whole and to the toilers of the range in particular.[34]

This general idea had been suggested as early as 1870 and continued to come up throughout the 1880s. In 1886 a letter to a New Mexico newspaper asked if the editor had "heard anything of the rumor about the Cowboy's Cattle Company, and their twenty thousand head of cattle [belonging to] three punchers, with lots of loose cash ... " The writer expressed concern that the new herd might further crowd the range in his area. He needn't have worried, for the "loose cash" could hardly have amounted to the four hundred thousand dollars required for a herd of that size. In 1887 there is another suggestion for "cooperative herding and joint ownership of a herd by many cowboys." The anonymous writer justifies the idea by noting that while previously (very previously) cowboys were allowed to run their own few head of stock along with his employers "in the course of time the big baron rebelled at this method and envious of his employee's success he put a veto to the custom until now it is infrequently practiced." The letter continues that this has deprived the cowboy of his one way "to get on in the world" and so is driving the best and most ambitious cowboys out of cattle raising and into something more promising. He suggests that a profit sharing plan would be the best way to keep them, but a company of their own was also a possibility.[35]

There is no indication that any of these schemes were ever put into operation; but the idea must have been attractive to cowboys and, at least as an idea, to cattlemen as well. For cowboys it meant participation on an equal footing with their employers, something they probably saw as more desirable than a brotherhood of workers. It was a hopeless dream for most, of course, but the few examples from the early days of cowboys successfully becoming small stock raisers were enough to encourage them.

In any case effective unionization among cowboys was equally hopeless, given the state of the labor market, technical difficulties of organization, and the power of corporate ranches and their stock associations. The few strikes and organizational attempts between 1883 and 1887 were all ultimately unsuccessful and only serve to underscore why cowboys usually did not even try to organize. Modernization and concentration in the industry after 1887 only made things worse, for then jobs were scarcer and starting up on one's own was even more difficult. In an urban context these factors might be conducive to unionization. If they fostered the desire for organization among cowboys, and the New Mexico resolutions indicate that they did, the facilitating conditions necessary to make unionization a reality were simply not present.

It is not entirely fanciful to suggest that the image of cowboy independence and rugged individualism was fostered by cowboy and cattleman alike precisely *because* cowboys were among the most dependent of workers. For one it was a salve to self-esteem, for the other a means to keep his workers quiet. But whatever the connection between myth and reality the latter is certainly a better if less appealing source for explaining cowboy behavior.

NOTES

1. Ernest Staples Osgood, *The Day of the Cattleman* (Minneapolis, 1929) is still the best account of the range cattle industry, even though it deals principally with only the northern plains. Gene Gressley, *Bankers and Cattlemen* (New York, 1960) tries to put the development of Wyoming ranching in a general political and economic perspective. Sympathetic accounts of particular ranches and cattlemen and popular general accounts of "cowboy days" are innumerable, but rarely shed much light on the historical cowboy. William Curry Holden, *The Spur Ranch* (Boston, 1934) is exceptional in its detailed treatment of ranch working conditions. Helen Huntington Smith, *The War on Powder River* (New York, 1966) provides a good description of the changing social conditions that led to a major conflict between large and small Wyoming ranchers in 1892.

2. For example, Joe B. Frantz and Julian E. Choate, *The American Cowboy: The Myth and the Reality* (Norman, 1955); Osgood; Lewis Eldon Atherton, *The Cattle Kings* (Bloomington, 1961); Edward Douglas Branch, *The Cowboy and His Interpreters* (New York, 1961).

3. For example, J. Evetts Haley, *Charles Goodnight: Cowman and Plainsman* (Norman, 1949), 374; Gressley, 123.

4. A recent example is William H. Hutchinson, "The Cowboy and the Class Struggle (Or, Never Put Marx in the Saddle)," *Arizona and the West*, 14 (Winter, 1972), 321–330. Also see Walter Prescott Webb, *The Great Plains* (New York, 1931) and compare Frantz and Choate, 71–131.

5. Julius Klien, *The Mesta* (Cambridge, Mass., 1920) and E. H. Carrier, *Water and Grass* (London, 1932) provide good accounts of Southern European stock raising. C. J. Bishko, "The Peninsular Background of Latin American Cattle Raising," *Hispanic American Historical Review*, 32 (November, 1952), 491–513, connects Old and New World stock raising techniques. Francois Chevalier, *Land and Society in Colonial Mexico* (Berkeley, 1963) and William H. Dusenberry, *The Mexican Mesta* (Urbana, 1963) describe the Mexican stock industry that was the immediate ancestor of cattle raising on the United States western plain. Ricardo Rodriguez Molas, *Historia social del gaucho* (Buenos Aires, 1968) provides some comparative material for Argentina. David E. Lopez, "Cowboys and Gauchos: the Cattle Workers of Argentina and the United States in the

Nineteenth Century" (unpublished Ph.D. diss., Harvard Univ., 1972) explicitly compares the situations of these cattle workers.

6. Frantz and Choate, 35–63; Holden, 93–100; Lopez, 205–209, which also contains additional documentation and discussion of all points made in this paper.

7. Klien, 24–25; Carrier, 39–42; Chevalier, 112–113; Dusenberry, 147.

8. Lopez, 181–183. Frantz and Choate 34, estimate twice this many cowboys, without explaining how they arrived at their estimate. My estimate comes from agricultural and population censuses and information about the ratio of stock to herders. It agrees closely with Joseph Nimmo, "The American Cow Boy," *Harpers New Monthly Magazine*, November, 1886, 880–884, the only contemporary estimate based on any actual research. Ranch work was not easily learned or endured by middle-class adventurers from the urban east, but it was no great challenge to the farm boys who constituted the vast bulk of recruits.

9. John Baumann, "On a Western Ranche," *Fortnightly Review* 47 (April, 1887), 516; Nimmo, 883; William A. Baillie-Grohman, *Camps in the Rockies* (London, 1882), 344; William T. Hornaday, "The Cowboys of the Northwest," *Cosmopolitan*, 2 (1887), 219–233; James Emmit McCauley, *A Stove-up Cowboy's Story* (Austin, 1943), 3–8. This last work, written in 1890, is a rare example of a cowboy autobiography that is actually by a cowboy rather than a rancher.

10. Clarence Gordon, "Special Report on Cattle, Sheep and Swine," *1880 Census of Agriculture*, 3 (Washington, D.C., 1883), 62, 71; George W. Romspert, *The Western Echo* (Dayton, 1881), 187. *Big Horn Sentinel*, November 21, 1885, in the Western Range Cattle Industry Study Archives, Denver, Colorado, hereafter WRCIS. Compare Frantz and Choate, 65, where winter is portrayed as a time of pleasant idleness for cowboys. Frantz and Choate are thinking of only the lucky minority with secure ranch positions over the winter. This exemplifies the common methodological error of mistaking the ideal for the typical.

11. *Big Horn Sentinel*, November 21, 1885 (WRCIS); Baillie–Grohman, 341; Romspert, 187. Harry E. Chrisman, *Lost Trails of the Cimarron* (Denver, 1961), 255–259, demonstrates an understanding of the dilemma of winter unemployment that is rare in the literature on cowboys. Holing up was a dangerous and unpleasant final alternative for those wanting to stay in the range country, desirable in order to get an early start job hunting in the spring, since towns welcomed cowboys only when they had money to spend on liquor and women. See Romspert, 187–217; Baumann, 532; Will James, *Cowboy North and South* (New York, 1931), 85–90; Lester F. Sheffy, *The Franklyn Land and Cattle Company* (Austin, 1963), 12.

12. *Daily Sentinel* (Laramie), December 19, 1873 and October 20, 1874 (WRCIS); Charles Guernsey, *Wyoming: Cowboy Days* (New York, 1936), 37–38, 97–102; Dulcie Sullivan, *LS Brand* (Austin, 1968), 128; John K. Rollinson, *Wyoming Cattle Trails* (Caldwell, Idaho, 1948), 243–249; Smith, 109–113, 149; Everett Dick, *The Sod-House Frontier, 1854–1890* (New York, 1937), 147–151.

13. Gressley, 123, refers to a third major strike, in Wyoming in 1884. The only primary reference to the 1884 strike that I have uncovered is in the unreliable John Clay, *My Life on the Range* (Chicago, 1924). From Clay's description it is obvious that he is really describing the 1886 strike and the date is only a typographical error.

14. See Haley, and Chrisman, for descriptions of cattle raising and working conditions in the Panhandle. Ruth Allen, *Chapters in the History of Organized Labor in Texas* (Austin, 1941), 33–42, provides the most complete previous account of the Panhandle strike, which she incorrectly believed to be the only cowboy strike.

15. *Texas Live Stock Journal* (Fort Worth), March 12, 1883, 6, April 28, 1883, 8, *The Denver Republican*, April 25, 1883, all reprinted in Clifford P Westermeier, *Trailing the Cowboy* (Caldwell, Idaho, 1955), a valuable compilation of stories about cowboys, mostly from western newspapers. See also Sullivan, 65, 153–154. *The Third Annual Report of the Commissioner of Labor* (Washington, D.C., 1888), 580–583, reports that 325 ranch workers were involved, but this is probably the total number of cowboys employed

at the outbreak of the strike, not the number of actual strikers. According to this report the strike was successful, but that is definitely incorrect.

16. Or apparently, race, though not explicitly mentioned. Black and brown cowboys usually worked for less than the prevailing wage, leading to protests by anglo cowboys that they be excluded from the range country or at least confined to certain low status jobs. The "cheap labor" referred to in the resolution of the New Mexican cowboys quoted later in this paper means Mexican cowboys and in the part of New Mexico adjacent to the Texas Panhandle their employment was a continuing issue. See John H. Cully, *Cattle, Horses and Men of the Western Range* (Los Angeles, 1940), 5.

17. Allen, 37–42; Sullivan, 64–68. Mavericks were unbranded young animals no longer with their mothers, making it impossible to determine their owners on the open range.

18. *Caldwell Commercial*, March 29, 1883 (reprinted in Westermeier).

19. The duration of the strike depends on what is measured. According to the *Third Annual Report of the Commissioner of Labor* it was only twelve days, from March 23 to April 4. But this is clearly incorrect as newspapers mention the strike as ongoing as late as April 28. Roundup with scab crews began in early May, about the same time the strikers were forced off the ranches. See *Texas Live Stock Journal*, April 28, 1883, 8 (reprinted in Westermeier), and Sullivan, 67–69. Allen, 38–40, states that the strike continued for an entire year. As animosity it lasted at least that long, but work was actually delayed for a few weeks at most. Picket lines were not practical on the open range.

20. Sullivan, 65–66, provides the best information about rancher reactions to the strike.

21. *Denver Republican*, April 25, 1883 (reprinted in Westermeier); Allen, 39; Sullivan, 69.

22. *Big Horn Sentinel*, November 21, 1885 (WRCIS); *Daily Boomerang* (Laramie), April 3, April 16, May 17, 1886 (WRCIS); *Field and Farm* (Denver), May 29, 1886, quoting the *Fort Collins Express*, n.d. (reprinted in Westermeier). Osgood, 131–132, agrees that the standard wage in the early 1880s was forty dollars.

23. Smith, 32–33. The Wyoming Stock Growers' Association letterbooks at the Western History Research Center in Laramie are notably thin around the time of the strike, just as they are essentially missing for 1892, the year the Association attacked small ranchers in Johnson County.

24. Sullivan, 69–72.

25. *Daily Boomerang*, July 28, 1886, 4 (WRCIS). Walking was more than just a blow to cowboy prestige; it was positively dangerous on the arid and featureless plains, especially since wild cattle sometimes attacked men on foot.

26. W. M. Pearce, *The Matador Land and Cattle Company* (Norman, 1964), 30.

27. Allen, 37.

28. *Field and Farm*, May 15, 1886, 8; *Topeka Capital Commonwealth*, April 18, 1889 (both reprinted in Westermeier).

29. *Wyoming Stock Growers' Association Incoming Letter Book*, January 1, 1892, Western History Research Center, Laramie. Osgood, 149–157, discusses blacklisting, but only with respect to rustling. He does inadvertently quote an Association discussion of blacklisting the 1886 Wyoming strikers, couched in vague but unmistakable terms.

30. Smith gives the best account of these conflicts in Wyoming. Sullivan gives the cattleman's view of small ranchers in the Panhandle. Chrisman leans more to the other side.

31. *Cattleman's Advertiser* (Trinidad, Colorado), March 18 and April 1, 1886 (reprinted in Westermeier).

32. *Daily Boomerang*, March 11, 1889 (WRCIS); Osgood, 83–113; Atherton, 46–64.

33. *Cattleman's Advertiser*, March 18, 1886 (reprinted in Westermeier).

34. *White Oaks Golden Era* (White Oaks, New Mexico), April 24, 1884 (reprinted in Westermeier); see also *Daily Boomerang*, May 27, 1884 (WRCIS).

35. *Daily Sentinel* (Laramie), September 17, 1870 and April 2, 1875 (WRCIS);

Socorro Bullion (Socorro, New Mexico), March 6, 1886 (reprinted in Westermeier); *Field and Farm*, May 7, 1887, 5 (reprinted in Westermeier). Suggestions for the cowboy cattle companies often sound as if they came from ranchers. The letters may have been conscious attempts to combat worker consciousness among cowboys, though there is no definite evidence for this.

11 "EVERYTHING I WANT IS HERE!": THE *DAKOTA FARMER'S* RURAL IDEAL, 1884–1934

Paula M. Nelson

Homesteading—the creation of small, independent farms and farm families—brought far more people into the American West than mining, soldiering, exploring, fur-trading, or any other occupation, until well into the twentieth century. From the 1630s in Massachusetts to the 1930s, homesteading or western settlement was the dream, and often the normal experience, of a great many Americans. Myth and legend has favored cowboys and gold miners, but the colorless mass of settlers far outnumbered them.

Why was the homesteading ideal so strong as to compel millions to try to realize it? Why did it last, despite all the hardships? Why especially did it keep drawing people to places where rainfall and groundwater were not dependably sufficient for small farms—which was true of the western part of the Dakotas and elsewhere in the Great Plains?

The ideology of homesteading was propagated for fifty years by the farm newspaper the Dakota Farmer. *The elements of this highly popular ideology, in its late-nineteenth-century forms, appeared over and over again, even into the era after 1915 when homesteading became more and more perilous economically. How did the editors explain this ideology, and how did they continue to rely on it despite mounting evidence that the glory days of homesteading were over? How did the editors try to "modernize" the ideology to fit changing conditions of weather, production methods, technology, and markets? How did editor Allen, in particular, relate farm values to family values?—editors*

I N 1881, at the peak of the Great Dakota Boom, James Baynes founded an agricultural paper, the *Dakota Farmer*, at Alexandria in southern Dakota Territory. It must have seemed like a wise thing to do. All throughout the plains, but especially in Dakota, the farmer's frontier was on the move in seeming fulfillment of the pioneer's oft-stated goal of subduing the wilderness while getting rich in the process.[1] All across the Northwest, new agricultural papers sprang up. Not all survived the ups and downs of American agriculture over the next decades. The *Dakota Farmer* did; in fact, it flourished. During the terrible days of the Great Depression and

Dust Bowl of the 1930s, when advertising was nil and the staff minimal, the *Dakota Farmer* had its largest number of subscribers, over ninety-six thousand.[2]

What allowed this farm paper to succeed where others failed? The answer lies largely in the personnel who staffed it over the years and the message it conveyed to its readers. The personnel included a twenty-six-year-old Illinois man, William F. T. Bushnell, who joined the paper as a partner in 1883 after its move to Huron in southern Dakota Territory and who became its sole proprietor in 1885. Until his untimely death in 1900, Bushnell *was* the *Dakota Farmer*. After his death, the mantle passed to his close friend, Millard F. Greeley. Greeley, who farmed near Gary, South Dakota, had written a column on sheep, as well as editorial commentary on rural life and values, for several years. Greeley edited the paper until 1910, when he became an associate editor, a position he held until his retirement in 1921. In 1902, William C. Allen joined the *Dakota Farmer* as "pressman," or mechanical engineer; within a few short years, he had become a director, manager, editor, and publisher. Allen, like Bushnell, would dominate the *Farmer*, becoming its voice in the trying days of the 1920s and 1930s.

The Greeley/Allen team made the *Dakota Farmer* a force in the Northern Great Plains. They took Bushnell's concept of a "farmer's paper," which he had just begun to develop at the time of his death, and made it the cornerstone of their operation. The "farmer's paper" had a reader orientation rather than the subject-matter orientation that traditional farm papers had. To these men, the distinction was important. A farmer's paper was practical, not theoretical. It did not brag of the professors on its staff but of the first-hand dirt-farmer experiences that came to life on its pages. A farmer's paper was personal, immediate, and of interest to every member of the family; it aspired, in fact, to be a member of the family. On occasion, editor Allen wrote to readers about the *Farmer's* business workings under the title "A Message from Home." All of the staff freely used the phrase "the *Dakota Farmer* family."[3] Although we, in our time, have become inured to patently commercial appeals to family values, the *Dakota Farmer* theory of a farming "family" was different and real.

Bushnell, Greeley, and Allen all confronted difficult and troubling issues during their days in the editor's chair. Each editor decided how to address the reality of the unpredictable plains environment in which his readers worked. Each came to terms with the forces leading to "modernization" and the destruction of traditional rural patterns of work and culture. Each also addressed the fundamental forces in American life then transforming the United States into an urban and industrial nation that accorded rural people lower status and less respect. The message that these editors gave to their subscribers was remarkably consistent over time: While they lived in a land that made farming more difficult, people with a wise "system" could triumph over the environment and live comfortably;

modern, progressive farmers who practiced diversified, adapted agriculture could enjoy an egalitarian family life, maintain pride in their fundamental role as agricultural producers, and further the best features of rural culture in the face of social change. Because they were Dakotans, the editors exhorted them, they had the strength and resiliency to build something out of nothing and to fight any enemy and win, whether it be nature or anonymous social forces.

This consistent vision of rural life in Dakota did not begin with the first publication of the *Dakota Farmer* but developed after the first trial of drought and hard times. In the beginning, W. F. T. Bushnell was an extravagant booster. The drought years of the late 1880s and the early 1890s converted him into a wise counselor who propagated the adaptation of agricultural knowledge and the faith that hard work and the proper attitude would bring the Dakotas to the forefront. His message was tempered with a hard dose of reality.

The *Farmer*'s initial attitude of unqualified boosterism was reflected in editorials and in exchange pieces (items taken from other papers) chosen for publication in the paper's columns. In April 1884, for example, Bushnell published a visionary piece entitled "Dakota in 1890," copied from an unidentified exchange. "But where is the country whose riches have been able to offer the stable inducements and the lasting benefits which our own Dakota offers to the pilgrim who would seek a new home?" the author asked. "The impulse that would seize the easterner and cause him to leave his friends and all the ties and associations that make home dear and voluntarily seek the climes of Dakota has been a wonder and an amazement to many. But it is not phenomenal nor even marvelous. When we come to reason about it and note the advantages offered here, and then think of the vicissitudes and discomforts that the early pioneer of our earlier States were subject to, the only wonder is that Dakota has not been overpopulated." The piece went on to forecast a population of two million by the year 1890, along with "the most perfect system of railroads in the world," flourishing cities, and two senators and twenty representatives in Congress to do the region's bidding.[4]

The population of the Dakotas in 1890 was only 519,808. The Great Dakota Boom had ebbed. By 1889, the year of statehood for North and South Dakota, drought parched the crops and desiccated the spirits of the pioneers. Several counties in the rich James River Valley reported average wheat yields that year of one bushel per acre. In 1890, the governor of South Dakota solicited relief money, food, and agricultural supplies for his citizens from more prosperous midwestern states. In North Dakota, the population had grown from 37,000 in 1880 to 152,000 in 1885, but growth slowed sharply after 1885. Many of the largest towns and counties actually lost population between 1885 and 1890. Fargo, for example, lost 1,730 people, 23 percent of its 1885 population. Over one thousand people migrated from Burleigh County, a loss of 20 percent. Cass and Grand Forks counties remained well populated at over eighteen thousand residents each but still experienced losses of 6 and 10 percent respectively. According to the state and federal census records of the time, the most populated counties of northern Dakota lost 10.5 percent of their people between 1885 and 1890.[5]

When the boom collapsed in the late 1880s, Bushnell came to terms with the situation by devising a solution for the problems of climate: the irrigation of Dakota lands from the artesian basins under the James River Valley. He began a regular irrigation feature in the *Farmer* and solicited written submissions from farmers in dry states such as Colorado. He also asked Dakotans who experimented with artesian wells to share their results. When such contributions were negative, he urged further efforts and admonished those who failed to try irrigation again.[6] As hopes rose and fell according to the weather in the last decade of the century, Bushnell also began to rail at the "blockheads who always toil at the rear end of any profession."[7] He visited successful farmers, reporting on their wealth and substance, and devoted an entire issue to detailed accounts of their agricultural techniques.[8] In soliciting their contributions, Bushnell wrote, "The writer believes that in every neighborhood in the Dakotas there is at least one farmer who has succeeded at farming and is fully satisfied with the country and its future promises. . . . It has been an easy matter in the past to obtain the discouraging reports of the less fortunate neighbors and publish them broad-cast to the detriment of the entire country." Bushnell noted that the *Dakota Farmer* might be more popular if it subscribed to the majority view of the Dakotas as a sham and a failure but concluded, "Our constant aim has been to get at the experience of the successful farmer and publish the report of his methods that his neighbors might profit thereby."[9]

In December 1893, after a dry and discouraging year, Bushnell's vision of a "farmer's paper" continued to evolve. "The *Farmer* has great faith in the agricultural possibilities of the Dakotas. Dry seasons have blasted many a hope and yielded many a harvest of discouragement. But through it all the *Farmer* has felt that when we get better acquainted with Nature as she appears to us here, and understand her more perfectly, so that we can work more in harmony with her our work will yield more satisfactory returns. . . . The *Farmer* believes it has a special mission to assist in this work."[10] Bushnell urged his readers to love their land and their work truly and to share their insights. He requested full reports of successes and failures for the columns of the *Farmer*. His invitation emphasized the deep relationship that he wanted Dakota farmers to have with their land. "We expect to receive a good lot of fresh practical reports from plow handle farmers," he wrote; "we mean farmers who love the business they are engaged in, and who are in it to stay; who love Dakota sod and who almost worship Dakota's conditions; who can see a bright side in the darkest cloud, but who believe that there are comparatively few dark clouds in the Dakotas. Men of faith, hope and charity."[11] Through hard work, proper mind set, adapted crops, diversified farming, and irrigation, he argued, "the Garden of Eden will . . . be reclaimed."[12]

The *Dakota Farmer* began publication at a time of major change in the place of agriculture in American life. The industrialization process, which had begun before the Civil War, reached maturity in the postwar period and led to tremendous growth in industry, the use of technology, and the population of the cities. In 1865, most Americans were small property owners; the majority were independent farmers. By 1900, most Americans had no attachment to the land and worked for others. Although census figures indicate that city people did not become a majority of the population until 1920, the trend toward urban dominance was clear much earlier. In the decade of the 1880s, for example, eighty-eight cities doubled in population. Chicago in 1880 had approximately half a million residents; in 1890 it had grown to over a million.

Along with the rise of industry, technology, and the city came economic changes that reduced the power of the individual farmer to control his own destiny. The technological revolution brought new machinery that eased the farm workload and allowed extensive cultivation of cash crops for a world market. Cash crops tied farm families into national and international economic swings. Unfortunately for rural people, the post–Civil War period brought several sharp economic downturns that adversely affected farm prices. In 1881, a farm family received $1.19 a bushel for wheat; by 1894, a bushel of wheat brought only $.49. Corn and other agricultural commodities experienced similar declines. Prices of nonagricultural goods also fell during this time, but agricultural prices fell faster and farther, leaving farm families in a state of relative poverty and unhappy over the decline. Agricultural debt began to increase as farm families borrowed money to mechanize their operations or to build new farms in the expanding frontiers of the Great Plains and the West. Farm tenancy grew as families were unable to repay loans and lost their property or were unable to purchase land in the first place. In a nation where the pride of landownership had been an enduring value, over one-third of all farmers were tenants in 1900. While problems on the farm stemmed from overproduction of agricultural commodities, depressed prices, and a variety of factors that led to increased costs for credit, railroad transportation, farm implements, and other necessary agricultural supplies, farmers targeted urban big business as the sole source of their suffering and reacted angrily to what they saw as the triumph of business monopolists.[13]

On the cultural level, a sense of anxiety and dislocation began to grow among farming people. American farm families came from a variety of backgrounds; many were recent European immigrants. Their incomes, religions, political beliefs, social conditions, and ways of life varied. Regardless of their diversity, however, in the late nineteenth century all rural people appeared to lag behind in the modernization process sweeping the rest of the nation. Urban life was in the ascendancy. Along with urbanization came new standards and values at every level of American society. For the family, the changes included an increased emphasis on individual happiness and autonomy for all members, which undermined the power of the patriarch. In the life of the mind, modernization created an emphasis on innovation, experimentation, planning, knowledge, education, open-mindedness, flexibility, and a broad view of issues that transcended the familial and local. Farm life, which had been centered on the patriarchal family, the neighborhood, and the traditions, customs, and folkways of centuries of rural history, did change in response to modernization but not as quickly or as dramatically as urban life did, and some farm families did not change at all. Because of the relative slowness of rural change, urban people and the intellectual and political leadership of the country were convinced that farm families were backward and in need of reform. Rural people, for their part, acknowledged their belief in urban superiority in three ways: demographically, by moving to the city en masse; psychologically, by developing a pronounced status anxiety; and sociologically, by organizing their own efforts to reform rural life.[14]

Bushnell appeared to accept many of the tenets of the modernization thesis. As editor of the *Dakota Farmer*, he had to reach an audience that was in one sense diverse, yet was, as a group, in decline vis à vis the changing standards and values of urban society and angry over its growing economic displacement. He succeeded in communicating with his readers by tying the modern to the traditional, advocating progressive, diversified modern agriculture in a practical package while also endorsing traditional rural values of independence and thrift. Using strong, descriptive language, he attacked "backward" agriculture and often compared good farmers with poor farmers as a teaching tool. "Success in any vocation that men follow almost always throws out some visible sign," he wrote. "When we see clean, well tilled fields, thrifty stock, good fences, houses and barns painted and in good repair; we can say pretty safely that it is the home of a prosperous man." On the other hand, he noted, "neglected fields and fences, poor stock and shabby buildings—is the equally sure sign of the improvident farmer."[15] In another editorial, Bushnell pondered "the slow man" in the neighborhood, a person he described as "a thing that started a little late in life, and never yet caught up to its place in the procession. ... he is behind time in his work constantly. ... Mr. Behind Times faces failure because he commenced today what should have been completed yesterday. He keeps the slow jog up through life and only occasionally catches a glimpse of the back platform of the train of prosperity as it sweeps around some distant curve."[16]

Bushnell also urged his readers to modernize family relationships and work patterns. In the early 1880's, the *Dakota Farmer* often included fictional morality tales in its columns. The overwork of farm women by unthinking husbands was a frequent subject. In these tales, the husbands had modern machinery, new outbuildings, blooded stock, and all the other trappings of agricultural success. The wives, however, toiled away without

12. In the settling of western Kansas in the 1870s and
1880s, buffalo or cow chips were commonly used for
fuel when wood was scarce. A Meade County editor
wrote in 1879: "It was comical to see how gingerly our
wives handled these chips at first. They commenced by
picking them up between two sticks, or with a poker.
Soon they used a rag, and then a corner of their apron.
Finally, growing hardened, a wash after handling them
was sufficient. And now? Now it is out of the bread,
into the chips, and back again—and not even a dust of
the hands!" *The Kansas State Historical Society,
Topeka, Kansas.*

hired help or household conveniences. In one story, the wife educated the
husband by refusing to cook his favorite foods in the name of the rigorous
economy that he required of her. Thus educated, her husband bought a
new stove, an efficient lightweight churn, and an innovative butter-making
utensil. He purchased sleds and skates for their sons, as well. In another
story, a woman barely survived a terrible illness brought on by overwork
before her husband recognized the unfairness of her workload.[17] After the
Dakota Farmer discarded its fiction section, Bushnell occasionally commented editorially about the need to recognize the labor of women and
children and give them some respite from it. He noted that too often
"there is a great tendency to make farm life slave life."[18]

Bushnell also tried to point the way out of economic turmoil. Although his involvement proved to be short-lived, he initially believed
that organization, and specifically the National Farmers' Alliance, was the
long-term solution to problems of the farmer's economic place. In July

1884, the editorial page aligned itself with the ideology of the alliance. "The *Farmer* is essentially a farmer's paper," the editor wrote, "not only in the matter of providing agricultural reading, but also in being ever ready to advocate the rights of the farmer and workman against those monopolies which are truly the enemy of all their truest interests. . . . They are the 'Hessians' of the nineteenth century."[19] In this statement, Bushnell equated farmers with the righteous yeomanry at the heart of the American Revolution and the "monopoly power" with the Hessian mercenaries who had fought for the British political monopoly. Later that year, the editor urged farmers to organize in order to solve the problems they confronted. "The weakness of the farming community," he argued, "is its lack of unity. . . . No class of industry is so completely at the mercy of the sharks."[20] In December 1884, Bushnell was one of three men who issued a call for a convention to form a territorial Farmers' Alliance organization. When the delegates met, they chose Bushnell as their secretary, and the *Dakota Farmer* became the official paper of the Dakota Farmers' Alliance. For the next three years, alliance news received prominent place in the paper as the editor greeted the organization of local alliances with enthusiasm. According to the *Dakota Farmer*, the organization hoped "in the near future to control the monopolists who have preyed on the farmer."[21]

The close relationship between the Dakota Farmers' Alliance and the *Farmer* lasted until December 1887, when alliance president Henry L. Loucks claimed that Bushnell was refusing to print official alliance documents. He prevented Bushnell from speaking in his own defense on the floor of the alliance convention, where delegates voted to drop the *Dakota Farmer* as their official paper. The rift had developed over the alliance's angry written attack on a rival group. In Bushnell's view, the submitted piece had not been official business but "a conglomeration of personal spleen." His lawyer had informed him that the *Dakota Farmer* would be liable for damages should he print the article, so he had refused. According to Bushnell, it was the only item received from the alliance that he had not printed.[22] His explanation, however, did not appease the angry followers of Loucks, who now apparently classed the *Dakota Farmer* editor as one with the money power.

Bushnell turned on the alliance leadership at this juncture, although he continued to pledge his support for the alliance concept. In stinging editorials, Bushnell decried the "political agriculturalist" who "agitates his own town or county, vividly portrays the wrongs of his class, [yet] neglects his own home and his farm."[23] For Bushnell and those who wrote in to support him, "political agriculturalists" were too willing to abrogate personal responsibility in favor of casting blame. From December 1887 on, the *Dakota Farmer* editor gravitated away from political solutions to agricultural problems but continued to use the heated antimonopoly rhetoric of the day. The columns of the *Farmer* began to emphasize the power of the individual to shape his or her own destiny through hard work, proper techniques, and attention to detail. Becoming largely apolitical and remaining that way through the rest of its first fifty years, the paper and its editors decried attachment to party and advocated instead that farmers vote the candidate and their own interests. Partisan political news never again graced the *Dakota Farmer*'s pages.[24]

During the Bushnell era, the *Dakota Farmer* became a paper of substance and influence. It emphasized practical experience and depended upon its readers to contribute pieces on all facets of farm and household work. It was Bushnell, a few years before his death, who began to describe the *Farmer* as a "farmer's paper" in order to distinguish it from the more theoretical journals available to farm families. During his years as owner of the *Dakota Farmer*, Bushnell expanded and enlarged the paper and, in the dark days of drought and despair in 1890, began to publish it on a semi-monthly rather than monthly basis, a sign of his faith in the future of Dakota. In 1893, he moved the paper to Aberdeen, South Dakota, believing it to be a better location for serving North Dakota readers, and he began plans for a large new building. For years, the publication lost money; in the depression years of the early 1890s, only unspecified "outside sources" of income kept the *Farmer* afloat. During hard times, Bushnell often extended subscriptions on credit. At one time, readers owed several thousands of dollars in past-due subscription money (the *Dakota Farmer* cost only one dollar a year). What kept him going was the conviction that his work was vital to the success of Dakota agriculture.[25]

In January 1900, in the last anniversary note he was to write Bushnell celebrated the start of the twentieth year of publication and some new-found prosperity that had come to the *Dakota Farmer* "because the farmers have believed in it and given it the substantial endorsement which it has received." He, in turn, believed in the farmers: "The farms of the Dakotas have been [my] pride—the pioneers of these prairies are [my] heroes." His conclusion stands as an emblem of his faith and of his paper's appeal. "By keeping everlastingly at it," he wrote, "[Dakotans] are now far in advance as a people, and by reviewing past experiences they will one day realize their greatest desires."[26] In August 1900, Bushnell traveled with his family to Colorado Springs to vacation and attend a national convention of farmers. He became ill with "cholera morbus," which led to a perforated bowel. Too weak to submit to potentially life-saving surgery, Bushnell died on 25 August 1900. He was forty-two years old.[27]

The men who took over the *Dakota Farmer* in 1900 after Bushnell's sudden death confronted circumstances in Dakota similar to those that Bushnell had faced throughout his career. The issues of climate and the economic potential of the Dakotas were again in the forefront as a new land boom in the western portion of both states attracted thousands of new settlers to the region. The early years of the century were unusually wet across the Dakotas, and railroad construction as well as government lotteries of Indian reservation lands lured the hopeful to the last frontier. Advocates of "dry-farming" techniques aided the rush with the promise that they held the key to agricultural success on the Great Plains. The failure of this last frontier movement a decade later, as drought dried the crops and the hopes of latter-day pioneers, created a second chapter in the long history of agricultural boom and bust in the Dakotas.[28] Periodic drought continued to afflict the *Farmer*'s circulation area as the twentieth century progressed. Economic turmoil continued, as well. World War I created huge markets for Dakota products, and land values soared. The agricultural depression that began in 1920 as markets contracted and land values fell destroyed many farm families. The effects of that devastating downturn still lingered when the entire nation plummeted to the economic depths in the 1930s. Editors Greeley and Allen had to respond to the heightened expectations and the crushing disappointments, just as Bushnell had done a generation before.

The editors also had to confront the troubling changes in American culture that accelerated during this period and pushed rural people even closer to the margins. Twentieth-century farm families recognized that their entire way of life was under attack by the values of the modern, urban age. This sense of losing ground, the feeling that farm life was no longer a good life, became especially pronounced in the post–World War I period. The rise of radio and film, then the triumph of the automobile made American culture markedly different from what it had been before. Open hostility towards the "rubes," "hicks," and "hayseeds" of the countryside became common. Describing the conflict of urban and rural cultures after World War I, James Shideler noted that while rural values included tradition, individuality, morality, hard work, thrift, and self-denial, the rising urban value system embraced "innovation, experiment, and creativity." The city was "fluid, profane, impersonal, and permissive." The redefinition of the good things in life for the majority of Americans changed. For rural people, the good things had always been "food, clothing, shelter, serene security, independence, and righteousness." With the rise of modern urban culture, the good things became "the command of mechanical power, style, variety, mobility, novelty, and things." As Shideler points out, the urban "good things" all had to be purchased; money, not character, became the dominant value. In the years between 1900 and 1934, rural people flooded out of the countryside to join the brave new urban world. Shideler quotes Finley Peter Dunne's famous Mr. Dooley series to explain the exodus. Dooley and his rural friend Hogan chatted about the changing world, with Hogan maintaining that people "ought to live where all th' good things iv life comes fr'm." Dooley, the city man, replied: "No, th' place to live in is where all th' good things iv life goes to."[29]

Millard F. Greeley took the editor's chair upon Bushnell's death in 1900 and was the first to cope with twentieth-century climatic crises. Although Greeley promoted the acquisition of small farms as a way for the masses to gain independence, he did not promote a new land boom. The *Dakota Farmer* maintained the optimistic but responsible position Bushnell had developed after the failure of the Great Dakota Boom in 1889.

Greeley discounted the popular theory that the rain belt had moved permanently west (a faith plains residents frequently held that cultivation of the land and the planting of trees had changed the climate) and instead advocated a heavy emphasis on stock raising for those who did venture into western Dakota lands. Caution was the watchword. "Plan for the dry years, as well as wet," Greeley wrote, "and . . . go slow."[30] When West River advocates wrote in to complain about the *Farmer*'s lukewarm endorsement of their section, Greeley replied, "A country where cactus is perfectly at home cannot be farmed just the same as where clover grows. . . . [T]he poor man who thinks it can be, has something to learn and we are only interested in making the lesson cost him as little as possible."[31] For the next thirty years, the *Dakota Farmer* editorial page carried occasional reminders of the boom and bust cycles of Dakota history, always under the heading "Lest We Forget."[32]

Notwithstanding his cautious reminders, Greeley maintained the belief that someday, with the proper agricultural techniques, the western Dakotas would "carry a fair, and in some places a very heavy and prosperous people."[33] As part of its efforts to be a practical farmer's paper, the *Dakota Farmer* carried detailed accounts of the successes and failures of dry-farming, announced new techniques as farmers and experts devised them, and offered sound, cautionary advice to new and experienced farmers alike. Greeley believed that while dry-farming could not "reverse the laws of nature," it might, after years of experimentation, be a successful system. When these techniques were applied, he wrote, "much, though not all of our western country, is going to show encouraging results."[34]

When William C. Allen became the editor in 1910, a terrible drought year in the western Dakotas, he adopted a more boosterish tone. Although he did not make extravagant claims about the Dakotas as a new Garden of Eden, he did celebrate the land and its resources and, most of all, the commitment of the valiant people who resided there. He worked to create pride in what was and in what could be. For the next twenty-nine years, Allen promoted the Dakota spirit of optimism, confidence, and "never say die." He believed that attitude was everything, that while the Dakotas were confronted with problems, they could be conquered by the hardy folk in his audience. Their spirit, he wrote, was the kind "that makes a people great." He argued that the resources of the northern plains were sufficient to make the region "the wealthiest of empires"; the character of the people would make it so.[35] In February 1912 as the western Dakota land boom fizzled and died, Allen adopted a new appellation for the region—the Dakota Farmer Empire—and used it until his death in 1939. Allen constantly reminded his readers of the progress that they had made since the Great Dakota Boom of the 1870s and 1880s. Occasionally, the cover of the *Farmer* juxtaposed pictures of the spare sod home of pioneer days with the comfortable tree-shaded farm of the present. Other times, the lesson was taught in vivid prose. The message was clear—Dakotans have done

much and should be proud, but the best is yet to be. To Allen, the resources were there to be tapped; the right people with the right system
could conquer all.[36]

While the proper farming system was important to the success that
the *Dakota Farmer* editors envisioned, their use of the terms "system"
or "method" did not imply that the paper espoused one sure-fire plan
for agricultural success. Instead, the editors encouraged farmers to study
their own land carefully, learning its capabilities, and then devise a systematic routine for its care. What worked on one farm might not work on
another; therefore, farmers had to be experimental, well-read, and open-
minded. The emphasis in the *Dakota Farmer* continued to be modern, progressive farming techniques, diversified agriculture, and a happy, balanced
partnership within the farm home. The editors believed that those who
followed such scientific, as opposed to traditional, ways had the greatest
chance of success.

An ongoing feature in the *Dakota Farmer* during 1911 and 1912 illus-
trated the editors' commitment to teaching proper work skills, attitudes,
adapted crop techniques, and diversification. The series was entitled
"Dakota Farmer Diary" and included a daily diary entry (which was structured as a family conversation) from each of two farm families, the Does
Things and the Lucks. The families were neighbors, and as the series progressed, the Luck family learned by observing the techniques and the attitudes of the Does Things family. The tone in each piece was didactic.
For example, in one entry, Mrs. Does Things asked her husband to purchase oyster shells, a source of calcium, to feed the hens to improve the
quality of egg shells. She went on to explain why: "A hen is just like a man
or woman, they can't make something out of nothing. If we get eggs we
must furnish the hens, which are the machines, the material from which
to make them." In the Luck family, Mr. Luck always wanted to do the
wrong things, and the family had already lost its oldest son to town living because of the unfortunate circumstances of their farm life. Mrs. Luck
and the remaining son and daughter seemed eager to learn new ways and
chided Mr. Luck for his errors. In one entry, Mr. Luck was unhappy because his hogs were not ready for market when prices were high, and he
envied Mr. Does Right for having so many to sell. His son reminded him
of the reason their hogs were behind: "Ours got a poor start out there in
the straw stacks."[37]

After a year of this instructional series, the editors changed the for-
mat. They believed that the Luck family had learned so well by example
that the paper no longer needed to feature diary entries from them. Instead, the Does Things family continued to produce a diary, while the
Shiftless family began to write letters to the editor to support yet another
approach to the land. The first letter from Mr. Shiftless embodied all that
the *Dakota Farmer* editors found troubling about nonprogressive farmers.
Mr. Shiftless began by announcing that he was the fount of all agricultural

wisdom in his neighborhood, but his brief personal history revealed problems: "My father gave me a farm [in Massachusetts] but there couldn't nobody make a living on it, it was so poor. I moved to Illinois in 1890. . . . [W]hile all of my neighbors had good farms, mine wasn't so good, so I came west then to Minnesota and got a piece of cheap land. There wouldn't nothing but weeds grow on that farm 'cause it hadn't been farmed good before I got it. . . . I sold . . . that place and came out west here and homesteaded. . . . Now I am going to show these western fellows how to do things, because I come from the east." Mr. Shiftless went on to tell how he kept little stock because he expected prices to go down, did not feed his calves much nor milk his cows in winter, allowed his hens to roost in trees where they had frozen to death, kept only one sow who had become a chicken killer, did not maintain his tools because he had left them outside where they had frozen to the ground, and grew no corn because the yields were not as high as they were in Illinois. He said that he was considering some corn for next year, however, because his children would be old enough to stay home from school and pick it for him. Mr. Shiftless planned to stick largely with wheat because he could then avoid work in the winter, unlike his foolish neighbors, who were busy on the farm all year round. He also refused to subscribe to the *Dakota Farmer*. "There can't nobody tell me nothing about farming," he concluded.[38]

The missives from the Shiftless family continued for the next several months, each full of excuses, mistakes, and general hubris. In later years, the *Farmer* ran a similar instructional comparison written by Helen B. Russell of Golden Valley County, North Dakota. This one featured the McSticker and O'Shucks families. The message was the same—hard work, proper attitude, open minds, and correct technique led to success and satisfaction. The series implied that only poor farmers had complete failures on the farm. Most readers applauded the *Dakota Farmer*'s emphasis on system, method, and attitude. The "Dakota Farmer Diary" became one of the most popular features of the paper at the time, and the readers voted to continue it when editor Allen asked their opinion.[39]

As part of their ongoing drive to modernize the farm, the *Dakota Farmer* editors also advocated the equality of individuals within the family. They used the "Dakota Farmer Diary" as one means to convey the message. Mrs. Does Things, for example, told son Charlie to bring town friends home from church to visit. "This is a home for the whole family," she reminded him.[40] The Does Things sent two of their children to a short course at the agricultural college in Brookings, and the entire family sat down together and conferred about the direction of the farm and the work at the start of each year. Mrs. Does Things mentioned only once that her stove was worn out; Mr. Does Things took her to town the next day to buy a new one. Even the Luck family recognized the need for proper family relationships. Mrs. Luck insisted that they borrow an extra fifty dollars from the bank, since they had to borrow anyway, to buy new clothes for the children to help halt their growing discouragement with farm life. The children were thrilled and appreciative of their parents' sacrifice and vowed to work hard to make the farm a going concern.[41]

Mr. Shiftless, on the other hand, described his wife as someone "who don't count for much" and snorted at the thought that she demanded some credit for raising their seven children. His children were a trial to him. He had to scold them and even "lick" them to get them to work, but he was proud to say that he was "certainly boss around here and no one questions it." The editor wrote back to Mr. Shiftless on occasion, and this letter about the children brought his ire. "You may be boss of the kids but are you master of yourself?" the editor asked, concluding: "It does not take much of a man to drive a child around, particularly when as you say, he 'licks' them occasionally. Any fool can do that. All cowards do it. . . . Our sympathies are with your children. They are not mules to be driven but human beings to be consulted and reasoned with and developed."[42]

While modern techniques and egalitarian family relations helped lay a strong foundation for an attractive farm life, the *Dakota Farmer* editors recognized that these were not enough to combat the overwhelming attractiveness of the city. They had to create an argument for the basic value of rural life. They did so with the concept of community. In the face of depersonalization and dreams imported from distant places, they reminded their readers of the solid foundations of rural life—family, friends, and community living in righteousness, independence, and harmony.

The very nature of the *Dakota Farmer*, depending as it did on first-person experiences, emphasized the concept of community. The publication had a personal tone that other farm papers did not have. Farmers wrote in with building or implement designs, offering them to others who might wish to duplicate them to save money or time, or they wrote to warn others of new diseases among their stock or of dangerous feeds. Others wrote to share techniques on the eradication of weeds or successes with certain crops. Sometimes they needed advice and asked other readers for help with a problem. Because women were usually in charge of poultry production on the farm, they also wrote frequently about problems and successes. Farm women and occasionally farm men wrote in to advise readers about such family matters as child-rearing and the division of labor in the home. Any letter that presented a problem or appeared to reveal a disheartened spirit prompted lengthy replies from subscribers eager to help someone else out of a rut.[43]

Editor Greeley emphasized to subscribers that their contributions really mattered. "When our experience can benefit others," he wrote, "we are public benefactors and state makers."[44] In 1918, the Home Department began a column called "Help One Another," which became an extremely popular forum for questions and answers on a wide variety of household problems from cooking to the eradication of bed bugs. The editorial page picked up the "Help One Another" theme and incorporated it into editorial notes as the guiding light of the *Dakota Farmer* and of community feeling. For several years, editor Allen urged readers to "Get acquainted with your neighbor, you might like him" and often concluded his remarks with "Be a good neighbor yourself."[45]

The paper itself became the focus of community feeling. At a time when other agricultural journals (and newspapers generally) became standardized, impersonal, and detached from their audience, the *Farmer's* personal, folksy style, its invitations to readers to visit the *Dakota Farmer* staff in Aberdeen, its open and unabashed interest in the daily lives of Dakotans, all made it a force for unity and common endeavor. The editors and associate editors even received personal correspondence and answered it themselves. In 1918, Greeley, then an associate editor with a column entitled "All Around the Farm," featured a sample of his personal mail in his column. One woman wrote about the landscape, another told of aiding a poor neighbor at Christmas, and another provided a detailed description of her sixth child.[46] Alfred Wenz, a popular field editor, quoted a letter written to him by a woman who had moved to the deep South with her husband and was homesick for Dakota and the *Dakota Farmer*. Wenz printed his reply: "Even though you have gone south, you are still in the Dakota Farmer Empire in spirit. . . . We feel that we have an outlying section of the Dakota Farmer Empire down your way."[47]

The warm personal tone encouraged readers to write in as if to family members. Many correspondents saw fellow readers as neighbors and friends, although they never met. As one woman wrote during an unexpected leisurely afternoon, "my thoughts went out to my other neighbors—my Dakota Farmer neighbors—who, though many miles away, are brought so close through its pages." On occasion a letter might note that it was almost midnight after a busy day, yet the writer wanted to take time to share thoughts with the *Dakota Farmer* family before retiring.[48] Proud of this role as community center, the *Dakota Farmer* worked hard to be of service to its readers and asked its readers to serve each other with the same joy and commitment. By working together, with the aid and the vision of the *Dakota Farmer* to guide them, farm families could create an appealing, harmonious world in sharp contrast to the ugly, impersonal city.[49]

The clearest expression of the *Dakota Farmer* themes of community, modernization within a rural context, and boosterish promotion of the Dakota spirit and character came in the "Everything I Want is Here!" advertising series that began in November 1926 and ran until 15 December 1931. Editor Allen explained the series as the fruition of the faith that the *Dakota Farmer* personnel had always maintained. "We believe," he wrote, "that the . . . great Dakota Farmer Empire offers everything any kind or class of folks can possibly want."[50] In another issue, he explained, "We want to build up in the two Dakotas a great, big neighborly community— a community where everybody knows everybody else to the extent of at least knowing the other fellow's problems and his knowing yours."[51] The series was made up of one- and two-page advertisements demonstrating the interdependence of Dakota farms and businesses and calling for cooperation and harmony among Dakota people generally. The first one described the Dakotas as a "vast empire in area and in gold, yet a self-contained, self-sustaining, interdependent *community* in thought and business.[52]

The advertisements that followed urged readers to get acquainted with area merchants, to trade at home, and to join hands in empire building. Cooperation was the watchword. "In fairness to your own self—your own interests—you should do all you can to build this fine neighborhood. . . . It is community cooperation that will make the Dakotas a better place in which to live.[53] In a 1927 installment, the editors proclaimed: "Now is the time to sow seeds of good will. Help your neighbor. . . . Boost the Dakotas and reap the great harvest of plenty that is sure to grow where there is whole-hearted community cooperation.[54]

The aim of the "Everything I Want is Here" campaign was to convince Dakotans that they had enough material comforts in Dakota and that conditions, having improved greatly in a generation, would continue to improve. In other words, the goal was "to sell ourselves to ourselves." One advertisement featured an elderly woman who compared her life on the farm with her daughter's life. Hers had been far more difficult—" 'Everything I want (was not) here then," but, the promotion continued, "the desire to have, intelligent planning and willingness to work" could win the comforts that improved farm life. "Know what you want—then go after it! . . . 'Everything I Want is Here'—if I want it sufficiently!" The piece concluded with a verbal drum roll: "Nowhere do the farms and farm homes average better—Nowhere do you find better farmers . . . Nowhere such a community spirit—Nowhere more contentment."[55]

The advent of the Great Depression changed the conditions under which the "Everything I Want" campaign was waged. Because the early years of the depression in the Dakotas did not bring the visible bread lines and occasional violence that occurred in urban areas of the United States, the national economic disaster gave editor Allen an opportunity for a fuller praise of the Dakota way of life. In January 1931, before severe drought destroyed the Dakota economy and made day-to-day survival precarious, Allen wrote a paean to agriculture and the Dakota spirit. He reminded his readers: "All Dakotans, of whatever manner of livelihood, finally must stand or fall together. . . . In Dakota, that has always been understood. With no great cities to confuse vision, and with but one great common industry, every man here has known the soil as the first source of new wealth. Farming and business together faced 'deflation' 10 years ago. Together they have spent a decade reshaping their common fortunes. . . . [The] Dakota situation today is comparatively better than elsewhere." The page concluded, as all of the advertisements did, with "Everything I Want is Here!" written in bold, clear type.[56]

As drought and depression became universal in 1931, it became clear that "Everything I Want" was not in the Dakotas of the 1930s. On one occasion, Allen reprinted a letter he had received from a disgruntled reader that concluded "Everything I Want is Here—if what I want is trouble!

Bah!"[57] The series faded and died in December 1931 with no public explanation or farewell. The ironies had been too obvious for several months.
By December 1934, 39 percent of the population of South Dakota was on
relief; 50 percent of South Dakota's farm population received aid in that
same month. South Dakota had a higher percentage of its population on relief than any other state in the Union. North Dakota had the second highest percentage. Real estate values in South Dakota plummeted 58 percent
between 1920 and 1930; by 1934, 71 percent of all South Dakota banks
had failed. In North Dakota in 1933, the annual per capita income was
$145, less than half the United States average. Over 121,000 people left
North Dakota in the 1930s; the farm population was hardest hit by the
loss, with over 17 percent of the agricultural population departing the
state. Only the New Deal relief programs and the Agricultural Adjustment
Administration allotment payments permitted many rural Dakotans to
hang on.[58]

Allen was not without ideas for a new promotional campaign, however. Although not invested with the formal design that the "Everything
I Want" campaign had featured, the ideas and goals that Allen promoted
in his regular columns were nevertheless clear. Allen worked vigorously
to build courage and hope in troubled times. He frequently harked back to
the pioneer past and the history of trials met and overcome by a hardy
Dakota people. He reported on the spirit that he saw around him. When
earlier Dakotans had faced drought, he wrote, they said, "So be it, . . . we
will get along as best we can; . . . we may have to dig in as did those who
came before us into this new country; we may have to endure severe hardships—but we will carry on."[59] According to Allen, his readers met the
future with confidence and optimism. "It's going to rain!" said a farmer
to Allen. "What makes you think so?" Allen asked. "Because it always
has," the reader replied.[60] When a shower did fall, Allen recorded the happiness he saw around him. "What a resilient lot we Dakotans are!" he
wrote. " 'Hope springs eternal in the human breast'—and nowhere more
so than in Dakota."[61]

Allen also suggested practical ways for Dakotans to survive hard
times. His five-step program involved hard work and proper attitude. First,
he recommended that farmers "dig in." "I don't have to tell you what that
means," he wrote; "old timers here who ground wheat in a coffee mill and
burned buffalo chips . . . knew what it was to 'dig in' and by so doing they
dug out again." His second point was equally succinct. "Make your head
save your back," he wrote; "these times require hard work—but it should
be intelligent work." Third, he advocated putting the farm into the best
possible shape for crop raising. "Next year may be THE year. . . . [T]he old
principle of making two blades of grass grow where one grew before will
help the individual farmer just as it always has." Fourth, Allen suggested
that farmers get together—cooperate—to improve their economic situation and place in American life. "I know that from past experience this
seems almost impossible," he wrote, but it was necessary for agricultural

success. Finally, Allen told his readers not to become discouraged; while agriculture was suffering, it could be worse.[62]

Initially willing to give Franklin D. Roosevelt and his New Deal an opportunity to succeed, Allen ultimately rejected the planned economy and government management of agriculture that the New Deal aid programs represented. To him, the power of the optimistic, hardworking individual could overcome any difficulty, no matter how daunting. The problems of the 1930s were certainly daunting, but Allen was too much a product of his time and place, too much imbued with the glorious, even mythical struggle of Dakotans to conquer the land, to change his ideological stance.

In 1931, the *Dakota Farmer* celebrated its fiftieth anniversary. At the time, editor Allen commented that while he had always heard that "the first hundred years are the hardest," he was most interested in "the comparative hardships of the first 50 years and the second 50." He went on to describe his faith. "While conditions are not so good just now, I firmly believe that the Dakotas are on the threshold of substantial and permanent progress; that our farming population will grow in numbers and prosperity, that those who are to follow the pioneers will reap richly from the efforts of those who have gone before."[63] Circumstances during the remaining years of his life, of course, belied that vision. Yet, until his death in 1939, Allen's faith never faltered. At Christmas time during the 1930s, he frequently urged his struggling readers to leave a light in their window on Christmas Eve. "It will hearten you to know," he wrote, "that it may bring hope to some weary wayfarer."[64] At a later Christmas season he wrote, "A light in the window. . . . Few so poor, that a light of some kind cannot be provided to send out rays of hope to all who may see it—the hope of better, brighter days."[65] For many in the Dakotas, the *Dakota Farmer* was the figurative light in the window, providing inspiration, education, and community in good times and bad.

NOTES

1. The Great Dakota Boom attracted thousands of eager homesteaders to the region between 1878 and 1887. In 1870, the population of all Dakota was 12,887. By 1890, the population of North Dakota stood at 191,000, and that of South Dakota at 328,808. For more information on the Dakota boom, see Elwyn B. Robinson, *History of North Dakota* (Lincoln: University of Nebraska Press, 1966), pp. 133–73, and Herbert S. Schell, *History of South Dakota*, 3d ed., rev. (Lincoln: University of Nebraska Press, 1975), pp. 158–88.

2. James F. Evans and Rodolfo N. Salcedo, *Communications in Agriculture: The American Farm Press* (Ames: Iowa State University Press, 1974), pp. 3–5; *Dakota Farmer*, 23 Dec. 1933, front page. Allen told his readers that the paper had 96,410 subscribers, 93,248 of them in the Dakotas.

3. The silver anniversary issue of the *Dakota Farmer*, 1 Jan. 1906, pp. 3–6, explains the history and philosophy of the paper, as does a lengthy piece by W. C. Allen entitled, "Why is The *Dakota Farmer*?: Facts in Reference to Dakota's Home Farm Paper," in the 1 Dec. 1909 edition, pp. 24–27. See also another Allen piece in the 15 Dec.

1912 issue, pp. 1122–23. Allen wrote such articles throughout his career. Bushnell used the term "farmer's paper" in 1900. See the issue of 1 May 1900, p. 8, for example. Allen used the phrase consistently and explained the concept in the 15 Jan. 1913 edition, p. 83, as well as the 6 Aug. 1932 paper, p. 395, and the front page of the 29 Oct. 1932 issue. The "Message from Home" appeared on 15 July 1909, p. 9. In June 1918, the paper began to distribute buttons to subscribers to identify them as members of the *Dakota Farmer* family (see 15 June issue).

4. *Dakota Farmer*, Apr. 1884, pp. 3–4.

5. Schell, *History of South Dakota*, pp. 343–44; Robinson, *History of North Dakota*, p. 153.

6. *Dakota Farmer*, 1 June 1890, p. 9, 1 Nov. 1890, p. 8, 1 Oct. 1891, p. 8, 1 June 1893, p. 8, 15 Jan. 1894, p. 8, 1 Jan. 1895, p. 9. Bushnell also created two special irrigation editions on 1 May 1891 and 1 Nov. 1895. Schell, *History of South Dakota*, pp. 344–45, briefly explains the history of the irrigation movement.

7. *Dakota Farmer*, 1 June 1898, p. 8.

8. Ibid., 15 May 1898, p. 8, 15 Feb. 1894, p. 8.

9. Ibid., 15 Dec. 1893, p. 8.

10. Ibid., 1 Dec. 1893, p. 8.

11. Ibid., 1 Dec. 1896, p. 8.

12. Ibid., 15 June 1900, p. 8.

13. Carl N. Degler, *The Age of the Economic Revolution, 1876–1900*, 2d ed. (Glenview, Ill.: Scott, Foresman & Co., 1977), pp. 1–3, 66–70; Paul W. Glad, *McKinley, Bryan, and the People* (Philadelphia: J. B. Lippincott Co., 1964), pp. 32–50.

14. David Danbom, *The Resisted Revolution: Urban America and the Industrialization of Agriculture, 1900–1930* (Ames: Iowa State University Press, 1979), pp. 3–22. Danbom is one historian who contends that farm families were tradition-bound. Roderick Cameron, *Pioneer Days in Kansas: A Homesteader's Narrative of Early Settlement and Farm Development on the High Plains Country of Northwest Kansas* (Belleville, Kans.: Cameron Book Co., 1951), pp. xiii–xviii, also describes his pioneer neighbors in Kansas as traditional and suspicious of change. Other writers argue that farmers were a diverse lot, with many being quite progressive. See Sally McMurry, *Families and Farmhouses in Nineteenth-Century America: Vernacular Design and Social Change* (New York: Oxford University Press, 1988), pp. 56–59, 82n.4. Steven Mintz and Susan Kellogg, *Domestic Revolutions: A Social History of American Family Life* (New York: Free Press, 1988), pp. 43–65, 113–31, explain the rise of the "democratic" family. William L. Bowers, *The Country Life Movement in America, 1900–1920* (Port Washington, N.Y.: Kennikat Press, 1974), pp. 7–30, discusses the rural crisis and the development of a reform movement to combat it.

15. *Dakota Farmer*, 15 Apr. 1892, p. 8.

16. Ibid., 15 Sept. 1898, p. 8.

17. Ibid., Sept. 1884, pp. 1–2, Oct. 1884, pp. 1–4.

18. Ibid., 1 Nov. 1893, p. 8.

19. Ibid., July 1884, p. 8.

20. Ibid., Nov. 1884, p. 7.

21. Ibid., Feb. 1885, p. 4.

22. Ibid., Jan. 1888, p. 8.

23. Ibid., July 1889, p. 13.

24. During the 1920s, the *Farmer* editors supported the McNary/Haugen Bill for farm price aid and also endorsed the Federal Farm Board during the Hoover years, but they did not do so as partisan political advocates but as spokesmen for an impartial, apolitical farmer's voice that transcended party. When W. C. Allen ran for governor of South Dakota on the Republican ticket in 1934, he made no mention of his campaign or his loss to Tom Berry in the *Dakota Farmer* columns. For examples of farm-policy editorials, see *Dakota Farmer*, 15 Feb. 1926, p. 207, 15 July 1926, p. 684, and 15 Aug. 1929, pp. 812–14.

25. Ibid., 1 Jan. 1890, p. 8, 15 Oct. 1893, p. 8, 15 Dec. 1899, p. 8, 1 Jan. 1895, p. 8, 1 June 1897, p. 8, 1 Jan. 1906, pp. 4–5.

26. Ibid., 1 Jan. 1900, p. 8.

27. *Aberdeen Daily News*, 25, 27, 28, 30 Aug. 1900.

28. For a discussion of the boom in western South Dakota, see Paula M. Nelson, *After the West was Won: Homesteaders and Town-Builders in Western South Dakota, 1900–1917* (Iowa City: University of Iowa Press, 1986). Dry-farming was the name given to the efforts to conduct unirrigated agriculture in semiarid regions. Hardy Webster Campbell, a farmer in Brown County in southern Dakota Territory, developed and publicized the techniques that came to be known as dry-farming. To Campbell and other dry-farming advocates, it seemed as if a way had been discovered to triumph over contentious nature on the plains, and the faithful promoted the method with religious fervor. Campbell had the basic concept right—that farmers had to conserve moisture to succeed. Early methods, however, were actually counterproductive. Campbell's deep plowing and loose surface mulch led to wind erosion in dry years. Over time, the agricultural experiment stations in the plains states developed more effective techniques, including minimal tillage, summer fallow, trashy fallow, and drought-resistant crops. Scientific agriculturalists believed that Campbell and other dry-farming advocates were mere promoters, tools of the railroads and land companies eager to settle the plains no matter the cost to settlers. See Mary Wilma M. Hargreaves, *Dry Farming in the Northern Great Plains, 1900–1925* (Cambridge, Mass.: Harvard University Press, 1957), pp. 1, 85–93, 537–47; *Dakota Farmer*, 1 Sept. 1907, p. 1, 15 Nov. 1909, pp. 20–21, 15 July 1910, p. 12; and Carl E. Kraenzel, *The Great Plains in Transition* (Norman: University of Oklahoma Press, 1955), pp. 308–16.

29. James H. Shideler, "Flappers and Philosophers, and Farmers: Rural–Urban Tensions of the Twenties," in *The Great Plains Experience: Readings in the History of a Region*, ed. James E. Wright and Sarah Z. Rosenberg (Lincoln: University of Mid-America, 1978), pp. 339–40.

30. *Dakota Farmer*, 15 July 1906, p. 10.

31. Ibid., 15 Aug. 1906, pp. 3–4.

32. Ibid., 15 July 1906, p. 11, 15 July 1909, p. 6.

33. Ibid., 15 Feb. 1910, p. 16.

34. Ibid., 15 July 1910, p. 12.

35. Ibid., 15 Nov. 1911, p. 1178.

36. Ibid., 15 Feb. 1912, p. 202. See the covers of the 1 Mar. 1918 and 1 Feb. 1907 issues.

37. Ibid., 1 Nov. 1911, p. 1120.

38. Ibid., 15 Jan. 1912, p. 64d. See also the 15 Feb. 1912 issue, p. 192.

39. Ibid., 15 Jan. 1912, p. 66. For an example of the McSticker family story, see the 15 May 1929 issue, pp. 570–71. Occasionally, the *Dakota Farmer's* perennial optimism and emphasis on personal responsibility could be frustrating. In a letter to the paper in 1912, a Moody County farmer noted that he had tried to follow the *Farmer's* instructions on sowing seed corn but the weather conditions during the early growing season had nullified the advice. He knew, he wrote, that the editors never accepted the excuse that the season was to blame, it was always the farmers' poor technique at fault. It "was no fault of the season," he thought the *Farmer* experts would say. "Had we only conserved the moisture in the spring of 1911, although there was none to conserve, or had we planted our grain fields on the north side of our corn fields, and better still had we planted a grove of trees on the south side of our fields twenty years ago . . . we would have raised a crop. . . . So don't tell me the season was to blame." A. E. Chamberlain responded to the frustrated farmer with words of praise for his abilities to think for himself and speak out on important issues. Chamberlain reminded him, however, that the *Dakota Farmer* had to supply general advice for a widely dispersed readership; farmers had to be responsible for its application according to the conditions in their localities. Ibid., 1 Oct. 1912, p. 842.

40. Ibid., 1 Nov. 1911, p. 1120.

41. Ibid., 15 Nov. 1911, p. 1176, 15 Jan. 1912, p. 64d. Editor Greeley always wrote sympathetically of the importance of women's role. In 1915, he commented that men would change their ways if they had to do their wives' work for six months (1 Jan. 1915, p. 1178).

42. Ibid., 15 Mar. 1912, p. 346.

43. Examples appear in most issues of the *Dakota Farmer*, especially after 1900.

44. Ibid., 1 Nov. 1906, p. 21.

45. Ibid., 1 Feb. 1931, p. 145, explains the twenty-year effort to promote neighborliness, and the slogan appeared frequently in the *Farmer*. The "Help One Another" column was suggested by a reader; it began on 15 Sept. 1918.

46. Ibid., 15 Mar. 1918, p. 436. Evans and Salcedo, *Communications in Agriculture*, pp. 34–35, and Sally Foreman Griffith, *Home Town News: William Allen White and the "Emporia Gazette"* (New York: Oxford University Press, 1989), pp. 211–39, explain in detail the changes that remade local journalism in the first decades of the twentieth century.

47. *Dakota Farmer*, 1 Mar. 1918, p. 364.

48. Ibid., 1 Sept. 1918, p. 1059.

49. The *Dakota Farmer* had a service department that answered agricultural and homemaking questions by personal letter at no charge to paid-up subscribers. In times of trouble, the paper did more. In 1917 and 1918 when stock feed was scarce, the *Dakota Farmer* acted as a clearinghouse to connect farmers with extra feed to those without feed, again for no charge. In 1914, the *Dakota Farmer* had a column called the "Sunshine Corner" in which aid to the poor could be solicited. The editor of the Home Department forwarded donations to the needy parties. Again in 1921, when many farm families were suffering severely due to the depression in agriculture, the Home Department editor invited families with extra clothing to send it to her and she would forward it to needy families who requested aid. See issues of 1 Jan. 1910, 15 Dec. 1914, 1 Sept., 1 Nov. 1917, 1 Aug. 1918, and 1 Jan. 1922.

50. Ibid., 1 Oct. 1926, p. 868.

51. Ibid., 1 Jan. 1927, p. 20.

52. Ibid., 1 Nov. 1926, pp. 956–57.

53. Ibid., 15 Feb. 1927, p. 169. The other themes are reflected in the issues of 1 Nov. 1926, p. 993, 1 Dec. 1926, p. 1031, and 15 Jan. 1927, p. 55.

54. Ibid., 15 Aug. 1927, p. 699.

55. Ibid., 15 July 1928, p. 719.

56. Ibid., 15 Jan. 1931, p. 66.

57. Ibid., 19 Mar. 1932, p. 141.

58. Schell, *History of South Dakota*, pp. 281–93; Robinson, *History of North Dakota*, pp. 400–401.

59. *Dakota Farmer*, 23 June 1934, cover.

60. Ibid., 26 May 1934, p. 244.

61. Ibid., 12 May 1934, p. 220.

62. Ibid., 2 Sept. 1933, p. 236.

63. Ibid., 1 Jan. 1931, p. 17.

64. Ibid., 15 Dec. 1930, p. 1077.

65. Ibid., 22 Dec. 1934, p. 516. That the *Dakota Farmer* staff saw themselves as a light to guide the community is indicated by an advertisement in the "Everything I Want is Here" series that included a full page of excerpts from readers' letters thanking them for services, advice, and courage. The title of the installment was "A lamp unto my feet and a light unto my path" (Feb. 1931, p. 125).

PART IV

THE
TWENTIETH
CENTURY

12

"THE MEN HAVE BECOME ORGANIZERS": LABOR CONFLICT AND UNIONIZATION IN THE MEXICAN MINING COMMUNITIES OF ARIZONA, 1900–1915

Phil Mellinger

Compared to the efforts of cowboys to unionize, western miners created a much more extensive set of labor organizations, and on many—though by no means all—occasions they succeeded in winning better wages, hours, and working conditions from mine owners. One of the greatest difficulties that industrial miners had to overcome in these efforts, aside from the bitter resistance of the corporations that owned the mines, was the ethnic division between Mexican mine workers and "Anglos"—a term that in fact included several mutually suspicious ethnic groups. Italian, Greek, Serb, and other south-European miners often felt discriminated against by miners from Ireland, England, or elsewhere in northern Europe. Mine managers understood these divisions and often used them as wedges to divide and conquer. The fundamental issue was whether "race" would divide workers, instead of "class," which should have united them against oppressive capitalist owners. "Race," however, meant something different and broader then than it does now. At that time, did it mean anything different from "ethnicity"? (And what does—or should—either term have to do with color?)

Between 1896 and 1915, according to Mellinger, "the great chasm" of "ethnic and racial divisiveness . . . was effectively bridged" among copper miners in the Southwest. How did that work? How did miners' efforts improve as they gradually bridged that chasm? In 1917, in their most famous defeat, 2,000 striking copper miners being organized by the Industrial Workers of the World at Bisbee, Arizona, were loaded on a train and shipped eastward across the New Mexico desert, where (according to historian Carlos Schwantes) "the deportees were simply abandoned." Probably half were foreign-born, and perhaps a quarter were Mexican. At other times, however, they did better. How does Mellinger relate ethnic unity to worker success?—editors

MEXICAN IMMIGRANTS and Mexican Americans began joining the United States southwestern copper industry labor force in the late nineteenth and early twentieth centuries. The copper industry and the railroads were the Southwest's industrial giants. Arizona was then becoming the most important metal mining state south of Montana, and its unskilled and semi-skilled industrial work force was predominantly immigrant (including many Europeans) and Mexican Americans. The Mexican and Mexican American workers in Arizona were performing difficult and dangerous tasks in the mines, mills, and smelters, often for inadequate wages. Toward 1915, many of the workers were joining labor unions and striking for better wages and improved working conditions.

According to the conventional explanation of labor organizing in the southwestern Mexican mining areas, an industrial labor movement began in early twentieth century organizing campaigns, grew large enough to include Mexican immigrants, Mexican Americans, and European immigrants, and then, just as it began to succeed, the movement fell prey to the combined First World War business and government counterreaction of 1917–1918. An implicit paradigm of growth supports this interpretation. In the paradigm, everything seems to lead to the 1917–1918 labor wars.

Growth explanations of the Mexican accession to American unionism either begin with the union confederations, or with the Mexican communities themselves. The two union confederations that conducted organizing drives among Arizona Mexicans and Mexican Americans before the First World War were the Western Federation of Miners (later called the International Union of Mine, Mill, and Smelter Workers), and the Industrial Workers of the World (IWW). Institutional histories of those organizations credit them with some degree of success in 1917.[1] Also, southwestern Mexican communities were internally organized. Beginning about 1900, there were fraternal societies, sickness-and-benefit societies (mutualistas), and community-based clubs with political connections to revolutionary activity in Mexico. Historians of Mexican revolutionary political activity credit these clubs and societies with labor-organizing success.[2] Both sets of explanations end with a 1917 climax treatment of Arizona labor history that is most convincingly presented in James Byrkit's standard work, Forging the Copper Collar: Arizona's Labor-Management War, 1901–1921. In his book, Byrkit explains Arizona labor relations from 1901 as a series of events that led to the Bisbee Deportation, an inevitable dramatic showdown in the union-breaking activities at Bisbee in the summer of 1917.[3]

This essay explains Arizona labor relations from 1901–1917 differently. There were frequent, intermittent labor organizational and strike activities both in Arizona and in other copper areas throughout the Southwest, beginning before 1900 and continuing after 1917. The Bisbee Deportation, and even the general counterreaction of 1917–1918, were two incidents in a sequential series of events, the most significant of which occurred in 1915. The question partially resolved at Miami, Ray, and Clifton–Morenci, Arizona, in 1915 was: Could the large Mexican and Mexican American copper industry work force, and to a lesser extent, the large immigrant European work force, be included within an organized labor movement in Arizona; alternatively, could the organized labor movement successfully *exclude* them and achieve its goals by reinforcing caste barriers against them?[4]

Universal inclusion is one of the great themes in all of United States labor history. During the first half of this century, many of the barriers based upon skill level, gender, ethnicity, and race fell away, and most of the United States working population gained access to potential affiliation with unionized labor. Mexican and European immigrant adherence to ethnically-based societies in the Southwest often, although not always, preceded their adherence to Western Federation of Miners unionism. But the WFM became a part of the American Federation of Labor in 1911, and in a sense, the AFL was the only game in town. American Federation of Labor union affiliates could provide their locals with access to the big, mainstream group of AFL unions, with their many connections to business and government and their ample funding and labor movement respectability. Joining the WFM meant joining the only strong metal-mining labor organization in the Southwest, both before and immediately after 1911; after 1911, it meant joining the mainstream of American organized labor as well.[5] There were advantages for Mexicans and Mexican Americans in joining organized labor. But the road to union affiliation was a rough one.

The series of events that led to the 1915 breakthrough began in 1896, at Globe, in Gila County, about halfway between the Clifton–Morenci area and Phoenix. Globe miners struck the Old Dominion mines that summer because management had reduced their wages. Most of the Globe strikers were Anglo or Irish Americans. S. A. Parnell, the newly hired Old Dominion superintendent, was known as a "Mexican pusher," and he intended to replace the striking miners with Mexicans or Mexican Americans. The enraged Anglo miners won the strike, and they forced the Old Dominion's owners to replace the hated Parnell.[6] Unionization came to Globe because of this strike, but it came by the back door. The mob that threatened Parnell made itself into a miners' union of one hundred twenty-five members. The miners contacted the new Western Federation of Miners for assistance. They got it. Ed Boyce, then the WFM's president, came to Globe, and soon Globe had the first Arizona WFM local, number 60, with about three hundred members. Globe also became, in reputation if not in fact, a white man's camp: a town in which relatively few or no perceived members of non-white ethnic groups could comfortably reside.[7] The angry crowd that instituted Globe Miners' Union's long and checkered career had ineluctably connected Arizona racism to unionism.

At Ray, Arizona, about twenty miles south of Globe, the situation was reversed. When Mexican and Mexican American workers struck there in 1900, management threatened that "hereafter . . . white miners will be employed exclusively."[8] Farther south at Pearce in Cochise County in 1901, a copper company fired an entire shift at a small mine because the men had begun to organize themselves into a miners' union. The company

announced that it would "probably make a Mexican camp of" Pearce.[9] At
Jerome, in Yavapai County, trouble began ten months later when the
United Verde Copper Company responded to a series of workers' com-
plaints by sending a carload of Mexican miners to Jerome.[10] But,

> they were en route . . . when the train reached a bridge underneath
> which had been placed a charge of dynamite, and but for a prema-
> ture explosion the entire train would have been blown to atoms.
>
> The car was backed down to Jerome Junction and that train with
> the Mexicans never came to camp.[11]

Ethnic trouble was a concomitant of labor conflict activity during the
next several years. Arizona WFM unionists began to divide on the ethnic
question in 1902. The locals at Jerome and Kofa (an acronym for the "King
of Arizona" gold mine) began recruiting Mexican mining workers in mid-
1902, encouraged to do so by J. T. Lewis, an old Arizona hand who had
become a WFM national executive board member.

Internal warfare broke out in the Globe local in September of 1902
over a constellation of issues connected to the ethnic question. Mining
company management and the Globe business community, including a
well-connected ex-mayor named George W. P. Hunt, backed the conservative miners against the radicals.[12] The winning conservatives signed a formal contract with copper company management that froze wages and
working conditions and sanctioned blacklisting. Miners who had made
wage demands, those who opposed the blacklist, and those who supported
ethnically inclusive unionism were all soundly defeated, and some of
them were forced out of town. Mexican American strikers who had sought
J. T. Lewis's help were refused access to union assistance at Globe. The
Anglo and Irish inclusionists soon lost at Kofa and Jerome too, and they
settled into disgruntled minority status for the next few years. In 1903,
the WFM national convention censured the Globe Miner's Union because
of its contract and because of its treatment of the minority faction the previous year.[13]

"Radical" and "conservative" were descriptive terminologies used by
members of the early WFM to delineate two opposing viewpoints within
the miners' union confederation. In 1902, WFM radicals generally supported extending the eight-hour day to a greater proportion of the work
force and vigorously opposed blacklisting. Some, but by no means all, radicals supported ethnic inclusionism. Conservatives were generally uninter-
ested rather than directly opposed to the radicals' stand on these issues,
but were opposed to the publication of lists of pro-union merchants (fair
lists), boycotts, and strikes in support of radical causes. The early twentieth century WFM miners did not generally espouse a fully developed, universally applicable radical ideology, despite the name given to those among
them who fought hardest for the WFM cause. Alan Dawley's book, *Class*

and Community, offers a similar cautionary note about the notion of working class radicalism. Dawley's study of nineteenth century workers' lives in Lynn, Massachusetts, concludes that "American wage earners can hardly be described as committed doctrinaires of class struggle. Taking tough-as-nails stands on economic battlefields is not the same thing as radical class consciousness."[14]

The biggest of all of the early twentieth-century Mexican versus Anglo labor confrontations was the great strike at Clifton–Morenci–Metcalf in 1903. Clifton, then a part of Graham County in eastern Arizona, smelted most of the copper ore from the nearby Morenci area. Morenci and neighboring Metcalf were mostly "Mexican towns," situated on copper company land near the Arizona, Detroit, and Shannon Copper Company mines high above Clifton. Morenci was a big company town, Metcalf a much smaller agglomeration of shacks and small houses. The two largest copper operators, the Arizona Company and the Detroit Company, were both managed by the James, Lewis, and Walter Douglas family and were affiliates of the Phelps–Dodge Corporation.

Trouble began at Clifton–Morenci when the Arizona territorial legislature passed an eight-hour law in 1903. The law stipulated that the maximum allowable shift time for underground mining workers was to be eight hours, beginning on 1 June 1903. Clifton–Morenci's Arizona and Detroit Copper Mining Company mines were the only big extractive operations in all of Arizona Territory that employed large numbers of exceptionally low-wage underground mining workers on ten–hour shifts in 1903. The two companies were also the largest employers of non-Anglo industrial labor in all of Arizona. The eight-hour law was deliberately aimed at the Clifton–Morenci copper companies, in the spirit of closed shop unionism. Its intent was to force the corporations to surrender the special advantages that they had accrued through the abuse of their immigrant work force, and to coerce the work force into either accepting Anglo and wage and hour standards, or quitting their jobs.[15]

The copper companies refused to obey the spirit of the new law, but they offered a last minute compromise. They offered "to pay underground men nine hours' pay for eight hours work."[16] The company's offer was a pay raise if calculated on an hourly basis, but it was actually a ten percent pay *cut* when calculated on a *daily* basis, which was the only meaningful calculation for the poorly paid Italian, Mexican, and Mexican American workingmen at Clifton–Morenci. The strike began on the morning of 1 June.[17]

There were about 3,500 strikers, according to one hostile Clifton resident. "It made a pretty big crowd—mostly Mexicans, but a lot of Dagoes, Bohunks, and foreigners of different kinds . . . no whites at all."[18] "Mexicans," which may have meant immigrant Mexicans, U.S. born men of Hispanic ancestry and even immigrant Spaniards, were probably a majority of the men on strike. Most of the other strikers were Italian immigrants.[19] Together, they constituted an overwhelming physical presence. Photo-

13. Strikers at the copper mines of Morenci, Arizona,
May–June 1903. *Arizona Historical Society/Tucson,*
#58785.

graphs of the scene show strikers, hundreds of them at a time, not only picketing, but occupying the mining properties. They stood on the streets, sat on railings, and leaned against buildings. Many were armed.[20]

Mexicans and Italians planned, led, and carried out the 1903 Clifton–Morenci strike entirely by themselves. Because there was no union activity associated with this big strike, it has been sometimes omitted from standard labor histories. It *is* included in studies of Mexican and Mexican American labor, and in histories of *La Raza* in the Southwest, but these generally err in another direction. They omit the Italian immigrants' important role in the 1903 strike. There is also the problem of the *mutualistas.*

Mutual sickness-and-benefit societies, of a type familiar in immigration history literature, and in Mexican American history in particular, were active in the Clifton–Morenci area when the big strike began. There were both Italian and Mexican and/or Mexican American societies at Clifton–Morenci in early 1903, and there was also a combined Mexican and Italian society in the Clifton district.[21] At least two months' worth of labor organizational activity preceded the strike, and some of these societies were a part of it.[22] Some of the leaders of the local ethnic societies were among the ten Mexican and Italian workingmen who were convicted of riot (though no riot occurred) and sent to Yuma Territorial Prison after the strike.[23]

Studies of *mutualistas* (Mexican and Mexican American mutual sickness-and-benefit societies) demonstrate that they sponsored a variety of social activities and that they tried to focus and exert political influence as well. But none of the *mutualista* studies has ever established the precise connection between *mutualistas* and specific labor organizing activity. Such connections certainly existed. At Clifton–Morenci in 1903, a mass of general evidence points to the connections between the Mexican and the Italian societies and labor activity there. But the evidence at Clifton–Morenci does not tell who organized the strike or when and how it was done. Understanding the Italian and Mexican societies may elucidate the process through which two distinct sets of ethnic workers combined their plans for a strike. That some of these societies were explicitly work-centered is demonstrable. A study of an Italian mutual society in a contemporary (1902) Utah coal camp indicates that it "functioned also as a labor union, expelling any of its members for scabbing."[24]

The 1903 Clifton area strike continued through June and into July. It was forcibly ended by a combination of local lawmen, Arizona Rangers, and U.S. cavalry dispatched by President Theodore Roosevelt. Meanwhile, the national convention delegates and officers of the Western Federation of Miners watched from the sidelines. Big strikes provided organizing opportunities, and the union confederation could have taken advantage of this one, but it did not. Big Bill Haywood received a wire at the WFM's Denver headquarters after the Clifton–Morenci–Metcalf strike had begun. It read, "One thousand men on strike in Morenci and vicinity, mostly Italians and Mexicans. . . . Good chance to organize. Received letter from Morenci today requesting me to send organizer." The organizer was sent, but he arrived when the strike was half finished.[25]

Two Arizona WFM inclusionists urged the WFM to take effective action. The report mentioned the special character of the 1903 Clifton–Morenci strike, which seemed to be causing the Western Federation to drag its feet:

> We believe that the conditions are such as would warrant and justify the Western Federation of Miners in taking immediate steps to organize this Camp. There has always been a peculiar condition existing in this camp, which up to the present has made it particularly difficult for the Western Federation of Miners to get a foothold, these conditions being that the company make [sic] a distinction between the wage of its different employees on account of nationality. Therefore we believe that these men, unorganized as they are, coming out as they have, shows to us that if the Western Federation of Miners takes advantage of the present conditions and sends a representative or representatives to this locality, the result

will be beneficial, not only to our unorganized brothers, who are struggling for the principles we contend for, but also will redound to the advancement and upbuilding of the Western Federation of Miners.[26]

The national convention was still making up its collective mind about whether or not it really wanted to attract foreign and Mexican American members. The fact that immigrant mining workers were sometimes imported as contract labor was a reason for the convention members' ambivalence. Shortly before the strike began, the WFM's *Miners' Magazine* reflected gloomily on the "threatened immigration" of "idle men of nations of Europe [who] are a grave menace to the working classes of this country."[27] But at the same time, the federation's executive board had voted to translate the union's ritual and constitution into the "Italian, Slavish, and Finnish languages."[28] The news from Clifton and Morenci helped push the convention toward soliciting immigrant membership. Convention delegates especially wanted to include Mexican workers in the union.[29] The WFM's 1903 national convention was a turning point, after which the union actively began to "organize the Mexicans." But WFM sympathy and enthusiasm came too late to help the Mexicans, Mexican Americans, Spanish, and Italians of the Clifton milling district, whose strike was lost.

The national convention's expressed intention to "organize the Mexicans" seemed to make no difference in Arizona. The inclusionists were quiet, and the series of violent ethnic incidents continued. At Colonel William Greene's Cananea mine just south of the border in Sonora, Mexico, in 1906, Mexican mining workers demanded justice and equality with Anglo American Cananea employees, rather than demanding a union.[30] The Western Federation of Miners worked to organize at Cananea before the advent of the strike there, but combining Anglo and Mexican workers into conjoint locals was an impossibility in the face of intense ethnic antagonism.[31] The WFM declared its staunch support for the Cananea strikers, but WFM verbal support was just as devoid of tangible benefit for the men at Cananea as it had been for the Clifton area strikers three years earlier.[32]

The next year there was inter-ethnic violence at Christmas, a small Gila County copper camp not far from Ray. The trouble at Christmas resembled that at Cananea. After an Anglo deputy sheriff shot and killed a Mexican miner, approximately three hundred Mexican mining workers armed themselves and tried to capture the deputy sheriff. Then, the Anglos at Christmas prepared to defend the sheriff. The two sides geared up for a "bloody race war," although Christmas eventually returned to "normal."[33]

WFM national headquarters tried to organize the Mexicans and Mexican Americans at Clifton–Morenci in 1906 and 1907. After a preliminary visit, the WFM asked the Industrial Workers of the World's Phoenix local to send organizers to the Clifton mining district, and Frank Little and

Fernando Velarde arrived there in late autumn. Little and Velarde established a Mill and Smelterman's local at Clifton, and a Miners' Union at Metcalf. Frank Little was an officer in both of them. Carmen Acosta, who became one of the Metcalf local's officers, was the only Mexican candidate elected in either union local.[34] But when a non-WFM strike broke out in July 1907, only the non-union Hispanic men joined it.[35] They struck as a group, and they disregarded WFM leadership. Some of the strikers invited Frank Little to one of their mass meetings. At the meeting, Little mounted the podium to make a speech, but the strike leaders refused to let him speak and escorted him outside.[36]

The strike failed, the Panic of 1907 deterred labor organizing all over the Southwest, and one of the two union locals disappeared almost as soon as Frank Little left the Clifton–Morenci area. The other local remained, but it was small and soon collapsed.[37] National Western Federation headquarters had little better luck when they sent organizers to Bisbee, Arizona, in February and March 1907. Many South Slavic mining workers joined Local 106 at Bisbee, but skilled Anglo and Irish craft workers and some local Anglo and Irish miners opposed the organizing effort. Local 106 survived, but remained small and ineffectual during its early years.[38]

The organizing efforts of 1906–1907 might be interpreted as growth or progress toward Mexican and Mexican American participation in organized labor and toward a universally inclusive labor movement in the U. S. But neither effort elicited any genuine enthusiasm among the majorities of Hispanic mining workers in the two camps where unionization was attempted, and neither effort led anywhere.

An alternative form of social activism was available to Clifton and Morenci Mexicans and Mexican Americans throughout the years preceding the 1910 revolution in Mexico. The Partido Liberal Mexicano (PLM), the revolutionary Mexican Liberal Party, was active in the Clifton district. Revolutionary activists, including Praxedis Guerrero, occasionally came to Clifton and Morenci. Lázaro Gutiérrez de Lara, who helped found the Club Liberal and helped plan the strike activity at Cananea in 1906, Mother Jones, and Father Thomas J. Hagerty all visited the Clifton–Morenci area. Abrán Salcido, one of the ten men jailed after the 1903 strike, returned to promote revolutionary activity in Morenci, and was there until at least September 1906.[39] There was both revolutionary political activity in the Clifton–Morenci–Metcalf area and the previously mentioned labor organizing activity. Some PLM district leaders in Arizona became WFM members and distributed IWW literature, and WFM leadership frequently expressed sympathy for PLM causes.[40] But this was mostly collaboration on an ideological level, without practical consequences. The organizational failures in Bisbee and in Clifton–Morenci attest to the lack of cooperation between the political revolutionary activists and the labor unionists.[41]

Nationally, the Western Federation of Miners continued to organize non-Anglo and non-Irish western mining workers, even developing a large new corps of ethnic organizers. Meanwhile, internecine fighting about the ethnic question arose in Jerome again in 1909. Exclusionists fought inclusionists to a stand-off for control of the Jerome Miners' Union. One group argued that "the union was getting too radical," particularly because "it was a mistake to have brought Ben Goggins [his name was actually Ben Goggin, and he was a Spanish-speaking organizer from Denver headquarters] here to try to get the Spaniards and Italians into the Union."[42] The nativist faction in Jerome was lumping Mexicans and Mexican Americans with the immigrant Spanish and Italian mining workers, intending to exclude all of them. The exclusionists disliked Goggin and an earlier organizer named Judich because the two organizers had successfully recruited new immigrant union members. The organizing drives managed by Goggin and Judich had temporarily doubled the Jerome Miners' Union's membership. The nativist faction wanted an end to immigrant recruiting. If not, they said, they were ready to quit the WFM and create an independent union local. They were opposed by an inclusionist faction that wanted to continue immigrant recruitment.[43]

The Globe Miners' Union also refought the ethnic question in 1910. Arizona was preparing for statehood, and four hundred community residents petitioned the constitutional convention, asking that the new state constitution include specific anti-ethnic language. The anti-ethnic provision would have excluded many of Globe's South Slavic, Spanish, and Italian immigrants, and also all Mexican immigrants, from work at the mines and mills. In July, the executive board of the Western Federation of Miners threatened the Globe Miners' Union with censure, just as it had in 1903, because of "conditions respecting the Latin workers of that section."[44] But this time, the inclusionist faction at Globe disassociated itself from the exclusionists. The non-nativist faction of Local 60 responded to the Western Federation's threat with a denial, announcing that Local 60 "knows nothing of [the immigrant exclusionists' plans], and that the matter has never been discussed by its members at any meeting."[45] Also, a neighboring WFM local, Number 70, newly opened at the town of Miami next to Globe, did not associate itself with the Globe residents' nativist petition.[46]

From 1911 to 1914, the Western Federation of Miners conducted major organizational campaigns in Utah and Nevada, and smaller ones in western New Mexico and El Paso, Texas. Also, the IWW tried to organize in El Paso, made a brief comeback at the site of a former local in Tonopah, Nevada, and did organizing work at the little gold camp of Oatman, Arizona. None of these efforts changed the status of the Mexican and Mexican American mining communities vis-à-vis the union organizations in Arizona.

The great change in Arizona ethnic relations began, improbably, in a series of incidents near the Ray Consolidated Copper Company's properties in August 1914. First, Pedro Smith, a sometime miner and woodcutter, was seen stealing a horse in Ray. Smith had been laid off at the mines when the price of copper fell earlier in 1914. He had been associated with "agitators among the Mexican miners thrown out of work," who had been accused of participating in a Mexican conspiracy and of possibly murdering an Anglo mine foreman. The Anglos from Ray who chased Smith into the mountains were ambushed and shot by Smith and his companions. In a sequence of related violence that lasted over a week, the Mexican boss of an all-Mexican mine work crew was stabbed to death while he slept, several more men were shot, a town riot broke out, and some men were arrested. The number of deaths is uncertain, but perhaps as many as sixteen people died, four of whom were Anglo, and twelve of whom were Mexican or Mexican American. Some of the fighting took place in the town of Ray and in nearby Sonora.[47]

After almost fifteen years of labor union activism and racial trouble in and near Ray, the Mexican portion of the mining work force was still unorganized. There was no union or fraternal benefits club to help the disadvantaged portion of the Ray mining camp community when they needed help. But the Mexicans at Ray did appeal for outside help. They contacted Lázaro Gutiérrez de Lara in Los Angeles, and told him that the Ray community was being persecuted. Gutiérrez de Lara responded by telegraphing George W. P. Hunt, the former mayor of Globe who had become governor of Arizona, with a request for intervention. Hunt's reply was cautious, but he promised to look into conditions at Ray. Gutiérrez de Lara was a former Mexican revolutionary activist and an old hand at southwestern organizing who had friends in both the national WFM and the Southern California IWW.[48] Governor Hunt's longtime home and power base were close to Ray. Both Hunt and Gutiérrez de Lara were ready to intervene when more trouble broke out in and around Ray in 1915.

The 1915 trouble at Ray was likely a continuation of the 1914 fighting. Approximately one hundred Hispanic men attended a meeting in late June 1915, at which they discussed the possibility that war might erupt between Mexico and the United States. The men at the meeting ended their discussion about war and began planning a strike against the Ray Consolidated Company before they went home that night.[49]

When the strike began, the racial component was its most salient feature. According to one source, the Hispanic strikers "did not want anything to do with the WFM and . . . they didn't care what they had to work for, provided the Americans had to work for the same rate . . . and the bitterness of the Americans against the strikers would have to be seen to be properly appreciated."[50] Practically all of the Mexican, Mexican American, and Spanish workers walked out, and all but perhaps ten Anglos opposed the strike. Most of the Anglos kept on working.[51] It was a story that went back to the 1890s.

The Ray strikers demanded the "Miami scale" of wages, which had been created during a brief, well-organized strike at Miami during January 1915. Local 70, some of the skilled trades AFL locals in Miami, and the Hispanic "Comité por Trabajadores en General" (General Workers'

Committee), about 1,500 men in all, had struck there. Management offered, and the strikers accepted, a sliding wage scale that was to be tied to
the price of copper on the New York wholesale market.[52]

After the non-Anglo work force walked out at Ray, picketing was effective because the Hispanic workers' homes, unlike those of the Anglos,
were away from company property, in segregated Mexican, Mexican
American, and Spanish communities called Sonora and Barcelona. Ray
Consolidated threatened to replace the Hispanics with more Anglos, but
the Hispanics ignored the threat.[53] By reputation, the Sonora and Barcelona
workers had been "notoriously non-union."[54] The Liga Protectora Latina,
an important *mutualista*, had recently been created in Phoenix and associated itself with the Ray strike.[55] The Ray strikers formed a "Workingmen's Committee," which was completely unconnected to the WFM or to
the Liga, late in the strike. But the strike's inspiration had been the June
"war" meeting. The WFM local at Miami also assisted the Ray strikers.[56]

During the first few days of the strike, Ray Consolidated began to negotiate. It quickly offered the strikers a sliding scale only slightly below
Miami rates. The scale included substantially higher pay for most Ray
mining workers. A vote to end the strike was taken in mid-July, and it
passed overwhelmingly.[57] The strike had lasted about two weeks and the
mainly Mexican contingent of the Ray work force had won.

The Ray strike was successful because disparate elements combined
into a labor movement for the first time in the history of the Southwest.
The combination was deliberate, if not felicitous, and in some respects, it
was enduring, rather than temporary.

In both Miami and Ray, the Mexican Comités por Trabajadores
planned and initiated strike activity, although the Miami Workers' Committee acted in concert with Miami's Local 70. In Ray, the Liga Protectora
Latina participated in the strike, but only *after* it had started. In Ray, also,
Local 70 participated at the midpoint and was extraordinarily useful at the
end of the strike.

The coalescing of Mexican with Anglo labor was a unique phenomenon. It began when several Ray strikers were driven out of town. Two of
them, Refugio Neyera and M. de J. Minoz (or more likely, Muñoz), were
beaten, brought to court, threatened with jail sentences, and then deported
from Ray.[58] A third Ray miner, A. N. Tribolet, was reportedly attacked by
three men, arrested, forced out of town under guard, and then given a train
ticket for a distant locale.[59] All three men went to Miami, where they were
welcomed.[60]

Two other men from Ray, C. L. Salcido and Jose Miranda, spoke to
Governor Hunt when he arrived in Miami. Hunt was invited to Miami by
Local 70, and in a speech there, he threatened to disarm the company's
guards and to declare martial law at Ray. One WFM organizer wrote, "[Al-
though] I have played a part in many strikes . . . I never saw one before
where the gunmen behaved so decently."[61] He believed this behavior was

a result of the governor's report. Miami also planned to raise money for the Ray strike. A benefit dance planned by two Miami men, E. Lopez and A. Gonzalez (Gonzalez owned a candy store in Miami) was called off "on account of the strike being settled."[62]

Local 70 was a refuge for Ray strikers, a conduit to Governor Hunt, and a general base of support. Local 70's officers also assisted at Ray. George Powell, already an ex-president of the Miami local, went to organize in Ray along with Henry S. McCluskey, who was the Miami Miners' Union regular organizer, and Guy Miller, who had come from the Western Federation's national headquarters.[63] At the end of the strike, the Ray Consolidated Company demanded that there be no union local at Ray. The Ray strikers agreed, and then many of them promptly joined the WFM locals at Miami and Globe. Immediately after the strike, the Miami local helped create a Ray branch, which soon became Local 72. Local 72 had at least 634 members by mid-July. Its business affairs were handled by two Miami Miners' Union officials, one of whom was Spanish-speaking. Miami collected initiation fees for Ray and disbursed funds for its use.[64] The predominantly Anglo Miami local had, in effect, become the sponsor and close affiliate of the predominantly Mexican Ray labor movement.

Guy Miller and A. N. Tribolet, a miner, went directly to the Clifton–Morenci area in mid-July.[65] Again, at Clifton–Morenci, local activists in the Mexican and Mexican American community clearly preceded them. El Club Cosmopolita began at Metcalf during mid-July with several hundred members at its inception. There were already several Mexican and Mexican American social organizations in the Clifton area. During the spring of 1915, the Clifton–Morenci Mexican clubs abruptly changed their meeting places. They seem to have gone underground.[66]

Most of Clifton–Morenci's 5,000-man work force struck the copper companies on 12 September. Again, it was a "Mexican" strike. This time an indigenous leadership, approximately half Mexican and half Anglo, directed the action. The two main ethnic groups in the Clifton district picketed, marched, and met together during the four month strike.[67]

George Powell of Miami went to Clifton–Morenci too. Again, he brought Governor Hunt, who spoke to a large, predominantly Mexican crowd, some of whom wore hats inscribed "Hurrah for Governor Hunt." Hunt promised that "when I come back to this community and have to bring troops, the principal officers of companies will be no different than the poorest Mexican they control."[68] For this strike, over $15,000 was raised in Globe and Miami. There was a union workers' subscription assessment, there were performances, dances, and other benefit activities, Ladies Aid contributions, clothing drives, businessmen's contributions, and there were even contributions collected from Miami schoolchildren.[69] Western Federation of Miners' national headquarters contributed only $1,000 toward the Clifton–Morenci strike, but in late 1915 that thousand dollars was approximately half of the money in the national organization's treasury.[70] In Clifton–Morenci, as at Ray, new WFM union locals were created, and they signed up new Clifton district members at the rate of over one hundred a day for part of September.[71]

Mexican and Mexican American labor activity, as well as joint Italian-Mexican club activity, was not new, it dated back to 1903. Neither was Western Federation of Miners' participation new; the Western Federation had been making a serious effort in Arizona since 1907. But nothing ever really worked until the Ray miners solicited, and were given, help from the Miami Miners' Union. Some of the reasons for this complete turnabout were connected to the Miami Miners' Union, and to Miami itself.

Much of Miami was new in 1914–1915. The Globe–Miami–Inspiration area was among the fastest growing copper regions in the United States. Two of the three copper companies in Globe–Miami–Inspiration were new. The huge International smelter, located between Globe and Miami, was completed only in May 1915. Miami was just incorporating as a town in 1915.[72]

Miami Miners' Union leadership was also new. The Miami men who figured prominently in the 1915 strikes had recently arrived in town. George Powell reportedly had attended law school and "a school of mines," had been an officer in various Arizona miners' union locals, a union delegate in Montana, and vice-president of the Arizona State Federation of Labor.[73] Henry S. McCluskey had been an international executive board member of a glassworkers' union in his native New York. McCluskey had suffered from tuberculosis and had come to Arizona for his health in 1914. He first appeared in Miami in February 1915, and by March he was Miami's new district organizer. He was only twenty-seven years old.[74]

Both the Globe and the Miami miners' unions were asserting their recently acquired power within the Arizona labor union movement. At the annual convention in October 1915, there were ten Miami delegates and five Globe delegates in the state total of thirty-seven. Miami's was by far the largest single contingent at the convention. Of the six convention delegates who were miners, four were Miami men. Also, Miami and Globe men introduced many, and perhaps most, of the important resolutions at the convention.[75] Both the Globe and Miami miners' unions owned large office buildings, and in both towns, most of the other local unions operated out of the miners' union buildings.[76] In Miami, the carpenters' union local asked the miners' union for assistance in organizing carpenters' helpers.[77]

Miami was leading a movement toward industrial unionism and ethnic tolerance in 1915 Arizona. After appointing Henry McCluskey district organizer, members decided, in a March 1915 meeting, "to take a more active campaign for [increased membership] throughout the entire Miami district."[78] In September, they opened Miami Miners' Union meetings "to all union men in good standing, irrespective of what organization they may be affiliated with." Shortly thereafter, another group of Arizona unions adopted a universal card system that enabled a cardholding union member of any of five different trades locals to seek work in any of the other affiliated trades.[79]

The rise of the Globe and Miami WFM men to preeminence caused a factional realignment in Arizona labor, beginning during the Ray and Clifton–Morenci struggles. Although many Mexican workers began joining Anglos in the WFM, organized Mexican opposition groups developed in several Arizona towns. There were at least two opposing factional subgroups within the Mexican American and Mexican communities in Arizona beginning in 1915. Lázaro Gutiérrez de Lara, veteran activist though he was, tried to speak to a crowd of mostly Mexican smelter workers in Douglas, Arizona, and was shouted down and forced to leave town.[80] A meeting of Mexicans at Metcalf itself was called off because of factional opposition.[81]

The position of Anglo workingmen had changed too. In Denver, WFM president Charles Moyer began to fear the power of the Miami Miners' Union and wanted to "send the Miami representatives home." Arizona WFM members began to choose sides: they either lined up behind the Moyer faction or behind the "new blood" faction, which was now being led by George Powell.[82]

This was the major change: inclusionists had become the new majority. The simple ethnic and racial division of previous years was gone because the Ray and Clifton–Morenci strikes had finally ended it. Anglo skilled trades locals called a joint meeting at Clifton–Morenci on 12 September, "realizing that for the first time in the history of the district, the Italians, Spaniards and Mexicans were united." Then, according to *Miners' Magazine*, "every craft voted unanimously to join the strike. For the first time the Americans were joining the foreigners in their struggle for organized labor."[83]

The 1915 events at Ray, Globe–Miami, and Clifton–Morenci led to the Bisbee Deportation, and the Red Scare of 1919. The Clifton–Morenci strikers forced a substantial set of concessions from the copper companies in the strike settlement. Then they continued to argue against work rules and for job control throughout 1916 and into 1917.[84] After one clash between a Mexican timberman and an Anglo shift boss, 2,500 men left their jobs for two weeks. There were nine relatively large strikes and many smaller ones, called "strikitos" by the Clifton–Morenci miners, as well some acts of sabotage through early 1917.[85]

The IWW had virtually vanished from Arizona as an organized force after 1910. The IWW's Metal Miners' Industrial Union 800 was not organized until early 1916. By the middle of 1916, IUMMSW Local 106 at Bisbee was soliciting funds for the IWW.[86] The IWW first reentered the copper industry labor battleground in a strike at the Humboldt smelter in Prescott early in 1917, and it began serious organizing at all of the bigger older copper areas in Arizona by April of that year.[87]

The Clifton, Morenci, and Metcalf WFM locals, which had been disbanded as a part of the 1915–1916 strike settlement, were reorganized late in 1917.[88] The principal officers of the Morenci and Metcalf unions were Spanish-surnamed, and the leading spokesman of all the Clifton–Morenci strikers during the big 1917 strike there was the Morenci local's president Pascual M. Vargas.[89] Of thirteen Clifton delegates to the Arizona Federation of Labor's 1917 convention, at least ten had Spanish surnames.[90] At least half of the Arizona Federation's total constituent membership was Mexican and Mexican American in 1917, as was one of the federation's vice-presidents.[91] One of the two Miami Miners' Union representatives to the national IUMMSW convention of 1917 was Hispanic, and in the 1918 convention, both of the men elected were Hispanic.[92] One of the two Jerome Miners' Union representatives to the convention was the much-traveled Lázaro Gutiérrez de Lara, who was soon afterward to become a vice-president of the Arizona Federation of Labor. Canuto A. Vargas of Metcalf, who was a $3.52-a-day mucker at Morenci in 1916, became the Morenci Miners' Union's secretary, and by late 1917, was co-editing a national American Federation of Labor Spanish-language newspaper. During 1918, he became the Spanish-language secretary of the AFL-sponsored Pan American Labor Federation in Washington.[93] Pascual M. Vargas, also of the Morenci Miners' Union, was appointed to the seven-member Arizona Council of Defense in January 1918.[94] Pascual Vargas, Canuto A. Vargas, and several other Arizona Mexican miners were the majority of the U.S. delegation to the Pan American Federation of Labor's first International Labor Conference in 1918. Both Pascual and Canuto Vargas were nominated for the post of conference chairman.[95] A series of Mexican and Mexican American success stories began with the ethnically conjoint activism of 1915.

The great chasm that had divided the Arizona mining labor movement since its inception in 1896, that of ethnic and racial divisiveness, was effectively bridged in 1915. Organized labor, at least in the southwestern mines, was open to unskilled European and Mexican workers for the first time. The organizing, strikes, Bisbee Deportation, and the series of defeats and deportations visited upon Mexicans and Mexican Americans at the war's end and thereafter were concerted counterattacks by corporate and political forces against the potent, ethnically unified work force which had been created in 1915. Some of the ethnic and racial achievements and some of the "new men" of 1915–1917 survived the battles of 1917–1927 and continued their labor activism thereafter.

NOTES

1. Vernon H. Jensen, *Heritage of Conflict: Labor Relations in the Nonferrous Metals Industry Up to 1930* (Ithaca, 1950), 381–429; and Melvyn Dubofsky, *We Shall Be All: A History of the Industrial Workers of the World* (Chicago, 1969), 369–86. See also James C. Foster, ed., *American Labor in the Southwest: The First One Hundred Years* (Tucson, 1982), 19–22 and esp. 27–28. Foster's essay "The WFM Experience in Alaska and Arizona, 1902–1908" focuses upon the institutional vicissitudes of the Western Federation, but posits the years 1914–20 as the period "when management brutally dismem-

bered the WFM," and the years after 1905 as the beginning of the Federation's decline. This approach does not lead the reader inevitably toward 1917, and it offers a careful explanation for the national institutional failure of the Federation. However, it does not consider some impressive WFM successes in local areas of the Southwest that occurred during these years.

2. Historians whose primary focus is the Mexican Revolution of 1910 have cited the organized community groups in southwestern towns during the pre-revolutionary and revolutionary years as examples of Mexican organized political activity. Examples of the literature that establishes connections between the U.S. Southwest and the Mexican Revolution include James D. Cockcroft, *Intellectual Precursors of the Mexican Revolution, 1900–1913* (Austin, 1976); James D. Cockcroft, *Outlaws in the Promised Land: Mexican Immigrant Workers and America's Future* (New York, 1986); W. Dirk Raat, *Revoltosos: Mexico's Rebels in the United States, 1903–1923* (College Station, 1981); Juan Gomez-Quiñones, *Sembradores: Ricardo Flores Magon y el Partido Liberal Mexicano: A Eulogy and a Critique* (Los Angeles,1973); and John M. Hart, *Anarchism and the Mexican Working Class, 1860–1931* (Austin, 1978).These new studies either implicitly or explicitly connect the political activity in southwestern Mexican communities with labor force activity; but none of them explains the nature of the connection. For an opposing view, see Rodney D. Anderson, *Outcasts in Their Own Land: Mexican Industrial Workers 1906–1911* (Dekalb, Ill., 1976). For further discussion on this see note 23, below.

3. James W. Byrkit, *Forging the Copper Collar: Arizona's Labor-Management War, 1901–1921* (Tucson,1982), 299, 326, 305, 312, 315, 317, 325. Byrkit discusses mining magnate Walter Douglas's "crusade against Arizona unionism itself," which he traces from a 1907 pledge to defeat labor "through the big Clifton–Morenci strike of 1915, and into 1917." He calls the Bisbee Deportation the climax of the entire span of copper industry labor history in Arizona from 1901 to 1921, and generally omits ethnic factors as causation for the 1917 Bisbee debacle.

4. Roy Rosenzweig, *Eight Hours for What We Will: Workers and Leisure in an Industrial City, 1870–1920* (Cambridge, Mass., 1983); Gwendolyn Rachel Mink, "The Alien Nation of American Labor: Immigration, Nativism and the Logic of Labor Politics in the United States, 1870–1925" (PhD. diss., Cornell University, 1982); and Tamara K. Hareven, *Family Time and Industrial Time: The Relationship between the Family and Work in a New England Industrial Community* (Cambridge, Mass., 1982). The terms "inclusion" and "exclusion" as used here refer to the incorporation or non-incorporation of a large group of immigrant Mexican, Mexican American, and immigrant European workers into a predominantly Anglo-Irish work force. In comparable current material the "inclusion process" described here is sometimes referred to as a struggle against "ethnic fragmentation," as the lessening of "ethnic cleavages," or as a struggle for "equality." The term "exclusion" is traditionally connected to nineteenth and early twentieth century "Chinese exclusion" legislation. The two terms used in this article are intended to provide a functional description of Arizona labor union operations, and are unrelated to federal work force legislation.

5. For a discussion of the barriers raised against non-Anglo or non-Irish union participation, see Mink, "The Alien Nation," 348–79; also Philip S. Foner, *The Politics and Practices of the American Federation of Labor 1900–1909*, Vol. 3, *The History of the Labor Movement in the United States* (New York, 1964, 1977).

6. Michael E. Casillas, "Mexicans, Labor, and Strife in Arizona, 1896–1917" (Master's thesis, University of New Mexico, 1979), pp. 35–40. The English and Irish in America are distinct groups and ought never to be confused with one another. Before the First World War there were readily identifiable groups of Cornish, other English, Catholic Irish, and men and women of many northern and western European nationalities living in U.S. western states and territories. There was frequent and especially bitter enmity between many of the Irish and the Cornish, as has been well explained in David Emmons's recent book on the Irish community in Butte, Montana, *The Butte Irish* (Urbana, 1989). Also, the Irish were the heart and soul of many WFM union locals, while

the Cornish seldom even joined them. In the Southwest, however, the term "Anglo" is intended to refer to people perceived as "white" and northern or western European, as distinguished from the term "Mexican," or "Mexican American," which is intended to describe people perceived as having wholly or partly Indian and Spanish racial and ethnic ancestry. "Anglo," as used here, is the southwestern culturally descriptive term, and includes persons perceived as being Cornish, English from areas other than Cornwall, Irish, and northern and western Europeans from areas other than England or southern Ireland.

7. Ibid.

8. *Arizona Daily Citizen* (Tucson), 2 February 1900, p. 2, and 3 February 1900, p.1; and Casillas, "Mexicans, Labor, and Strife," p. 39.

9. *Arizona Daily Citizen* (Tucson), 30 October 1901, p. 3; and *Arizona Republican* (Phoenix), 2 November 1901, p. 3.

10. *Jerome (AZ) Mining News*, 23 July 1900, p. 3; and Kenneth F. Clark, "Unions, Wobblies, and the Jerome Deportation: A Labor Relations Problem" (Master's thesis, Arizona State University, 1989).

11. *Arizona Republican* (Phoenix) 25 August 1902, p. 1.

12. Western Federation of Miners [WFM], *Proceedings of the Tenth Annual Convention, 1902, Proceedings of the Eleventh Annual Convention, 1903,* and *Proceedings of the Fifteenth Annual Convention, 1907.*

13. WFM, "Report of the Executive Board," in *Proceedings, 1903,* 95–6, 230–32; *Jerome (Ariz.) Mining News,* 23 July 1900, p. 3.; *Arizona Silver Belt* (Globe), 25 September 1902, p. 1, and 9 October 1902, p. 2; James David McBride, "Organized Labor in Globe: Building a Gibraltar in the Desert, 1884 to 1912," a paper presented at the Arizona State Historical Society Annual Conference in Globe, 4 May 1991, pp. 11–19; and Edward Crough, Notebooks, n.p., privately held, Phoenix, Arizona, entry dating from 1907. I am indebted to Professor James Foster for suggesting the importance of the Kofa information.

14. WFM, *Proceedings, 1902; Proceedings, 1903;* and *Proceedings, 1907;* Alan Dawley, *Class and Community: The Industrial Revolution in Lynn* (Cambridge, Mass., 1976), p. 236.

15. *Arizona Republican* (Phoenix), 11 June 1903, p. 2; and *Arizona Silver Belt* (Globe), 5 March 1903, p. 1; Joseph F. Park, "The History of Mexican Labor in Arizona During the Territorial Period" (Master's thesis, University of Arizona, 1961), especially pp. 189–190, 256. Park presents a thorough discussion of the eight hour law and its organized labor and Democratic Party support in Arizona, and writes that the law was intentionally "directed against the companies employing Mexican and contract labor." There were also several smaller companies operating in the Clifton district.

16. *Arizona Republican* (Phoenix), 11 June 1903, pp. 1, 8.

17. Ibid. Like United Verde's William A. Clarke, Phelps–Dodge's Lewis W. Douglas claimed to have the workingmen's interest at heart. In his, "Autobiographical Recollections," Tms, part V, p. 5, AZ290, Box 2, Lewis W. Douglas Collection, Special Collections, University of Arizona Library, Tucson, Douglas writes that "for motives of humanity," management had reduced working hours at Bisbee's big Copper Queen mine from ten to eight, *before* the eight hour law was passed. But, Douglas argued, most of the work in Bisbee was done in exceptionally wet or hot mining shafts, while the Morenci mines were generally dry and well ventilated; so management decided on the formula of eight hours of work for nine hours of pay in Morenci. The Clifton–Morenci workers, he explained, refused his offer, "as they had a perfect right to do."

18. J. H. Bassett, "Notes Dictated for the Arizona Archives while he was in the Arizona Pioneers Home, 15 March 1936," Tms, p. 1, Arizona State Archives, Phoenix.

19. U.S. Bureau of the Census, "Graham County, Arizona Territory (1900)," Ms. (Washington, D.C., 1900). The census returns do not show the Italian immigrant influx, much of which occurred after the 1900 census was taken. Census information is only

occasionally useful in discussion of people and events which attained significance during the years between decennial census-taking. Also, "Payroll" and "Time Book" records, 1902–04, Detroit Copper Mining Company, Special Collections, University of Arizona Library; and Douglas, "Autobiographical Recollections," part V, p. 5. Microfilmers destroyed some of the original handwritten payroll and time book records from years preceding 1903 without microfilming them. This writer used the payroll and time book material before the microfilming process began.

20. "Scene at Morenci during Strike 1903" and "Strike at Morenci 1903," photographs, La Moine collection, Arizona Historical Society, Tucson.

21. Greenlee County Recorder's Office, *Incorporations*, Book 1 (transcribed record of Graham County Incorporations), Clifton, Arizona; and *Arizona Republican* (Phoenix), 19 June 1903, p. 1.

22. Evidence of serious planning for labor action is implied in plans made by the Detroit Copper Mining Company in response to impending trouble, in March or April 1903. A letter discusses payment to the Theil Detective Service Company "for the services of two men in Morenci April May June [*sic*] and for part of July." One of the men hired was reportedly Italian, the other thought to be Mexican. They were told to get jobs in Morenci, and provide intelligence to company management while there. Earlier correspondence indicates that the Detroit Company had not hired detectives previously, at least not during 1902–1903. C. E. Mills, superintendent, Morenci, to Professor James Douglas, President of Detroit Copper Mining Company of Arizona, 30 July 1903, Lewis Douglas Collection, AZ290. Box 12b, Special Collections, University of Arizona Library.

23. *Arizona Republican* (Phoenix), 13 June 1903, p. 1; and "Register and Descriptive List of Convicts in the Territorial Prison, Arizona," 1903, Arizona State Archives, Phoenix. The entries are listed as "Graham County," "miner," and "Riot."

24. Recent studies include Mario Barrera, *Beyond Aztlan: Ethnic Autonomy in Comparative Perspective* (New York, 1988), esp. pp. 13–15; Jose Amaro Hernandez, *Mutual Aid for Survival: The Case of the Mexican American* (Malabar, Fla., 1983), esp. pp. 34–40; and Kay Lynn Briegel, "Alianza Hispano Americana, 1894–1965: A Mexican American Fraternal Insurance Society" (Ph.D. diss., University of Southern California, 1974). All of these studies suggest connections between *mutualista* and labor activity, but none of them details such activity. Other studies of Mexican and Mexican American labor activity simply assume that *mutualistas* promoted labor activism, and then predicate further statements about labor and political activity upon that assumption. This assumption can be extremely ill-founded because many sickness-and-benefit societies were obviously just that and probably little more. There is no evidential basis for assuming that other *mutualistas*, in other mining areas, functioned the way that the Clifton–Morenci Mexican and Italian societies did in 1903. Examples of this assumption can be found in Raat, *Revoltosos*, pp. 43–44; and Gomez-Quiñones, *Sembradores*, p. 30. Studies that discuss *mutualistas* without generalizing about unprovable labor activism include James D. McBride, "The Liga Protectora Latina: A Mexican-American Benevolent Society in Arizona," *Journal of the West* 14, (October 1975): pp. 82–90; and Mario T. García, *Desert Immigrants: The Mexicans of El Paso, 1880–1920* (New Haven, 1981), pp. 223–28. The study of the Italian mutual society, the "Fratellanza Minatori" of Sunnyside, Utah, is Philip Frank Notarianni, "Tale of Two Towns: The Social Dynamics of Eureka and Helper, Utah" (Ph.D. diss., University of Utah, 1980), p. 95.

25. WFM, *Proceedings*, 1903, p. 224; and *Weekly Republican* (Phoenix) 11 June 1903, p. 1.

26. WFM, *Proceedings*, 1903, p. 224.

27. John Higham, in his *Strangers in the Land: Patterns of American Nativism 1860–1925* (New York, 1963), pp. 48–49, argued that, at least through the 1890s, U.S. labor union leadership distinguished sharply between "voluntary immigration and that induced or controlled by capitalists," that is, so called "contract labor." The unions, according to Higham, were not anti-immigrant: they were anti-contract labor. A *Miners'*

Magazine (Denver), March 1903, p. 35, editorial indicated plainly nativist sentiment, rather than principled opposition to contract labor.

28. WFM, *Proceedings*, 1903, Executive Board Report, 25 May 1903, pp. 123, 260. The full convention adopted the recommendation.

29. Ibid., pp. 262–68.

30. Anderson, *Outcasts*, 110.

31. WFM, *Proceedings of the Thirteenth Annual Convention, 1905*, pp. 253–54; David M. Pletcher, *Rails, Mines, and Progress: Seven American Promoters in Mexico, 1867–1911* (Ithaca, 1958), p. 237; *Miners' Magazine* (Denver), 8 March 1906, p. 3, 15 March 1906, p. 13, and 12 April 1906, p. 3, and WFM, *Proceedings of the Fourteenth Annual Convention, 1906*, p. 220.

32. WFM, *Proceedings, 1906*, p. 136.

33. *Bisbee (AZ) Daily Review*, 14 April 1907, p. 2.

34. WFM, *Proceedings, 1907*, pp. 148, 6; *Miner's Magazine* (Denver), 9 January 1908, p. 15; Detroit Copper Mining Company, records, May–August 1908, Detroit Copper Mining Company; and "Payroll" and "Time Book" records, May–August 1908, Arizona Copper Mining Company, Special Collections, University of Arizona Library.

35. *Morenci (Ariz.) Leader*, 27 July 1907, p. 1. The strikers included some of the better-paid Mexican and Mexican American employees, including some who were earning over three dollars a day.

36. Ibid.

37. Ibid., 15 June 1907, p. 2; WFM and International Union of Mine, Mill, and Smelter Workers (WFM and IUMMSW), "Official Charter Book of the Western Federation of Miners and the International Union of Mine, Mill, and Smelter Workers," Western Historical Collection, University of Colorado, Boulder. Metcalf Miners' Union disappeared in early 1909.

38. *Bisbee (Ariz.) Daily Review*, February–April, 1907; *Bisbee (Ariz.) Evening News*, 12 April 1907, p. 1; and *Morenci (Ariz.) Leader*, 13 April 1907, p. 1.

39. Retyped clipping from *Graham (Ariz.) Guardian*, 28 September 1906 sent to the author by Yuma Territorial Prison State Historical Park staff, Yuma, Arizona, 15 August 1981; and Luis Araiza, *Historia del Movimiento Obrero Mexicano* (Mexico City, 1964), 2: 48.

40. Raat, *Revoltosos*, pp. 44–50.

41. *Copper Era* (Clifton), 1905–09; *Morenci (Ariz.) Leader*, 1907; Isidro Fabela, ed., *Documentos Históricos de la Revolución Mexicana*, vol. 2 (Mexico City, 1960); and Manuel González Ramírez, ed., *Epistolario y textos de Ricardo Flores Magón* (Mexico City, 1964), pp. 77–81, 122–41, 182–239. Clifton area newspapers reported on both political and labor organizing activity, and nothing in them indicates that political and labor activities had combined in the Clifton-Morenci area. Also, documentary evidence of *magonista* (PLM) activities indicates much political activity but substantially nothing about job-connected organizing.

Michael Casillas, in his M. A. thesis, "Mexicans, Labor, and Strife," 65–76, cites extensive documentary research, and states that "the Flores Magón group . . . was the only viable political and economic union open to Mexican workers in Arizona and the only organization that concerned itself with the needs of these workers during the period 1906-1909," but he offers no instances of actual labor organizing by the *magonistas* in the Clifton district.

42. Letter from Joseph D. Cannon, Jerome, Arizona, to Charles Moyer, 5 July 1909, pp. 3, 4, Arizona Collection, Arizona State University.

43. Ibid.

44. Tru Anthony McGinnis, "The Influence of Organized Labor on the Making of the Arizona Constitution" (Master's thesis, University of Arizona, 1930), 83–85; WFM, *Executive Board Minutes* 45 (27 July 1910): n.p.; and *Miami (Ariz.) Silver Belt*, 26 October 1910, p. 1.

45. *Miami (Ariz.) Silver Belt*, 28 October 1910, p. 8.

46. WFM and IUMMSW, "Official Charter Book"; and *Miami (Ariz.) Silver Belt*, October–November, 1910.

47. *Arizona Republican* (Phoenix), 20 August 1914, pp. 1, 4; 21 August 1914, pp. 1, 7; 22 August 1914, pp. 1, 5; and 23 August 1914, pp. 1, 8; *Miami (Ariz.) Silver Belt*, 13 January 1915, p. 2; and letter from P. C. Harris, Phoenix, Arizona, to Roscoe Willson, 14 November 1955, Roscoe Willson files, Arizona Historical Foundation, Tempe.

48. *Arizona Republican* (Phoenix), 22 August 1914, p. 5.

49. *Miami (Ariz.) Silver Belt*, 29 June 1915, p. 4, and 30 June 1915, p. 2.

50. Ibid., 9 September 1915, p. 1.

51. Ibid.; and *Miners' Magazine* (Denver), 5 August 1915, p. 3.

52. *Miami (Ariz.) Silver Belt*, 16 January 1915, p. 1, 18 January 1915, p. 4, 19 January 1915, p. 1, 20 January 1915, p. 1, 21 January 1915, p. 1, and 23 January 1915, p. 1. The Comité por Trabajadores was *not* a *mutualista*. The beginning base rate for a Miami miner was $3.50 in February 1915.

53. *Miami (Ariz.) Silver Belt*, 9 September 1915, p. 1.; and Leonor Lopez, *Forever Sonora, Ray, Barcelona: A Labor of Love* (privately published, 1984), pp. 3, 7, 8, 15, 16, 19.

54. *Deseret Evening News* (Salt Lake City), 1 November 1912, p. 10.

55. Thomas E. Sheridan, *Los Tucsonenses: The Mexican Community in Tucson, 1854–1941* (Tucson, 1986), p. 170; and McBride, "The Liga Protectora Latina," p. 84.

56. Clipping dated 1 July 1915, unknown newspaper, n.d., Scrapbook Number 16, May–June 1915, George W. P. Hunt Collection, Special Collections, University of Arizona Library.

57. *Arizona Record* (Globe), 13 July 1915, p. 3.

58. *Miami (Ariz.) Free Press*, 9 September 1915, p. 2.

59. Ibid., 19 July 1915, p. 4.

60. Ibid., and 9 September 1915, p. 2.

61. *Miners' Magazine* (Denver), 15 August 1915, p. 3.

62. *Miami (Ariz.) Free Press*, 19 July 1915, p. 8; and *Arizona State Business Directory*, 1915–16 (Denver, 1914), 374.

63. *Daily Arizona Silver Belt* (Globe), 9 July 1915, p. 1; *Miami (Ariz.) Free Press*, 19 July 1915, p. 8, and 22 July 1915, p. 1. Powell was replaced as organizer for Ray by W. E. Burleson shortly thereafter. That summer, Guy Miller made the remark that is part of this article's title.

64. *Arizona Record* (Globe), 13 July 1915, p. 3; *Miners' Magazine* (Denver), 15 August 1915, p. 3; and WFM, "Meetings of the Executive Board of the Western Federation of Miners," 1902–17, Tms, Western History Collection, University of Colorado, Boulder 20 (15 July 1915): 20–23.

65. WFM, "Executive Board Minutes," 20 (15 July 1915). Tribolet was probably the same A. N. Tribolet who had come to Miami from Ray during the Ray strike, but WFM records describe him as William Tribolet. The only Tribolet of record in the vicinity was *Fred* Tribolet, who owned a meat market in the town of Ray, itself. (*Arizona State Business Directory*, p. 527.) The Tribolet who accompanied Guy Miller, A. N. Tribolet, spoke and understood Spanish, but he may have been either a Spanish immigrant, a Mexican immigrant, or a Mexican American (*Miami Free Press*, 19 July 1915, p. 4.)

66. *Clifton Morenci (Ariz.) Mining Journal*, 22 July 1915, p. 2; and *Bills of Sale, Greenlee County*, Book 2, Recorder's Office, Greenlee County, Arizona.

67. Philip Mellinger, "The Beginnings of Modern Industrial Unionism in the Southwest: Labor Trouble among Unskilled Copper Workers, 1903–1917" (Ph.D. diss., University of Chicago, 1978), 172–73.

68. *Outlook*, 2 February 1916, p. 251; and *Arizona Republican* (Phoenix), 1 October 1915, p. 1.

69. James R. Kluger, *The Clifton-Morenci Strike: Labor Difficulties in Arizona, 1915–16* (Tucson, 1970), p. 41; and *Miami (Ariz.) Free Press*, 21 October 1915, p. 5.

70. WFM, *Executive Board Minutes* 34 (26 November 1915).

71. *Miami (Ariz.) Free Press*, 16 September 1915, p. 2.

72. Robert Bigando, *Globe, Arizona: The Life and Times of a Western Mining Town, 1864-1917* (Globe, 1989), 69, 101, 104; and *Arizona Record* (Globe), 10 January 1915, p. 3; 21 May 1915, p. 1., and 22 May 1915, p. 1.

73. *Arizona Labor Journal* (Phoenix), 21 October 1915, p. 6.

74. James David McBride, "Henry S. McCluskey: Workingman's Advocate" (Ph.D. diss., Arizona State University, 1982), 3, 8-11, 15, 20, 26, 31. McCluskey was also an Arizona State Federation of Labor delegate that October. (*Miami (Ariz.) Free Press*, 14 October 1915, p. 2.)

75. *Miami (Ariz.) Free Press*, 14 October 1915, pp. 1-2. The convention also helped to raise money for the Clifton–Morenci strike.

76. *Globe (Ariz.) Leader*, 4 June 1913, p. 3.

77. *Miami (Ariz.) Free Press*, 15 July 1915, p. 3.

78. McBride, "Henry S. McCluskey," 31.

79. *Miami (Ariz.) Free Press*, 16 September 1915, p. 8.

80. *El Paso Morning Times*, 20 October 1915, p. 1.

81. *Clifton Morenci Mining Journal*, 26 August 1915, p. 1.

82. WFM, *Executive Board Minutes* 29 (26 November 1915) and 24 (11 September 1915). Some Western Federation locals threatened to leave the federation in February 1916, blaming Charles Moyer for, among other things, "failure to make progress in organizing our industry." Globe and Miami separatists led this "new blood" movement at the 1916 WFM convention and tried to elect George Powell to the federation's presidency in place of Moyer. Moyer won, in a fairly close vote. *Miners' Magazine* (Denver), 3 February 1916, pp. 1, 2, 5; and Jensen, *Heritage of Conflict*, pp. 371-77.

83. *Miners' Magazine* (Denver), 7 October 1915, p. 7.

84. Kluger, *The Clifton-Morenci Strike*, pp. 67-71.

85. *Engineering and Mining Journal* (New York), 21 July 1917, p. 136, and 13 October 1917, p. 641; and *The Copper Era and Morenci Leader* (Clifton, Ariz.), March–May, 1916, and 9 October 1917, p. 5.

86. *Solidarity* (Chicago), 19 February 1916, p. 4, 13 May 1916, p. 1, and 5 August 1916, p. 1. The Western Federation of Miners renamed itself the International Union of Mine, Mill, and Smelter Workers (IUMMSW) in mid-1916.

87. Ibid., 9 May 1917, p. 1, 10 March 1917, pp. 1, 4, and 14 April 1917, p. 4.

88. IUMMSW, *Proceedings, 1918*, pp. 48-50.

89. *Miners' Magazine* (Denver), October 1917, p. 8.

90. *The Copper Era and Morenci Leader* (Clifton, Ariz.), 10 August 1917, p. 1.

91. Ibid.

92. Ibid.; IUMMSW, *Proceedings, 1918*, p. 32.

93. "Longfellow Mine" payroll, 1-16 June 1916, Arizona Copper Mining Company; *The Copper Era and Morenci Leader* (Clifton, Ariz.), 10 August 1917, p. 1; and Philip Taft, *The AF of L in the Time of Gompers* (New York, 1957), p. 325.

94. *The Copper Era and Morenci Leader* (Clifton, Ariz.), 4 January 1918, p. 1.

95. Pan American Federation of Labor, *Report of the Proceedings, Meeting of the International Labor Conference at Laredo, Texas* (Laredo, Tex.), 13 November 1918, pp. 18, 24-25, 41. Both men declined the nomination, which ultimately devolved upon Samuel Gompers.

13 IDAHO AND THE GREAT DEPRESSION

Leonard J. Arrington

Leonard Arrington, an economic historian of the intermountain West and of the Mormon Church, lived as a child on an irrigated farm in Idaho's Snake River Valley. With his family, he survived the Great Depression of 1929–1941. Here he asks whether the West consumes more than its fair share of federal tax money collected from Easterners, or, on the other hand, whether Easterners plunder the West of its natural resources. During the Depression, Idaho ranked eighth among the states in per-capita federal funding—which seems to argue that the West got more than it should have.

Arrington says, not so. He compares Idaho's drop in income with New England's and finds that Idaho suffered much worse. How badly hit was it? Did Idaho deserve even greater support from Washington? What explains the drop in his father's returns on Idaho potatoes, from $1.50 a bushel in 1929 to ten cents in 1932, while grocery shoppers still had to pay $1.85? Who got the money? How did farmers deal with this situation? How did Idaho farmers protect their neighbors' tax sales, and why did unemployed young men even set forest fires to create firefighter jobs? Many people left Idaho in those years; but others, ruined by drought on the Great Plains, arrived in the hope of surviving, and required relief.

Anti-depression programs helped farmers, youths, and the unemployed, and provided construction jobs which created roads, bridges, schools, and other permanent benefits. Yet for all the spending, the total during the 1930s was only $57 per person per year. How does that compare to the nuclear, space, and military aircraft spending that came a decade or so later when the Cold War got under way? Arrington concludes, however, that New Deal federal aid crucially helped Idaho regain its economic footing.—editors

SEVERAL YEARS AGO, while doing research at the Henry E. Huntington Library and Art Gallery in Southern California, I became personally acquainted with one of the "greats" in American economic history. A confirmed New England Yankee, he-who-shall-be-nameless irreverently suggested that our beloved West was hardly more than a gigantic fed-

eral boondoggle—a mechanism by which the taxes paid by frugal and industrious Easterners were siphoned off to support impractical settlement
projects better left to the coyotes and rattlesnakes. The reason for the continuation of this national scandal, he declared, was that each poorly populated Western state had two senators—just as many as each of the populous productive states in the East. To these blasphemous exaggerations I
replied, somewhat indignantly, that Eastern monopolies had continually
plundered the West of its resources—that these resources contributed
mightily to the prosperity of the East—and that any financial support
which the West managed to obtain through means of the government in
Washington was really ours to begin with.

Some documents recently "discovered" make possible a rather precise
measurement of the assistance rendered by the national government to
Idaho and other Western states during the Great Depression of the 1930s.
Prepared in 1939 by the Office of Government Reports for the use of
Franklin Roosevelt during the presidential campaign of 1940, these documents—one for each state—give statistical and descriptive information on
the activities and achievements of the various federal economic agencies
within each of the states for the years 1933 to 1939. The obvious intent
of these reports was to dramatize the accomplishments within each state
of the various anti-depression agencies of the New Deal. After the invasion
of Poland in September, 1939, however, Dr. Win-the-War replaced Dr. New
Deal, and America's interests shifted from domestic policies to international affairs. The state reports were pushed aside and, apparently, have
not been used by historians of the West.

The discovery that the New Deal recovery agencies benefited Idaho
and other western states more than they did other sections of the nation
was a surprise. If one reduces New Deal expenditures to a per capita basis,
Idaho ranked eighth among the forty-eight states in the expenditures of
the anti-depression agencies of the New Deal, ranking first in Rural Electrification Administration expenditures, second in Civilian Conservation
Corps expenditures, second in Civil Works Administration expenditures,
fourth in public works grants, sixth in public roads subsidies, ninth in Federal Emergency Relief, eighteenth in Reconstruction Finance Corporation
grants, and twenty-first in Works Progress Administration expenditures.
All told, from 1933 to 1939, federal agencies made grants to Idaho of $209
million and loans of $112 million, for total assistance of $321 million.
If the more than $10 million worth of loans insured by government agen-
cies is added, the grant total of federal financial assistance to Idaho during
these years was more than $331 million.[1]

What were the justifications for these expenditures? First, despite a
number of contemporary statements to the contrary, Idaho's economy
was in desperate straits during the 1930s. The three principal supports of
Idahoans had been agriculture, mining, and lumbering. Under the substantial incentives of high prices and patriotic urgings during World War I, each
of these activities was greatly expanded. New land was opened for farming

which, from a long-term point of view, should never have been brought under cultivation. Old mines were resuscitated which had better lain in desuetude. Forests were exploited in a manner that was to bring later regret. No sooner had this expansion taken place than the war ended, and with no planned withdrawal the result was catastrophic. Idaho suffered probably as much as any state in the Union from the depression of 1921, and Idaho's recovery from that depression not only was slow, but in fact never did take place. Wheat, for example, sold for $2.50 in 1919, and brought only $1.30 in 1929. Sugar beets, another important source of support, sold for $22 per ton in 1919, and only $15 per ton in 1929. Idaho's wonderful potatoes sold for $1.51 a bushel in 1919, sank to a low of $.31 a bushel in 1922, and rose only gradually thereafter. Thus, a good case can be made for the fact that Idaho and other western states did not participate fully in the prosperity of the 1920s. This helps to account for the fact that Idaho, next to Montana, had the highest rate of emigration of any western state in the 1920s.[2]

Then came the depression of the 1930s. Looking back on it, one wonders that Idaho could have experienced so much distress. One supposes that agricultural states would not suffer heavily; farmers could always eat, and they were seldom unemployed. Nevertheless, in terms of income lost the economies of the agricultural states exhibited more affliction than the more heavily industrialized states. The state which suffered the greatest drop in income from 1929 to 1932 was North Dakota, followed by South Dakota, Mississippi, Oklahoma, Alabama, Montana, and Idaho. The states which had the least percentage decline in income were the heavily industrialized states of New England, New York, and New Jersey. From 1929 to 1932, the incomes of New Englanders dropped by about a third, while those of Great Plainsmen and Westerners fell by approximately one half. The income of average Idahoans dropped by 49.3 percent, compared to a decline of only 30.5 percent for the average Massachusetts resident.[3]

The evidence for the decline in Idaho's income between 1929 and 1932 is not hard to find. The price of wheat dropped to 26 cents per bushel, while cattle brought less than $20 a head in 1932—the lowest average price since the 1890s. Sheep, similarly, sold for $2.25 per head in 1932—the lowest in the century. Prunes were down from $22 per ton in 1929 to $6.50 a ton at the bottom of the depression. Sugar beets sank to $4 per ton in 1932, while wool declined from 36 cents per pound in 1929 to 9 cents per pound three years later.

With respect to lumber, there was virtually no demand at any price in 1932 because people were not building. The production of Idaho's famous white pine dropped from 438 million board feet in 1929 to 169 million board feet in 1933. The total production of mineral products declined from $32 million in 1929 to less than $10 million in 1933—again, the lowest in the twentieth century. The price of silver fell from $1.39 an ounce in 1919 to 24 cents an ounce in 1933. This was the lowest price silver had brought in Idaho's history.

It is instructive to observe the differing behavior of silver and gold during the early years of the depression. The production of silver fell drasti-
cally; but inasmuch as the United States was on the gold standard until
1934, the decline in the general price level after 1929 caused gold to become more valuable. This induced a surge in the production of gold from
21,000 ounces in 1929 to 62,000 ounces in 1933. The combination of the
rise in price and rise in production caused the value of Idaho's gold crop
to spurt from $429,000 in 1929 to $1,641,000 in 1933. As a contemporary
observer pointed out, the depression of the 1930s induced a rejuvenated
gold industry comparable to the boom period of the 1860s.[4] Indeed, it is
unfortunate that the New Deal did not try to help out matters by taking
the gold out of Fort Knox, burying it in various centers of unemployment,
and letting the unemployed go out and dig it up to put in circulation for
the benefit of trade!

In terms of aggregates, the cash income of Idaho farmers dropped from
$116 million in 1929 to $41 million in 1932. Similarly, wages and salaries
fell from $139 million in 1929 to $81 million in 1932. Total income payments of all kinds in Idaho moved downward from $235 million in 1929
to $123 million in 1932. This was a drop in per capita income from $529
in 1929 to $268 in 1932.[5] Manufacturing employment was cut back from
15,644 men in 1929 to 7,682 men in 1933, and Idaho's manufacturing payroll declined from $22.5 million to $7.1 million during the same period.

Perhaps a word of personal recollection may not be inappropriate. My
father—a farmer east of Twin Falls—decided that 1929 was a good year to
expand his farming acreage, and after much soul-searching he finally purchased a tract of sixty acres of rich apple orchard land, paying $300 per
acre. He planned to raise potatoes, and Grade A potatoes in 1929 were selling for $1.50 per bushel. At such a price, and considering his big family of
boys, he could envision paying for the land within a few years. But in 1930
when he harvested the first crop, potatoes were selling for only 75 cents
a hundred. In 1931 the land yielded well, but potatoes were down to 50
cents per hundred. In 1932, as the depression continued to deepen, run-of-
the-field "spuds" brought 10 cents per sack. I was 15 years old at the time,
and while helping to load several truckloads of these ten-cent "spuds," I
asked my father, "What do you suppose people will pay for these potatoes
in grocery stores?" My father said he didn't know, but why didn't I find
out?

Under my father's direction I prepared ten letters which were placed
in representative sacks on different truckloads. The letters indicated where
the potatoes were produced, mentioned the ten-cent price per sack, included a self-addressed envelope, and asked the final purchaser to reply
what he had paid. As I recall, we received five replies from the ten we had
enclosed in the sacks. All of the replies were from California, and the price
paid by the ultimate purchaser had varied from a low of $1.50 per sack to
a high of $2.15 per sack. I still have in my possession one of the letters.
Mailed from Oceanside, California, the letter carried this message: "You

14. Run on the bank: depositors rushing to get their
money from a bank in Boise, 1932. *Idaho State Historical Society, #72-2.14.*

say you received 10 cents for this sack of potatoes. I paid $1.85, although
the freight from Twin Falls to here is only 76 cents. Something is wrong
here!"

It was precisely in order to discover just what was wrong there that
this former Future Farmer of America later enrolled as an agricultural economics major at the University in Moscow [Idaho], and later switched to
economics. The answer, as I inevitably discovered, was complex. But one
thing was clear. My father had obligated himself in 1929 to pay $300 per
acre for land on the assumption that it would produce an abundance of
potatoes worth $1.50 per hundred-pound sack. He was still having to make
the agreed payments on that land when the potatoes worth harvesting
were bringing only ten cents a sack. Something was wrong there, too! How
my father ever held on to the land and made the payments I was never able
to find out. My mother said it was by the labor of her boys, but that may
have been her way of making us feel important.

There were persons in our neighborhood who had made similar investments who did not have the boys to do the work nor wives who could manage to "get along" on virtually no income. Sometime during the winter
of 1932–1933 a family acquaintance was foreclosed by his creditor, and a
sheriff's sale ordered for a certain Monday. All the farmers in his neighborhood gathered together on Sunday evening and agreed upon a plan to
help their friend. They would attend the sale and refuse to bid against each
other. The next day, as the auctioneer went through his accustomed chant,

a splendid team of horses sold for $1.50; a grain binder, $2.00; a hay mover, $1.00. Prices of other animals and equipment ran from a low of 50 cents to a high of $3.00. The farmers duly paid the sums they had bid, received the items purchased, and promptly turned them back to the farmer who had been foreclosed.

There were many examples of such conspiracies. Michael Malone, in his splendid dissertation on C. Ben Ross and the New Deal, states that in Gem, Boise, Idaho, Valley, Adams, and Lemhi counties arsonists systematically ignited fires in the forests in order to obtain employment as fire fighters. The situation became so serious that Governor Ross declared those counties to be in a state of insurrection, placed them under martial law, and ordered the National Guard to close off the forests to public access.[6]

One other factor which explains the severity of the depression years in Idaho is the drought of 1934. The report of the Governor's Emergency Drought Relief Committee, dated May 22, 1934, states that on the basis of reports from 45 water districts, representing 80 percent of the irrigated land of Idaho, the general average water supply was 56 percent of normal.[7] Crop losses were estimated at $22.4 million. About 30,000 people required relief in the 45 districts.

The reports from six weather observation stations in southern Idaho showed that from October 1933 to April 1934 there was a precipitation of less than 65 percent of the long-term normal for that period, and that there was already a heavy crop loss of potatoes, beets, beans, peas, and hay. According to the report, 1934 was already the driest year in southern Idaho since the stations had started keeping records in 1909.

The report estimated that approximately 75,000 Idaho citizens would need aid on account of the drought, and that $2 million in emergency relief funds were needed to remove beaver dams obstructing the flow of streams; to pump water from lakes, marshes, sloughs, ponds, and streams into irrigation ditches and canals; to straighten creek and river channels; to pump from wells; to clean canals and ditches; and for direct relief.

In a telegram to the Universal News Service in Chicago on July 26, 1934, Governor Ross declared: "In Idaho the drought is serious, the worst in the history of the white man in this territory. Rivers and creeks are drying up which in previous years furnished irrigation. Thousands of springs that have been used for watering livestock in the mountains have become dry, and water must be furnished from other sections. While people in the affected areas will not be required to evacuate, feed must be shipped in to save the livestock. . . . with assistance of the Federal Government we will be able to sustain our people in their homes without evacuation." The files of Ross Administration in the State Archives contain many applications for drought relief.

The problems of the drouth pyramided as the drouth in the Great Plains region caused thousands of families to move into the Far West. Idaho received many thousands of these migrants—from Nebraska, Kansas, Oklahoma, Arkansas, Missouri, and Texas. Thus, although Idaho's economy was incomparably more distressed in the 1930s than in the 1920s, the net emigration of the 1920s was converted by *Grapes of Wrath* folk into a net in-migration in the depressed thirties. The newcomers, who went principally into the Snake River Valley in Southern Idaho and the cut-over area in Northern Idaho, created a mounting relief load. Clearly, conditions in Idaho, as in other states, required a sustained program of relief and recovery.

The federal aspects of the anti-depression program in Idaho included unemployment relief, agricultural loans and benefits, programs for youth, social welfare assistance, works programs, and lending programs. All of these measures were extensive in their coverage, and a review of the activities of federal agencies in Idaho is instructive. But the most surprising thing is how really small the expenditures of the various New Deal agencies proved to be. Accepting the political folklore of the 1930s, one gets the impression that Franklin Roosevelt staged a giant barbecue which supported millions of people and forced the nation irretrievably into debt. Somehow or other, the most easily remembered quotation is one attributed to Harry Hopkins: "We will spend and spend and elect and elect." Compared with expenditures of recent years, however, New Deal expenditures were quite modest. Although Idaho, as mentioned previously, ranked eighth among the forty-eight states in per capita federal expenditures during the period 1933 to 1939, the total expenditures in Idaho of all New Deal agencies during those seven years was only $399 per capita, or an average of $57 per person per year. That is less than half the estimated annual per capita expenditures of the National Reactor Testing Station of the U.S. Atomic Energy Commission at Arco.

Of course, the dollar was worth more in those days. But to convert to present prices, the figures are still far less than Apollo 8—or, for that matter, some of our model custom-produced bombers. One reason the nation failed to recover from the depression of the 1930s until the advent of World War II was the small magnitude of the effort made. In all the years of the New Deal, the total expenditures of the federal government on recovery programs were approximately $24 billion. That is a stout sum, but in the first year of World War II the federal government spent more than twice that figure. One of the lessons of World War II was that our recovery effort had been inadequate.

Looking back at the 1930s, we are amazed at the things the nation was able to do with the expenditures made by the various antidepression agencies. In Idaho alone:

The Civilian Conservation Corps provided healthful and productive outdoor labor for almost 20,000 sons of poor families.

The National Youth Administration provided part time employment for some 5,000 needy high school and college students.

The Reconstruction Finance Corporation, Federal Emergency Relief Administration, and other agencies provided relief for some 20,000 destitute Idaho families during most of these years. Approximately 20,000 to 30,000 Idaho farmers signed contracts with the Agricultural Adjustment Administration and received payments to help sustain their incomes. Another 9,000 low income farmers were given more substantial help by the Farm Security Administration. More than $50 million was loaned Idaho farmers by agricultural loan agencies.

Some 4,000 Idaho laborers were employed on an expanded highway program, involving thousands of miles of new and improved roads.

Other Idaho workers constructed the Owyhee Reclamation Project, several storage reservoirs, 78 educational buildings, 25 airports in the state, 125 public buildings, the sewer systems of several dozen cities, the municipal waterworks for other cities, and hundreds of athletic fields, fairgrounds, and parks throughout the state.

Creative Idahoans, directed by Vardis Fisher, put out the first of the state guides, an *Idaho Encyclopedia,* an *Idaho Folklore,* and an *Idaho Digest and Blue Book.*[8]

All of this, of course, cost money—but only a small percent of it came from Idahoans, whose incomes had fallen so low that their federal taxes were minimized. The *Idaho Digest and Blue Book* indicates that in 1935 Idaho paid only $904,000 in internal revenue to the federal government while receiving some $39,900,000 in emergency relief. Only one state (South Dakota) paid a smaller percentage in taxes in relation to what it received.[9]

As the result of the inflow of federal funds, Idaho's economy did improve. The following summary is suggestive:

Individual income taxes in Idaho rose from $138,000 in 1933 to $628,000 in 1939.

Corporate taxes rose from $265,000 in 1933 to $1,384,000 in 1939.

Bank deposits rose from $41 million in 1933 to $90 million in 1939.

Income per capita rose from $287 in 1933 to $452 in 1939.

Farm marketings rose from $52 million in 1933 to $80 million in 1939.

Silver production rose from $2 million in 1933 to $15 million in 1939.[10]

As did other Americans, Idahoans slowly improved in wealth and welfare. By the outbreak of World War II, Idahoans were in a reasonably good position to participate effectively in the struggle for national survival against the menaces of German Nazism, Italian Fascism, and Japanese expansionism.

NOTES

1. See Leonard J. Arrington, "The New Deal in the West: A Preliminary Statistical Inquiry," forthcoming in *Pacific Historical Review*, and the data presented in Table 1 of this article.

2. Earl Pomeroy, *The Pacific Slope: A History of California, Oregon, Washington, Idaho, Utah, and Nevada* (New York, 1965), 295.

3. Frederick M. Cone, "Income Payments by States," *Survey of Current Business* (August 1941), 21:14.

4. G. C. Hobson, comp., *The Idaho Digest and Blue Book* (Caldwell, Idaho, 1935), 566–571.

5. Cone, "Income Payments," 14.

6. Michael P. Malone, "C. Ben Ross and the New Deal in Idaho" (unpublished Ph.D. dissertation, Washington State University, 1966), 51–52.

7. The report may be found among the papers of the Ross Administration, Box 27, folder entitled "Drouth Relief, 1934–1935." Idaho State Archives, Boise. The chairman of the committee was R. W. Faris, the Idaho Commissioner of Reclamation.

8. These summaries have been compiled from Office of Government Reports, Statistical Section, Report No. 10, Idaho, Vol. II (Washington, D.C., 1940). A Xerox copy of this 54-page mimeographed report is in the Utah State University Library.

9. *Idaho Digest and Blue Book*, 296–301.

10. These summaries are compiled from Office of Government Reports, Report No. 10.

14 THE IMPACT OF THE SECOND WORLD WAR ON LOS ANGELES

Arthur C. Verge

Los Angeles County in 1941, on the eve of Pearl Harbor, already had a population of about 3,000,000, making it decidedly the largest metropolis west of Chicago. Arthur Verge describes in this essay how "the war"—which many still call it, because it was the greatest such event in modern American history—changed Los Angeles. Besides sheer growth, what were these changes? What was the metropolis like before the war, and how was it different after the war? Did the war truly transform Los Angeles or just accelerate changes already under way? The city's history certainly did not begin in 1941—it was founded in 1781—and the elements of explosive growth were already there when the war began. Nevertheless, the changes of wartime were profound.

The early months of the war saw the city's Japanese-American people, the largest such community in the country, uprooted and shipped off to detention centers. When they returned, "home" was no longer there. In 1940 and 1941, before Pearl Harbor, and on through 1943, African Americans flocked to Los Angeles for the first time in the tens of thousands, seeking and finding jobs in war industries, especially the aircraft plants and the docks and shipyards. For them and the many Anglos and Mexicans who also migrated to the area, housing became an acute problem. What connection did the internment of the Japanese Americans have to the wartime housing shortage? Wages and incomes were never better, and the recent Depression of the 1930s became only a memory. How did this prosperity-amid-wartime affect people's lives?

The author also traces the impact of the war effort on the port of Los Angeles/Long Beach and other parts of the Los Angeles economy. He also describes how public works like Hoover Dam and the Colorado River Aqueduct and the creation of Union Station changed the metropolis. What impact did they have?—editors

"THE WAR." Two simple words that are often still uttered with deep emotion. For millions of Americans, the Second World War was the most transformative event of their lives. In the swirl of the most devastating conflict in human history, many Americans found that their participation in the war effort had a redemptive impact upon their lives, in sharp contrast to the faith shattering years of the Great Depression. They emerged from the war with a renewed sense of confidence in themselves and in the nation's democratic institutions. The popular description of World War II as the "Last Good War" gives testament to the conflict's mixed legacy of national unity and shared purpose in the face of the hundreds of thousands wounded and killed.

Nowhere was the war's mixed legacy seen more graphically than in the nation's cities. While bread lines gave way to crowded factory gates, municipal authorities frequently found themselves nearly overwhelmed by the magnitude of changes unprecedented in their scope and impact. The legacy of these changes often proved to be completely transforming. Most dramatically, the war spelled prosperity for many urban centers as aging, rust-ridden factories gave way to new modernized manufacturing plants, whose design and assembly technologies were often the envy of the world. In addition, the industrial production demands of the war created record numbers of new jobs that served to lift millions of Americans out of poverty and into a middle-class existence.

While the impact of the Second World War was felt throughout the American homefront, no other American urban center was so transformed by the war as was Los Angeles. Once perceived as a distant western outpost, isolated and separated by 3,000 miles from the nation's industrialized East, Los Angeles, bolstered by massive federal defense spending, emerged in the war as an industrial giant whose production of vital defense goods, such as warships and planes, helped turn the war in the Allies' favor.

Yet the war proved to be a mixed legacy. Los Angeles paid for its rise to industrial greatness largely at the expense of its environment and quiet, "small town" prewar character. In addition, wartime Los Angeles struggled with acute racism, most notable of which was the widespread support for the forced removal and internment of the city's large Japanese-American community. Blacks, Mexican Americans, and Mexican nationals also suffered, struggling under the burden of racially restrictive housing covenants, widespread job discrimination, and segregated public facilities such as pools and beaches. Yet the war also provided new opportunities for women and minorities. Access to jobs in the previously closed high-paying defense industries helped to encourage a renewed and stronger civil rights movement.

The Second World War's impact on Los Angeles proved to be nothing short of a social and industrial revolution. While it is true that the war greatly accelerated several social and economic forces already in motion, it is this article's contention that the Second World War brought forth a new, substantially different, and much more economically powerful Los Angeles than the one that would have developed without the war.[1] Once in the shadow of its Gold Rush neighbor to the north, Los Angeles emerged unchallenged from the Second World War as the leading urban center of not only California, but also of the new American West.[2]

On the eve of the Second World War Los Angeles was moving from its rural past into its urban future. Physically, large open spaces and vacant city lots checkered much of the Los Angeles basin. The city known today as the "freeway capital of the world" did not have a single mile of freeway in 1939. Visitors to prewar Los Angeles often described it in romantic terms, deeming it "The land of sunshine," "A Tourist's Mecca," or quite simply, "Small town Los Angeles."[3] Several professional surveyors of the region's prewar industrial and manufacturing capacity concurred. Their 1939 report observed "that characteristically Los Angeles is a small plant town."[4]

The physical appearance of prewar Los Angeles, however, was as deceptive as one of the region's carefully crafted movie sets. For beneath the small town veneer was a large and blossoming economy. As early as 1937, Los Angeles was successfully competing with the nation's more established eastern seaboard cities. That year Los Angeles ranked third among American cities in the number of manufacturing establishments and fifth in the value of manufactured output.[5] By 1939, Los Angeles County led the nation in the number of predominant industries, ranking first in the production of aircraft, motion pictures, sportswear, oil well equipment, and food products.[6]

Much of the city's economic success by 1939 can be traced to farsighted investment of eastern manufacturers who built branch plant operations in southern California. Eastern manufacturers such as R.C.A. Victor, Firestone Tire, and Bethlehem Steel were attracted to Los Angeles because of the region's near perfect climate, its large tracts of vacant affordable land, a rapidly growing population, and strong local petroleum industry that offered inexpensive power. Further, after locating operations in Los Angeles, several manufacturers took advantage of the city's strategic Pacific Coast location. Lying on the Pacific Rim, Los Angeles served as an ideal distribution point for Asian and Latin American destinations.[7]

The geographic potential of Los Angeles was not lost on the United States Navy. Following the First World War, Los Angeles had become the home port of the Pacific Fleet in 1919. Since naval authorities considered the port of San Diego too shallow for the fleet's largest ships, such as battleships and new developing aircraft carriers, naval leaders selected the ports of San Pedro (Los Angeles Harbor) and Long Beach as the fleet's new home.[8] By 1936, San Pedro Bay was headquarters to one of the world's greatest naval armadas in history. (Included in the fleet's two hundred plus ships was the legendary "battleship row" which later fell prey to the Japanese attack at Pearl Harbor.)[9]

With much of the firepower of the United States Navy berthed within San Pedro, an already interdependent relationship between Los Angeles and the federal government deepened. It had earlier increased significantly with the onset of the Great Depression as local Angelenos looked past City

Hall and towards Washington, D.C., for needed relief assistance. Subsequent federal intervention had an important twofold effect. First federal expenditures helped create local jobs which, in turn, eased Los Angeles's historic feeling of separation and isolation from the nation's capital. Second, these depression–era public works programs did much to improve the physical infrastructure of the city. Key among them were the building of Hoover Dam and the Colorado River Aqueduct, without whose electricity and water the southland could not substantially expand, and completion of the Union Railroad Station which would serve as the central transit point for rapid railroad service between the West and eastern sections of the country.[10]

With the onset of the Second World War, in September 1939, cooperative interdependence between the federal government and Los Angeles heightened. Although local aircraft producers relied on foreign defense contracts to expand their operations in the early days of the war, the massive infusion of federal defense spending in 1939 almost caused the city to explode. Nowhere was the pressure of expansion more impressive than in the aircraft industry. Employment in Los Angeles soared from 15,930 at the end of 1938 to over 120,000 in December 1941, when the United States entered the War.[11]

Though aircraft expansion was impressive, it was not the sole beneficiary of America's defense buildup. Since World War I the area's shipbuilding industry had been inactive, but as defense orders arrived, the shipyards of Los Angeles embarked on a remarkable expansion program. The industry, which averaged a thousand employees in 1939, grew to 22,000 by October 1941.[12]

The continued influx of defense orders after 1939 caused the Los Angeles industrial area to grow at a startling pace, earning it distinction as the nation's fastest growing region.[13] Not everyone was pleased with the unprecedented growth. Local writer Sarah Comstock complained: "Towns do not develop here, they are instantly created, synthetic communities of a strangely artificial world."[14]

The rapid industrial growth of Los Angeles continued to accelerate following the surprise Japanese attack at Pearl Harbor on December 7, 1941. While military authorities in Washington rushed troops and supplies to the West Coast, the city's "Big Six" aircraft companies—Douglas, Lockheed, North American, Northrup, Vega, and Vultee—quickly expanded their operations through an increased inflow of federal defense dollars. One federal agency that played a key role in governing these defense investment dollars was the Reconstruction Finance Corporation (RFC). Given the need for rapid wartime response, and the blessing of cheap available land, the RFC encouraged the expansion of existing facilities over the construction of new ones. Through its subsidiary, the Defense Plant Corporation (DPC), it oversaw the expenditure in Los Angeles of more than $312 million in plant expansion efforts between 1939 and 1944. The DPC also spent $142 million on the construction of new plants. In all, more than a thousand plants expanded in Los Angeles County during the war years while, during the height of the war from 1942 to 1944, 479 new defense plants joined the region's manufacturing base.[15]

The beneficiaries of this massive wartime federal investment ranged from the already large aircraft plants to small manufacturing concerns. The Defense Plant Corporation supplied the capital for 71 percent of the aircraft factories, 58 percent of the aluminum plants, and 96 percent of new rubber plants for the western region of the United States. Further, it financed fourteen of the fifteen largest aircraft plants built during the Second World War.[16]

Los Angeles's proximity to the Pacific war and its growing industrial capacity created fears among many Angelenos that the city would become the target of Japanese attacks. Actor and writer Buck Henry humorously recalls the city's then trepidation: "We imagined parachutes dropping. We imagined the hills of Hollywood on fire. We imagined hand-to-hand combat on Rodeo Drive."[17] Yet given the city's strategic value and its emotional ties to the heavily damaged fleet at Pearl Harbor, the fear remains understandable. Within nine months of the attack on Pearl Harbor more than 165,000 volunteers, nearly one in ten of the city's residents, had become active members of the Citizen's Defense Corps. Trained by the city's police and fire departments, these resident volunteers took positions as air raid wardens, fire reporters, messengers, and auxiliary police officers.[18]

While Los Angeles did not have to contend with an actual Japanese attack, Japanese submarines did operate effectively off the West Coast. On December 23, 1941, Japanese submarines sank the Los Angeles-based Union Oil tanker *Montebello* off the California central coast.[19] The next day, on Christmas Eve 1941, the American lumber carrier SS *Absaroka* was torpedoed just off the coast of Los Angeles by a Japanese submarine operating in the Catalina Channel. The attack, which was witnessed by onlookers from White Point in San Pedro, killed one crewman, but failed to sink the ship.[20]

These offshore attacks not only served to panic the local populace but also stirred increasing resentment towards the city's Japanese-American community. Even the respected *Los Angeles Times*, whose lead articles on the day following the attack on Pearl Harbor had assured readers that many local Japanese Americans were "loyal Americans," began reversing its posture. The paper in heated competition with the Hearst Newspaper Corporation soon took to calling these same Japanese American residents "Japs" and "Nips."

Los Angeles's normally stoic mayor, Fletcher Bowron, also became swept up in the anti-Japanese American hysteria. Playing to local sentiments, Bowron demanded that the federal government take immediate action against the local Japanese American community before, in his words, "it is too late." In a February, 5, 1942, radio address, Bowron stated that Los Angeles, with the nation's largest concentration of Japanese, had become "the hotbed, the nerve center of the spy system, of planning for sabotage." Warning his listeners that "each of our little Japanese friends will know his part in the event of any possible attempted invasion or air raid," Bowron argued in support of removing all persons of Japanese descent from the city. Otherwise, he told his radio audience, "We are the ones who will be the human sacrifices."[21]

In response to continued public pressure and demands for a complete removal of Japanese Americans from the West Coast by such political leaders as California Governor Culbert Olsen and California Attorney General Earl Warren, President Franklin Delano Roosevelt took action. On February 19, 1942, he issued Executive Order 9066 which authorized the forcible evacuation of Japanese Americans from the West Coast. As a result, an estimated 60,000 Los Angeles Japanese American residents were quickly forced out of their homes and businesses. The misery of many of them increased during the two months they had to live in horse stables at both Santa Anita and Hollywood Park race tracks while the permanent internment camps were being constructed.[22]

As if to justify the forced evacuation, the Los Angeles Times continued to print news stories claiming that the local Japanese American community was still in deep alliance with the Japanese war machine. On February 23 1942, the paper carried news of weekend raids that broke up "secret societies organized as espionage centers" and resulted in the capture of "scores of alien reserve officers, particularly Japanese." The raids, described as "the first triumphs of the war in the Pacific Coast States" were alleged to have "ended the careers of many saboteurs before they began." Unfortunately for Los Angeles's Japanese-American community, a Japanese submarine shelled the oil storage area of Ellwood, twelve miles north of Santa Barbara, only hours after the article appeared. Although the attack inflicted little damage, it substantially heightened citizen fears of a Japanese attack and it unfortunately served to increase the credibility of those favoring the removal of Japanese Americans from the West Coast.[23] Lampooning any remaining doubters, the Los Angeles Times ran an editorial cartoon showing a complacent citizen being shelled from offshore and carrying the words, "It could happen here" emblazoned on the projectile's trail.[24]

On February 25, two nights after the submarine's shelling of Ellwood, army officials warned Los Angeles civil defense authorities that enemy aircraft were seen approaching the city. At 2:25 a.m. the region's defenses went into full alert, with antiaircraft guns firing into searchlight-swept skies. Many witnesses to the event believe that the authorities mistook a wayward weather balloon for a Japanese plane. Although the raid's authenticity became a source of debate among military officials, no bombs were dropped and no planes were shot down.[25] However the event, known today as the "Battle of Los Angeles," gave the city's residents a genuine feeling of being at war.[26]

Although the only shells that actually fell on Los Angeles that night were from the city's own antiaircraft guns, local residents felt that they were beginning to experience the full impact of the war. City streets became increasingly crowded with sailors, marines, and soldiers. The once nearly empty newspaper "Help Wanted" ad sections became filled with job advertisements as defense plants sought to fill vacancies continually being created by the nation's military draft. Increasing the demand for war workers was the widespread resistance of many of the city's war industries to the hiring of women and minorities. Several plant operators in the early months of the war claimed that females would prove inept at war production work. Several others argued that women on the assembly line would distract male workers from the work at hand. There was also large-scale resistance to women workers from males in the work force. With the Depression still fresh in their minds, many males perceived women workers as potential threats to fair wages and job security.[27]

But the demands of fighting a two-front war necessitated dramatic societal change. As one War Department official bluntly told a gathering of southern California defense officials, "Women are as capable and productive as men and they must be so used. Prejudice, convenience and inertia can no longer bar their full employment."[28] With large contracts and federal defense dollars dangling before them, many aircraft and ship building companies suddenly saw the "light" and began actively recruiting women for war production jobs. Minorities in wartime Los Angeles, in contrast, did not fare as well.

While the war effort brought forth a spirit of cooperation and participation among Los Angeles citizens, serious undercurrents of racial tension continued to plague the region. Despite its long history as a migratory center, Los Angeles remained a city divided and segregated along racial lines. According to Floyd C. Covington, director of the Los Angeles Urban League, the city's racial divisions hardened with the arrival of thousands of white southerners, who had come to Los Angeles in search of war work.[29] "The southernizing of California," one observer noted, "is becoming a real factor in mitigating against employment opportunities for the Negro. . . . On all sides," he concluded, "can be sensed a general change of attitude toward the Negro, due to the impress of this southern influence on almost every activity within the community."[30]

The failure of most Los Angeles defense plants to hire blacks can be traced to the attitudes of both organized labor and management. By restricting its initiation ritual to whites only, the aircraft industry's principal union, the AFL International Association of Machinists, barred blacks from membership until 1942.[31] Management policies were equally restrictive. When members of the Los Angeles Council of the National Negro Congress inquired about the racial policies of Vultee Aircraft in August 1940, Gerald Tuttle, manager of industrial relations for the company, sent a curt reply: "I regret to say that it is not the policy of this company to employ people other than of the Caucasian race, consequently, we are not in a position to offer your people employment at this time."[32]

In Pasadena, the director of the California State Employment Service declared that his office was continually approached by competent black mechanics desiring work in the aircraft industry. Although the black mechanics often possessed the very skills the firms were looking for, the vast majority could not be placed. The personnel representative of a large aircraft plant admitted that although the company had hired many thousands of men in the previous year and was still in desperate need of skilled workers "there isn't a Negro in the entire plant." The company maintained its restrictive racial policy, he wrote, because "many of the white men would object to working with a Negro."[33] In the spring of 1941 J. H. Kindelberger, president of North American Aviation, took an equally hard line. "While we are in complete sympathy with the Negroes," he declared, "it is against the Company policy to employ them as mechanics or aircraft workers. . . . There will be some jobs as janitors for Negroes." He insisted, however, that "Regardless of their training as aircraft workers, we will not employ them in the North American Plant."[34]

For blacks in Los Angeles, and for that matter, throughout the nation, the incongruity of fighting a war for democratic ideals abroad while maintaining segregationist policies at home led to large-scale protests. Ironically, the most successful of these was a march that never took place. The proposed march, organized by A. Philip Randolph, was to have brought to Washington, D.C. on July 1, 1941, more than 100,000 blacks demanding equal rights. The march was called off when President Franklin D. Roosevelt met with Randolph and agreed to issue an executive order outlawing discrimination. Roosevelt's Executive Order 8802, issued June 25, 1941, forbade "discrimination in the employment of workers in defense industries or government because of race, creed, color or national origin." The President then created the Fair Employment Practices Committee (FEPC) to enforce the order.

In Los Angeles, which even prior to the Great Depression had a substantial black community, black protest between 1940 and 1942 gained strength as a result of the "Double V" campaign.[35] National in scope, the "Double V" campaign signified black America's efforts to win victory over the Axis powers overseas and over discrimination at home. To help attain these ends a variety of black organizations worked together documenting instances of discrimination against minorities in the work place.

Among the most successful of these groups was the Negro Victory Committee. Formed in April 1941, the Los Angeles Victory Committee sought to remind the city's white majority of the American black community's historic loyalty to the nation while at the same time aggressively pursuing the cause of equal rights.[36] Under the leadership of Rev. Clayton D. Russell, the local Victory Committee organized five black-owned markets into the Victory Markets Cooperative. The cooperative functioned throughout the war years, helping to solidify black support behind both the war effort and the fight for equality at home.

Black solidarity against hiring discrimination also received strong support from the community's two leading black newspapers, the *California*

Eagle and the *Los Angeles Sentinel*.[37] Discrimination against blacks in Los Angeles also received national attention from *Fortune* magazine. Its March, 1943, issue accused Los Angeles defense plants of "almost universal prejudice against Negroes" with "little concealment about the anti-Negro policy."[38] And as historian James Wilburn has noted, "In June, 1941, there were exactly four Negro production workers in the aircraft industry in southern California."[39]

The black solidarity forged by Russell and other leaders soon became evident on the streets. In July 1942, a local official of the United States Employment Service tried to justify discriminatory hiring practices by claiming that black women were not interested in working in defense production and were better suited for employment as domestic servants and cooks. The statement awakened long-smoldering resentment among blacks over their inability to find jobs despite the region's massive shortage of war workers. The Negro Victory Committee encouraged black women to flood the agency with job applications, organized a protest march, and finally forced federal officials from the War Manpower Commission to enter into negotiations over the job issue. A joint statement followed announcing that discrimination would no longer be tolerated in the defense industry.[40]

The Victory Committee's march played a paramount role in breaking down the barriers that had confronted blacks in the defense industry. Although Executive Order 3809 forbade discriminatory hiring practices, leaders throughout the black community felt the only hope for enforcement of the order was strong public pressure by blacks. Arguing patriotically from the position of "we want to aid in the war effort but are prevented from doing so," the Negro Victory Committee avoided charges of subversion and anti-Americanism.

Fortunately for blacks and other minorities, Los Angeles began to suffer acute labor shortages in 1942. The aircraft industry, for example, had nearly 20,000 workers who either enlisted in or were drafted into the military by August 1949. Further, industrial expansion in the Los Angeles area between 1940 and mid-1943 accounted for the creation of 550,000 new jobs. In sharp contrast to the Depression years, women and minorities soon found themselves with a wide array of job choices. So dramatic was the change that the number of women employees in the six southern California aircraft plants went from 143 in 1941 to nearly 65,000 by the summer of 1943.[41]

Los Angeles, however, despite gaining substantially in its labor supply by employing women and minorities, still faced large shortages of workers in 1943 and late into 1944. Part of the problem was rapid industrial expansion, where the number of new job openings often outstripped the number of workers entering the labor force. Job turnover, too, contributed to lagging production schedules. Many women entering the work force for the very first time, for example, found factory work unappealing and often left it for employment in service sector work. Others, quite understandably, found juggling a full-time job, while raising children and maintaining a

15. Rosie-the-Riveters in a defense factory, Los Angeles, 1942. *Courtesy of the Huntington Library, San Marino, California.*

home, to be too difficult. Still others cited the lack of adequate child care as the cause for their leaving defense work.

The continual loss of valuable workers forced the defense industry to completely rethink its employment practices. Several Los Angeles aircraft plants responded to the loss of women workers by redesigning their assembly lines to include conveyor belts, streamlined tools, chain hoists, and load lifts.[42] The industry also effectively lobbied for the 1942 passage of the Lanham Act.[43] The act, which provided federal funding for an extensive array of on-site child-care centers, reduced significantly the loss of women war workers.[44]

In turn, women employees proved to be the backbone of the city's wartime industrial expansionism. At the peak of worker shortages, women comprised 42 percent of the aircraft industry's total work force. In fact, in several companies their numbers made up over 50 percent of those employed.[45] Thus, the large-scale incorporation of women in the industrial work force proved to be the single greatest factor in easing the war's severe "manpower" shortage.

Despite apparent gains made by blacks in defense hiring, they received a disproportionate share of jobs when compared to their population. In June 1944 blacks composed 5.3 percent of the war workers in Los Angeles yet blacks constituted 7.1 percent of the city's population.[46] Nonetheless, the open hiring of blacks in the high-paying defense industry did lead to the greatest black migration in Los Angeles history. By the summer of 1943 blacks were arriving in Los Angeles at a rate of between 10,000 to 12,000 a month, or approximately 50 percent of new migrants to the city.[47] From 55,114 in 1940, the black population of Los Angeles swelled to 118,888 by April 1944.[48]

The subsequent war production by the people of Los Angeles proved remarkable. Perhaps no other Los Angeles industry was impacted as much from the war as the area's shipbuilding industry. Local shipyards, which until 1940 had not constructed a large ship in twenty years, were by late December 1941 the second largest manufacturing industry in the Los Angeles area.[49] Henry J. Kaiser played a prominent role in the area's shipbuilding success. In 1940, Kaiser and his associates, backed by the Maritime Commission, organized from scratch the California Shipbuilding Corporation. Known as Calship, the yard was located on 175 acres of semitidelands on Los Angeles's Terminal Island. Beginning production of Liberty ships in May 1941, the yard thirteen months later broke the existing world's record by delivering fifteen Liberty ships in June 1942.[50] By standardizing the design and specifications for all its government ordered ships Calship was able to launch 111 ships in 1942, more than any other yard in the United States.[51] Ship production at Calship was further accelerated with the completion of Kaiser's Fontana steel plant in August 1943. As a result, Calship was the country's second largest emergency shipyard, launching 467 ships between September 27, 1941, and September 27, 1945.[52]

Los Angeles was also the home of several other major shipyards. Consolidated Steel Corporation delivered more than 500 vessels, while the Bethlehem Shipbuilding Corporation repaired and returned to service an average of two large naval vessels for every work day during the war. Todd Shipyards took over the previously failed Los Angeles Shipbuilding and Drydock Company and converted 2,376 ships during the last three years of the war.[53] During the war the shipyards of Los Angeles handled more than one and one-half billion dollars in shipbuilding contracts.[54] At the war's peak they employed some 90,000 employees, including 55,000 at Calship.[55]

The rapid use of Los Angeles's shipbuilding industry from 1939 to 1945 gives testimony to the region's adaptability for wartime industrial growth. However, the greatest beneficiary of this adaptability was the aircraft industry. By 1944, the aircraft production sector led Los Angeles's second largest industry, shipbuilding, by a six-to-one ratio in payroll and employee figures.[56] Its development affected the region as no other wartime industry and unlike maritime construction, its impact was longstanding.

As the dominant force in wartime Los Angeles, the aircraft industry played a prominent role in shaping the local economy. At its wartime high, the industry employed 228,000 workers.[57] These substantial numbers of employees, many of whom had families, helped to continue the economic growth of service-related industries during the war. Much of the financing of the large payrolls came from defense orders. The United States government by June 1945 had placed more than $7 billion worth of aircraft orders.[58]

The financial impact on Los Angeles was nothing short of phenomenal. For small manufacturers, the plane orders were a "boon" as they quickly expanded their operations to meet the sub-contract demands of an already overwhelmed aircraft industry. By 1944, an estimated 4,000 separate "war plants" were located in Los Angeles with the large majority involved in aircraft manufacturing.[59] By producing a wide variety of vital defense goods, ranging from planes to ships and uniform clothing, Los Angeles as early as July 1942 had won 47.1 percent of the nearly five billion federal defense dollars invested in California since 1940. In comparison, the San Francisco–Oakland industrial area captured only 20.4 percent, and San Diego County, due in large part to its growing aviation production, received 21.8 percent.[60] As a result, Los Angeles, which many federal authorities still considered a branch plant town, emerged in the summer of 1942 as the nation's second most productive industrial area based on the size and number of government war contracts awarded.[61]

Los Angeles, like most boom towns during the war, found itself contending with a wide array of societal ills linked to its rapid growth. The influx of massive numbers of hopeful job seekers and their families simply overwhelmed the city's physical infrastructure. Chief among Los Angeles's war-related problems was the increasing lack of available housing for newly arriving defense workers. Ironically, prior to 1939, Los Angeles had a substantial surplus of available housing. Blessed with a decentralized base, large open spaces, and a history as a migratory center, pre-war Los Angeles was able to handle large numbers of new arrivals. Home building, however, quickly slowed with the American entrance into the war. Builders found themselves stymied by wartime restrictions on building supplies and the loss of large numbers of their construction workers to the war effort.

Especially hard hit by the region's housing shortages was the black community of central Los Angeles. Because blacks had been forcibly segregated by racial covenants into approximately 5 percent of the city's residential area, newly arriving blacks had great difficulty in finding housing within the established black communities of Central Avenue, West Jefferson, and Watts.[62] Many of the migrants had to live instead in the city's "Little Tokyo" section which had been emptied because of the internment of Japanese Americans. Renamed by locals as "Bronzeville," this section became the worst wartime housing in Los Angeles. Deputy City Mayor Orville Caldwell was so appalled at the conditions there that he testified to federal investigators that if they visited the area, as he had, "You will see life as no human is expected to endure it." A member of the

Los Angeles Women's War Chest Committee echoed Caldwell's sentiments: the conditions in Bronzeville "almost require the help of missionaries."[63]

Overcrowding, particularly in the central city area, led to record crime rates. The Los Angeles Police Department, already severely hampered by the loss of experienced personnel to the war effort, saw felonious assaults and robberies increase by more than 50 percent between 1942 and 1943.[64] The problem of juvenile delinquency was most clearly linked to the war's impact. Between 1940 and 1943 the numbers of those arrested under age eighteen in Los Angeles doubled. The lack of proper parental supervision and overcrowded housing conditions contributed to the rise. The situation became so bad in parts of the city that parents of those repeatedly arrested were prosecuted for allowing their children on the streets again.[65]

Also plaguing law-enforcement officials was the open confrontation between military service personnel and groups of young Mexican-American males, many of whom were outfitted in the then popular "zoot suit." On the night of June 3, 1943, large-scale fighting broke out between the zoot suiters and servicemen. While the tension between the two groups had been mounting for some time, the exact origins of zoot suit riots are unclear, although racism played a large part in instigating the violence. The uniforms of each group seemed to take on meaning. Many servicemen saw the zoot suit as a symbol of open defiance of society. Further, many military personnel considered the zoot suiters draft dodgers. In contrast, many of the zoot suiters resented the constant traffic of servicemen through their neighborhoods and the impolite attention the servicemen gave to their girl friends. For some Mexican Americans, the military uniforms symbolized dominant Anglo society invading their closed world.

While no one was killed during the riots, police were unable to control the mobs of servicemen who swarmed into the downtown area in search of zoot suiters. Their invasion was precipitated by rumors that Mexican hoodlums had openly attacked servicemen near a dance hall in Venice on the night of June 3, 1943. For at least ten days military officials were unable to control the servicemen despite efforts by local and military police authorities. There were simply too many service personnel involved in the riots to be controlled. The rioters marched through the downtown area stripping zoot suiters of their outfits. They even entered a movie theatre, turned on the lights, and attacked persons they considered to be zoot suiters. Most of the victims were Mexican Americans, but there were cases of attacks on blacks as well. The riots stopped after the commanding officers of southern California military bases put the barrio and downtown areas on off-limits status.[66]

While local police and military officials contended with a growing epidemic of crime, city and county health departments fared little better in their fight against the increasing spread of communicable discuses. The shortage of adequate essential care facilities, for example, raised serious concerns that an epidemic in Los Angeles could affect the nation's war effort. Such fears were not unfounded. Wartime Los Angeles received thousands of new residents and transients, a substantial percentage of whom had never been inoculated against communicable diseases. Further, overcrowding and lack of adequate sanitation in many parts of the region raised the threat of rodent- and insect-borne diseases such as bubonic plague, typhus, and malaria.[67]

Moreover, rapid wartime industrialization and population growth of Los Angeles created serious environmental problems. Most adversely affected were the adjacent Pacific Ocean and the air over the city. In terms of ocean pollution, Los Angeles's large population growth during the war years overtaxed regional sewer systems to the point that dumping of raw sewage in neighboring Santa Monica Bay became commonplace. The beaches of southern California, the region's number one tourist attraction, were often closed during the war due to the presence of raw sewage along the shore. Elmer Belt, president of the California State Board of Health, complained of "massive, gross contamination" of the Los Angeles shoreline by the raw sewage, and he subsequently led efforts to quarantine beaches most seriously affected by sewage dumping. Still, the quarantines were not always effective and local Santa Monica Bay area doctors reported large increases in intestinal diseases in proportion to the numbers of ocean swimmers.[68]

Adding to public health woes was the dramatic wartime change in the region's air quality. Much of the change was due to the growth of new industries in the region. In 1940 and 1941 a total of 233 new industrial plants sprang up in Los Angeles. In the next two years industrial usage of the Los Angeles Department of Water and Power soared from 400 million to over a billion kilowatt hours. Literally, while area production statistics brightened, the skies over Los Angeles darkened.[69]

Despite its poor wartime environmental record, Los Angeles continued to gain stature as the leading city of the newly industrialized West. Although the cessation of hostilities in 1945 prompted fears that Los Angeles would be plagued by war plant closures and large unemployment, the city's ties to technological innovation assured it a bright future. Just as the city quickly adapted itself to wartime production, it rapidly and successfully adjusted to a postwar economy.

Thus, the Second World War changed nearly every facet of life in Los Angeles, and many of the most dramatic changes occurred in the expansion of local industry. Although some 175,000 wage earners were dropped from local manufacturers' payrolls between August 1944 and September 1945, substantial wartime employment gains were retained by nearly every local industry.[70] The aircraft industry, for example, at its lowest postwar employment level was still nearly 400 percent above its 1939 prewar level.[71] The shipbuilding industry, which suffered an 81 percent decline in employment between its wartime peak and October 1945, nevertheless exceeded its 1939 level by over 500 percent. Other industries experiencing substantial growth during the war years (petroleum, steel, and electric) survived postwar downturns in employment only to quickly recover with dramatic gains over their 1939 prewar levels.[72] The growth of local industry was so substantial that even as production reached its lowest postwar levels in December 1945, local manufacturing employment exceeded that of 1939 by nearly 80 percent.[73]

Among the chief factors influencing the wartime industrial growth of Los Angeles were federal government investment capital, a large work force, and the region's abundant natural resources. The federal government's interest in developing industry in Los Angeles also stemmed from the city's location and its manufacturing potential. Los Angeles proved worthy of federal investment dollars. The area's several hundred small concerns, which characterized the manufacturing base of Los Angeles in 1939 quickly converted to wartime production needs. They proved instrumental in supplementing the needs of the area's most important wartime industries: aircraft production and shipbuilding.

Federal defense dollars were also used to finance industries that produced locally needed unfinished items, especially those requiring steel and aluminum. Perhaps most notable was the federally-financed Kaiser steel plant in Fontana. The Fontana mill, second largest in the West, helped Los Angeles to break the domination of eastern-based industries whose high cost for raw and basic materials had hindered the city's industrial development. As a result of these investments, Los Angeles emerged from the war confident that it could produce locally many of the items needed to carry on its expansive industrial program.

Los Angeles's confidence in its post-war future was further spurred by the wartime gains made in harnessing the abundant natural resources of the area. Substantial progress was made in oil recovery and in chemical and electrical production. In addition, gains made in technological developments added to the city's growing industrial strength. The most important natural resource, though, was the people of Los Angeles. Despite wartime stresses and strains, many Angelenos worked well beyond the forty-eight hour average work week. Still others worked the mandatory forty-eight hour work week and then used their free time as civilian defense volunteers. Despite these heroic efforts, there never seemed to be enough workers to meet wartime industrial needs. The chronic shortages were eased only by the constant influx of first-time workers.

Given the vacuum in defense industry employment, previously neglected groups, notably women, blacks, and Hispanics, made their way aggressively into the ranks of well-paying occupations for the first time, representing social changes that bordered on revolutionary. For the first time in the history of Los Angeles these groups worked in large numbers in positions that had been dominated by white males. Although each of these groups experienced sharp downturns in employment near the end of the war due to the return of white male workers, fiscal cutbacks, and other cultural and social factors, the maintenance of second-class status for women and minorities thereafter was unacceptable to both groups.[74]

It must be stressed that the federal government played an integral role in helping women and minorities obtain employment in the wartime industries of Los Angeles. Through its chief agency for minority groups, the Fair Employment Practices Commission (FEPC), the government exerted pressure on employers to end discriminatory hiring practices. Although the agency was considered weak and ineffective, its hearings on working conditions and labor practices encouraged minority groups to continue their fight for equal employment. The intervention of the federal government on their behalf kept growing numbers of minorities committed to the ideals of democracy.

Another important aspect in the fight for equal employment and working conditions was the continued development of organized minority groups. Groups such as the Negro Victory Committee achieved important gains for their causes. By maintaining a mainstream patriotic strategy, these organizations were able to press their demands for job opportunities. Among their successful approaches were large war bond rallies, where leaders not only raised money for the war but also pleaded for war industry jobs for minorities. The irony of large worker shortages and the continued refusal by industries to hire minorities was not lost on the press or the public.

Minority community organizations also played a vital role in pointing out the problems of their neighborhoods exacerbated by the war. Local minority leaders, such as Charlotta Bass, editor and publisher of the black newspaper, the *California Eagle*, made known the needs and problems in the black community by serving on public boards and organizing peaceful protests.[75] Although government help remained limited, inroads were made in the segregated and discriminatory features of Los Angeles society. One of the most important new starts was the work begun to end housing-covenant restrictions. Strong efforts to repeal this policy were begun in the minority communities during the war years when the racially segregated communities were overrun with in-migrants.[76]

The vast migration of aspiring war workers and their families dramatically altered the population characteristics of the Los Angeles area. The United States Bureau of the Census in January 1946 conducted a special census of Los Angeles City. It found that the total population had grown by 20 percent since 1940. The most dramatic changes, however, occurred in the minority communities. The black community grew by an astounding 108.7 percent. In contrast, mostly due to the removal of the Japanese Americans, other racial groups not classified under white or black (except for Hispanics who were classified by census takers as white) declined by nearly half.[77]

As a result of the strong population growth of the city of Los Angeles and an estimated wartime population increase of 31 percent for Los Angeles County, the region appeared destined for a bright future.[78] Adding to the encouraging picture was the easing of restrictions on building materials. With plenty of open space remaining outside the central city, Los

Angeles expected to handle its burgeoning population growth by building new residences. During the first nine months of 1945, a total of 21,916 building permits were issued by the city, a number more than double that of either Detroit or New York City.[79]

Another positive indicator of Los Angeles's post-war economic strength was the large-scale conversion of war production plants into peacetime factories.[80] Many of those buying and converting war plants were companies from outside the region. During the war, thirty-one eastern and midwestern manufacturers bought property in Los Angeles County. Following the war's conclusion, such companies as Sylvania Electric, General Motors, and Quaker Oats all opened large branch factories in Los Angeles. Approximately one-eighth of all the new businesses started in the United States in 1946 were begun in southern California, thus adding to the region's economic promise.[81]

Despite the termination of large war contracts following the war's conclusion in August 1945, Los Angeles retained its close ties with the federal government. Among the key developments emanating from the war experience was the establishment of a large aerospace industry in southern California with an important economic relationship with the military. At the war's conclusion, military authorities chose Los Angeles as the site for the government's first "think tank," the RAND Corporation. Standing for "Research and Development," RAND brought military authorities and scientists together to discuss military contingencies and defense strategies.[82]

Los Angeles also remained throughout the war a leading fashion center. Between 1940 and 1945 employment in the city's garment industry grew by approximately 20 percent. Ironically, the greatest boom during the war in the garment industry came not from its tremendous production of parachutes, life preservers, and military outfits, but in the production of clothing that reflected the outdoor and informal living style characteristic of Los Angeles. Among the best individual customers were visiting military personnel, many of whom were taken with the region's temperate climate and natural beauty.[83]

Also benefitting from the war was the city's entertainment industry. It lured some of the world's greatest talent to Los Angeles by offering high paying work and a place of refuge from the destruction of Europe. According to cultural historian Peter Gay, "The exiles Hitler made were the greatest collection of transplanted intellect, talent, and scholarship the world has ever seen."[84] Hollywood, in particular, benefitted from this great talent because of the employment opportunities it offered for writers, musicians, and artists. Although the number of European war refugees in southern California totaled no more than ten thousand, the presence of such emigres as Arnold Schoenberg, Thomas Mann, Bertolt Brecht, Ernest Gold, and Erich Korngold helped Los Angeles break out of its cultural provincialism and ascend to the ranks as one of the world's cultured cities.[85]

Upon the war's conclusion, Los Angeles remained a popular destination for those in search of better lives and economic opportunity. Even with the city's well publicized problems of smog-filled air, congested streets, inadequate housing, racial tension, and a broken sewer system, to name but a few of the wartime afflictions, newcomers continued to pour in. Much of the city's attraction remained the industrial base that had been developed by the war. No longer dependent on the investment monies and raw materials from the regions east of the Rockies, Los Angeles, in partnership with the federal government, developed a self-sustaining economy that was oriented toward future regional growth and technological innovation. As the *Los Angeles Times* explained in late December 1945:

> The story of the west's great industrial future has spread over the nation and like the story of the discovery of gold, it is luring hopeful men whose dreams are spun of golden opportunity.[86]

In summation, the Second World War brought forth a new West, a new Los Angeles. So powerful was the war's impact that the once small town of Los Angeles had by 1943 become home to one in forty Americans.[87] And unlike most war boom areas, Los Angeles's new inhabitants decided to remain in the city. Indeed, many invited friends and relatives to join them. This new population of footloose people sought government housing and jobs and looked for the urban advantages of good schools, pleasant neighborhoods, and a California lifestyle of automobiles and easy access to work, shops, and recreation. The Second World War consequently gave them a taste of paradise. Thus, in reducing the war's impact on Los Angeles to the simplest of terms, it is correct to say, "The 'war' made Los Angeles."

NOTES

1. The leading proponent of the Second World War's transformative power on the development of the American West is Gerald D. Nash, *The American West Transformed: The Impact of the Second World War* (Bloomington, 1985); and Nash, *World War II and the Reshaping of the Economy* (Lincoln 1990). In contrast to what has become known as the "Nash thesis" is the seminal work of Roger W. Lotchin. Lotchin makes a strong case for the "evolution," rather than "revolution" school of thought in *Fortress California, 1910–1961: From Warfare to Welfare* (New York, 1992).

2. Los Angeles, in fact, had surpassed San Francisco in population by 1920 and had by 1939 some 172,000 industrial workers within its metropolitan corridor as compared to 101,000 for the San Francisco-Oakland metropolitan district. Still, a strong argument can be made that on the eve of the Second World War, Los Angeles was often perceived by many Americans, and particularly by federal authorities in Washington, D.C., as California's second city.

3. Willard E. Motley, "Small Town Los Angeles," *Commonweal*, (June 1939), 251–252.

4. Phillip Neff, Lisette C. Baum, and Grace E. Heilman, *Favored Industries in Los Angeles: An Analysis of Production Costs* (Los Angeles, 1948), 7.

5. John Parke Young, "Industrial Background" in George W. Robbins and L. Deming Tilton, eds., *Preface to a Master Plan* (Los Angeles, 1941), 61.

6. Los Angeles County Chamber of Commerce, Industrial Department, "Eco-

nomic Background of Los Angeles County," in *Collection of Eight Studies in the Industrial Development of Los Angeles County* (Los Angeles, n.d.), 6.

7. Young, "Industrial Background," 69–72.

8. Harvey M. Beigel, *Battleship Country: The Battle Fleet at San Pedro–Long Beach, California 1919–1940* (Missoula, 1983), 1.

9. Ibid., 71.

10. Leonard Leader, *Los Angeles and the Great Depression* (New York, 1991), 266–269.

11. The aircraft industry went from employing 5 percent of industrial workers in Los Angeles County in 1937 to employing more than 40 percent in 1942. Arthur G. Coons and Arjay R. Miller, *An Economic and Industrial Survey of the Los Angeles and San Diego Areas* (Sacramento, 1941), 184.

12. Ibid., 198.

13. Ibid., 125.

14. Carey McWilliams, *Southern California Country: An Island on the Land* (New York, 1946), 233.

15. Created by Congress in August 1940, the DPC became the largest investor in the defense industries of Los Angeles. Within the first two years of its existence, the agency invested nearly a third of a billion dollars constructing not only aircraft plants but shipyards, aluminum plants, steel mills, and other industrial facilities throughout southern California as well. Security-First National Bank of Los Angeles, *Monthly Summary of Business Conditions In Southern California* (Los Angeles, Jan. 1945).

16. Nash, *American West Transformed*, 19.

17. *Los Angeles Times*, Sept. 1, 1992.

18. "Civilian Defense in Los Angeles," *Western City*, 18 (Sept. 1942), 30.

19. *Los Angeles Times*, Dec. 24, 1941.

20. Torrance *Daily Breeze*, Feb. 23, 1992.

21. Radio speech given on February 5, 1942. Congressman John Costello inserted the speech in the *Cong. Rec.*, 77 Cong. 2 Sess. (1942), 457–459. For a more thorough examination of Fletcher Bowron's role in the events leading up to the evacuation of the Japanese, see Morton Grodzins, *Americans Betrayed, Politics and the Japanese Evacuation* (Chicago, 1949), 100–106.

22. An excellent study of America's decision to evacuate the Japanese is Roger Daniels, *The Decision to Relocate the Japanese* (Malabar, 1975).

23. Bert Webber, *Silent Siege: Japanese Attacks Against North America in World War II* (Fairfield, 1984), 105–111.

24. *Los Angeles Times*, Feb. 25, 1942.

25. Webber, *Silent Siege*, 111–115; *Jack Smith's L. A.* (New York, 1980), 90–94.

26. It also gave "locals" a story that is still recounted as a fond wartime memory. Comedian Bob Hope recalled that during the "attack" two air-raid wardens in Beverly Hills, the Austrian–born movie director Otto Preminger, and German–born producer Henry Blake, ran up and down Rexford Drive screaming, "Close de vindows! Close de vindows!" In response, a frightened movie star ran out of his front door yelling, "Run for your lives! The Germans are here!"

27. James Richard Wilburn, "Social and Economic Aspects of the Aircraft Industry in Metropolitan Los Angeles during World War II" (Ph.D. dissertation, University of California, Los Angeles, 1971), 203.

28. *Los Angeles Times*, Dec. 11, 1941.

29. Carnegie-Myrdal Study, "Survey of the Negro," Los Angeles Urban League Papers, form 1, 2, collection 203, box 1, Department of Special Collections, University Research Library, University of California, Los Angeles.

30. Ibid., form 4.

31. Lawrence Brooks de Graaf, "Negro Migration to Los Angeles, 1930 to 1950" (Ph.D. dissertation, University of California, Los Angeles, 1962), 167.

32. As quoted in National Negro Congress, Los Angeles Council, *Jim Crow in National Defense* (Los Angeles, 1940), 13.

33. James E. Crimi, "The Social Status of the Negro in Pasadena, California" (M.A. thesis, University of Southern California, 1941), 38–39.

34. Lester B. Granger, "Negroes and War Production," *Survey Graphic*, 31 (Nov. 1942), 470.

35. A good summation of Los Angeles's substantial black community before the Second World War can be found in Lawrence de Graaf, "The City of Black Angels: Emergence of the Los Angeles Ghetto, 1890–1960," *Pacific Historical Review*, 39 (1970), 323–352.

36. E. Frederick Anderson, *The Development of Leadership and Organization Building in the Black Community of Los Angeles from 1900 through World War II* (Saratoga, Calif., 1980), 85–86.

37. Issues of the *Los Angeles Sentinel* are not available for the years 1941–1945.

38. *Fortune Magazine*, 33 (March 1943), 98.

39. Wilburn, "Aircraft Industry," 165.

40. Anderson, *Leadership and Organization Building*, 88–91.

41. Sherna Berger Gluck, *Rosie the Riveter Revisited: The War and Social Change* (Boston, 1987), 203–204.

42. Carleton Champe, "Women Only," *North American Skyline* (May–June 1944), 10–11.

43. Karen Anderson, *Wartime Women: Sex Roles, Family Relations, and the Status of Women during World War II* (Westport, Conn., 1981), 125; D'Ann Campbell, *Women at War with America: Private Lives in a Patriotic Era* (Cambridge, Mass., 1984), 13–14.

44. House Subcommittee of Committee on Naval Affairs, *Hearings in Congested Areas*, 78 Cong., 1 Sess. (1944), 1794, 2036.

45. Wilburn, "Aircraft Industry," 236–237.

46. Ibid., 270.

47. *Hearings on Congested Areas*, 1761.

48. De Graaf, "Negro Migration to Los Angeles," 263. In total numbers, between April 1940 and April 1944, an estimated 780,000 persons migrated into the Los Angeles area. Nearly 80 percent of these immigrants were under the age of forty-five, and they were responsible for increasing Los Angeles's wartime labor supply by 25 percent. U.S. Bureau of the Census, "Wartime Changes in Population and Family Characteristics, Los Angeles Congested Production Area, April 1944," Series CA-2, No. 5, 1–3.

49. Security-First, *Monthly Summary* (Feb. 1943).

50. Charles F. Queenan, *The Port of Los Angeles: From Wilderness to World Port* (Los Angeles, 1982), 87.

51. Security-First, *Monthly Summary* (Feb. 1943).

52. Queenan, *Port of Los Angeles*, 87; City of Los Angeles, Board of Harbor Commissioners, *Annual Report: For the Fiscal Year Beginning July 1, 1946, and Ending June 30, 1947* (Los Angeles, 1947).

53. Queenan, *Port of Los Angeles*, 52.

54. City of Los Angeles, Board of Harbor Commissioners, *Annual Report*, 1946–1947 (Los Angeles, 1947).

55. Queenan, *Port of Los Angeles*, 91.

56. Wilburn, "Aircraft Industry," 68.

57. Ibid., 47.

58. Nash, *American West Transformed*, 26.

59. Wilburn, "Aircraft Industry," 54–55.

60. Security-First, *Monthly Summary* (Aug. 1942).

61. Ibid.

62. Mignon E. Rothstein. "A Study of the Growth of Negro Population in Los Angeles and, Available Housing Facilities between 1940 and 1946" (M.A. thesis, Univer-

sity of Southern California, 1950), 36–44. As late as 1950 the United States census showed that the city of Los Angeles contained 78 percent of the blacks in the county.

63. *Hearings in Congested Areas*, 1761.

64. Ibid., 1770–1771.

65. Ibid.

66. For accounts of the "Zoot Suit Riots," see Mauricio Mazón, *The Psychology of Symbolism: The Zoot Suit Riots* (Austin, 1984); Richard Romo, *East Los Angeles: History of a Barrio* (Austin, 1983), 165–167; Nash, *American West Transformed*, 115–121.

67. *Hearings on Congested Areas*, 1773–1780, 1816–1827.

68. Elmer Belt, "A Sanitary Survey of Sewage Pollution of the Surf and Beaches of Santa Monica Bay," *Western City*, 19 (June 1943), 17–22.

69. Marvin Brienes, "Smog Comes to Los Angeles," *Southern California Quarterly*, 53 (1976), 515–532.

70. Frank L. Kidner and Phillip Neff, *Los Angeles: The Economic Outlook* (Los Angeles, 1946), 5. Particularly hard hit by aircraft industry lay-offs were thousands of women defense workers. A post-war survey conducted by the *Los Angeles Times* found that the number of women in the city's five largest aircraft plants had dropped from 37 percent on August 5, 1945, to 27 percent by December 16, 1945. While it is true that some of these women left voluntarily, other women found themselves forcibly removed from company payrolls by lay-off notices and social mores that demanded that returning male war veterans be given any available jobs in the high-paying industry.

71. Wilburn, "Aircraft Industry," 247.

72. Security-First, *Monthly Summary* (Dec. 1946).

73. Ibid. (Jan. 1946).

74. Wilburn, "Aircraft Industry," 236–237.

75. Charlotta Bass, *Forty Years: Memoirs from the Pages of a Newspaper* (Los Angeles, 1960).

76. The United States Supreme Court in 1948 ruled in *Shelly v. Kraemer*, and *Hurd v. Hodge* that the enforcement of restrictive covenants against selling residential properties to minorities was in violation of the Fourteenth Amendment and the Civil Rights Act of 1866. A Los Angeles case, *Barrows v. Jackson* (1953), closed an important loophole by ruling out damage suits against the seller of a property covered by restrictive covenant. For description and background on the Los Angeles case, see Loren Miller, "Scotching Restrictive Covenants," in John W. Caughey and Laree Caughey, eds., *Los Angeles: Biography of a City* (Berkeley, 1976), 388–391.

77. Special U.S. census figures on population characteristics of Los Angeles City on January 28, 1946 are broken down in Security-First, *Monthly Summary* (Sept. 1946).

78. Ibid.

79. In comparison, Detroit was ranked second nationally with 9,965 permits followed by New York City with 9,707. *Los Angeles Times*, Special edition Mid-Winter Edition, Jan. 2, 1946.

80. Security-First, *Monthly Summary* (Feb. 1946).

81. "The Undiscovered City," *Fortune*, 34 (June 1949), 160.

82. Fred Kaplan, "Scientists at War: The Birth of the RAND Corporation," *American Heritage*, XXIV (1983), 49–64.

83. The garment industry in Los Angeles in 1944 employed 35,000 workers and was selling 85 percent of its product east of the Rockies. Carey McWilliams, *California the Great Exception* (New York, 1949), 218–220: "Los Angeles' Little Cutters," *Fortune*, 31 (May 1945), 134–139.

84. Peter Gay, "Weimar Culture: The Outsider as Insider," in Donald Fleming and Bernard Bailyn, eds., *The Intellectual Migration* (Cambridge, Mass., 1969), 11–12.

85. Nash, *American West Transformed*, 195.

86. *Los Angeles Times*, Dec. 18, 1945.

87. *Hearings on Congested Areas*, 1761.

15　JAPANESE–AMERICAN WOMEN DURING WORLD WAR II

Valerie Matsumoto

The internment of 110,000 Japanese–Americans by the U.S. government in 1942 is a shameful chapter in American history. Popular hysteria, shared by civilian and military officials, about espionage and Japanese naval and air attacks on the West Coast, provoked the removal of these people from their homes, jobs, and businesses with scarcely any compensation or warning. The army and local law enforcement took them first to "staging areas"—places such as the stables of the Santa Anita race track near Los Angeles—and then to a dozen camps in the intermountain West and in Arkansas. These amounted to minimum- or medium-security prisons, and there these people (one-third of them born in Japan, two-thirds of them natural-born American citizens) stayed, in most cases, until the war was over. How can we explain how fear of an Asian minority provoked such a reaction? How could authorities and the public justify it?

Much has been written about the internment. In this essay, Matsumoto focuses on how deportation, internment, and release particularly affected Nisei women, the teenage and twentyish daughters of the immigrants. She describes camp life and how these daughters adapted to what it offered them in the way of job training and education. How did the experience have a "silver lining" for these young women? How did the immigrant generation's practices regarding family-arranged marriages give way to more Americanized ideas? How did certain professions and occupations open up to them, which before the war were closed? What were these new options? How did these young women manage to combine Issei discipline with their own self-reliance and the support networks which they constructed among themselves, often in spite of internment conditions?—editors

The life here cannot be expressed. Sometimes, we are resigned to it, but when we see the barbed wire fences and the sentry tower with floodlights, it gives us a feeling of being prisoners in a "concentration camp." We try to be happy and yet oftentimes a gloominess does creep in. When I see the "I'm an American" editorial and writeups, the "equality of race etc."—it seems to be mocking us in our faces. I

just wonder if all the sacrifices and hard labor on [the] part of our parents has gone up to leave nothing to show for it?
—*Letter from Shizuko Horiuchi,*
Pomona Assembly Center, May 24, 1942

THIRTY YEARS after her relocation camp internment, another Nisei woman, the artist Miné Okubo, observed, "The impact of the evacuation is not on the material and the physical. It is something far deeper. It is the effect on the spirit."[1] Describing the lives of Japanese American women during World War II and assessing the effects of the camp experience on the spirit are complex tasks: factors such as age, generation, personality, and family background interweave and preclude simple generalizations. In these relocation camps Japanese American women faced severe racism and traumatic family strain, but the experience also fostered changes in their lives: more leisure for older women, equal pay with men for working women, disintegration of traditional patterns of arranged marriages, and, ultimately, new opportunities for travel, work, and education for the younger women.

I will examine the lives of Japanese American women during the trying war years, focusing on the second generation—the Nisei—whose work and education were most affected. The Nisei women entered college and ventured into new areas of work in unfamiliar regions of the country, sustained by fortitude, family ties, discipline, and humor. My understanding of their history derives from several collections of internees' letters, assembly center and relocation camp newspapers, census records, and taped oral history interviews that I conducted with eighty-four Nisei (second generation) and eleven Issei (first generation). Two-thirds of these interviews were with women.

The personal letters, which comprise a major portion of my research, were written in English by Nisei women in their late teens and twenties. Their writing reflects the experience and concerns of their age group. It is important, however, to remember that they wrote these letters to Caucasian friends and sponsors during a time of great insecurity and psychological and economic hardship. In their struggle to be accepted as American citizens, the interned Japanese Americans were likely to minimize their suffering in the camps and to try to project a positive image of their adjustment to the traumatic conditions.

PREWAR BACKGROUND

A century ago, male Japanese workers began to arrive on American shores, dreaming of making fortunes that would enable them to return to their homeland in triumph. For many, the fortune did not materialize and the shape of the dream changed: they developed stakes in small farms and businesses and, together with wives brought from Japan, established families and communities.

The majority of Japanese women—over 33,000 immigrants—entered the United States between 1908 and 1924.[2] The "Gentlemen's Agreement" of 1908 restricted the entry of male Japanese laborers into the country but sanctioned the immigration of parents, wives, and children of laborers already residing in the United States. The Immigration Act of 1924 excluded Japanese immigration altogether.

Some Japanese women traveled to reunite with husbands; others journeyed to America as newlyweds with men who had returned to Japan to find wives. Still others came alone as picture brides to join Issei men who sought to avoid army conscription or excessive travel expenses; their family-arranged marriages deviated from social convention only by the absence of the groom from the *miai* (preliminary meeting of prospective spouses) and wedding ceremony.[3] Once settled, these women confronted unfamiliar clothing, food, language, and customs as well as life with husbands who were, in many cases, strangers and often ten to fifteen years their seniors.

Most Issei women migrated to rural areas of the West. Some lived with their husbands in labor camps, which provided workers for the railroad industry, the lumber mills of the Pacific Northwest, and the Alaskan salmon canneries.[4] They also farmed with their husbands as cash or share tenants, particularly in California where Japanese immigrant agriculture began to flourish. In urban areas, women worked as domestics[5] or helped their husbands run small businesses such as laundries, bath houses, restaurants, pool halls, boarding houses, grocery stores, curio shops, bakeries, and plant nurseries. Except for the few who married well-to-do professionals or merchants, the majority of Issei women unceasingly toiled both inside and outside the home. They were always the first to rise in the morning and the last to go to bed at night.

The majority of the Issei's children, the Nisei, were born between 1910 and 1940. Both girls and boys were incorporated into the family economy early, especially those living on farms. They took care of their younger siblings, fed the farm animals, heated water for the *furo* (Japanese bath), and worked in the fields before and after school—hoeing weeds, irrigating, and driving tractors. Daughters helped with cooking and cleaning. In addition, all were expected to devote time to their studies: the Issei instilled in their children a deep respect for education and authority. They repeatedly admonished the Nisei not to bring disgrace upon the family or community and exhorted them to do their best in everything.

The Nisei grew up integrating both the Japanese ways of their parents and the mainstream customs of their non-Japanese friends and classmates—not always an easy process given the deeply rooted prejudice and discrimination they faced as a tiny, easily identified minority. Because of the wide age range among them and the diversity of their early experiences in various urban and rural areas, it is difficult to generalize about the Nisei. Most grew up speaking Japanese with their parents and English with their siblings, friends, and teachers. Regardless of whether they were Buddhist or Christian, they celebrated the New Year with traditional foods and visiting, as well as Christmas and Thanksgiving. Girls learned to knit, sew, and embroider, and some took lessons in *odori* (folk dancing). The Nisei, many of whom were adolescents during the 1940s, also listened to the *Hit Parade*, Jack Benny, and *Gangbusters* on the radio, learned to jitterbug, played kick-the-can and baseball, and read the same popular books and magazines as their non-Japanese peers.

The Issei were strict and not inclined to open displays of affection towards their children, but the Nisei were conscious of their parents' concern for them and for the family. This sense of family strength and responsibility helped to sustain the Issei and Nisei through years of economic hardship and discrimination: the West Coast anti-Japanese movement of the early 1920s, the Depression of the 1930s, and the most drastic ordeal—the chaotic uprooting of the World War II evacuation, internment, and resettlement.

EVACUATION AND CAMP EXPERIENCE

The bombing of Pearl Harbor on December 7, 1941, unleashed war between the United States and Japan and triggered a wave of hostility against Japanese Americans. On December 8, the financial resources of the Issei were frozen, and the Federal Bureau of Investigation began to seize Issei community leaders thought to be strongly pro-Japanese. Rumors spread that the Japanese in Hawaii had aided the attack on Pearl Harbor, fueling fears of "fifth column" activity on the West Coast. Politicians and the press clamored for restrictions against the Japanese Americans, and their economic competitors saw the chance to gain control of Japanese American farms and businesses.

Despite some official doubts and some differences of opinion among military heads regarding the necessity of removing Japanese Americans from the West Coast, in the end the opinions of civilian leaders and Lieutenant General John L. DeWitt—head of the Western Defense Command—of Assistant Secretary of War John McCloy and Secretary of War Henry Stimson prevailed. On February 19, 1942, President Franklin Delano Roosevelt signed Executive Order 9066, arbitrarily suspending the civil rights of American citizens by authorizing the removal of 110,000 Japanese and their American-born children from the western half of the Pacific Coastal States and the southern third of Arizona.[6]

During the bewildering months before evacuation, the Japanese Americans were subject to curfews and to unannounced searches at all hours for "contraband" weapons, radios, and cameras; in desperation and fear, many people destroyed their belongings from Japan, including treasured heirlooms, books, and photographs. Some families moved voluntarily from the Western Defense zone, but many stayed, believing that all areas would eventually be restricted or fearing hostility in neighboring states.

Involuntary evacuation began in the spring of 1942. Families received a scant week's notice in which to "wind up their affairs, store or sell their possessions, close up their businesses and homes, and show up at an assembly point for transportation to an assembly center."[7] Each person was allowed to bring only as many clothes and personal items as he or she could carry to the temporary assembly centers that had been hastily constructed at fairgrounds, race tracks, and Civilian Conservation Corps camps: twelve in California, one in Oregon, and one in Washington.

The rapidity of evacuation left many Japanese Americans numb; one Nisei noted that "a queer lump came to my throat. Nothing else came to my mind, it was just blank. Everything happened too soon, I guess."[8] As the realization of leaving home, friends, and neighborhood sank in, the numbness gave way to bewilderment. A teenager at the Santa Anita Assembly Center wrote, "I felt lost after I left Mountain View [California]. I thought that we could go back but instead look where we are."[9] Upon arrival at the assembly centers, even the Nisei from large urban communities found themselves surrounded by more Japanese than they had ever before seen. For Mary Okumura, the whole experience seemed overwhelming at first:

> Just about every night, there is something going on but I rather stay home because I am just new here & don't know very much around. As for the people I met so many all ready, I don't remember any. I am not even going to try to remember names because its just impossible here.[10]

A Nisei from a community where there were few Japanese felt differently about her arrival at the Merced Assembly Center: "I guess at that age it was sort of fun for me really [rather] than tragic, because for the first time I got to see young [Japanese] people. . . . We signed up to work in the mess hall—we got to meet everybody that way."[11]

Overlying the mixed feelings of anxiety, anger, shame, and confusion was resignation. As a relatively small minority caught in a storm of turbulent events that destroyed their individual and community security, there was little the Japanese Americans could do but shrug and say, "*Shikata ga nai*," or, "It can't be helped," the implication being that the situation must be endured. The phrase lingered on many lips when the Issei, Nisei, and the young Sansei (third generation) children prepared for the move—which was completed by November 1942—to the ten permanent relocation camps organized by the War Relocation Authority: Topaz, Utah; Poston and Gila River, Arizona; Amache, Colorado; Manzanar and Tule Lake, California; Heart Mountain, Wyoming; Minidoka, Idaho; Denson and Rohwer, Arkansas.[12] Denson and Rohwer were located in the swampy lowlands of Arkansas; the other camps were in desolate desert or

semi-desert areas subject to dust storms and extreme temperatures reflected in the nicknames given to the three sections of the Poston Camp:
Toaston, Roaston, and Duston.

The conditions of camp life profoundly altered family relations and
affected women of all ages and backgrounds. Family unity deteriorated in
the crude communal facilities and cramped barracks. The unceasing battle
with the elements, the poor food, the shortages of toilet tissue and milk,
coupled with wartime profiteering and mismanagement, and the sense of
injustice and frustration took their toll on a people uprooted, far from
home.

The standard housing in the camps was a spartan barracks, about
twenty feet by one hundred feet, divided into four to six rooms furnished
with steel army cots. Initially each single room or "apartment" housed an
average of eight persons; individuals without kin nearby were often moved
in with smaller families. Because the partitions between apartments did
not reach the ceiling, even the smallest noises traveled freely from one end
of the building to the other. There were usually fourteen barracks in each
block, and each block had its own mess hall, laundry, latrine, shower facilities, and recreation room.

Because of the discomfort, noise, and lack of privacy, which "made a
single symphony of yours and your neighbors' loves, hates, and joys,"[13]
the barracks often became merely a place to "hang your hat" and sleep.
As Jeanne Wakatsuki Houston records in her autobiography, *Farewell to
Manzanar*, many family members began to spend less time together in the
crowded barracks. The even greater lack of privacy in the latrine and
shower facilities necessitated adjustments in former notions of modesty.
There were no partitions in the shower room, and the latrine consisted of
two rows of partitioned toilets "with nothing in front of you, just on the
sides. Lots of people were not used to those kind of facilities, so [they'd]
either go early in the morning when people were not around, or go real
late at night. . . . It was really something until you got used to it."[14]

The large communal mess halls also encouraged family disunity as
family members gradually began to eat separately: mothers with small
children, fathers with other men, and older children with their peers.
"Table manners were forgotten," observed Miné Okubo. "Guzzle, guzzle,
guzzle; hurry, hurry, hurry. Family life was lacking. Everyone ate wherever he or she pleased."[15] Some strategies were developed for preserving
family unity. The Amache Camp responded in part by assigning each family a particular table in the mess hall. Some families took the food back
to their barracks so that they might eat together. But these measures were
not always feasible in the face of varying work schedules; the odd hours of
those assigned to shifts in the mess halls and infirmaries often made it
impossible for the family to sit down together for meals.

Newspaper reports that Japanese Americans were living in luxurious
conditions angered evacuees struggling to adjust to cramped quarters and
crude communal facilities. A married woman with a family wrote from
Heart Mountain:

16. In the internment camps: a Nisei girl brings rice into the mess hall of a camp at Shelley, Idaho, July 1942. *The Library of Congress.*

Last weekend, we had an awful cold wave and it was about 20° to 30° below zero. In such a weather, it's terrible to try going even to the bath and latrine house. . . . It really aggravates me to hear some politicians say we Japanese are being coddled, for it isn't so!! We're on ration as much as outsiders are. I'd say welcome to anyone to try living behind barbed wire and be cooped in a 20 ft. by 20 ft. room. . . . We do our sleeping, dressing, ironing, hanging up our clothes in this one room.[16]

After the first numbness of disorientation the evacuees set about making their situation bearable, creating as much order in their lives as possible. With blankets they partitioned their apartments into tiny rooms and created benches, tables, and shelves as piles of scrap lumber left over from barracks construction vanished; victory gardens and flower patches appeared. Evacuees also took advantage of the opportunity to taste freedom when they received temporary permits to go shopping in nearby towns. These were memorable occasions. A Heart Mountain Nisei described what such a trip meant to her in 1944:

for the first time since being behind the fences, I managed to go out shopping to Billings, Montana—a trip about 4 hours ride on train and bus. . . . It was quite a mental relief to breathe the air on the outside. . . . And was it an undescribable sensation to be able to be dressed up and walk the pavements with my high heel shoes!! You just can't imagine how full we are of pent-up emotions until we leave the camp behind us and see the highway ahead of us. A trip like that will keep us from becoming mentally narrow. And without much privacy, you can imagine how much people will become dull.[17]

Despite the best efforts of the evacuees to restore order to their disrupted world, camp conditions prevented replication of their prewar lives. Women's work experiences, for example, changed in complex ways during the years of internment. Each camp offered a wide range of jobs, resulting from the organization of the camps as model cities administered through a series of departments headed by Caucasian administrators. The departments handled everything from accounting, agriculture, education, and medical care to mess hall service and the weekly newspaper. The scramble for jobs began early in the assembly centers and camps, and all able-bodied persons were expected to work.

Even before the war many family members had worked, but now children and parents, men and women all received the same low wages. In the relocation camps, doctors, teachers, and other professionals were at the top of the pay scale, earning $19 per month. The majority of workers received $16, and apprentices earned $12. The new equity in pay and the variety of available jobs gave many women unprecedented opportunities for experimentation, as illustrated by one woman's account of her family's work in Poston:

First I wanted to find art work, but I didn't last too long because it wasn't very interesting . . . so I worked in the mess hall, but that wasn't for me, so I went to the accounting department—timekeeping—and I enjoyed that, so I stayed there. . . . My dad . . . went to a shoe shop . . . and then he was block gardener. . . . He got $16. . . . [My sister] was secretary for the block manager; then she went to the optometry department. She was assistant optometrist; she fixed all the glasses and fitted them. . . . That was $16.[18]

As early as 1942, the War Relocation Authority began to release evacuees temporarily from the centers and camps to do voluntary seasonal farm work in neighboring areas hard hit by the wartime labor shortage. The work was arduous, as one young woman discovered when she left Topaz to take a job plucking turkeys:

The smell is terrific until you get used to it. . . . We all wore gunny sacks around our waist, had a small knife and plucked off the fine feathers.

This is about the hardest work that many of us have done—but without a murmur of complaint we worked 8 hours through the first day without a pause.

We were all so tired that we didn't even feel like eating. . . . Our fingers and wrists were just aching, and I just dreamt of turkeys and more turkeys.[19]

Work conditions varied from situation to situation, and some exploitative farmers refused to pay the Japanese Americans after they had finished beet topping or fruit picking. One worker noted that the degree of friendliness on the employer's part decreased as the harvest neared completion. Nonetheless, many workers, like the turkey plucker, concluded that "even if the work is hard, it is worth the freedom we are allowed."

Camp life increased the leisure of many evacuees. A good number of Issei women, accustomed to long days of work inside and outside the home, found that the communally prepared meals and limited living quarters provided them with spare time. Many availed themselves of the opportunity to attend adult classes taught by both evacuees and non-Japanese. Courses involving handcrafts and traditional Japanese arts such as flower arrangement, sewing, painting, calligraphy, and wood carving became immensely popular as an overwhelming number of people turned to art for recreation and self-expression. Some of these subjects were viewed as hobbies and leisure activities by those who taught them, but to the Issei women they represented access to new skills and a means to contribute to the material comfort of the family.

The evacuees also filled their time with Buddhist and Christian church meetings, theatrical productions, cultural programs, athletic events, and visits with friends. All family members spent more time than ever before in the company of their peers. Nisei from isolated rural areas were exposed to the ideas, styles, and pastimes of the more sophisticated urban youth; in camp they had the time and opportunity to socialize—at work, school, dances, sports events, and parties—in an almost entirely Japanese American environment. Gone were the restrictions of distance, lack of transportation, interracial uneasiness, and the dawn-to-dusk exigencies of field work.

Like their noninterned contemporaries, most young Nisei women envisioned a future of marriage and children. They—and their parents—anticipated that they would marry other Japanese Americans, but these young women also expected to choose their own husbands and to marry "for love." This mainstream American ideal of marriage differed greatly from the Issei's view of love as a bond that might evolve over the course of an arranged marriage that was firmly rooted in less romantic notions of compatibility and responsibility. The discrepancy between Issei and Nisei conceptions of love and marriage had sturdy prewar roots; internment fostered further divergence from the old customs of arranged marriage.

In the artificial hothouse of camp, Nisei romances often bloomed quickly. As Nisei men left to prove their loyalty to the United States in the 442nd Combat Team and the 100th Battalion, young Japanese Americans strove to grasp what happiness and security they could, given the uncertainties of the future. Lily Shoji, in her "Fem-a-lites" newspaper column, commented upon the "changing world" and advised Nisei women:

> This is the day of sudden dates, of blind dates on the up-and-up, so let the flash of a uniform be a signal to you to be ready for any emergency. . . . Romance is blossoming with the emotion and urgency of war.[20]

In keeping with this atmosphere, camp newspaper columns like Shoji's in *The Mercedian*, *The Daily Tulean Dispatch*'s "Strictly Feminine," and the *Poston Chronicle*'s "Fashionotes" gave their Nisei readers countless suggestions on how to impress boys, care for their complexions, and choose the latest fashions. These evacuee-authored columns thus mirrored the mainstream girls' periodicals of the time. Such fashion news may seem incongruous in the context of an internment camp whose inmates had little choice in clothing beyond what they could find in the Montgomery Ward or Sears and Roebuck mail-order catalogues. These columns, however, reflect women's efforts to remain in touch with the world outside the barbed wire fence; they reflect as well women's attempt to maintain morale in a drab, depressing environment. "There's something about color in clothes," speculated Tule Lake columnist "Yuri"; "Singing colors have a heart-building effect. . . . Color is a stimulant we need—both for its effect on ourselves and on others."[21]

The evacuees' fashion columns addressed practical as well as aesthetic concerns, reflecting the dusty realities of camp life. In this vein, Mitzi Sugita of the Poston Sewing Department praised the "Latest Fashion for Women Today—Slacks," drawing special attention to overalls; she assured her readers that these "digging duds"[22] were not only winsome and workable but also possessed the virtues of being inexpensive and requiring little ironing.

The columnists' concern with the practical aspects of fashion extended beyond the confines of the camps, as women began to leave for life on the outside—an opportunity increasingly available after 1943. Sugita told prospective operatives, "If you are one of the many thousands of women now entering in commercial and industrial work, your required uniform is based on slacks, safe and streamlined. It is very important that they be durable, trim and attractive."[23] Women heading for clerical positions or college were more likely to heed Marii Kyogoku's admonitions to invest in "really nice things," with an eye to "simple lines which are good practically forever."[24]

RESETTLEMENT: COLLEGE AND WORK

Relocation began slowly in 1942. Among the first to venture out of the camps were college students, assisted by the National Japanese American Student Relocation Council, a nongovernmental agency that provided invaluable placement aid to 4,084 Nisei in the years 1942–46.[25] Founded in 1942 by concerned educators, this organization persuaded institutions outside the restricted Western Defense zone to accept Nisei students and facilitated their admissions and leave clearances. A study of the first 400 students to leave camp showed that a third of them were women.[26] Because of the cumbersome screening process, few other evacuees departed on indefinite leave before 1943. In that year, the War Relocation Authority tried to expedite the clearance procedure by broadening an army registration program aimed at Nisei males to include all adults. With this policy change, the migration from the camps steadily increased.[27]

Many Nisei, among them a large number of women, were anxious to leave the limbo of camp and return "to normal life again."[28] With all its work, social events, and cultural activities, camp was still an artificial, limited environment. It was stifling "to see nothing but the same barracks, mess halls, and other houses, row after row, day in and day out, it gives us the feeling that we're missing all the freedom and liberty."[29] An aspiring teacher wrote: "Mother and father do not want me to go out. However, I want to go so very much that sometimes I feel that I'd go even if they disowned me. What shall I do? I realize the hard living conditions outside but I think I can take it."[30] Women's developing sense of independence in the camp environment and their growing awareness of their abilities as workers contributed to their self-confidence and hence their desire to leave. Significantly, Issei parents, despite initial reluctance, were gradually beginning to sanction their daughters' departures for education and employment in the Midwest and East. One Nisei noted:

> [Father] became more broad-minded in the relocation center. He was more mellow in his ways. . . . At first he didn't want me to relocate, but he gave in. . . . I said I wanted to go [to Chicago] with my friend, so he helped me pack. He didn't say I could go . . . but he helped me pack, so I thought, "Well, he didn't say no."[31]

The decision to relocate was a difficult one. It was compounded for some women because they felt obligated to stay and care for elderly or infirm parents, like the Heart Mountain Nisei who observed wistfully, "It's getting so more and more of the girls and boys are leaving camp, and I sure wish I could but mother's getting on and I just can't leave her."[32] Many internees worried about their acceptance in the outside world. The Nisei considered themselves American citizens, and they had an allegiance to the land of their birth: "The teaching and love of one's own birth place, one's own country was . . . strongly impressed upon my mind as a child. So even though California may deny our rights of birth, I shall ever love her soil."[33] But evacuation had taught the Japanese Americans that in the eyes of many of their fellow Americans, theirs was the face of the enemy. Many Nisei were torn by mixed feelings of shame, frustration, and bitterness at the denial of their civil rights. These factors created an atmosphere of anxiety that surrounded those who contemplated resettlement: "A feeling of uncertainty hung over the camp; we were worried about the future. Plans were made and remade, as we tried to decide what to do. Some were ready to risk anything to get away. Others feared to leave the protection of the camp."[34]

Thus, those first college students were the scouts whose letters back to camp marked pathways for others to follow. May Yoshino sent a favorable report to her family in Topaz from the nearby University of Utah, indicating that there were "plenty of schoolgirl jobs for those who want to study at the University."[35] Correspondence from other Nisei students shows that although they succeeded at making the dual transition from high school to college and from camp to the outside world, they were not without anxieties as to whether they could handle the study load and the reactions of the Caucasians around them. One student at Drake University in Iowa wrote to her interned sister about a professor's reaction to her autobiographical essay, "Evacuation":

> Today Mr.—, the English teacher that scares me, told me that the theme that I wrote the other day was very interesting. . . . You could just imagine how wonderful and happy *I* was to know that he liked it a little bit. . . . I've been awfully busy trying to catch up on work and the work is so different from high school. I think that little by little I'm beginning to adjust myself to college life.[36]

Several incidents of hostility did occur, but the reception of the Nisei students at colleges and universities was generally warm. Topaz readers of *Trek* magazine could draw encouragement from Lillian Ota's "Campus Report." Ota, a Wellesley student, reassured them: "During the first few days you'll be invited by the college to teas and receptions. Before long you'll lose the awkwardness you might feel at such doings after the months of abnormal life at evacuation centers."[37] Although Ota had not noticed "that my being a 'Jap' has made much difference on the campus itself," she offered cautionary and pragmatic advice to the Nisei, suggesting the burden of responsibility these relocated students felt, as well as the problem of communicating their experiences and emotions to Caucasians.

> It is scarcely necessary to point out that those who have probably never seen a nisei before will get their impression of the nisei as a whole from the relocated students. It won't do you or your family and friends much good to dwell on what you consider injustices when you are questioned about evacuation. Rather, stress the contributions of [our] people to the nation's war effort.[38]

Given the tenor of the times and the situation of their families, the pioneers in resettlement had little choice but to repress their anger and minimize the amount of racist hostility they encountered.

In her article "a la mode," Marii Kyogoku also offered survival tips to the departing Nisei, ever conscious that they were on trial not only as individuals but as representatives of their families and their generation. She suggested criteria for choosing clothes and provided hints on adjustment to food rationing. Kyogoku especially urged the evacuees to improve their table manners, which had been adversely affected by the "unnatural food and atmosphere" of mess hall dining:

> You should start rehearsing for the great outside by bringing your own utensils to the dining hall. It's an aid to normality to be able to eat your jello with a spoon and well worth the dishwashing which it involves. All of us eat much too fast. Eat more slowly. All this practicing should be done so that proper manners will seem natural to you. If you do this, you won't get stagefright and spill your water glass, or make bread pills and hardly dare to eat when you have your first meal away from the centers and in the midst of scrutinizing caucasian eyes.[39]

Armed with advice and drawn by encouraging reports, increasing numbers of women students left camp. A postwar study of a group of 1,000 relocated students showed that 40 percent were women.[40] The field of nursing was particularly attractive to Nisei women; after the first few students disproved the hospital administrations' fears of their patients' hostility, acceptance of Nisei into nursing schools grew. By July 1944, there were more than 300 Nisei women in over 100 nursing programs in twenty-four states.[41] One such student wrote from the Asbury Hospital in Minneapolis: "Work here isn't too hard and I enjoy it very much. The patients are very nice people and I haven't had any trouble as yet. They do give us a funny stare at the beginning but after a day or so we receive the best compliments."[42]

The trickle of migration from the camps grew into a steady stream by 1943, as the War Relocation Authority developed its resettlement program to aid evacuees in finding housing and employment in the East and Midwest. A resettlement bulletin published by the Advisory Committee for Evacuees described "who is relocating":

> Mostly younger men and women, in their 20s or 30s; mostly single persons or couples with one or two children, or men with larger families who come out alone first to scout opportunities and to secure a foothold, planning to call wife and children later. Most relocated evacuees have parents or relatives whom they hope and plan to bring out "when we get re-established."[43]

In early 1945, the War Department ended the exclusion of the Japanese Americans from the West Coast, and the War Relocation Authority announced that the camps would be closed within the year. By this time, 37 percent of the evacuees of sixteen years or older had already relocated, including 63 percent of the Nisei women in that age group.[44]

For Nisei women, like their non-Japanese sisters, the wartime labor shortage opened the door into industrial, clerical, and managerial occupations. Prior to the war, racism had excluded the Japanese Americans from most white-collar clerical and sales positions, and, according to sociologist Evelyn Nakano Glenn, "the most common form of nonagricultural employment for the immigrant women (issei) and their American-born daughters (nisei) was domestic service."[45] The highest percentage of job offers for both men and women continued to be requests for domestic workers. In July 1943, the Kansas City branch of the War Relocation Authority noted that 45 percent of requests for workers were for domestics, and the Milwaukee office cited 61 percent.[46] However, Nisei women also found jobs as secretaries, typists, file clerks, beauticians, and factory workers. By 1950, 47 percent of employed Japanese American women were clerical and sales workers and operatives; only 10 percent were in domestic service.[47] The World War II decade, then, marked a turning point for Japanese American women in the labor force.

Whether they were students or workers, and regardless of where they went or how prepared they were to meet the outside world, Nisei women found that leaving camp meant enormous change in their lives. Even someone as confident as Marii Kyogoku, the author of much relocation advice, found that reentry into the Caucasian dominated world beyond the barbed wire fence was not a simple matter of stepping back into old shoes. Leaving the camps—like entering them—meant major changes in psychological perspective and self-image.

I had thought that because before evacuation I had adjusted myself rather well in a Caucasian society, I would go right back into my former frame of mind. I have found, however, that though the center became unreal and was as if it had never existed as soon as I got on the train at Della, I was never so self-conscious in all my life.

Kyogoku was amazed to see so many men and women in uniform and, despite her "proper" dining preparation, felt strange sitting at a table set with clean linen and a full set of silverware.

I felt a diffidence at facing all these people and things, which was most unusual. Slowly things have come to seem natural, though I am still excited by the sounds of the busy city and thrilled every time I see a street lined with trees I no longer feel that I am the cynosure of all eyes.[48]

Like Kyogoku, many Nisei women discovered that relocation meant adjustment to "a life different from our former as well as present way of living"[49] and, as such, posed a challenge. Their experiences in meeting this challenge were as diverse as their jobs and living situations.

"I live at the Eleanor Club No. 5 which is located on the west side," wrote Mary Sonoda, working with the American Friends Service Committee in Chicago:

> I pay $1 per day for room and two meals a day. I also have maid service. I do not think that one can manage all this for $1 unless one lives in a place like this which houses thousands of working girls in the city. . . . I am the only Japanese here at present. . . . The residents and the staff are wonderful to me . . . I am constantly being entertained by one person or another.
>
> The people in Chicago are extremely friendly. Even with the Tribune screaming awful headlines concerning the recent execution of American soldiers in Japan, people kept their heads. On street cars, at stores, everywhere, one finds innumerable evidence of good will.[50]

Chicago, the location of the first War Relocation Authority field office for supervision of resettlement in the Midwest, attracted the largest number of evacuees. Not all found their working environment as congenial as Mary Sonoda did. Smoot Katow, a Nisei man in Chicago, painted "another side of the picture":

> I met one of the Edgewater Beach girls. . . . From what she said it was my impression that the girls are not very happy. The hotel work is too hard, according to this girl. In fact, they are losing weight and one girl became sick with overwork. They have to clean about fifteen suites a day, scrubbing the floors on their hands and knees. . . . It seems the management is out to use labor as labor only . . . The outside world is just as tough as it ever was.[51]

These variations in living and work conditions and wages encouraged—and sometimes necessitated—a certain amount of job experimentation among the Nisei.

Many relocating Japanese Americans received moral and material assistance from a number of service organizations and religious groups, particularly the Presbyterians, the Methodists, the Society of Friends, and the Young Women's Christian Association. One such Nisei, Dorcas Asano, enthusiastically described to a Quaker sponsor her activities in the big city:

> Since receiving your application for hostel accommodation, I have decided to come to New York and I am really glad for the opportunity to be able to resume the normal civilized life after a year's confinement in camp. New York is really a city of dreams and we

are enjoying every minute working in offices, rushing back and
forth to work in the ever-speeding sub-way trains, counting our ration points, buying war bonds, going to church, seeing the latest
shows, plays, operas, making many new friends and living like our
neighbors in the war time. I only wish more of my friends who are
behind the fence will take advantage of the many helpful hands offered to them.[52]

The Nisei also derived support and strength from networks—formed
before and during internment—of friends and relatives. The homes of
those who relocated first became way stations for others as they made the
transition into new communities and jobs. In 1944, soon after she obtained
a place to stay in New York City, Miné Okubo found that "many of the
other evacuees relocating in New York came ringing my doorbell. They
were sleeping all over the floor!"[53] Single women often accompanied or
joined sisters, brothers, and friends as many interconnecting grapevines
carried news of likely jobs, housing, and friendly communities. Ayako
Kanemura, for instance, found a job painting Hummel figurines in Chicago; a letter of recommendation from a friend enabled her "to get my foot
into the door and then all my friends followed and joined me."[54] Although
they were farther from their families than ever before, Nisei women maintained warm ties of affection and concern, and those who had the means
to do so continued to play a role in the family economy, remitting a portion of their earnings to their families in or out of camp, and to siblings
in school.
    Elizabeth Ogata's family exemplifies several patterns of resettlement
and the maintenance of family ties within them. In October 1944, her
parents were living with her brother Harry who had begun to farm in
Springville, Utah; another brother and sister were attending Union College
in Lincoln, Nebraska. Elizabeth herself had moved to Minneapolis to join
a brother in the army, and she was working as an operative making paja-
mas. "Minn. is a beautiful place," she wrote, "and the people are so nice.
. . . I thought I'd never find anywhere I would feel at home as I did in Mt.
View [California], but I have changed my mind."[55] Like Elizabeth, a good
number of the 35,000 relocated Japanese Americans were favorably impressed by their new homes and decided to stay.
    The war years had complex and profound effects upon Japanese Ameri-
cans, uprooting their communities and causing severe psychological and
emotional damage. The vast majority returned to the West Coast at the
end of the war in 1945—a move that, like the initial evacuation, was a
grueling test of flexibility and fortitude. Even with the assistance of old
friends and service organizations, the transition was taxing and painful;
the end of the war meant not only long-awaited freedom but more battles to be fought in social, academic, and economic arenas. The Japanese
Americans faced hostility, crude living conditions, and a struggle for
jobs. Few evacuees received any compensation for their financial losses,

estimated conservatively at $400 million, because Congress decided to appropriate only $38 million for the settlement of claims.[56] It is even harder to place a figure on the toll taken in emotional shock, self-blame, broken dreams, and insecurity. One Japanese American woman still sees in her nightmares the watchtower searchlights that troubled her sleep forty years ago.

The war altered Japanese American women's lives in complicated ways. In general, evacuation and relocation accelerated earlier trends that differentiated the Nisei from their parents. Although most young women, like their mothers and non-Japanese peers, anticipated a future centered around a husband and children, they had already felt the influence of mainstream middle-class values of love and marriage and quickly moved away from the pattern of arranged marriage in the camps. There, increased peer group activities and the relaxation of parental authority gave them more independence. The Nisei women's expectations of marriage became more akin to the companionate ideals of their peers than to those of the Issei.

As before the war, many Nisei women worked in camp, but the new parity in wages they received altered family dynamics. And though they expected to contribute to the family economy, a large number did so in settings far from the family, availing themselves of opportunities provided by the student and worker relocation programs. In meeting the challenges facing them, Nisei women drew not only upon the disciplined strength inculcated by their Issei parents but also upon firmly rooted support networks and the greater measure of self-reliance and independence that they developed during the crucible of the war years.

NOTES

For their invaluable assistance with this paper, I would like to thank Estelle Freedman, Mary Rothschild, and members of the women's history dissertation reading group at Stanford University—Sue Cobble, Gary Sue Goodman, Yukiko Hanawa, Gail Hershatter, Emily Honig, Susan Johnson, Sue Lynn, Joanne Meyerowitz, Peggy Pascoe, Linda Schott, Frances Taylor, and Karen Anderson.

1. Miné Okubo, Miné Okubo: An American Experience, exhibition catalogue (Oakland: Oakland Museum, 1972), p. 36.

2. The very first Japanese women to arrive in the United States before the turn of the century were the ameyuki-san—prostitutes—of whose lives little is known. For information, see Yuji Ichioka, "Ameyuki-san: Japanese Prostitutes in Nineteenth Century America," Amerasia Journal, 4, No. 1 (1977). A few references to the ameyuki-san appear in Mildred Crowl Martin's biography, Chinatown's Angry Angel, The Story of Donaldina Cameron (Palo Alto: Pacific Books, 1977).

3. In Japan, marriage was legally the transfer of a woman's name from her father's registry to that of the groom's family. Even through the Meiji Era there was enormous diversity in the time period of this formalization; it might occur as early as several days before the wedding ceremony or as late as seven or more years later, by which time the bride should have produced several sons and proven herself to be a good wife and daughter-in-law. For a detailed cross-cultural history of the Issei women, see Yukiko Hanawa, "The Several Worlds of Issei Women," Thesis, California State University at Long Beach, 1982.

4. Yuji Ichioka. "*Amerika Nodeshiko: Japanese Immigrant Women in the United States, 1900–1924*," *Pacific Historical Review*, 69, No. 2 (May 1980), p. 343.

5. Evelyn Nakano Glenn has examined the lives of Issei and Nisei domestic workers in the prewar period in her study, "The Dialectics of Wage Work: Japanese-American Women and Domestic Servants, 1905–1940," *Feminist Studies*, 6, No. 3 (Fall 1980), pp. 432–71.

6. Sources on evacuation: Roben A. Wilson and Bill Hosokawa, *East to America: A History of the Japanese in the United States* (New York: William Morrow, 1980); Audrie Girdner and Anne Loftis, *The Great Betrayal: The Evacuation of the Japanese-Americans during World War II* (Toronto: Macmillan, 1969); Daisuke Kitagawa, *Issei and Nisei: The Internment Years* (New York: Seabury Press, 1967); Roger Daniels, *The Decision to Relocate the Japanese Americans* (Philadelphia: J. B. Lippincott, 1975).

7. Wilson and Hosokawa, p. 208.

8. Bettie to Mrs. Jack Shoup, June 3, 1942, Mrs. Jack Shoup Collection, Hoover Institution Archives (hereafter referred to as HIA), Stanford, California.

9. May Nakamoto to Mrs. Jack Shoup, November 30, 1942, Mrs. Jack Shoup Collection, HIA.

10. Mary Okumura to Mrs. Jack Shoup, May 30, 1942, Mrs. Jack Shoup Collection, HIA.

11. Miye Baba, personal interview, February 10, 1982, Turlock, California.

12. Many of the Japanese community leaders arrested by the FBI before the evacuation were interned in special all-male camps in North Dakota, Louisiana, and New Mexico. Some Japanese Americans living outside the perimeter of the Western Defense zone in Arizona, Utah, etc. were not interned.

13. Miné Okubo, *Citizen 13660* (New York: Columbia Univ. Press, 1946), p. 66.

14. Chieko Kimura, personal interview, April 9, 1978, Glendale, Arizona.

15. Okubo, *Citizen 13660*, p. 89.

16. Shizuko Horiuchi to Henriette Von Blon, January 24, 1943, Henriette Von Blon Collection, HIA.

17. Shizuko Horiuchi to Henriette Von Blon, January 5, 1944, Henriette Von Blon Collection, HIA.

18. Ayako Kanemura, personal interview, March 10, 1978, Glendale, Arizona.

19. Anonymous *Topaz Times*, October 24, 1942, p. 3.

20. Lily Shoji, "Fem-a-lites," *The Mercedian*, August 7, 1942, p. 4.

21. "Yuri," "Strictly Feminine," September 29, 1942, p. 2.

22. Mitzi Sugita, "Latest Fashion for Women Today—Slacks," *Poston Chronicle*, June 13, 1943, p. 1.

23. Sugita.

24. Marii Kyogoku, "a la mode," *Trek* (February 1943), p. 38.

25. From 1942 to the end of 1945 the Council allocated about $240,000 in scholarships, most of which were provided through the donations of churches and the World Student Service Fund. The average grant per student was $156.73, which in that era was a major contribution toward the cost of higher education. Source: National Japanese American Student Relocation Council, Minutes of the Executive Committee Meeting, Philadelphia, Pennsylvania, December 19, 1945.

26. Robert O'Brien, *The College Nisei* (Palo Alto: Pacific Books, 1949), pp. 73–74.

27. The disastrous consequences of the poorly conceived clearance procedure have been examined by Wilson and Hosokawa, pp. 226–27, and Girdner and Loftis, pp. 342–43.

28. May Nakamoto to Mrs. Jack Shoup, November 20, 1943, Mrs. Jack Shoup Collection, HIA.

29. Shizuko Horiuchi to Henriette Von Blon, December 27, 1942, Henriette Von Blon Collection, HIA.

30. Toshiko Imada to Margaret Cosgrave Sowers, January 16, 1943, Margaret Cosgrave Sowers Collection, HIA.

31. Ayako Kanemura, personal interview, March 24, 1978, Glendale, Arizona.

32. Kathy Ishikawa to Mrs. Jack Shoup, June 14, 1942, Mrs. Jack Shoup Collection, HIA.

33. Anonymous Nisei nurse in Poston Camp to Margaret Finley, May 5, 1943, Margaret Finley Collection, HIA.

34. Okubo, *Citizen 13660*, p. 139.

35. *Topaz Times*, October 24, 1942, p. 3.

36. Masako Ono to Atsuko Ono, September 28, 1942, Margaret Cosgrave Sowers Collection, HIA. Prior to the war, few Nisei had college experience: the 1940 census lists 674 second-generation women and 1,507 men who had attended or were attending college.

37. Lillian Ota, "Campus Report," *Trek* (February 1943), p. 33.

38. Ota, pp. 33–34.

39. Kyogoku, "a la mode," p. 39.

40. O'Brien, p. 84.

41. O'Brien, pp. 85–86.

42. Grace Tanabe to Josephine Duveneck, February 16, 1944, Conard Duveneck Collection, HIA.

43. Advisory Committee for Evacuees, *Resettlement Bulletin* (April 1943), p. 2.

44. Leonard Broom and Ruth Riemer, *Removal and Return, The Socio-Economic Effects of the War on Japanese Americans* (Berkeley: University of California Press, 1949), p. 36.

45. Glenn, p. 432.

46. Advisory Committee for Evacuees, *Resettlement Bulletin* (July 1943), p. 3.

47. 1950 United States Census, Special Report.

48. Marii Kyogoku, *Resettlement Bulletin* (July 1943), p. 5.

49. Kyogoku, "a la mode," p. 39.

50. *Poston Chronicle*, May 23, 1943, p. 1.

51. *Poston Chronicle*, May 23, 1943.

52. Dorcas Asano to Josephine Duveneck, January 22, 1944, Conard Duveneck Collection, HIA.

53. Okubo, *An American Experience*, p. 41.

54. Ayako Kanemura, personal interview, March 24, 1978, Glendale, Arizona.

55. Elizabeth Ogata to Mrs. Jack Shoup, October 1, 1944, Mrs. Jack Shoup Collection, HIA.

56. Susan M. Hartmann, *The Home Front and Beyond: American Women in the 1940s* (Boston: Twayne Publishers, 1982), p. 126. There is some debate regarding the origins of the assessment of evacuee losses at $400 million. However, a recent study by the Commission on Wartime Relocation and Internment of Civilians has estimated that the Japanese Americans lost between $149 million and $370 million in 1945 dollars, and between $810 million and $2 billion in 1983 dollars. See the *San Francisco Chronicle*, June 16, 1983, p. 12.

16 FROM ESTEBAN TO RODNEY KING: FIVE CENTURIES OF AFRICAN AMERICAN HISTORY IN THE WEST

Quintard Taylor

In this essay, Taylor sketches the history of African Americans in the West from 1539, when the slave Esteban traveled north with the Coronado expedition from central Mexico into what is now the American Southwest, to the tragic riots of 1992, which were triggered by the acquittal of Los Angeles police officers who were being tried for the beating of a black citizen, Rodney King, in 1991. Race, Taylor maintains, has always been part of the history of the West, as it has been in other parts of the country; but western race relations, he says, have been different. How does he explain this difference?

African Americans have been present in the West not only since the ephemeral Coronado expedition (Esteban and Coronado, after all, did not stay very long). Others, however, have been part of the West's people since Spain colonized New Mexico after 1598 (twenty-one years before Africans were brought to Jamestown, Virginia). They arrived with the Spanish in Texas in 1716, and in California in 1769. Many, perhaps most, of the first settlers of San Diego (1769) and Los Angeles (1781), Taylor points out, were black. They were also free under Spanish and Mexican law. An interesting question is how, when, and under whose auspices African-American slaves were brought into Texas, yet— another question worth pondering—slaves were never present in California, whether Spanish, Mexican, or American.

Following the Civil War and Emancipation, African Americans came to the West in a number of ways—as cowboys, as homesteaders in the Indian Territory, Kansas, and states as far northwest as Idaho, as miners, as railroad workers (from ordinary laborers to Pullman-car porters), and as the founders of the black communities of Denver, Los Angeles, San Francisco, and Seattle (to name only the largest) before World War I. How did the onset of World War II change the size and structure of black communities in the West? How did western African Americans struggle for civil rights and equal treatment, and how did their struggle differ because of the presence of Asian and Latino minorities?—editors

IN APRIL 1992, South Central Los Angeles exploded in a maelstrom of anger and rage. Although Los Angeles is by far the largest metropolis in the West, those scenes of carnage, no less than the city itself, belie the regional self-image most westerners prefer—placid valleys or broad vistas populated by a proud, self-reliant citizenry, jealously guarding its individual rights, equality, and freedom "under an open sky."[1] Yet black western history, much like the Los Angeles uprising, intrudes itself onto our sensibilities and forces reexamination of the imagined West.[2] That history, with its examples of resistance, negotiation, conflict, and cooperation between African Americans and other westerners, can be celebrated or critiqued, but no longer can it be ignored.

It is tempting to credit the New Western History, with its emphasis on race, class, and gender, as primarily responsible for the growing recognition of the African American past in the region. Indeed, any bibliography on the black West would find most of the entries dating from the past two decades when new methodologies, interpretations, and debates reinvigorated the field. Yet for all that is new in the scholarship of African Americans of the region, black western history is, in fact, nearly a century in the making. One thinks, for example, of the early articles analyzing slavery in Texas, California, and Oregon, which appeared in 1898, 1905, and 1908, respectively, or the essays by W. Sherman Savage in 1928 and Kenneth W. Porter in 1932, which initiated long careers of reconstructing African American history "on the frontier." Of course, the post-1970 period witnessed the rapid proliferation of studies of discrete aspects of black western history as historians ask, and answer, more profound questions about the region's past.[3]

Much of New Western History scholarship easily reconciles Asian American, Chicano, or most of nineteenth- and twentieth-century Native American history, which are axiomatically "western" in orientation. Yet anomaly continues to define black western history. There is the uneasy sense that it is imposed on regional historiography to appease contemporary sensibilities rather than because it is central to the historical narrative. Scholarship on African American westerners continues to be viewed by many western regional historians and historians of African America as an interesting footnote to a story focused largely on the rural South, the urban East, and the Midwest. The ghost of Walter Prescott Webb's 1955 comment that the West is defined by its scarcity of "water, timber, cities, industry, labor, and Negroes" continues to intrude onto the region's popular consciousness. This "dearth" argument, long a central tenet in the marginalization of black western scholarship, is particularly surprising considering the size of the affected population. As early as 1870 African Americans constituted 19 percent of the region's inhabitants—some 284,000 people who resided in every western state and territory. By 1910, the percentage had dropped to 5.7, but that still represented 941,000 blacks, and in 1990, there were 5.2 million African Americans in the West, constituting 7.1 percent of the region's population. If the percentages have fluctuated through the decades, they nonetheless show black westerners represented a substantial component of the western populace.[4]

African American History in the West tests the validity of western exceptionalism originally advanced by Frederick Jackson Turner and posited in a quite different context by many New West historians. Was the West significantly different for African Americans? That answer is a qualified yes as exemplified in the success of post-Civil War western blacks who gained and kept voting rights everywhere in the region except Texas, but no, if we consider the emergence of postbellum discriminatory legislation symbolized by antimiscegenation statutes and public school segregation in states as diverse as Montana, Arizona and Kansas. Such ambiguity surely renders more complex the region's past.[5]

That complexity begins with the earliest African arrivals. Consider the lives of Esteban, the black slave who ventured to New Spain's northern frontier in 1539 in a futile search for the fabled Seven Cities of Cíbola, or of Isabel de Olvera, a member of the Juan Guerra de Resa colonization expedition to New Mexico in 1600, who became the first free black woman to enter the West (predating by nineteen years the landing of twenty Africans at Jamestown). These accounts should be removed from the "contributions" school of ethnic history and allowed to suggest myriad possibilities for reconceptualizing the region's past. Esteban's travels, for example, initiated the meeting of Indian and Spanish cultures, which in turn shaped much of the region's history. Moreover, Esteban, Isabel de Olvera, and the hundreds of other Spanish-speaking black settlers who populated cities and towns from San Antonio to San Francisco, and who in 1781 comprised a majority of the founders of what was to become the greatest of the region's cities, Los Angeles, confirm the "multicultural" West as the meeting place of diverse races and cultures long before the arrival of nineteenth-century English-speaking settlers. From the sixteenth through the eighteenth centuries, persons of African ancestry who migrated to what now constitutes the West were far more likely to move north from central Mexico than west from the Atlantic seaboard. Their experiences call for a reinterpretation of Spanish Mexican history in the Southwest to illustrate the enigmatic role of race in shaping social and cultural traditions in colonial and post-colonial Mexican society. Those traditions, in turn, confounded Anglo sensibilities on proper racial attitudes long after the Treaty of Guadalupe Hidalgo established American sovereignty over the region.[6]

African American history in the West often reveals paradoxes, as in revolutionary-era Texas where the liberty of Anglo slaveholders was in direct opposition to the freedom of black people. Mexico's constitution of 1821 renounced black slavery and proclaimed political equality for all the nation's inhabitants. The promise of freedom and equality proved a powerful attraction for African Americans "from the states." Many were fugitive slaves, but the African American immigrants also included free blacks determined to live under what they viewed as Mexican liberty rather than American tyranny. Samuel H. Hardin, for example, wrote that he had moved to Texas because Mexico's laws "invited his emigration and guaranteed his right to own property." Yet the aspirations of free blacks and their supporters for a free, racially tolerant Texas soon clashed with the

17. Esteban, the first known African American in what is now the American West. In Spanish uniform, he took part in the ill-fated expedition of Cabeza de Vaca and was killed by Indians in 1539. *Courtesy of Prof. David J. Weber.*

goal of southern white planters to transform the Mexican province into an empire for slavery. By 1835 Texas slaveholders had duplicated the slave system of the United States, increasing the servile population to 10 percent of English-speaking Texans. With growing numbers of slaveholders demanding protection for their property while openly selling black slaves, Anglo Texans and the Mexican government were on a collision course that led to the Alamo.[7]

African Americans were soon engulfed in the tumultuous creation of an independent Texas. For many Texas slaves the flag of Mexico rather than the revolutionary "lone star" seemed the banner of liberty. In February 1836, one month before his siege of the Alamo, General Antonio López de Santa Anna, commander of the Mexican army, queried government officials in Mexico City about the liberation of the slaves. "Shall we permit those wretches to moan in chains any longer in a country whose kind laws protect the liberty of man without distinction of cast [*sic*] or color?" Mexico's minister of war, José María Tornel, provided an answer on March 18. While affirming that "the philanthropy of the Mexican nation" had already freed the slaves, he directed commanding general Santa Anna to grant their "natural rights," including "the liberty to go to any point on the globe that appeals to them," to remain in Texas, or to relocate to another part of Mexico. The Mexican army seemed poised to become a legion of liberation. As that army crossed the Colorado and Brazos rivers, moving into the region heavily populated by slaves, the boldest of the bondspeople took flight toward Santa Anna's forces both when they marched into Texas and when they retreated. In return for Mexican protection, fugitives served as spies, messengers, and provocateurs for their liberators.[8]

The victory of the Texas revolutionaries over the Mexican army set in motion political events that in the next decade resulted in all of Mexico's northern territories being added to the United States. But it also initiated a decline in the status of free blacks who sought refuge in Texas, and fixed African slavery as the state's predominant labor system. With guarantees of governmental protection, Texas's "peculiar institution" grew from three thousand African Americans held in bondage in 1835 to a quarter of a million slaves by the time of the Civil War almost three decades later.

African slavery was central to the political economy of Texas. Yet few western historians have ever linked slavery with the rest of the region. When the Civil War began in 1861 only four western states had been admitted to the Union, and the Euramerican inhabitants of the vast western territories considered themselves physically and psychologically removed from the labor system that generated the turmoil engulfing the nation. The West's claims of innocence on slavery are muted, however, by the presence of African American bond servants in virtually every state and territory in the region prior to the Civil War, and by the intense local debates about the suitability of slavery in Oregon, California, Utah, Nebraska, New Mexico, and particularly "bleeding Kansas," where political discourse gave way to armed conflict in the 1850s. The ninety-eighth meridian may have represented the farthest advance of slave-based plantation agriculture as it was practiced in the Old South, but the meridian was not an insurmountable barrier to the development of some variation of the servile institution in the West. The region was saved from slavery by antislavery, antiblack "free soil" farmers, who were always more numerous than proslavery advocates or slaveholders, rather than any environmental barrier or any particular commitment by westerners to universal liberty or equality.[9]

Yet the significance of the western debate over slavery extended far beyond the valleys of California, Oregon or the prairies of eastern Kansas and Nebraska. The arrival of just a few black slaves in territories often immediately transformed the intense political debate east of the Mississippi between *sections* into a contentious *local* struggle between neighbors. By the 1850s the West remained the only region in the nation where the fate of slavery had not been determined. Both pro- and antislavery interests felt compelled to compete for its allegiance in a contest that ultimately brought on the Civil War.

The first significant numbers of African Americans who entered the West from the older states came as slaves. The largest servile population resided in Texas, where the federal 1860 census reported 182,556 bondspeople comprising slightly over 30 percent of the state's total population.[10] Like Texas, the Five Indian Nations in what would become Oklahoma had an economy that rested on slave labor. Eight thousand bondspeople in Indian Territory in 1860 comprised 14 percent of the total population. Their subjugation by another "people of color" cautions our propensity to view the institution only in terms of white masters and black slaves. (In yet another irony of western exceptionalism, black slavery in New Mexico was rendered superfluous by the availability of Mexican peons and Indian slaves.) Slavery was legal in only one other western territory—Utah—yet the historical record is replete with accounts of black bond servants held illegally throughout the region.[11]

Western slaveholders did not anticipate the role that a dedicated minority of black and white abolitionists, particularly in California and Kansas, would play in undermining the "peculiar institution." Through the 1850s white abolitionists such as Cornelius Cole, Joseph C. Zabriskie, Edwin Bryan Crocker (brother of Charles Crocker), and Mark Hopkins utilized the courts to free Californians illegally held in bondage. Their efforts were joined by an aroused African American community willing to employ legal and extra-legal means to ensure the freedom of black slaves. Unlike Texas and the Indian Territory, where abolitionist sentiment was virtually nonexistent, California slaves and antislavery activists resided in the same urban communities or worked side by side in the mining fields. The close proximity of slave and abolitionist gave bond servants direct contact with their champions, a position virtually impossible in the eastern United States. That proximity also heightened the sense of urgency for antislavery activists who could witness the horrors of the servile institution on a daily basis. Peter Lester, a former Philadelphia abolitionist who arrived in San Francisco in 1850, invited black slaves into his home to lecture them on their rights. "When they left," he declared, "we had them strong in the spirit of freedom. They were leaving [slavery] every day." The active role of blacks in challenging slavery prompted one contemporary German observer to remark: "The wealthy California Negroes . . . exhibit a great deal of energy and intelligence in saving their brethren."[12]

Kansas blacks challenged slavery through flight. Indeed black Kansas was virtually created by the Civil War itself. Although the late 1850s battle for "bleeding Kansas" resulted in a victory for free state partisans, the territory in 1860 had only 627 African Americans. By 1865 more than 12,000 blacks resided in Kansas, comprising nine percent of the population. A combination of politics and geography explains the explosion of black population in Kansas. As a sparsely populated territory adjacent to the Missouri counties with the largest slave populations, Kansas was an obvious destination.[13] After passage of the Kansas–Nebraska Act in 1854, the territory attracted a small group of ardent abolitionists who established Underground Railroad "stations" in the region. Although only a minority of Euramericans approved of their actions, antislavery partisans such as James H. Lane, James Montgomery, and John Brown, who briefly resided in Kansas before returning east to direct the fateful raid on Harper's Ferry, led bands of "Jayhawkers" into Missouri in the late 1850s on raids for slaves who were then led back across the border and directed toward northern states, creating what one historian described as the "golden age of slave absconding." If northern black and white abolitionists mounted rhetorical campaigns against slavery and occasionally protected fugitives who fled the South, some white Kansans actually entered a slaveholding state to rescue black men and women from bondage.[14]

Slaves also acted on their own, seeking to cross the Kansas–Missouri border and then reach Lawrence, "the best advertised antislavery town in the world." While both Kansas abolitionists and Missouri slaveholders exaggerated the figures of escaped slaves for their own purposes, it was clear that the western Missouri slaveholding counties, isolated from other major slaveholding regions and in close proximity to free, sparsely populated western territories, were particularly susceptible to servile flight. Freedom for such bondspeople, unlike their counterparts in the Deep South, lay a short trip to the west rather than a long, circuitous journey through slaveholding states to the north.[15]

Opportunities for flight increased dramatically with the coming of the Civil War. Kansas entered the Union on January 29, 1861, barely two months before Lincoln's inauguration and five weeks after South Carolina seceded. The state legislature chose as one of its two United States senators James H. Lane, a passionate, volatile abolitionist who assumed leadership in the defense of his adopted state and quickly fused his military responsibilities with his antislavery goals. In August 1861 Lane mounted a brief incursion into southwest Missouri. News of his presence encouraged fugitive slaves to seek out his military camp near Springfield. Without authorization from higher military or civilian authorities, Lane enlisted the male fugitives into his command and arranged for the women and children to be sent to Kansas "to help save the crop and provide fuel for the winter." His impetuous and largely symbolic act emancipated slaves and unofficially created the first African American troops in the Union army during the Civil War.[16]

When word of Lane's action as a "liberator" spread, other Missouri slaves as well as refugees from Arkansas and Indian Territory made their way toward Kansas. Henry Clay Bruce, the brother of future Mississippi Senator Blanche K. Bruce, recounted in his autobiography how he and his fiancée escaped from Missouri to Kansas in 1863. Bruce strapped around his waist "a pair of Colt's revolvers and plenty of ammunition" for the run to the western border. "We avoided the main road and made the entire trip . . . without meeting anyone," he wrote. "We crossed the Missouri River on a ferry boat to Fort Leavenworth, Kansas. I then felt myself a free man."[17]

After 1862, both Lawrence's established white residents and black newcomers engaged in activities that suggested their recognition of the permanence of black settlement. "The Negroes are not coming. They are here. They will stay here," asserted abolitionist Richard Cordley. "They are to be our neighbors, whatever we may think about it, whatever we may do about it."[18] The newcomers certainly heeded Cordley's words. Despite their relatively short residence in the Sunflower State, African American men soon demanded the right to vote and to serve on juries. Both black women and men called for an end to discrimination in public transportation and accommodations, initiating a century-long struggle to extend the prewar promise of freedom for slaves into the post-Civil War prospect of equal rights for all of the state's citizens.

African American agricultural history on the high plains during the post-Civil War decades provides another opportunity to explore the western promise of success and upward mobility for the free people. On a thousand-mile frontier from North Dakota to Oklahoma, African American homesteaders, propelled by twin desires for land and political freedom, confronted the Great Plains. The Langston City *Herald*, the newspaper for the famous all-black town in Oklahoma Territory, proclaimed as much in 1893 when it called on African American southerners to avail themselves of the last chance to secure "free homes" on government domain. "Everyone that can should go to the [Cherokee] strip . . . and get a hundred and sixty, all you need . . . is a Winchester, a frying pan, and the $15.00 filing fee." In Graham County, Kansas, in 1879, Logan County, Oklahoma in 1891, or Cherry County, Nebraska, in 1904, African American women and men tried and often failed to "conquer" the plains. A sense of the daunting challenges they faced are found in the words of one settler, Willianna Hickman, who wrote of navigating across Kansas by compass in the summer of 1878, destined for Nicodemus, the first of the high plains black settlements. When fellow emigrants exclaimed: "There is Nicodemus!" she anxiously surveyed the landscape. Expecting to find buildings on the horizon, she said, "I looked with all the eyes I had. 'Where is Nicodemus? I don't see it.'" Her husband pointed to the plumes of smoke coming out of the ground. "The families lived in dugouts," she dejectedly recalled. "We landed and struck tents. The scenery was not at all inviting and I began to cry."[19]

Success for black western farmers rested on a tenuous foundation of ample credit and rain. The absence of either could spell disaster. Gilbert Fite did not have African American farmers in mind when he wrote that "homesteaders battered and defeated by nature and ruined by economic conditions over which they had no control . . . who filed on government land soon found that natural and human-made barriers defeated their hopes and aspirations." Yet the statement reflected the experience of a disproportionate number of African American agriculturalists on the high plains as well. Statistics indicate that the general poverty of black homesteaders from the South prevented their acquiring the land necessary to sustain farming in the West. In Oklahoma, which received the largest number of African American homesteaders, black farm ownership peaked at thirteen thousand in 1910. Perhaps more telling, 38 percent of these farmers had less than 50 acres. In a region where large landholding was a necessity, the small size of these farms ensured a rapid exit from western agriculture.[20]

The experience of black homesteaders in northwestern Nebraska suggests that farm size alone did not ensure success. The Kinkaid Homestead Act of 1904, which threw open thousands of acres in the Nebraska Sandhills, provided the last opportunity for black homesteading in the state. Recognizing the land's aridity, the federal government provided homestead claims of 640 rather than 160 acres. The first African American to file a claim, Clem Deaver, arrived in 1904. Other blacks followed and by 1910 twenty-four families filed claim to 14,000 acres of land in Cherry County. Eight years later 185 blacks held 40,000 acres. Yet much like Oklahoma and Kansas, black farm families, unable to render the land productive enough for sustainable incomes, began leaving the isolated region in the early 1920s for Denver, Omaha, or Lincoln. The disappearance of black homesteaders from the high plains constitutes one of many crucial areas in need of scholarly investigation.[21]

No debate in black western history has been more contentious than that surrounding the "buffalo soldiers," the approximately 25,000 men who served in four regiments, the Ninth and Tenth Cavalry and the Twenty-fourth and Twenty-fifth Infantry, between 1866 and 1917. Along with cowboys, these troops were the first African American western historical figures to capture public attention in the 1960s when a nation eager to accept black heroes embraced the saga of the western regiments. Indeed, long before the nation recognized them, some black soldiers were highly conscious of their role in the "pacification" of the region. "We made the West," boasted Tenth Cavalry Private Henry McCombs. "[We] defeated the hostile tribes of Indians; and made the country safe to live in." William Leckie, the first biographer of the black cavalry regiments, reiterated that view when he wrote in 1967 that "the thriving cities and towns, the fertile fields, and the natural beauty [of the West] are monuments enough for any buffalo soldier." But by the 1970s Jack Forbes and other historians began to probe the moral dilemma posed by the actions of these men. Were they not instruments in the subjugation of native peoples for a society that went on to "erect thriving *white* cities, grow fertile *white* fields and leave no real monuments to the memory of brave, but denigrated-in-their-lifetime soldiers?"[22]

Forbes's critique rests on the presumption of an Indian-*fighting* army. Until 1890 that presumption was generally correct, although on occasion black soldiers defended Indian people from the depredations of Euramericans, as black troops did in 1879 when they were dispatched to protect Kiowas and Comanches from Texas Rangers or when they repeatedly removed hundreds of the white "boomers" who illegally occupied Indian lands between 1879 and 1885. After 1890 black soldiers were far more likely to confront angry white strikers than native warriors. Beginning with the Coeur d'Alene mining district shutdown in 1892 through the national railroad strike two years later, and the second confrontation in the Coeur d'Alene district in 1899, African American troops were called upon to defend life and property and to maintain law and order, a curious paradox in light of antiblack violence common in the South during this period. At the height of the Johnson County War in 1892, for example, the Wyoming Stockgrowers Association exploited the longstanding hostility between black soldiers and white Texans as well as the belief that poor whites' hostility toward black workers would ensure African American loyalty in the coming battle between the social classes. When local law enforcement officials sided with small ranchers, the stockgrowers association wired Wyoming Senator Joseph M. Carey, on June 1, 1892, asking him to arrange for stationing black troops in the area. "We want cool level-headed men whose sympathy is with us," the telegram read. "Send six companies of Ninth Cavalry. . . . The colored troops will have no sympathy for Texan thieves . . . these are the troops we want.[23]

Historians have provided nuanced accounts of black soldiers in the West that reveal the texture of military life. We know now, for example, that as soldiers were posted at various forts, wives and children accompanied them as did single black women and men—laundresses, cooks, prostitutes, gamblers, and laborers. As Virginia Scharff has written elsewhere, these military communities resembled a "traveling village, more like the bands of Plains Indians who inhabited the same territory." Eventually the traveling stopped as retired soldiers and their families settled in towns such as Havre, Montana, near Fort Assinniboine, and Douglas, Arizona, near Fort Huachuca, or they augmented black populations in larger communities such as Salt Lake City and Spokane.[24]

We also know now that black soldiers were not always "heroic," and that boredom, isolation, and racism emanating from both officers and civilians took a toll in alcoholism, desertion, suicide, and internalized violence such as the 1887 murder of Sergeant Emanuel Stance, a Congressional Medal of Honor winner. Stance's repeated verbal and physical abuse of his men at Fort Robinson, Nebraska, led to his death at their hands. The historical record even occasionally shows soldiers in sympathy with those they were sworn to fight. Private W. H. Prather, one of the Ninth Cavalry troopers who guarded the Sioux in the winter of 1891 after the Wounded Knee confrontation, summarized his anger over the inadequate supplies left for both the Indians and the soldiers in a poem, the last lines of which read: "In a warm barracks our recent comrades take their ease, while we poor devils, and the Sioux are left to freeze."[25]

The explosion of scholarship on Euramerican women in the West in the 1970s shattered the myth that the region, even in its "pioneering" period, was a particularly male preserve. Several historians are examining the region's African American women comprehensively to answer the often unstated assumption that their history simply parallels the experiences of white women or of black men. As with many fundamental assumptions concerning the West, the evidence indicates otherwise. Isabel de Olvera's saga, for example, shows black women in the West from the seventeenth century in various roles and capacities. Sex ratios suggest that African American women were neither isolated from other women of their race or overwhelmingly outnumbered by black men. By 1860 African American women comprised half of the black population in Texas, Indian Territory, Utah Territory, and the Pacific Northwest. Only in gold rush California was there initially a huge imbalance between black women and men. Of the 952 blacks counted in the 1850 census, only 90 were women. Ten years later, when black California numbered slightly more than 4,000 inhabitants, black women comprised 31 percent of the total population. Post-Civil War settlement patterns of African American homesteaders in Nebraska, Kansas, and Oklahoma also show a balanced ratio as black women came both as single homesteaders and in families. Unfortunately we know far more about the numbers of women on the plains than about their experiences.[26]

We know a great deal more about nineteenth-century urban black women. Accounts of Mary Ellen Pleasant in San Francisco, Biddy Mason in Los Angeles, and Lutie Lytle in Topeka, when coupled with studies of organizations such as the black women's clubs in Colorado, Kansas, Wyoming, and Montana, help provide a composite image of African American women as crucial pillars in the maintenance and defense of the black community. Bridget "Biddy" Mason, for example, founded Los Angeles's First African Methodist Episcopal Church in 1872, the oldest black church in the city, and singlehandedly supported it during the crucial first years by paying all taxes and expenses, including the minister's salary. Businesswoman Mary Ellen Pleasant challenged streetcar segregation in San Francisco in the 1860s and used her influence with prominent white politicians such as California governor Newton Booth (who was elected while a resident of her boardinghouse) to promote civil rights for African Americans. Lutie Lytle, only the second black female attorney in the nation, was a Populist campaigner and organizer in Topeka, Kansas. African American women in Lawrence organized the Ladies Refugee Aid Society in 1864 to collect food, clothing, and money and to assist destitute ex-slaves. A decade later, the Colored Ladies Legal Rights Association, a group of middle-class black Denverites, made highly visible protests of racial discrimination such as the exclusion of African Americans from the Tabor Opera House. That pattern of service and protest carried forward into the twentieth century and was embodied in the activities of individuals such as Los Angeles newspaper editor Charlotta Bass, who in 1952 became the first African American woman to be nominated on a presidential party ticket (the Progressive Party), or Clara Luper, who in 1958 organized one of the first sit-in protests of the modern civil rights movement, when she led black students into Katz Drug Store in Oklahoma City, and in myriad organizations such as the hundreds of black women's clubs stretching from Montana to Arizona.[27]

Today the vast majority of African American women and men reside in the region's cities. The origins of these contemporary black western urban communities can be found in the rise of the nineteenth-century African American urban population. In 1885, when black cowboys were trailing cattle from Texas to Dodge City, Kansas, when black homesteaders were trying to grow wheat from stubborn west Kansas soil, or when buffalo soldiers were patrolling the Southwest desert, far more women and men entered Denver, San Francisco, Seattle, and Los Angeles, anxious to assume the various jobs they believed the urban economy made available. The contrasting images of black cowboys, homesteaders, buffalo soldiers, and urban workers reminds us that multiple "Wests" often existed side by side.

The nineteenth-century black urban community expanded in the larger cities—San Francisco (which had the only significant antebellum black urban population), Los Angeles, Denver, Seattle, Salt Lake City, Omaha, Portland, Houston, Dallas, Fort Worth, and San Antonio. But black communities also evolved in smaller towns and cities such as Topeka, Kansas, Virginia City, Nevada, Helena, Montana, Yankton, South Dakota, and Pocatello, Idaho. It was here that churches, fraternal organizations, social clubs, even fledgling civil rights organizations established the fabric of community life. Some black urban populations, such as those in Helena and Yankton did not survive into the twentieth century. Others, such as those in Houston, Dallas, Oakland, Denver, and Los Angeles, became the final destinations for tens of thousands of migrants inspired by the belief that their piece of the urban West would provide the political and social freedom that had evaded them in their former homes.[28]

The late-nineteenth- and early-twentieth-century black urban West population was small. The combined African American population of the five largest western cities in 1910—San Francisco, Los Angeles, Seattle, Denver, and Portland—totaled just 18,008 people, only slightly more than one-fifth the black population of Washington, D.C., the nation's largest black community. Such small numbers, however, did not keep western urban blacks from organizing a rich social and cultural life or prevent them from continuing the battle for racial justice. Despite the different local economies, blacks in western cities performed surprisingly similar work. Men and women were personal servants for wealthy households, and black men worked as hotel waiters, railroad porters, messengers, cooks, and janitors. The seaports had some sailors and dock workers. A small number of blacks were independent entrepreneurs operating barbershops, restaurants, and boardinghouses. By the 1890s most western cities had handfuls of black doctors, lawyers, and newspaper editors who, along with ministers and private schoolteachers, comprised the "elite." This elite often urged separation from impoverished blacks. Some of them anticipated following the advice of one Kansas newspaper editor who exhorted middle-class black westerners to "make a line, and keep within it . . . to ostracize them from our society."[29]

Most pre–World War II western urban populations proved too small, however, to successfully segregate themselves into distinct social classes, as had been done in Washington, D.C., Baltimore, New York, and other eastern cities. Despite their small numbers, black urban westerners usually established churches, fraternal organizations, social clubs, newspapers, and literary societies. These fledgling nineteenth-century institutions and organizations immediately addressed the spiritual, educational, social, and cultural needs of the local inhabitants. But such "race" organizations also provided African Americans with respite from a hostile world, a retreat where blacks could lose their anonymity and gain some control over their lives. While these desires were hardly unique to black westerners, the small size of the region's population, the vast distances between black communities in the West, and from the South, increased the importance of these organizations.

As early as 1862, the San Francisco *Pacific Appeal* called on its readers to create political, religious, and moral organizations "wherever there are half a dozen Colored people." This network of organizations did not end at the city's boundaries. Indeed, its most important function was to link small, isolated black western populations with the larger African American world. Such linkages were far more crucial for western communities separated by huge distances and by their even greater remoteness from the large African American populations of the South and eastern cities. Thus, the creation of the Puget Sound African Methodist Episcopal Conference, which embraced black churches in Oregon, Washington, Alaska, Idaho, and British Columbia in 1900, or the founding of National Association for the Advancement of Colored People (NAACP) chapters in places as diverse as Houston, Portland, Albuquerque, Omaha, El Paso, Oklahoma City, Tucson, San Antonio, Salt Lake City, and Boise, all by 1919, or the establishing of Marcus Garvey-inspired Universal Negro Improvement Association Chapters by 1926 in Denver, Dallas, Kansas City, Tulsa, San Francisco, San Diego, Phoenix, Oakland, and smaller towns such as Prescott, Colorado Springs, Fresno, Muskogee, Ogden, and Waco, served as vital reminders that however isolated they might be in individual cities or towns, African Americans were part of a much larger black community that stretched across the region, the nation, and the world.[30]

Whether the activity involved building a church, mounting a political campaign, organizing a women's club, or protesting a lynching, black urban westerners generated a sense of cooperation and shared destiny that was impossible to establish among the region's African American cowboys, soldiers, miners, or farmers. Thus, the urbanites were the first black westerners who could be accurately depicted as constituting a "community." Their activities and aspirations would shape the black West for generations. There were consequences, of course. One was that urbanization made black westerners a less distinct group as they melded into an emerging national African American culture.

It was in the western cites that these intrepid newcomers fought for the full democratization of American society. Indeed California's "Rosa

Parks" emerged when the rest of the nation was still in the throes of the Civil War. On April 17, 1863, Charlotte Brown was ejected from a San Francisco streetcar because of her race. In her subsequent suit against the Omnibus Company for $200 in damages, the jury awarded her just five cents—the cost of the fare. Three days after the trial she was again ejected from an Omnibus streetcar and brought a second suit for $3,000 in damages. The case ended on January 17, 1865, with a jury awarding her $500. Brown's victory did not permanently abolish streetcar exclusion. In 1868 the California Supreme Court reversed on appeal lower court judgments against Mary E. Pleasant and Emma J. Turner, who had brought similar suits against the North Beach and Mission Railroad, another San Francisco streetcar company.[31]

The right to vote epitomized complete African American political emancipation in the urban West as well as the rural South. In 1865 black women and men in Virginia City, Nevada, initiated a series of meetings that led to the formation of the Nevada Executive Committee, which in turn petitioned the next legislature for voting rights. The following year a convention of black men meeting in Lawrence, Kansas, challenged the widely held idea that black voting was a privilege that the white male electorate could embrace or reject at its pleasure. The convention then issued this warning to the Euramerican majority in the state:

Since we are going to remain among you, we believe it unwise
to . . . take from us as a class, our natural rights. Shall our presence
conduce to the welfare, peace, and prosperity of the state, or . . . be
a cause of dissention, discord, and irritation. We must be a constant
trouble in the state until it extends to us equal and exact justice.[32]

The victory black westerners gained in their campaign for suffrage in the Colorado Territory had national implications. Between 1864 and 1867 Denver's 150 African Americans, including Lewis Douglass, son of the national civil rights leader Frederick Douglass, waged a relentless campaign to press Congress to delay statehood for the territory until their suffrage rights were guaranteed. Denver barber William Jefferson Hardin, who had arrived from Kentucky in 1863, quickly assumed leadership of the effort, contacting Massachusetts senator Charles Sumner by letter and telegram in 1866 to outline the grievances of the territory's African Americans. Hardin issued an ominous warning in his letter to Senator Sumner: "Slavery went down in a great deluge of blood, and I greatly fear, unless the american [sic] people learn from the past to do justice now & in the future, that their cruel prejudices will go down in the same crimson blood." Senator Sumner read Hardin's telegram to the United States Senate in a speech opposing Colorado statehood. The ensuing debate over black suffrage restrictions in Colorado prompted Congress to pass the Territorial Suffrage Act in January 1867, which gave black male residents the right to vote. Consequently black male Coloradans and those in other western territories gained suffrage months before similar rights were extended to African American males in the southern states and three years before ratification of the Fifteenth Amendment insured those rights for black men in northern and western states.[33]

Although they had to wait much longer, other black westerners were equally determined to win voting rights. In 1921 black urban Texans began their campaign for the restoration of the voting rights they had gradually lost after Reconstruction. Charles Norvell Love, editor of the *Texas Freedman*, filed suit against the Harris County Democratic Party for its prohibition of African Americans from voting in primary elections. The Love lawsuit sparked a war of litigation between black urban political activists in Houston, Dallas, San Antonio, and El Paso, and the state Democratic Party. The legal conflict that ensued produced four United States Supreme Court rulings between 1927 and 1944, culminating in *Smith v. Allwright*, the decision that outlawed the all-white Democratic primary and guaranteed voting rights to the state's African Americans.[34]

The unprecedented migration of African Americans to the West during World War II fused the campaigns for civil rights and economic opportunity. Wartime migrants believed their access to jobs, to housing, and to the voting booth were all components of racial and individual advancement. The numbers suggest the scale of change in the African American West. During the 1940s the region's African American population increased by 443,000 persons or 33 percent. The three Pacific Coast states and Nevada led the region (and the nation) in percentage growth with virtually all of the newcomers concentrated in five major metropolitan regions: Seattle–Tacoma, Washington, and Portland, Oregon–Vancouver, Washington, in the Pacific Northwest; the San Francisco Bay area, including San Francisco, Oakland, and smaller cities such as Berkeley and Richmond; the Los Angeles–Long Beach area; and San Diego. These regions saw black population increases ranging from 798 percent for San Francisco to 168 percent for Los Angeles. Las Vegas, although three hundred miles inland, also saw its population grow rapidly. Between 1940 and 1950 the African American population of Las Vegas exploded from 178 to 2,888, a 1,622 percent increase. Although their numbers were less dramatic, Denver, Omaha, Phoenix, Wichita, Kansas City, Tucson, Houston, and Honolulu also saw surging black populations. The migration signaled a significant shift in the intraregional concentration of African Americans. In 1940, Texas, Oklahoma, and Kansas accounted for 86 percent of the region's blacks. Ten years later their share dropped to 67 percent. Conversely, the Pacific Coast states of California, Oregon, and Washington saw their regional share jump from 10 percent to 28 percent.[35]

Expanding populations were only the initial indicators of change. After decades of labor in menial positions on the periphery of the economy, black workers throughout the region finally gained access to the industrial workplace. By 1943 thousands of black women and men, old residents and newcomers alike, worked in aircraft factories, shipyards, munitions plants, and related industries. Thousands more African American military personnel were stationed at western military facilities that also hired numerous black civilian employees. Black service personnel frequently ended their enlistments in the West, sent for family members, and settled permanently in the region. Marilyn Johnson's conclusion that World War II-era migration made the East Bay area population "younger, more southern, more female, and noticeably more black" than ever before, applies with equal force to other western communities from Omaha to San Diego.[36]

The World War II migration enlarged and intensified the campaign for civil rights. Determined to challenge local and national racial restrictions and obtain a double victory over the Axis and Jim Crow, black activists from Houston to Honolulu launched a full-scale assault on western citadels of racial discrimination, including some of the most powerful labor unions in the nation. In Seattle, for example, the enlarged black community, supported by white and Asian allies and ultimately the federal government, challenged the exclusionary practices of the International Association of Machinists Local 751. Their efforts forced the local to admit people of color and white women on a nondiscriminatory basis at Boeing Aircraft and prompted the IAM itself to remove its color bar at its national convention in 1946. Similar campaigns by black shipyard workers against the International Boilermakers' Union in Portland, the San Francisco Bay area, Los Angeles, and Honolulu led to the union's postwar admission of African American workers and put in place important legal precedents that would be used in the 1960s and 1970s to challenge workplace discrimination throughout the nation.[37]

Black western urbanites continued their campaign for full political equality into the Cold War. In 1951, Oliver Brown filed suit in Topeka, Kansas, on behalf of his daughter, Linda, against her exclusion from a nearby racially segregated elementary school. The case would reach the United States Supreme Court in 1954 as *Brown v. Board of Education* and would inspire a national effort toward racial equality whose repercussions are felt to this day. Although *Brown* received international notoriety for the societal change it initiated, few scholars have explored the seventy-year campaign by Topeka activists that culminated in the decision. Nor do most scholars know of the decades-old effort by blacks in Phoenix and Tucson that led to a 1953 Arizona State Supreme Court decision providing a crucial legal precedent for *Brown*.[38]

A decade before *Brown*, other black and white westerners were employing "direct action"—sit-ins and boycotts of public facilities that discriminated against African Americans. The impetus for these efforts came from the creation of the multiracial Congress of Racial Equality (CORE). Formed in Chicago in 1942 by peace and civil rights advocates, it was initially active mainly on college campuses. CORE mounted brief campaigns in the West, including a sit-in against a downtown Denver movie theater in 1943 and in 1948 against a restaurant in Lawrence, Kansas. By 1951, the DePorres Club, a CORE affiliate based at Creighton University in

Omaha, launched successful direct action campaigns against employment and housing discrimination in the city. Independent of the CORE actions, University of New Mexico students in 1947 initiated successful boycotts against discrimination in Albuquerque-area public accommodations. These efforts were a prelude to large-scale direct-action campaigns beginning in 1958 with sit-ins in Wichita and Oklahoma City against public accommodations segregation. The sit-ins in the southern plains cities preceded by two years the much heralded Greensboro protests credited with initiating the direct-action phase of the 1960s civil rights movement.[39]

By the early 1960s, the campaign that began on the southern plains swept across the region. From San Antonio to Seattle, African Americans took to the streets as an integral part of the national campaign that attempted to eradicate racism, empower black communities, and achieve the full and final democratization of the United States. The Seattle "Movement," for example, an entirely local effort mounted by blacks and sympathetic whites and Asians, employed sit-ins, economic boycotts, protest marches, and other forms of nonviolent demonstrations to confront the three major community grievances—job discrimination, housing bias, and de facto school segregation. When Reverend John H. Adams, a local activist, proudly proclaimed in 1963 that "the Civil Rights Movement has finally leaped the Cascade Mountains," he was simply confirming the rise of a nonviolent crusade that already had engaged the energies and aspirations of thousands of Seattleites. Although the "direct action" efforts of western black civil rights activists and their allies did not eliminate all of their racial grievances, as became apparent in Los Angeles in 1992, the campaign nonetheless demolished decades-old barriers to opportunity and equality, confirming what nineteenth-century black westerners had long known: that the struggle for racial justice was not simply a southern campaign, it had to be waged everywhere in the nation, including the American West.[40]

The 1992 Rodney King uprising in Los Angeles should remind historians of the complex, uncertain, evolving relationships between peoples in the modern urban West. The 1992 conflagration was not simply a reprise of the 1965 Watts Riot, which pitted angry black ghetto residents against a largely white police force and National Guard. The 1992 confrontation revealed tensions that divided Angelenos by class as much as by race (impoverished blacks, Latinos, and whites engaged in looting and burning), as well as conflicts and rivalries between people of color (black and Latino hostility toward Korean American merchants). Yet the multiple sources of that relationship are rooted in five centuries of encounters between racially and culturally diverse peoples both as individuals and distinct populations. A careful reading of African American history in the West reveals the numerous ways in which Asian Americans, Native Americans, and Latinos have been allies or competitors for land, jobs, and political power, and how each group has, in its own particular fashion, incorporated racist beliefs against other people of color to further its own interests. This view was bluntly advanced by nineteenth-century San Francisco newspaper editor Philip A. Bell, who attempted to distance the post-Civil War black suffrage campaign from "heathen . . . idolatrous" Chinese. "We make no issue in the Chinese question," Bell proclaimed, "let them paddle their own canoe." The record also reveals how people of color have overcome what appeared to be insurmountable cultural chasms to forge bonds of friendship and fidelity as occurred in the 1850s when *Tejanos* (Texans of Mexican ancestry) aided black slaves via an underground railroad that ran south across the Rio Grande, or the 1930s when a remarkable coalition of Asian Americans and African Americans forestalled enactment of anti-marriage laws in Washington state. These examples, at the very least, confirm the obsolescence of the model of race relations that centers on Euramerican interaction with each group. Historians must now ask how the groups faced each other in the West.[41]

In an influential article published in 1986, Richard White argued that the peculiar pattern of race relations in the region provides much of the foundation for western distinctiveness. Without it, the West, White maintained, "might as well be New Jersey with mountains and deserts." Indeed, from the sixteenth-century encounter of Esteban with native peoples to the Rodney King uprising eight years before the beginning of the twenty-first century, "race" in the West has mattered, although its specific impact and consequence has varied as much as the regional landscape. African American history in this region affords us an opportunity to view this contested racial terrain and to understand how the contest itself, as it unfolded through the centuries, shaped the destiny of all westerners.[42]

NOTES

1. Westerners disagree on whether Los Angeles should be included in the region. See Walter Nugent, "Where Is the American West? Report on a Survey," *Montana The Magazine of Western History*, 42 (Summer 1992), 8.

2. I define the West as the nineteen states from North Dakota south to Texas and West to Alaska and Hawaii.

3. The early articles on slavery are Lester G. Bugbee, "Slavery in Early Texas," *Political Science Quarterly*, 13 (September 1898), 389–412; Clyde Duniway, "Slavery in California After 1848," *American Historical Association Annual Reports*, 1 (1905), 243–48; and T. W. Davenport, "Slavery Question in Oregon," *Oregon Historical Quarterly*, 9 (September 1908), 189–253. See also, W. Sherman Savage, "The Negro in the History of the Pacific Northwest," *Journal of Negro History*, 13 (July 1928), 255–64; and Kenneth W. Porter, "Relations between Indians and Negroes within the Present Limit of the United States," *Journal of Negro History*, 17 (July 1932), 287–367.

4. On black western population see Bureau of the Census, *Negro Population in the United States, 1790–1915* (Washington, D.C., 1918), 43–45; and Bureau of the Census, *1990 Census of Population, General Population Characteristics by States* (Washington, D.C., 1992), table 3. The "scarcity" quote appears in Walter Prescott Webb, "The American West: Perpetual Mirage," *Harper's Magazine* (May 1957), 30.

5. See for example, Donald A. Grinde, Jr., and Quintard Taylor, "Red vs. Black: Conflict and Accommodation in the Post-Civil War Indian Territory, 1865–1907," *American Indian Quarterly*, 8 (Summer 1984), 211–29: and Quintard Taylor, "Blacks and

Asians in a White City: Japanese Americans and African Americans in Seattle, 1890–1940," *Western Historical Quarterly*, 22 (November 1991), 401–29.

6. See Arnoldo De Leon, *They Called Them Greasers: Anglo Attitudes toward the Mexicans in Texas, 1821–1900* (Austin, 1983), 75–102. On Esteban, see A.D. F. Bandelier, ed., *The Journey of Alvar Nuñez Cabeza de Vaca* (New York, 1905), 8–9, 30–34, 53–54. On Isabel de Olvera see George P. Hammond and Agapito Rey, eds., *Don Juan de Oñate: Colonizer of New Mexico, 1595–1628* (Albuquerque, 1953), 560–62.

7. The Hardin quote appears in George Ruble Woolfolk, *The Free Negro in Texas, 1800–1860: A Study in Cultural Compromise* (Ann Arbor, Mich., 1976), 23. See also Paul Lack, *The Texas Revolutionary Experience: A Political and Social History, 1835–1836* (College Station, Tex., 1992), 238–52.

8. Quoted in Lack, *Texas Revolutionary Experience*, 244.

9. The "natural limits" of slavery debate has a long history and only a slightly shorter historiography. See for example Charles W. Ramsdell, "The Natural Limits of Slavery Expansion," *Mississippi Valley Historical Review*, 16 (September 1929), 151–71; Allen Nevins, *Ordeal of the Union*, 2 vols. (New York, 1947), 116–24; and Charles Desmond Hart, "The Natural Limits of Slavery Expansion: Kansas–Nebraska, 1854," *Kansas Historical Quarterly*, 34 (Spring 1968), 32–50. On the race-slavery-politics nexus in antebellum West, see Eugene Berwanger, *The Frontier against Slavery: Western Anti-Negro Prejudice and the Slavery Extension Controversy* (Urbana, Ill., 1967).

10. Campbell, *Empire for Slavery*, 55–56, 251.

11. On the extent of slavery in normally free states and territories see James A. Rawley, *Race and Politics: "Bleeding Kansas" and the Coming of the Civil War* (Philadelphia, 1969), 87; James R. Harvey, "Negroes in Colorado" (master's thesis, University of Denver, 1941), 15–17; Quintard Taylor, "Slaves and Free Men: Blacks in the Oregon Country, 1840–80," *Oregon Historical Quarterly*, 83 (Summer 1982), 165–69; and Albert S. Broussard, "Slavery in California Revisited: The Fate of a Kentucky Slave in Gold Rush California," *Pacific Historian*, 29 (Spring 1985), 17–21.

12. The Lester quote appears in the *Pennsylvania Freeman*, December 5, 1850. The quote of the German observer is in Ruth Frye Ax, ed., *Bound for Sacramento* (Claremont, Calif., 1938), 144. See also Rudolph Lapp, *Blacks in Gold Rush California* (New Haven, 1977), 137–39, 155–56.

13. See Richard B. Sheridan, "From Slavery in Missouri to Freedom in Kansas: The Influx of Black Fugitives and Contrabands into Kansas, 1854–1864," *Kansas History*, 12 (Spring 1989), 30–31, 37; and Gunja SenGupta, "Servants for Freedom: Christian Abolitionists in Territorial Kansas, 1854–1858," *Kansas History*, 16 (Autumn 1993), 200–13.

14. The "golden age" quote is from Harrison Anthony Trexler, "Slavery in Missouri, 1804–1865," *Johns Hopkins University Studies in Historical and Political Science*, 32 (no. 2, 1914), 384.

15. Sheridan, "From Slavery in Missouri to Freedom in Kansas," 29–31.

16. The quote is from H. D. Fisher, *The Gun and the Gospel: Early Kansas and Chaplain Fisher* (Chicago, 1896), 42–43.

17. Quoted in Henry Clay Bruce, *The New Man: Twenty-Nine Years a Slave, Twenty-Nine Years a Free Man* (New York, 1969), 108–9.

18. The quote is from Richard Cordley, *Pioneer Days in Kansas* (New York, circa 1903), 150–51.

19. The Hickman quote appears in Glen Schwendemann, "Nicodemus: Negro Haven on the Solomon," *Kansas Historical Quarterly*, 34 (Spring 1968), 14.

20. The Fite quotation appears in Gilbert Fite, "A Family Farm Chronicle," in *Major Problems in the History of the American West*, ed. Clyde A. Milner (Lexington, Mass., 1989), 431–32. See also Jimmie Lewis Franklin, *Journey toward Hope: A History of Blacks in Oklahoma* (Norman, 1982), 22–23.

21. Bish, "Black Experience in Selected Nebraska Counties," 157, 209–20.

22. The Leckie and Forbes quotes are taken from Lawrence B. De Graaf, "Recognition, Racism, and Reflections on the Writing of Western Black History," *Pacific Histori-*

cal Review, 44 (February 1975), 37; McCombs's statement appears in Frank N. Schubert, ed., *On the Trail of the Buffalo Soldier: Biographies of African Americans in the U.S. Army, 1866–1917* (Wilmington, Del., 1995), xviii.

23. Quoted in Frank N. Schubert, "The Suggs Affray: The Black Cavalry in the Johnson County War," *Western Historical Quarterly* 4 (January 1973), 60. On the Coeur d'Alene strikes and other civil disturbances, see United States Senate, *Federal Aid in Domestic Disturbances, 1787–1903*, 57th Cong., 2nd Sess., 1902–1903. Senate Doc. 209, pt. 10, pp. 222–25, 246–53; and Clayton D. Laurie, "The United States Army and the Labor Radicals of the Coeur d'Alenes: Federal Military Intervention in the Mining Wars of 1892–1899," *Idaho Yesterdays*, 37 (Summer 1993), 14–17, 24. On the protection of Native American land see "Oklahoma," *Harper's Weekly Magazine* 29 (March 28, 1885), 199; and William L. Leckie, *Buffalo Soldiers: A Narrative of the Negro Cavalry in the West* (Norman, 1967), 28, 166–68, 246–51.

24. Virginia Scharff, "Gender and Western History: Is Anybody Home on the Range?" *Montana The Magazine of Western History*, 41 (Spring 1991), 62.

25. The Prather quote appears in Jack D. Foner, *The United States Soldier between Two Wars: Army Life and Reforms, 1865–1898* (New York, 1970), 135.

26. See Ruthe Winegarten, *Black Texas Women: 150 Years of Trial and Triumph* (Austin, 1995); Paul Spickard, "Work and Hope: African American Women in Southern California during World War II," *Journal of the West*, 32 (July 1993), 70–79; and Gretchen Lemke-Santangelo, *Abiding Courage: African American Migrant Women and the East Bay Community* (Chapel Hill, N.C., 1996). On California population, see Bureau of the Census, *Seventh Census of the United States: 1850* (Washington, D.C., 1853), xxxiii; Bureau of the Census, *Eighth Census of the United States, 1860, Population* (Washington, D.C., 1864), 33.

27. See Delores Hayden, "Biddy Mason's Los Angeles, 1856–1891," *California History*, 69 (Fall 1989), 97–98. See Lynn M. Hudson, "A New Look, or 'I'm not Mammy to Everybody in California': Mary Ellen Pleasant, a Black Entrepreneur," *Journal of the West*, 32 (July 1993), 37. Lytle is described in Thomas C. Cox, *Blacks in Topeka, Kansas, 1865–1915: A Social History* (Baton Rouge, La., 1982), 94–95. See also Sheridan, "From Slavery in Missouri to Freedom in Kansas," 40. On the Colored Ladies Legal Rights Association, see Brian R. Werner, "Colorado's Pioneer Blacks: Migration, Occupations, and Race Relations in the Centennial State" (master's thesis, University of Northern Colorado, 1979), 13, 25. On other women's organizations, see Marilyn Dell Brady, "Kansas Federation of Colored Women's Clubs: 1910–1930," *Kansas History*, 9 (Spring 1986), 19–30; and Lynda Fae Dickson, "The Early Club Movement among Black Women in Denver, 1890–1925" (doctoral diss., University of Colorado, 1982). Charlotta Bass is described in Gerald R. Gill, "'Win or Lose—We Win,' The Vice-Presidential Campaign of Charlotta A. Bass," in *The Afro-American Woman: Struggles and Images*, ed. Sharon Harley and Rosalyn Terborg-Penn (Port Washington, N.Y., 1978), 109–18. Luper is profiled in Franklin, *Journey toward Hope*, 187–89.

28. See William Lang, "The Nearly Forgotten Blacks on Last Chance Gulch, 1900–1912," *Pacific Northwest Quarterly*, 70 (April 1979), 50–51; C. Robert Haywood, "No Less a Man: Blacks in Cow Town Dodge City, 1876–1886," *Western Historical Quarterly*, 19 (May 1988), 161–82; Quintard Taylor, "The Emergence of Afro-American Communities in the Pacific Northwest, 1865–1910," *Journal of Negro History*, 64 (Fall 1979), 342–51.

29. Quoted in the Fort Scott *Colored Citizen*, June 14, 1878. On the elites in western cities, see Willard Gatewood, *Aristocrats of Color: The Black Elite, 1880–1920* (Bloomington, Ind., 1990), 138.

30. The quote is from a *Pacific Appeal* editorial, June 7, 1862, p. 2. On regional church networks, see Taylor, *Forging*, 37–38. For representative examples of western NAACP chapter activities, see Barr, *Black Texans*, 144; Elizabeth McLagan, *A Peculiar Paradise: A History of Blacks in Oregon, 1788–1940* (Portland, 1980), 123; Franklin, *Journey toward Hope*, 52; and Ronald Coleman, "Blacks in Utah History: An Unknown Leg-

294 The Twentieth Century

acy," in *The People of Utah*, ed. Helen Z. Papanikolas (Salt Lake City, 1976), 139. For a listing of UNIA branches in the West, see Tony Martin, *Race First: The Ideological and Organizational Struggles of Marcus Garvey and the Universal Negro Improvement Association* (Westport, 1976), 361–368.

31. See Robert J. Chandler, "Friends in Time of Need: Republicans and Black Civil Rights in California during the Civil War Era," *Arizona and the West*, 24 (Winter 1982), 333–34.

32. Quoted in the *Kansas Tribune*, October 28, 1866. See also Elmer Rusco, *"Good Time Coming?" Black Nevadans in the Nineteenth Century* (Westport, Conn., 1975), 73–75.

33. See Eugene Berwanger, *The West and Reconstruction* (Urbana, Ill., 1981), 145–55, and Eugene Berwanger, "William J. Hardin: Colorado Spokesman for Racial Justice, 1863–1873," *Colorado Magazine*, 52 (Winter 1975), 55–56.

34. See Richard Kluger, *Simple Justice: The History of Brown v. Board of Education and Black America's Struggle for Equality* (New York, 1975), 234–37.

35. Overall the region's African American population increased 33 percent from 1.3 million to 1.8 million between 1940 and 1950. See Bureau of the Census, *Sixteenth Census of the United States: 1940, Population*, vol. 2, *Characteristics of the Population*, pt. 1 (Washington, D.C., 1943), 52; and Bureau of the Census, *Census of Population: 1950*, vol. 2, *Characteristics of the Population*, pt. 1, (Washington, D.C., 1953), 1–106.

36. See Marilyn S. Johnson, *The Second Gold Rush: Oakland and the East Bay in World War II* (Berkeley, 1993), 58.

37. On Seattle see Taylor, *Forging*, 164–65, 170. On campaigns in Portland, Los Angeles, San Francisco, and Honolulu, see Alonzo Smith and Quintard Taylor, "Racial Discrimination in the Workplace: A Study of Two West Coast Cities during the 1940s," *Journal of Ethnic Studies*, 8 (Spring 1980), 35–54; Albert Broussard, *Black San Francisco*, (Lawrence, Kansas, 1993), 158–65; and Beth Bailey and David Farber, "The 'Double-V' Campaign in World War II Hawaii: African Americans, Racial Ideology, and Federal Power," *Journal of Social History*, 26 (Summer 1993), 831–35.

38. On *Brown v. Board*, see Kluger, *Simple Justice*, 367–424. On the Arizona case, see Mary Melcher, "Blacks and Whites Together: Interracial Leadership in the Phoenix Civil Rights Movement," *Journal of Arizona History*, 32 (Summer 1991), 201.

39. On CORE demonstrations in Denver, Lawrence, and Omaha, see August Meier and Elliott Rudwick, *CORE: A Study in the Civil Rights Movement, 1942–1968* (New York, 1973), 27, 56–57, 60. See also George Long, "How Albuquerque Got Its Civil Rights Ordinance," *Crisis*, 60 (November 1953), 521–24; Ronald Walters, "Standing Up In America's Heartland: Sitting in Before Greensboro," *American Visions* 8 (February), 20–23; and Carl R. Graves, "The Right to Be Served: Oklahoma City's Lunch Counter Sit-Ins, 1958–1964," *Chronicles of Oklahoma*, 59 (Summer 1981), 152–66.

40. The Adams quote appears in Taylor, *Forging*, 198.

41. The Bell quote appears in Leigh Dana Johnsen, "Equal Rights and the 'Heathen Chinee': Black Activism in San Francisco, 1865–1875," *Western Historical Quarterly* 11 (January, 1980), 61.

42. See Richard White, "Race Relations in the American West," *American Quarterly*, 38 (Fall 1986), 396–97; Patricia Nelson Limerick, *The Legacy of Conquest: The Unbroken Past of the American West* (New York, 1987), 349.

17 REGIONAL CITY AND NETWORK CITY: PORTLAND AND SEATTLE IN THE TWENTIETH CENTURY

Carl Abbott

Until recently, the Pacific Northwest was to many Americans "a well-kept secret," a geographically large but culturally hazy region whose image, if there was one, included trees, mountains, and water. Its abundant water, especially, exempted it from most mythology about the West—no desert, no cowboys, hardly any gold rushes, and (until "Twin Peaks") virtually no mention in television or film. (Is it truly part of the West?) In recent years, however, the Seattle World's Fair of 1962, the eruption of Mt. St. Helens in 1981, and the prominence of corporations like Intel in Portland and Boeing and Microsoft in Seattle have helped remove the Northwest's secret character. This essay explores how the Northwest's leading cities, Portland and Seattle, have grown, competed, and functioned in the twentieth century.

In different ways, the author finds, Portland and Seattle have exerted leadership and reached maturity. As the twentieth century opened, the two were almost equal in population and economic activity; if anything, Portland led. During the twentieth century, Seattle outpaced Portland in population and prominence. The author offers several explanations: Did Seattle's closer location to the Yukon–Klondike gold rush of the late 1890s jump-start its lead over Portland? How did one become a "regional city" and the other a "network city," and does this explain the faster "progress" of Seattle? (Is growth equivalent to progress, in any case?)

Assuming that "network" status is advantageous, what does it involve, particularly in Seattle's case? What does it have to do with trade, transportation, and manufacturing? (Boeing is the major case of an internationally effective Seattle company, but it was not the only one, and Portland has some too.)

It appears that most citizens of each city are satisfied with the style of the one where they live. Portland, the author says, presents "moralistic politics," while Seattle's style is "individualistic politics." How do these differ? Which is preferable? May other distinctions be made between the two cities?—editors

ECONOMIC AND social interactions in the United States have undergone a massive expansion of scale since the mid-nineteenth century.

The change is apparent in the size and scope of business enterprise, government operations, and organized social movements. As Kenneth Boulding pointed out nearly forty years ago, the result has been an "organizational revolution." The relatively isolated and self-contained "island communities" described by Robert Wiebe have been encompassed by a web of national institutions, obligations, and interactions. One result has been the intensification of extra-local ties and connections at the expense of local relationships.[1]

Scholars interested in the elaboration of organization and the expansion of scale have given particular attention to the industrial transformation of the United States between 1870 and 1920. Understanding modernization as the interactive development of mass production, industrial cities, and bureaucracy, these scholars help us understand both the rise of the central state and the cultural process of nation-building. In detail, many of their studies deal with the emergence of national organizations, institutions, and fields of action: corporations, universities, federal agencies, labor unions, professions, industrial sectors, and policy arenas.[2] For the twentieth century, mainstream social science has tended to assume the continuing expansion of social scale and to explore the erosion of local and regional affiliations.[3]

The expanding scale of economic activity, in contrast, raises the question of differentiation as well as homogenization. In the twentieth century, further transitions of economic organization have depended upon the ability of corporations to use new technologies of distribution and control to manage multilocational enterprises. The results can be viewed as a redefinition of specialization within increasingly complex national and global systems.[4] This redefinition opens the basic historical question of differential impacts on individual communities. Local heritage, local character, and conscious local choices have all mediated the effects of economic scale-change.

Specifically, American cities have responded differently to opportunities created by the rise of an interconnected world economy. This essay examines the range of such responses by analyzing the experiences of twentieth-century Portland and Seattle. Separated by 175 miles of highway or rail line, the cities have similar early histories, analogous economic bases, and parallel demographic profiles, and have long competed against each other for regional dominance. Nevertheless, they have diverged in their connections with the changing national and world economy. I use quantitative measures to define contrasting regional and network orientations that reflect the relative localization or nationalization of community economic life. Between 1900 and 1950, Seattle and Portland were both regional capitals. Since the 1950s, however, Seattle has assumed functions that reach beyond the Pacific Northwest for inputs and markets. While Portland has pursued its traditional role, and even gained ground as a regional metropolis, Seattle has grown into a network city involved in the long-distance transfer of goods, services, and ideas.

The character of civic enterprise shapes this divergence. Faced with the same economic environment between 1955 and 1970, Portland responded with hesitancy, while Seattle acted with greater flexibility and initiative. Comparisons of parallel public decisions in the two cities allow us to weigh the effects of government institutions and political values on growth. For the crucial years around 1960, Seattle's tendency to make network-oriented choices can best he explained by studying the decision-making styles grounded in each city's political culture.[5]

A century ago, Portland and Seattle had an equal partnership in the Pacific Northwest. In the mercantile model of urban growth suggested by Richard Wade and elaborated by James Vance, they were points of entry for capital and labor in a developing frontier.[6] Portland's eight-year head start as an American settlement—1843 versus 1851—gave it an initial edge in trade with gold-rush California, but both cities soon developed as importers or suppliers of manufactured goods and processed foods and as exporters of raw materials within a commercial and financial system dominated by San Francisco.[7] By the time the transcontinental railroad reached the Northwest, Portland's jump on Seattle was down to the single year between 1883 and 1884, although Seattleites waited until the early 1890s for fully competitive service.

In the common version of the history of the Northwest, the Klondike gold rush of 1897 permanently upset the commercial balance between cities. Through a combination of boosterism, luck, and previous trading connections, Seattle made itself the entrepôt for the Far North. Portland and other West Coast cities had equal ambitions, but publicist Erastus Brainerd and the Seattle Chamber of Commerce identified Seattle with Alaska in the public mind.[8] Captured initially in the flush times, the story goes, Alaska business stayed in the pocket of Seattle merchants, bankers, and boat builders, and triggered an inevitable process of economic agglomeration that pushed Seattle's population past Portland by 1910 and kept it in the lead.[9] As early as 1921, historians such as Ezra Meeker perceived that "without Alaska Washington would not now have attained the commanding development that is her pride." Murray Morgan said it even more directly: "In Seattle, gold spurred growth, and growth battened on growth."[10]

In both thematic and chronological coverage, the story, as outlined, is typical of historical explanations of the relative fortunes of American cities. It treats differential urban growth as the product of an intraregional competition that was over by the twentieth century. On closer examination, however, the Portland–Seattle case does not match the standard model as closely as supposed. The recent experience of the two cities demonstrates the continued volatility of urban fortunes within a regional context, as new sources and avenues of growth have emerged with the expanding scale of economic activity. The case invites an alternative explanation for differential urban growth that emphasizes national and international connections, in addition to regional roles. The history of the two cities reconfirms the importance of specific events and choices, but the point of divergence lies sixty years closer to the present than often thought. In addition, many of the crucial decisions have involved the public, rather than the private, sector.

The "Alaska thesis" of Seattle's ascendancy fits within the common historical model of interurban competition in the nineteenth century United States. Baltimore and Philadelphia, St. Louis and Chicago, and scores of other urban rivals provide comparable stories in which active and foresightful entrepreneurs in one city capitalized on commercial opportunities potentially available to both. In turn, the trade of the newly acquired hinterland supported further growth of the successful city and increased its competitive advantage in future rivalries. The model is especially apt for the era of continental expansion, when the progress of settlement involved the allocation of newly opened frontiers among new commercial centers.[11] Indeed, historical studies of urban rivalries and urban imperialism mirror the nineteenth-century understanding of urban growth as the product of territorial control of resources and trade.[12]

A spatially-rooted explanation of differential urban growth also matches the basic assumptions of central place theory. One of the key models in modern quantitative geography, central place theory, was developed in Germany in the 1930s, introduced in the United States in the 1940s, and tested against American evidence in the 1950s and 1960s. The theory argues that there is a correspondence between the size of a city, the variety of functions it performs for a surrounding hinterland, and the size or purchasing power of the hinterland. The wider a city's spatial reach, the broader its range of businesses and the larger its population. A city that captures a new customer base (such as Alaska) or enjoys a rapidly developing hinterland (such as the Columbia Plateau) positions itself for economic diversification and growth in the level of economic activity. The final result in a developing region is a nested hierarchy of towns and hinterlands that builds successively from crossroads stores through small towns to comprehensive regional centers.[13]

The structured propositions of central place theory recognize the resources and demands of a city's hinterland as the essential engine of that city's growth.[14] In historical terms, the process of interurban competition has determined relative positions in the hierarchy of central places. For newly settled frontiers such as the Pacific Northwest, where each ambitious town started nearly equally, it requires historical analysis to understand how Seattle eclipsed Everett, or how Portland squeezed out Oregon City. This regional approach to urban growth has been particularly congenial to American urban historians because it emphasizes local decisions and sources of information, and is compatible with practical case studies. It also ties the subfield of urban history to the wide historical interest in the expansion of the continental resource frontier.[15]

An alternative model that emphasizes extra-regional networks as key determinants of urban growth may offer greater relevance to the processes of urban development in the twentieth century, which has been marked by basic changes in the sectoral composition and spatial patterns of economic activity. Several historians who have taken on topics with broad spatial and temporal sweep have described dual urban systems in which a set of regionally based cities coexists with a second set of cities oriented to national or transnational networks. Studying late imperial China, G. William Skinner found that one hierarchy of towns and cities served regional trading needs with few connections outside their local hinterlands. The hierarchy developed from the bottom up with the expansion of local and provincial commerce in accord with the assumptions of central place theory. A second hierarchy of administrative centers, in contrast, was created from the top down by imperial agents and functioned as a single network of centers for control and information transmission.[16] Edward W. Fox divided premodern France into two subareas and urban systems based on different patterns of exchange. Central and interior France was a territorial society organized around local trade between provincial cities and regional agricultural hinterlands. The commercial society of the western coast, in contrast, was dominated by Atlantic seaports tied more closely to interregional and international flow of goods than to their own backcountry. Bordeaux and Nantes coexisted with interior cities in the same political unit, but also participated in a network of trading cities that extended from Amsterdam and London to Lisbon, Barcelona, and Naples.[17]

In *The Making of Urban Europe*, Lynn Lees and Paul Hohenberg elaborated Fox's idea of regional and commercial systems as a major explanatory concept. They argued that western European urbanization produced parallel systems that coexisted in time and often in space. Cities in the central place system were rooted in a close relationship with their agricultural environs, expressed indigenous or provincial culture, and tied the locality to the state through a defined hierarchy of towns and cities. Network cities took their life from long-distance commerce and served as "centers, nodes, junctions, outposts, and relays" within complex sets of economic and social linkages that crossed political borders. They transmitted values and ideas from one culture to the next. Lees and Hohenberg have presented the two systems not as exclusive categories but as heuristic concepts that focus attention on one or the other aspects of urban growth. Major cities, indeed, could fill roles simultaneously in both regional and network systems.[18]

Historians of United States cities have sporadically stressed the importance of extraregional connections. In his classic study, *The Rise of New York Port*, Robert G. Albion argued that New York's early roles in coastal shipping, trans-Atlantic trade, and wholesaling were more important than its capture of a regional hinterland. For the twentieth century, Roger Lotchin and Gerald Nash have focused attention on the ways in which federal spending and investment in federal facilities functioned as sources of rapid growth in western cities. Other historians of sunbelt cities have also begun to examine international connections during the postwar decades.[19]

Extra-regional sources of urban growth have received theoretical attention in the social sciences. Geographer Allan Pred has offered empirical support for a model of urban growth that parallels the historical idea of the dual system, arguing that central place theory is far too limited for understanding the wide ranging connections of modern cities. In Pred's "asymmetric" model, a city's transactions with its regional hinterland are likely to be less important for its future than its unpredictable and idiosyncratic set of extra-regional connections. To support his argument, he points to the large proportion of jobs in every major city now controlled by multilocational businesses and government organizations. A detailed, empirical description of the corporate control patterns of Seattle, Portland, and four other western cities as of 1974–1975 shows that extra-regional ties equal or outweigh those within traditional hinterlands.[20]

Pred's data are often cited by an emerging school of urban analysis that emphasizes a city's role in the global economy as the prime determinant of local economic change. In particular, fundamental changes in the world economic system during the 1970s have created a "new international division of labor" that has established a new and controlling context for urban growth programs.[21] In specific applications, Joe Feagin has described twentieth-century Houston as being tied to international markets and multinational corporations through decisions of Detroit auto executives, congressional committees, and foreign oil producers. Edward Soja and his co-workers have detailed the transition of Los Angeles from a regionally-based metropolis, oriented to domestic markets, to "a global capitalist city of major proportions" that participates fully in the finance and production networks of the Pacific Rim.[22]

These alternative conceptions of regional and network cities help to define specific questions about the comparative development of twentieth-century Seattle and Portland. Both cities entered the century having developed after two generations into regional centers for Puget Sound and the Columbia Basin. The common understanding of Northwest history suggests that both have retained their regional roles, but that Seattle has made a better job of it, edging further ahead until it has left Portland behind. The suggestion that Seattle may have grown by gaining new trans-regional network functions, however, provides an alternative framework for understanding change within an urban system. A variety of accessible quantitative data allow a structured evaluation of Seattle's relative success.

In 1900, the Twelfth Census counted 9,555 more Portlanders than Seattleites. Eighty years later Seattle's margin over Portland was either 365,000 (using Standard Metropolitan Areas [SMSA]) or 795,000 (using Consolidated Metropolitan Areas). For the years between, the changing population ratio provides a standardized measure that directly reflects the relative growth of the two cities (see Table 17.1). The first decade of the twentieth century shows the expected surge for Seattle, with carry-over into the 1910s. Between 1920 and 1950, however, the two cities grew at the same pace. Not until the 1950s and 1960s did Seattle begin again to outpace Portland. The pattern since 1970 depends on the chosen defini-

Table 17.1
Seattle and Portland Population

	Seattle	Portland	Seattle:Portland
1880	3,553	17,577	
1890	42,837	46,385	.92
1900	80,871	90,426	.89
1910	237,174	207,214	1.14
1920	357,950	299,882	1.19
1930	420,663	378,728	1.11
1940	452,639	406,406	1.11
1950	844,572	704,829	1.20
1960	1,101,213	821,897	1.35
1970	1,421,869	1,009,129	1.41
1980a	1,607,469	1,242,594	1.29
1990a	1,972,961	1,412,344	1.40
1980b	2,093,000	1,298,000	1.61
1990b	2,559,164	1,477,895	1.73

1880–1910:	Cities
1920–1940:	Metropolitan Districts
1950–1990a:	Populations within 1960 SMSA boundaries
1980b—1990b:	Standard Consolidated Metropolitan Areas

tion for the Seattle and Portland metropolitan areas. Use of Consolidated Metropolitan Areas, which adds Tacoma to Seattle, shows Portland losing more ground after 1970. Comparison of growth within 1960 SMSA boundaries, however, shows relatively slower growth for Seattle in the 1970s, followed by recovery in the 1980s.

This aggregate population comparison directs the search for critical turning points in the Seattle–Portland rivalry to the 1950s and 1960s. Information on the structure of the two Metropolitan economies supports the same conclusion by showing significant changes in the sources of economic growth for Seattle, but not for Portland, after 1950.

Apart from the Alaskan bonanza, Seattle and Portland retained more structural similarities than differences between 1900 and 1920. Both benefited from the shift of the American timber industry to the Northwest and from an agricultural boom in the Columbia Basin that was triggered by new railroad lines, private and public irrigation projects, stock raising, and dryfarming.[23] Both cities' bankers controlled roughly equal amounts of capital when new federal reserve banks were located in 1913.[24] Both downtowns experienced building booms to provide office space for commercial, financial, and professional service sectors. Successful international expositions in 1905 (Portland's Lewis and Clark Centennial Exposition and Oriental Fair) and 1909 (Seattle's Alaska–Yukon–Pacific Exposition) symbolized the cities' arrivals as mature communities that could command the respectful attention of easterners.[25]

Given the similar roles of the two cities, Seattle's more rapid growth tied directly to the development of its hinterland. For comparative analy-

Table 17.2
Relative Population and Personal Income:
Ratios of Seattle and Portland Hinterlands

	Population		Income	
	(1)	(2)	(3)	(4)
1900	1.44	1.58		
1910	1.73	1.94		
1920	1.71	1.97		
1930	1.57	1.80	1.62	1.82
1940	1.48	1.63	1.56	1.76
1950	1.43	1.58	1.49	1.66
1960	1.50	1.60	1.58	1.64
1970	1.50	1.56	1.62	1.67
1980	1.41	1.49	1.54	1.61

(1): Population in OR and WA weighted 1, population in AK, ID and MT weighted 0.5.
(2): Same as (1), less Seattle and Portland city populations (1900–1910), metropolitan district populations (1920–40), or populations within 1960 SMSA boundaries (1950–80).
(3): Personal income in OR and WA weighted 1, personal income in AK, ID, and MT weighted 0.5 [WA per capita income used for AK for 1930 and 1940]
(4): Same as (3), less Seattle and Portland city populations (1900–10), metropolitan district populations (1920–40), or populations within 1960 SMSA boundaries (1950–80).
For hinterland definitions, see Note 26.

sis, Portland's primary hinterland is defined as Oregon and three adjacent counties in southwestern Washington, with southwestern Idaho as its secondary hinterland. Seattle's primary hinterland is the remainder of Washington, while Alaska, the Idaho panhandle, and western Montana are its secondary hinterland.[26] As an estimate of effective market size, population is weighted at 1.0 in the primary hinterlands and at 0.5 in the secondary hinterlands, where other cities competed for market share (see Table 17.2). Between 1900 and 1920, Seattle's trading region grew more rapidly than Portland's, reflecting the development of Alaska and the Columbia Plateau and the climax of activity in the northern Rocky Mountain mining region. The completion of additional transcontinental railroads in 1893 and 1909 also helped Seattle cut into Portland's business in eastern Washington. The Seattle:Portland population ratio increased by 34 percent over the two decades while the comparable hinterland ratio increased by 20 percent (see Table 17.2, Column 1). If the populations of the two cities themselves are excluded from the hinterland totals, the ratio increased by 25 percent (see Table 17.2, Column 2).

There was little change in the standing of the two cities between 1920 and 1950. Portland drew closer to Seattle in population in the 1920s, held its gains in the 1930s, and slipped only as far as its relative position of 1920 during the turbulent 1940s. Data on industrial structure support the picture of regional stability. Regionally-based manufacturing makes direct and essential use of regional resources and raw materials.[27] Although the basis for data compilation changed in 1930 and again in 1940, the Seattle–

Table 17.3
Employment in Regionally Based Manufacturing

	Regionally Based Manufacturing as Percentage of All Employment		
	Seattle	Portland	Seattle:Portland
1909	4.7	5.7	.82
1919	4.8	6.2	.69
1930	3.1	4.7	.66
1940	9.0	13.0	.69
1950	6.8	12.4	.55
1960	6.9	11.5	.60
1970	4.8	7.9	.61
1980	3.6	6.2	.58

See Note 27 for definition of category and sources. The figures for 1909–19, for 1930, and for 1940–80 were derived from data compiled according to different principles.

Portland ratios in Table 17.3 suggest that such industries account for a stable proportion of the total employment in each city from 1920 to 1940. War production jobs and wartime growth were also comparable.[28] As late as the 1950s, outside observers thought that the two cities competed on an equal basis for the trade of the Pacific Northwest, with Portland gaining shipping and wholesaling at the expense of Seattle, and Seattle building a more diversified manufacturing base.[29]

Another indicator of regional relationships is the extent to which economic activity and population concentrate in a single "primate" city. High concentration may reflect both the absence of strong secondary cities, as in lesser developed nations, and the "overdevelopment" of a dominant city through participation in trading systems or other exchange networks external to its regional hinterland, as with medieval Venice or modern Miami.[30] Table 17.4 summarizes the standard Ginsburg Index of urban primacy, calculated by dividing the population of a region's largest city by the combined population of its four largest cities. An index that approaches 1.0 indicates that the largest city far overshadows its nearest rivals. An index of .50 or less shows the presence of substantial secondary cities, a pattern that is characteristic of developed economies.[31]

The primacy indices for Portland and Seattle are striking for their stability between 1920 and 1950. Just as neither metropolis gained or lost population relative to the other, so neither gained nor lost significantly, relative to the secondary cities in its hinterland. Seattle's lower index reflects the size of its hinterland cities of Tacoma, Spokane, and Butte, which outranked Boise, Eugene, and Salem until after World War II. By implication, Seattle's well-developed hinterland offered a wide range of opportunities for growth as a regional city.

Portland's strong competitive showing in the 1920s and 1930s was tied to continued growth in its farming hinterland in Oregon and southern Idaho. In contrast, the mining regions of Alaska, northern Idaho, and

Table 17.4
Seattle and Portland as Primate Cities

	Ginsburg Index	
	Seattle	Portland
1900	.44	.81
1910	.51	.83
1920	.55	.85
1930	.57	.85
1940	.58	.84
1950	.58	.86
1960	.63	.82
1970	.65	.76
1980	.75	.73

Ginsburg Index = population of largest city in region divided by total population of four largest cities in region.
Seattle and Portland regions defined as in Table 17.2 (see Note 26).
Metropolitan district populations used when designated for 1920–40; metropolitan area populations for 1950–70; consolidated metropolitan area populations for 1980.

Montana were stagnating (see Table 17.2). The Seattle:Portland ratios of hinterland population declined by 13 to 17 percent between 1920 and 1940, showing the more rapid growth of Portland's trading zone. Data available since 1930 allow the population totals to be weighted by state per capita personal income, which gives a closer approximation of hinterland purchasing power. The weighting alters the individual ratios but not the trend (see Table 17.2, Columns 3–4).

After a century of relatively stable competition, the regional sources of Seattle's advantage over Portland began to erode in the 1950s. If anything, Portland, rather than Seattle, reaped the greatest benefit from regional development and regionally-oriented activities. Even though Seattle's population margin over Portland grew from 20 percent in 1950 to 41 percent in 1970, the two hinterlands grew at essentially the same pace (Table 17.2). Seattle's increasing primacy after 1950 suggests that it has become less dependent on regional connections. Portland's decreasing primacy, in contrast, is caused by the more rapid development of its hinterland with resulting opportunities for regional trade and services.

Trends in specific industrial sectors support the conclusion that Portland, rather than Seattle, benefited most from regional functions after 1950. Before World War II, for example, Seattle's wholesale business was half again as great as Portland's. Seattle's lead shrank to a few percentage points in the 1940s and 1950s and disappeared completely in the 1960s and 1970s. Although a portion of wholesale trade involved log and lumber brokerage for national markets, the majority represented regional distribution.[32] Most federal employment outside the Department of Defense similarly involves local services such as mail delivery and veterans' assistance or regional resource management through the Forest Service, National Park Service, Bonneville Power Administration, and similar agencies. Despite Seattle's status as a federal regional center, the same proportion of Portlanders and Seattleites worked in such jobs in 1980.[33]

The most obvious contrast with Seattle's stable or declining regional role was the rapid growth of aerospace manufacturing employment as Boeing captured the dominant share of commercial jetliner production for national and overseas airlines. After the failure of the Stratocruiser in the immediate postwar decade, Boeing introduced the highly successful 707 in 1950s, following with the 727, the 737, and the 747, which began to roll off production lines in Everett in 1970. Aircraft manufacturing jobs in metropolitan Seattle increased steadily from 1949 to 1958. For the next fifteen years, however, Boeing's employment fluctuated widely. Three quick cycles of boom and bust culminated in the deep "Boeing depression" of 1969–1971, when the corporation's local employment fell from 105,000 to 38,000. In addition, Boeing procured only 10 percent of its processing inputs from the Seattle area during the 1960s, limiting its capacity to stimulate local economic diversification, though shielding the city from multiplier effects of production slowdowns. The major *developmental* impact of Boeing, in short, was felt with national rearmament in the early 1950s, rather than in the booming 1960s.[34]

Equally important in the long run were additional changes that tied Seattle into national and international networks. The growth sectors included tourism, higher education, research and development, finance, and foreign trade. In concert with Boeing's expansion in response to world markets, a set of public decisions in Seattle between 1955 and 1970 confirmed its participation in a variety of long-distance networks. The remainder of this essay explores these decisions and their results in comparison with Portland. Although the numbers point to the 1950s as the decade when the fortunes of the two cities began to diverge, direct comparison of their governmental capacity would have offered little encouragement for an ambitious Seattle. Both cities had fiscally conservative "caretaker" governments that placed greatest emphasis on the smooth delivery of routine services.[35] Portland mayors Earl Riley (1941–1948), Fred Peterson (1953–1956), and Terry Schrunk (1957–1972) maintained close ties with important local market businesses. Seattle mayors Arthur Langlie (1938–1942), William Devin (1942–1952), and Gordon Clinton (1956–1964) were even more clearly the picks of the local economic establishment. Reform-minded mayors who entered office hoping to activate local government— Dorothy Lee in Portland (1949–1953) and Alan Pomeroy in Seattle (1952–1956)—found themselves frozen out of the action by the downtown establishment and City Hall cronies.[36]

Both city administrations were also buffered against vigorous central direction. Individual elected officials and bureaucrats constituted functional fiefdoms within each city government. Under Portland's commission charter, the mayor and each of four independently elected city commissioners managed separate sets of city departments. Seattle had achieved the same fragmentation by institutionalizing a system in which the chairs of city council committees controlled the budgets for specific functional areas and dominated council discussions with expertise and access to specialized information. The result, as Edward Banfield noted in *Big City Politics*, was to force any analysis of Seattle politics to start with the question: "Anybody in Charge?"[37]

Despite these formal similarities, Seattle mounted a series of public initiatives between 1958 and 1968 that Portland was unable to match. Community efforts assured a successful world's fair, developed convention and sports facilities, provided essential infrastructure to support a growing metropolis, and revitalized the port. The cumulative effect was to move Seattle into new roles in long range networks of exchange. Over the same decade, Portland faced similar opportunities and attempted parallel projects but failed to act effectively to promote economic growth.

Contemporary observers commented on the contrasting approaches to public business. Journalists such as Neil Morgan and Neil Pierce and such scholars as Earl Pomeroy and Dorothy Johansen all perceived different spirits of public and private enterprise. "Unlike Seattle, which is in its own promotional vocabulary a 'go-ahead' city," Johansen wrote in 1967, "Portland moved in 1965 as slowly and deliberately as it did in 1865, and there remains considerable sentiment ... to 'keep things as they are.'"[38] These styles of public action expressed distinct valuations of community entrepreneurship. Each city inclined to a particular way of doing business by a well-established understanding of acceptable behavior and by institutions that codified those customs and traditions. Assumptions about the proper way to carry out the public business conditioned specific responses to scale change in the American economy. Portland was process-centered, cautious, and localized. Seattle was project-centered, entrepreneurial, and expansive. While Seattleites built in anticipation of growing business, Portlanders judged facility needs by current demand and by the potential of purely local and regional markets. In the broadest sweep, Seattle leaders viewed the expansion of economic scale as an opportunity and measured their ambitions by Chicago, Philadelphia, and Pittsburgh. Portlanders viewed the expansion of economic networks as irrelevant or even threatening to stable commercial relationships.[39]

Different experiences with major expositions illustrate the contrast. The two cities began by competing not only for regional and national attention but also for the same date. Led by the Portland Chamber of Commerce, Oregonians decided in December 1954 to commemorate the centennial of statehood with a celebratory exposition in Portland in 1959. Within a few months, Seattleites began to explore a fifty-year follow-up to the Alaska–Yukon–Pacific Exposition of 1909. As second in line, Seattle reluctantly ceded 1959 to Portland and shifted its target to 1961 (later 1962).[40]

The parallels ended with the timing. The scope of the Seattle exposition grew steadily from a regional reaffirmation of the Alaska connection to "a means of recapturing prestige . . . as the gateway to the Orient" and, finally, to the global theme of "the wonders of the 'space age' science" and the future of "Century 21," a newly created non-profit branch of the Washington State fair commission that managed the fair.[41] The fair's advocates recruited strong business leadership and political backing in Olympia and used Century 21 to insulate their operation from local politics. The promoters tapped the city for $15 million in site and building improvements, secured $7.5 million from the State of Washington, and obtained $9 million for federal participation. The federal commitment forced postponement to 1962, but it enabled fair chairman Joseph Gandy to argue successfully for designation as a world's fair by the Bureau of International Expositions.[42] Official sanction also allowed the planners to attract international exhibits and to draw on the best national expertise, ranging from the Walt Disney organization to an advisory board representing the National Science Foundation, National Academy of Sciences, and American Association for the Advancement of Science. Reams of favorable publicity and 9,600,000 paid visits made it arguably the most successful of all postwar American world's fairs. The renovated site and buildings, about a mile north of downtown, became Seattle Center, with a science museum, renovated auditorium, and major convention facilities. Just as importantly, the fair symbolized Seattle's arrival as a national city and taught outsiders that the Northwest's metropolis started with an "S."[43]

Portland had preempted 1959 but lost its chance to upstage Seattle by planning the Oregon Centennial Exposition on the cheap. While Seattle steadily broadened the scope and appeal of its effort, Portland whittled its vision to the comfortable model of local "pioneer days." Despite early national publicity and a small international trade fair, the celebration had little to attract Portlanders, let alone visitors from out of state. Planned initially to utilize a new Portland coliseum and convention center, the exposition had to turn to the Oregon Legislature when the Portland facility bogged down in the city's neighborhood politics. The parsimonious state doled out $2.6 million in two grudging installments in 1958 and 1959 barely in time to remodel a livestock exhibition hall into display space. Downstate jealousies were manifested in a penny-pinching Oregon Centennial Commission that determined to show an operating profit, and diverted effort to ancillary events around the state. Political conflicts between the state commission and newly elected Governor Mark Hatfield hobbled local managers in the last months of preparation.[44] Portlanders themselves quickly learned to stay away from what turned out to be little more than an interminable county fair without the plum preserves and Future Farmers. The 900,000 paid admissions embarrassed civic leaders who had hoped for 5-7 million visitors. The event left a slightly improved facility for the privately operated Pacific International Live Stock Exposition rather than any equivalent of Seattle Center.[45]

A delay in the construction of a coliseum and convention center handicapped the centennial exposition. As early as 1954, a mayor's advisory committee had recommended a Columbia River site for an exposition-arena campus that could accommodate the Pacific International stock show, as well as other events. In May 1954, Portland voters approved a charter amendment that created an Exposition-Recreation Commission and authorized an $8 million bond issue. The assurance of funding brought the city's sectional conflicts into the open. Reports from the Planning Commission and Stanford Research Institute argued for a centrally located alternative. The leading site, in the view of downtown investors, was an under-utilized area south of the downtown—land that would later be incorporated into Portland's first urban renewal project. In October 1955, the Exposition-Recreation Commission voted three to two for the Columbia River location. The city council then refused, by one vote, to make available the necessary city land. The stalemate was broken by a successful initiative measure that restricted any coliseum to the east side of the Willamette River (an area that included the Columbia River shoreline). The city finally compromised with a location on the east bank of the Willamette River within view of downtown. The openness of the deliberations and Oregon's easy use of the voter-initiated referendum allowed different economic interests to derail the project in sequence. When finally built, the new coliseum was too small to compete for large national conventions; and, ironically, voters rejected expansion in 1962 as too risky.[46]

The differing fates of proposals for covered sports stadiums also revealed contrasting approaches to growth. Portland's proposed "Delta Dome" (named for its site in Delta Park near the Centennial Exposition grounds) would have been the nation's second covered multipurpose stadium. Despite strong backing from Mayor Terry Schrunk and other politicians, from newspapers, and from utility companies, Multnomah County bonds proposals for a Delta Dome failed in both May and November 1964, with substantial opposition in every part of the county.[47] In addition to their concerns about site access, many voters were unwilling to risk national competition by building a stadium without a previous commitment from a major league baseball franchise.[48]

Defeat at the polls opened the doors for city and suburban politicians to float competing proposals for a new site near the Columbia River, for suburban locations, and for expansion of existing facilities. Advocates for each scheme for new construction were able to veto the competition without being able to develop a coalition around their own proposal.[49] Under heavy pressure from downtown hotels and retailers, the City of Portland purchased an inadequate 28,000 seat stadium located on the downtown fringe from private owners in 1966. By committing Portland to an interim measure, the action killed hope of a new, nationally competitive facility. It also expressed a deep unwillingness to speculate on the long-term expansion of professional sports. The city maintained a venue for Triple-A baseball and high school football playoffs, but dropped off the list for major league baseball or football.[50]

Seattle started the 1960s with similar problems. Efforts to court the

Cleveland Indians in 1964 foundered on inadequate facilities and lack of enthusiasm at City Hall.[51] The commercial-civic elite incorporated a major stadium in the massive 1968 bond issue that voters approved under the rubric Forward Thrust. Use of a state-appointed Washington Stadium Commission to evaluate locations in the suburbs, near Seattle Center, and south of downtown deliberately took the decision on site out of open politics. The appointment of Joe Gandy, the former president of the Century 21 corporation, kept the civic elite in control of the process. A glance at Gandy's incoming correspondence shows the intense advocacy for competing sites that might have derailed a more open process (as had happened in Portland).[52] Indeed, the initial Stadium Commission choice near Seattle Center was defeated by referendum in 1970, bringing reactivation of the commission, another detour around open politics, and a new site on the southern edge of the central business district. The resulting Kingdome gets few points for design excellence, but its availability for American League and National Football League teams confirmed Seattle's public standing as a "major league" city.

Underlining the different success in project planning and implementation was a contrasting willingness to pay for basic infrastructure. After meeting immediate postwar needs, voters in both cities were reluctant to spend money on anything but bare maintenance of public facilities. From 1952 through 1962, Portlanders said yes to eight tax base, tax levy, and bond measures proposed by the city, county, and school district and no to twenty. Seattle's voters accepted only three bond issues and rejected eight between 1952 and 1958.[53] In the latter year, however, Seattle and King County residents took the bold step of creating the Municipality of Metropolitan Seattle to build the sewers and treatment plants necessary to preserve the attractions of Lake Washington. Although Seattle and King County voters turned down a multipurpose regional agency in March, they agreed in September to spend $125 million on the single problem of water quality.[54] Ten years later, business and political leadership coordinated Forward Thrust, an ad hoc process to develop a prioritized list of metro area capital needs. Forward Thrust was developed outside the structures of local government explicitly to force the support of local rival politicians. As attorney James Ellis commented during the Forward Thrust campaign, "some of us have just gotten sick and tired of trying to change the structure of local government. I tried myself for fifteen years, and I'm damned if I'm going to wait another fifteen before anything actually gets done." Again, Seattle and King County responded by approving $324 million for highways, sewers, neighborhood improvements, fire protection, parks, and recreation.[55]

Portland was not so much cheap as it was slow in pursuing new port investment. Through the 1950s, Portland outpaced Seattle in general cargo movements and the bulk shipments of farm and forest products that traditionally constituted most of the trade over northwest docks.[56] Portlanders supported new maritime facilities by voting $6.5 million for

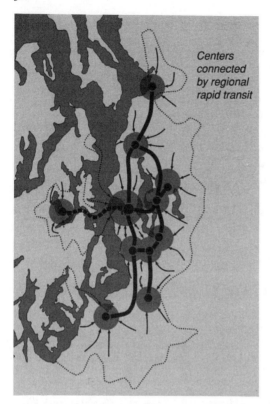

18. The interconnectedness of the Puget Sound area, from Everett on the north, through Seattle (largest node), to Tacoma in the south. *Courtesy of the Puget Sound Regional Council.*

the city's Commission of Public Docks in 1954 and $9.5 million in 1960. However, the 1960 figure covered less than half of the needs list prepared by consultants.[57] Lacking the stable funding of a dedicated tax base and with no comprehensive plan in place, the Docks Commission waited three cautious years before it began to spend the money. Since the established operators in the Columbia River trade who dominated the Docks Commission agreed with outside consultants that the new technology of containerization was inappropriate for traditional regional bulk commodities, the funds finally went to improve familiar general cargo docks.[58]

The careful preservation of split decision-making further hampered effective port development. The city-appointed Docks Commission and the state-appointed Port of Portland divided responsibilities until they merged in 1970. The former maintained public marine terminals and built new ones, when it could pull together the money. Originally created to dredge the Willamette River channel, the latter agency added industrial development and operation of the regional airport. The Docks Commission saw itself as a scrappy agency that spoke for the ship captains and barge owners who knew the rivers. The Port of Portland represented the more Olympian views of bankers, clubmen, and inheritors of old wealth whose eyes were alert to real estate deals. Given the poor record of cooperation, the divided

Table 17.5
Seattle-Everett and Portland-Vancouver Waterborne
Foreign Trade ($1 Millions)

	Exports			Imports		
	Seattle	Portland	S:P	Seattle	Portland	S:P
1967	$203	$385	.53	$205	$173	1.18
1972	348	388	.90	1655	350	4.73
1977	833	765	1.15	3966	1159	3.42
1982	2759	2048	1.35	10,251	2167	4.86
1986	4194	1873	2.24	19,084	3940	4.84

Source: U.S. Department of Commerce, U.S. Waterborne Exports and General Imports.

control of port development institutionalized caution through multiple veto points.[59]

Simultaneously, Seattle turned to facilities for containerized cargo out of a sense of necessity. A series of consultant studies and a KING-TV documentary on "Lost Cargo" articulated a growing crisis of confidence in Port of Seattle management in 1959, setting off several years of bureaucratic infighting and contests for the elected seats on the Port Commission. Firmly in place by 1963, a new growth-oriented majority spent more than $100 million to modernize and upgrade marine terminals and industrial land as a way to bypass Portland's historic advantage, and to compete directly with Oakland. The Port Commission gambled on the development of long range business in which containerized cargoes would move through Seattle in transit between Asia and the ports on the Atlantic. A reactivated Mayor's Maritime Advisory Committee after 1963 promoted port-based economic development and lobbied state and federal officials. The rhetoric of the revitalized port reflected its new energy, "catapulting" to "record-breaking performance" by the mid-1960s and "barreling full bore" in its "relentless escalation" toward full success.[60]

The results of the Portland and Seattle approaches were apparent in import-export data. The relative value of both import and export trade shifted to the advantage of Seattle between 1967 and 1997 (see Table 17.5). Portland retained its historic western role as an exporter of high bulk, low value commodities such as minerals, wood products, and farm products while gaining selected high tonnage imports such as automobiles. Seattle developed as a comprehensive international port that shipped and received extensively-processed high-value goods. A key step came in 1970, when the development of new container terminals convinced a consortium of six Japanese shipping lines to make Seattle their first port of call on the West Coast. In 1967, Seattle exports carried an average value of $.05 per pound compared with $.04 for Portland. The comparable figures for 1986 were $.36 for Seattle and $.08 for Portland.[61]

Seattle also emerged as the Northwest's air-travel hub. Into the 1950s, the two cities had equal rail access to the East, while Portland enjoyed greater proximity to California. Both cities produced equal numbers of air passengers per thousand residents.[62] When American carriers adopted passenger jets during the 1960s, however, Seattle gained a majority of direct long-distance flights. Airport expansion, starting in 1969, and aggressive competition for new route designations allowed Seattle to double Portland's air passenger miles and passengers per day by the early 1980s. Present day Seattle can virtually match Portland's time-distance to California and offers superior access outside the West.[63]

One reason for Seattle's greater willingness to pursue extra-regional opportunities lies in the timing of generational transition. The expansion of Boeing with Korean War orders, Cold War contracts, and the 707 passenger jet required the recruitment of thousands of engineers and managers from beyond the Northwest.[64] Expansion of the University of Washington multiplied this "Boeing effect." After divisive internal battles over political loyalty oaths during the early 1950s, the university hired a new president with a new agenda in 1958. Enrollment had edged up from 12,271 in 1940 to 13,675 in 1956 and then exploded to 29,977 by 1968. President Charles Odegaard encouraged faculty to tap the rapidly growing pool of federal research funds in medicine and science.[65] A growing university helped to attract a Battelle Institute think tank in 1965. By 1977, Seattle occupied eighth place among all metropolitan areas in receipt of federal research and development dollars to universities and sixth place for total federal research and development funds. The university itself had changed from a regional educator to a national information producer.[66]

As utility executive Thomas Bolger pointed out during the Forward Thrust campaign, the growth of Boeing, the University of Washington, and business and university related activities made Seattle "a net importer of people and talent."[67] Politically active citizens now included college educated professionals and managers with experience and connections outside Seattle. In contrast, statewide institutional and community jealousies retarded the evolution of Portland State College into a major university. Portland lacked the economic multiplier from a large body of out-of-town students and from faculty research grants. It also lacked Seattle's dense network of connections within national educational and research systems. Something comparable to the impact of Boeing did not appear in Portland's stable industrial structure until the rapid growth of the electronics industry in the 1970s.[68] The results can be read from census data on the proportion of adults twenty-five years or older with four or more years of college. In 1950, Portland's 7.5 percent lagged behind Seattle's 9.7 percent. The gap had widened by 1970, with 12.8 percent of Portlanders and 15.9 percent of Seattleites holding college degrees.[69]

Patterns of internal migration also show the importance of newcomers for setting Seattle's civic tone. Census reports include data on migration among state economic areas from 1955 to 1960 and from 1965 to 1970 (see Table 17.6). During both periods, Seattle drew a higher proportion of its

Table 17.6
Origins of Domestic Immigrants to Seattle and Portland,
1955–60 and 1965–70

	Oregon and Washington	Other Pacific or Northwest States	Other U.S.
1955–60			
Seattle SEA (163,916 total)	46%	21%	33%
Portland SEA (105,237 total)	50%	26%	24%
1965–70			
Seattle SEA (218,935 total)	36%	33%	31%
Portland SEA (137,044 total)	44%	34%	22%

Seattle State Economic Area: King County.
Portland State Economic Area: Multnomah, Washington, and Clackamas counties.
Sources: U.S. Census of Population, 1960, Subject Report PC (2E): Migration between State Economic Areas; U.S. Census of Population, 1970, Subject Report PC(2)-2E: Migration between State Economic Areas.

residents from beyond the Pacific states and greater Northwest (Nevada, Idaho, Montana, Utah, Wyoming, and the Dakotas). In 1960, roughly 54,000 King County residents had arrived from the more distant parts of the United States since 1955, but only 25,000 new residents of metropolitan Portland. For 1970, the parallel figures were 68,000 and 30,000. The contrasting totals reflect the greater need and ability of Seattle enterprises to tap national labor markets and the city's greater attraction for footloose migrants. In turn, the newcomers found both a guide book and a voice in *Seattle Magazine* (1964–1971), whose articles and columns exposed local issues, profiled politicians and businessmen, reviewed neighborhoods, and introduced new Seattleites to their city.[70] A growing and changing community supported a spirit of civic optimism in Seattle in the 1960s. The weekly *Argus* mounted a vigorous campaign to energize city politics. The venerable Municipal League changed from the conservative voice of what the *Argus* called the "mature oligarchy" to a more active advocate of government reform.[71] Metro's visible success with Lake Washington and the underpinning of prosperity during the 1960s created a window of opportunity for civic action. Community activist James Ellis later recalled the origins of Forward Thrust:

> The business leadership had been so successful with the World's Fair, the civic leadership had been successful with Metro in cleaning up Lake Washington, and both of those big initiatives, which were citizen-led, had tremendously effective public official participation. . . . The public generally had the view then that there was al-

most nothing that this community couldn't tackle and win. It was a very upbeat time in this area, and I've lived here all my life, and I don't know of any other times when I've seen so much optimism generally shared by the public.[72]

If generational change and community confidence help to explain the greater responsiveness of Seattle voters to civic initiatives, historical continuities seem more relevant to different attitudes in club rooms and board rooms. Portland in the 1960s confirms Daniel Elazar's characterization of Oregon as a state of moralistic politics. Government was seen as an enforcer of rules and barrier against impetuous action. Reasoning by analogy from the realm of individual ethics, conservative Portland tended to regard public debt as a flaw of civic character. At best, Portland's moralistic politics have prompted open decision-making and public processes that have ensured careful planning.[73] At its least effective, the same emphasis on process has meant a distrust of active government and a willingness to accept multiple vetoes by popular referendum, legislative inaction, and conflicting economic interests.[74]

Seattle's contrasting tradition of individualistic politics treated active government as an instrument for creating economic value. The Seattle system was open to self-interest and corruption, as with labor–management collusion in the 1940s.[75] It was also amenable to the definition and pursuit of a positive common good. Seattleites in the 1960s accepted ad hoc decision-making in the interest of accomplishing their development agenda. The city's project orientation allowed its commercial civic leadership to detour around the potential delays and vetoes of the formal political process. In a sense, Seattle leaders accepted a set of operating rules that looked back to the Alaska myth as legitimation of active community entrepreneurship.[76]

By the time Portland felt the equivalent of Seattle's civic energy in the 1970s, Seattle's evolution into a network city had a ten- or twelve-year lead.[77] Historical analysis confirms and provides a context for recent studies that emphasize Seattle's extra-regional ties in specific industrial sectors such as manufacturing and services.[78] The results can be summed up as the contrast between a "Northwest city" and a "Pacific city." As it did a century ago, Portland still functions as a gateway for regional commerce and as a service center for portions of three states. Seattle increasingly participates in the long-range network of finance, investment, tourism, and trade that link the North American and East Asian core regions of the world economy. It outranks Portland not only in the volume and value of overseas trade, but also in the number of direct overseas flights, number of foreign bank offices, amount of foreign investment, number of professional consular officers, and proportion of foreign born residents.[79]

Examination of urban growth in the Pacific Northwest confirms that urban rivalry remains a fruitful topic for historians interested in twentieth-century cities. A number of historians, most prominently Roger Lotchin, have explored the definition of network-oriented growth strategies as city boosters have looked to federal spending or international trade. This essay offers a framework for measuring the relative importance of such transregional connections. The dual system model may be applicable to the changing fortunes of cities in other parts of North America. Pairs of cities that may be comparable to Portland and Seattle include Birmingham and Atlanta, Cincinnati and Columbus, Cleveland and Pittsburgh, or San Antonio and Dallas. Across the northern border, the rise of Toronto relative to Montreal is similarly attributed to the shifting location of network activities.[80]

Attention to the role of network factors in urban rivalries suggests a way to structure the historical analysis of local responses to the changing scale of activity and the changing range of opportunities in the national and international economies.[81] Many specialists now recognize "world cities" as a distinct type of metropolis that absorbs a disproportionate share of economic and political control functions. The world city or global city is a specialized producer of financial and business services and a wholesaler of the nonregionalized resources of public information, private intelligence, and capital.[82] Most writers, however, are content to inventory the distribution and character of world cities while ignoring the question of origins. They are much better at detailing what such cities do and what they are like than at explaining why Hong Kong is on everybody's list but Panama City is not. For one nation, at least, attention to the changing balance of regional, national network, and international network functions over several decades may be an appropriate avenue for exploring the way in which the United States has structured its developing participation in the world urban system.

NOTES

1. In Kenneth Boulding, *The Organizational Revolution* (New York, 1952), the author explored the social and cultural consequences of the expansion of institutional scale since the early twentieth century. Robert Wiebe made the increasing scale and integration of American institutions the central theme for interpreting the transition from nineteenth to twentieth century in Robert H. Wiebe, *The Search for Order, 1877–1920* (New York, 1967) and restated the same interpretation for a longer time span in Robert H. Wiebe, *The Segmented Society* (New York, 1975). Organizational change as a synthesizing principle for United States history has been proposed by Louis Galambos, "The Emerging Synthesis in Modern American History," *Business History Review* 44 (Autumn 1978): 279–90; in Louis Galambos, "Technology, Political Economy, and Professionalization: Central Themes of the Organizational Synthesis," *Business History Review* 57 (Winter 1983): 471–93; and Louis Galambos, *America at Middle Age: A New History of the United States in the Twentieth Century* (New York, 1982). The "organizational synthesis" has been examined by Robert F. Berkhofer, Jr., "The Organizational Interpretation of American History: A New Synthesis," *Prospects* 4 (1979): 611–29; and Robert D. Cuff, "American Historians and the 'Organizational Factor,'" *Canadian Re-*

view of American Studies 4 (Spring 1973): 19–31. This approach can be viewed as a refinement or specification of modernization theory, which was developed by Emile Durkheim, Georg Simmel, Max Weber, and others to explain the broad outlines of societal change.

2. Alfred D. Chandler, Jr., *The Visible Hand: The Managerial Revolution in American Business* (New York, 1977); Laurence R. Veysey, *The Emergence of the American University* (Chicago, 1965); Stephen Skowronek, *Building a New American State: The Expansion of National Administrative Capacities, 1877–1920* (New York, 1982); Thomas I. Haskell, *The Emergence of Professional Science: The American Social Science Association and the Nineteenth-Century Crisis of Authority* (Urbana, Ill., 1977); Burton J. Bledstein, *The Culture of Professionalism: The Middle Class and the Development of Higher Education in America* (New York, 1976); Olivier Zunz, *Making America Corporate, 1870–1920* (Chicago, 1990).

3. Robert A. Nisbet, *The Quest for Community* (New York, 1953); Maurice R. Stein, *The Eclipse of Community: An Interpretation of American Studies* (Princeton, 1960); Arthur J. Vidich and Joseph Bensman, *Small Town in Mass Society: Class, Power and Religion in a Rural Community* (Princeton, 1968); Roland I. Warren, *The Community in America* (Chicago, 1963); and Melvin Webber, "Order in Diversity: Community without Propinquity," in *Cities and Space*, ed. Lowdon Wingo (Baltimore, 1963), 23–54. For a critique and summary see Albert Hunter, "Persistence of Local Sentiments in Mass Society," in *Handbook of Contemporary Urban Life*, ed. David Street (San Francisco, 1978), 133–62.

4. John Kenneth Galbraith, *The New Industrial State* (Boston, 1971); Paul Kantor with Stephen David, *The Dependent City: The Changing Political Economy of Urban America* (Glenview, Ill., 1988), 164–70; John Mollenkopf, *The Contested City* (Princeton, 1983); Michael Storper, "Toward a Structural Theory of Industrial Location," in John Rees, Geoffrey J. D. Hewings, and Howard A. Stafford, eds., *Industrial Location and Regional Systems* (New York, 1981), 17–41; Thomas Stanback and Thierry Noyelle, *The Economic Transformation of American Cities* (Totowa, N.J., 1983); Allen J. Scott and Michael Storper, eds., *Production, Work, Territory: The Geographical Anatomy of Industrial Capitalism* (Boston, 1986).

5. The distinction between structural and cultural determinants of community decision-making follows Michael Aiken and Robert R. Alford, "Comparative Urban Research and Community Decision-Making," in Willis D. Hawley and Frederick M. Wirt, eds., *The Search for Community Power*, 2d. ed. (Englewood Cliffs, N.J., 1974), 271, and J. Rogers Hollingsworth and Ellen Jane Hollingsworth, *Dimension in Urban History: Historical and Social Science Perspectives on Middle-Size American Cities* (Madison, 1979), 10–12.

6. Richard C. Wade, *The Urban Frontier: The Rise of Western Cities, 1790–1830* (Cambridge, Mass., 1959); James E. Vance, Jr., *The Merchant's World: The Geography of Wholesaling* (Englewood Cliffs, N.J., 1970). Nineteenth-century Portland and Seattle can also be viewed as gateway cities in the sense developed in William Cronon, *Nature's Metropolis: Chicago and the Great West* (New York, 1991).

7. Rodman Paul, *Mining Frontiers of the Far West, 1848–1890* (New York, 1963); D. W. Meinig, "American Wests: Preface to a Geographical Interpretation," *Annals of the Association of American Geographers* 62 (June 1972): 164; E. Kimbark MacColl with Harry Stein, *Merchants, Money and Power: The Portland Establishment, 1843–1913* (Portland, 1988) 4–41; Norbert MacDonald, *Distant Neighbors: A Comparative History of Seattle & Vancouver* (Lincoln, 1987), 12–14.

8. Jeannette Paddock Nichols, "Advertising and the Klondike," *Washington Historical Quarterly* 13 (January 1922): 20–26; Norbert MacDonald, "Seattle, Vancouver, and the Klondike," *Canadian Historical Review* 49 (September 1968): 234–46; Murray Morgan, *Skid Road: An Informal Portrait of Seattle*, rev. ed. (Sausalito, Calif., 1971), 156–63.

9. WPA Writers' Program, *Washington: A Guide to the Evergreen State* (Tacoma, 1941), 218–20; Howard H. Martin, "Urban Patterns of Western Washington," in Otis W. Freeman and Howard H. Martin, eds., *The Pacific Northwest: An Overall Appreciation* (New York, 1954), 459–62; Edwin J. Cohn, Jr., *Industry in the Pacific Northwest and the Location Theory* (New York, 1954), 26; Constance McLaughlin Green, *American Cities in the Growth of the Nation* (New York, 1965),177–79; Gordon B. Dodds, *The American Northwest* (Arlington Heights, Ill., 1986), 134–35; and Carlos A. Schwantes, *The Pacific Northwest: An Interpretive History* (Lincoln, 1989), 195–98.

10. Ezra Meeker, *Seventy Years of Progress in Washington* (Seattle, 1921), 328; Murray Morgan, *Puget's Sound: A Narrative of Early Tacoma and the Southern Sound* (Seattle, 1979), 301. Also see the treatment of Portland in Roger Sale, *Seattle Past to Present* (Seattle, 1976), 50–93, and MacDonald, *Distant Neighbors*, 58, 70.

11. For an introduction to the literature on inter-urban competition and urban imperialism, see Charles N. Glaab, "Historical Perspective on Urban Development Schemes" in *Social Science and the City*, ed. Leo F. Schnore (New York, 1968), 197–219.

12. Wade, *Urban Frontier*, 322–36; Carl Abbott, *Boosters and Businessmen: Popular Economic Thought and Urban Growth in the Antebellum Middle West* (Westport, Conn., 1981), 198–208; Charles N. Glaab and A. Theodore Brown, *A History of Urban America*, 2d. ed. (New York, 1976), 59–65; J. Christopher Schnell and Catherine B. Clinton, "The New West: Themes in Nineteenth Century Urban Promotion," *Bulletin of the Missouri Historical Society* 30 (January 1974): 75–88.

13. Walter Christaller, *Central Places in Southern Germany* (Englewood Cliffs, N.J., 1966); August Lösch, *The Economics of Location* (New Haven, 1954); Edward Ullman, "A Theory of Location for Cities," *American Journal of Sociology* 46 (May 1941): 835–64; Brian J. E. Berry and Allan Pred, *Central Place Studies: A Bibliography of Theory and Applications* (Philadelphia, 1965); Brian J. E. Berry, *The Geography of Market Centers and Retail Distribution* (Englewood Cliffs, N.J., 1967).

14. Although they start with large metropolitan centers rather than small towns, functional classifications of American cities have shared an interest in the regional sources of urban growth. Otis Dudley Duncan et al., *Metropolis and Region* (Baltimore, 1960) described a national urban hierarchy with a handful of truly national cities and a second tier of eight "regional metropolises" including Portland and Seattle. This second group is characterized by its special dependence on commercial and financial services performed for regional hinterlands. More recently, Thomas Stanback and Thierry Noyelle, in *The Economic Transformation of American Cities*, identified nineteen "regional diversified advanced service centers" that again include Seattle and Portland. The economies of such cities are dominated by regionally oriented transportation, utility, retail, banking, and wholesaling services.

15. Carl Abbott, "Frontiers and Sections: Cities and Regions in American Growth," in Howard Gillette, Jr. and Zane L. Miller, eds., *American Urbanism: A Historiographic Review* (Westport, Conn., 1987), 271–90.

16. G. William Skinner, "Urban Development in Late Imperial China" and "Cities and the Hierarchy of Local Systems," both in *The City in Late Imperial China*, ed. G. William Skinner (Stanford, 1977), 3–27, 275–352.

17. Edward W. Fox, *History in Geographic Perspective: The Other France* (New York, 1971).

18. Paul Hohenberg and Lynn H. Lees, *The Making of Urban Europe, 1000–1950* (Cambridge, Mass., 1985). Also see Eugene Genovese and Leonard Hochberg, eds., *Geographic Perspectives in History* (London, 1989).

19. Robert Greenhalgh Albion, *The Rise of New York Port: 1815–1860* (New York, 1939); Roger W. Lotchin, *Fortress California, 1910–1961: From Warfare to Welfare* (New York, 1992); Gerald D. Nash, *The American West Transformed: The Impact of the Second World War* (Bloomington, 1985); Spencer C. Olin, "Globalization and the Politics of Locality: Orange County, California in the Cold War Era," *Western Historical Quarterly*

22 (May 1991): 143–62; Carl Abbott, "International Cities in the Dual Systems Model: The Transformations of Los Angeles and Washington," *Urban History Yearbook* No. 18 (Leicester, England, 1991).

20. Allan Pred, *City-Systems in Advanced Economies* (New York, 1977), 98–165.

21. Doreen Massey, *The Spatial Division of Labor* (London, 1984); David Harvey, *The Urbanization of Capital* (Baltimore, 1985); Joe R. Feagin and Michael Peter Smith, "Cities and the New International Division of Labor," in *The Capitalist City*, ed. Joe R. Feagin and Michael Peter Smith (Oxford, England, 1987), 3–36; Jeffrey Henderson and Manuel Castells, eds., *Global Restructuring and Territorial Development* (London, 1987); John R. Logan and Harvey L. Molotch, *Urban Fortunes: The Political Economy of Place* (Berkeley, 1987); Mark Gottdiener and Joe R. Feagin, "The Paradigm Shift in Urban Sociology," *Urban Affairs Quarterly* 24 (December 1988): 163–87; Robert A. Beauregard, ed., *Economic Restructuring and Political Response* (Newbury Park, Calif., 1989).

22. Joe R. Feagin, "The Global Context of Metropolitan Growth: Houston and the Oil Industry," *American Journal of Sociology* 90 (May 1985): 1204–30; and Joe R. Feagin, *Free Enterprise City: Houston in Political-Economic Perspective* (New Brunswick, N.J., 1988); Edward Soja, Rebecca Morales, and Goetz Wolff, "Urban Restructuring: An Analysis of Social and Spatial Change in Los Angeles," *Economic Geography* 59 (April 1983): 195–230.

23. D. W. Meinig, *The Great Columbia Basin: A Historical Geography 1805–1929* (Seattle, 1968); John Fahey, *The Inland Empire: Unfolding Years, 1879–1929* (Seattle, 1986); Thomas R. Cox, *Mills and Markets: A History of the Pacific Coast Lumber Industry to 1900* (Seattle, 1974); Robert E. Ficken, *The Forested Land: A History of Lumbering in Western Washington* (Seattle, 1987); James O. Oliphant, *On the Cattle Ranges of the Oregon Country* (Seattle, 1968); and Dodds, *American Northwest*, 137–48.

24. In 1913, national banks in Seattle had a capital stock surplus of $5,560,000 and in Portland, $6,675,000. See Richard Franklin Bensel, *Sectionalism and American Political Development, 1880–1980* (Madison, Wis., 1984), 426–31. Citing a different measure, Dorothy O. Johansen and Charles M. Gates, *Empire of the Columbia: A History of the Pacific Northwest* (New York, 1957), 435, report that national banking resources in 1909 totaled $38 million for Seattle and $32 million for Portland.

25. Carl Abbott, *Portland: Planning, Politics and Growth in a Twentieth Century City* (Lincoln, 1983), 33–70; George Frykman, "The Alaska–Yukon–Pacific Exposition, 1909," *Pacific Northwest Quarterly* 53 (July 1962): 89–99; Sale, *Seattle*, 78–86, 92.

26. Portland's primary hinterland is defined as Oregon plus Clark, Cowlitz, and Skamania counties, Washington. Seattle's primary hinterland is defined as the remainder of Washington. Portland's secondary hinterland is Ada, Adams, Boise, Camas, Canyon, Elmore, Gem, Gooding, Owyhee, Payette, Twin Falls, and Washington counties, Idaho. Seattle's secondary hinterland is Alaska; Benewah, Bonner, Boundary, Clearwater, Idaho, Kootenai, Latah, Lewis, Nez Perce, and Shoshone counties, Idaho; and Beaverhead, Broadwater, Cascade, Deer Lodge, Flathead, Gallatin, Glacier, Granite, Lewis and Clark, Lincoln, Madison, Meagher, Mineral, Missoula, Park, Pondera, Powell, Ravalli, Sanders, Silver Bow, Teton, and Toole counties, Montana. The allocation of these territories is based on patterns of rail and water transportation, retail trade, and newspaper circulation. Several studies are useful for defining the outer limits where the Seattle and Portland hinterlands have shaded into those of San Francisco, Salt Lake City, and Minneapolis-St. Paul. These include John R. Borchert, *America's Northern Heartland* (Minneapolis, 1987); Mildred Hartsough, *The Twin Cities as a Metropolitan Market* (Minneapolis, 1925); Chauncy Dennison Harris, *Salt Lake City: A Regional Capital* (Chicago, 1940); D. W. Meinig, "The Mormon Culture Region: Strategies and Patterns in the Geography of the American West," *Annals of the Association of American Geographers* 55 (1965): 191–220; and A. Philip Andrus et al., *Seattle* (Cambridge Mass., 1976), 1–3.

27. Regionally oriented manufacturing industries include lumber and wood products, paper and related products, foodstuffs, textile mills, furniture and related products,

leather products, and primary metals. Metals are included because of the importance of local iron ore for small iron producing industries at the turn of the century and because of the role of regionally generated hydro-electric power as the essential resource input for aluminum production. The data were drawn from: *Twelfth Census of the United States, Vol. 8: Manufactures, Pt. 2, States and Territories and Special Reports: Occupations* (Washington, D.C.); *Thirteenth Census of the United State Vol 9: Manufactures: Reports by States* (Washington, D.C.); *Fourteenth Census of the United States, Vol. 4: Population: Occupations* and *Vol. 9: Manufactures: Reports for States* (Washington, D.C.); *Fifteenth Census of the United Slates, Vol. 4: Occupations by States* (Washington, D.C.); *Sixteenth Census of the United States: Characteristics of the Population* (Washington, D.C.), Table 51; *Seventeenth Census of the United States: Characteristics of the Population* (Washington, D.C.), Table 79; *Eighteenth Census of the United States: Characteristics of the Population* (Washington, D.C.), Table 12; *Nineteenth Census of the United States: Characteristics of the Population* (Washington, D.C.), Table 184; *Twentieth Census of the United States: Detailed Population Characteristics* (Washington, D.C.), Table 228.

28. Carl Abbott, "Planning for the Home Front in Seattle and Portland, 1940–45," in *The Martial Metropolis*, ed. Roger Lotchin (New York, 1984), 163–89.

29. John Gunther, *Inside U.S.A.* (New York, 1947), 92; and Neil Morgan, *Westward Tilt: The American West Today* (New York, 1963), 210–12.

30. Brian J. L. Berry, "City Size Distribution and Economic Development," *Economic Development and Cultural Change* 9 (July 1961): 573–87; Clyde Browning, "Primate Cities and Related Concepts," in *Urban Systems and Economic Development*, ed. F. R. Pitts (Eugene, Ore., 1962); Brian J. L. Berry and Frank E. Horton, *Geographic Perspectives on Urban Systems: With Integrated Readings* (Englewood Cliffs, N.J., 1970), 64–93; Michael Timberlake, ed., *Urbanization in the World-Economy* (Orlando, Fla., 1985).

31. Norton Ginsburg, *Atlas of Economic Development* (Chicago, 1961); Kingsley Davis, *World Urbanization, 1950–1970*, Vol. 1, *Basic Data for Cities, Counties and Regions* (Berkeley, 1976); Pamela Barnhouse Walters, "Systems of Cities and Urban Primacy: Problems of Definition and Measurement," in *Urbanization*, ed. Timberlake, 63–85.

32. J. Dennis Lord, "Shifts in the Wholesale Trade Status of U.S. Metropolitan Areas," *Professional Geographer* 36 (1984): 51–63; Morgan, *Westward Tilt*, 210. The Seattle:Portland ratios for wholesale sales were 1.50 in 1930; 1.42 in 1940; 1.05 in 1949; 1.04 in 1958; .90 in 1967; and .86 in 1977. Data are from *Fifteenth Census of the United States, Distribution Vol. II: Wholesale Distribution* (Washington, D.C.); *Census of Business: 1939 Vol. II: Wholesale Trade* (Washington, D.C.); *County and City Data Books*, 1952–77; *State and Metropolitan Area Data Book*, 1982.

33. U.S. Office of Personnel Management, *Federal Civilian Workforce Statistics: Report of Employment by Geographic Area: December 31, 1980* (Washington, D.C.).

34. Rodney A. Erickson, "The Regional Impact of Growth Firms: The Case of Boeing, 1963–68," *Land Economics* 50 (May 1974): 127–36; and Rodney A. Erickson, "The Spatial Pattern of Income Generation in Lead Firm, Growth Area Linkage Systems," *Economic Geography* 51 (January 1975): 17–26; U.S. Arms Control and Disarmament Agency, *A Case Study of the Effects of the Dyna-Soar Contract Cancellation upon Employees of the Boeing Company in Seattle Washington* (U.S. ACDA Publication No. 29, 1965); Laurence S. Kuter, *The Great Gamble: The Boeing 747* (University, Ala., 1973).

35. Oliver P. Williams, "A Typology for Comparative Local Government," *Midwest Journal of Political Science* 5 (1961): 150–64; Oliver P. Williams and Charles R. Adrian, *Four Cities: A Study of Comparative Policy Making* (Philadelphia, 1963). Caretaker governments contrast with those that actively pursue economic development, provide a wide range of amenities, or try to redistribute resources and services among groups and neighborhoods.

36. The results of electoral politics in Seattle are discussed in Edward C. Banfield,

Big City Politics: A Complete Guide to the Political System of Atlanta, Boston, Detroit, El Paso, Los Angeles, Miami, Philadelphia, St. Louis, Seattle (New York, 1965), 132–45; James Halpin, "Our Musty, Crusty City Council," *Seattle Magazine,* May 1965, 12–16, 46–48; and David Brewster, "The Making of a Mayor, 1969," *Seattle Magazine,* May 1969, 21–25, 47–50. For Portland, see E. Kimbark MacColl, *The Growth of City: Power and Politics in Portland, 1915–1950* (Portland, 1979), 609–60, and Paul Pitzer, "Dorothy McCollough Lee: The Successes and Failures of 'Dottie-Do-Good'" *Oregon Historical Quarterly* 91 (Spring 1990): 5–42.

37. Banfield, *Big City Politics,* 132.

38. Johansen and Gates, *Empire of the Columbia,* 564; Earl Pomeroy, *The Pacific Slope: A History of California, Oregon, Washington, Idaho, Utah, and Nevada* (New York, 1965), 139; Neal Pierce, *The Pacific States of America* (New York, 1972), 215; Morgan, *Westward Tilt,* 212; Sale, *Seattle,* 189, 213.

39. Central Association of Seattle, Annual Report for 1960–61, Box 10, Dingwall Papers, University of Washington Manuscript Division, University of Washington, Seattle, Washington (hereafter Dingwall Papers).

40. For Seattle, see Murray Morgan, *Century 21: The Story of the Seattle World's Fair* (Seattle, 1963); John M. Findlay, "The Off-center Seattle Center: Downtown Seattle and the 1962 World's Fair," *Pacific Northwest Quarterly* 80 (January 1989): 2–11; Cyrus Noe, "Innocence Revisited: Twenty Years after the Fair," *Pacific Northwest* 16 (April 1982): 24–32; and substantial materials in the Dingwall Papers and Joseph Gandy Papers, University of Washington Manuscripts Department, University of Washington, Seattle, Washington (hereafter Gandy Papers). The story of the Oregon Centennial Exposition must be pieced together from newspaper accounts and from the Oregon Centennial Commission Papers, Oregon Historical Society, Portland, Oregon (hereafter Commission Papers), the Ted Hallock Papers, Oregon Historical Society, Portland, Oregon (hereafter Hallock Papers), and the Anthony Brandenthaler Papers, Oregon Historical Society, Portland, Oregon (hereafter Brandenthaler Papers).

41. Minutes of the Board of Trustees World Fair Corporation 28 January and July 22 1958, Box 14, Dingwall Papers; Design Standards Advisory Board, "Preliminary Site Plan Report," 1958, Box 13, Dingwall Papers.

42. Transcript of interview of Ewen Dingwall by John Findlay, 19 August 1985, Dingwall Papers (hereafter Dingwall interview); "Historical Features" file, Box 1, Gandy Papers; Minutes of Board of Trustees, World's Fair Corporation, 27 March 1958 and 30 October 1959, Box 14, Dingwall Papers.

43. "Report of the Century 21 Commission, State of Washington, 1961," Box 13, Dingwall Papers; and Dingwall interview. For typical discussions of the fair as a boost for Seattle, see Russell Lynes, "Seattle Will Never be the Same," *Harpers,* July 1962, 20–25; and Charles N. Stabler, "Seattle World's Fair Likely to be First One in 30 Years to Profit," *Wall Street Journal* (New York), 13 July 1962.

44. Stanford Research Institute, Study of the Economic Feasibility and Preliminary Planning Requirements for the Proposed Oregon Centennial Celebration, June 1955, Box 1, Accession Group 1603-1, Commission Papers; Final Report of Oregon Centennial Commission (draft, 1960), Box 2, Accession Group 1603, Commission Papers; Ted Hallock to John Simpson, 27 July 1959, Hallock Papers; transcript of KATU-TV news report by Tom McCall on Mark Hatfield's questions about Centennial Commission spending, Brandenthaler Papers; Lillie Sweetland (Centennial Commissioner) to the editor, *Oregonian* (Portland), 13 August 1958; *Oregon Journal* (Portland), 13 March and 4 April 1957; *Oregonian* (Portland), 5 October and 23 December 1958.

45. *Oregonian* (Portland), 24 July and 5 August 1959; Final Report, Commission Papers.

46. Progress Notes on the Exposition-Recreation Center, 23 July 1956, Ormond Bean Papers, Oregon Historical Society, Portland, Oregon; statements on Exposition-Recreation Center by James Richardson, October 1955, and William Bowes, 25 October

1955, and report of Exposition-Recreation Commission to Mayor Terry Schrunk, 3 July 1957, all in Box 1, William Bowes Papers, Oregon Historical Society, Portland, Oregon; "Report on Exposition-Recreation Bonds, New Series," *Portland City Club Bulletin* 43 (2 November 1962).

47. "Report on Authorizing County Bonds to Construct a Covered Stadium," *Portland City Club Bulletin* 45 (23 October 1964) "Report on Multnomah Stadium Acquisition Bonds," *Portland City Club Bulletin* 47 (21 October 1966); Terry Schrunk to R. W. DeWeese, 31 August 1964, Box 1, Terry Schrunk Papers, Oregon Historical Society, Portland, Oregon (hereafter Schrunk Papers); *Oregon Journal* (Portland), 14 November 1964.

48. "Report . . . September–November 1964," opposition statement by Citizens Against Delta Dome, and "General Summary of Data Analysis on Delta Dome Election, November 1964," in Volunteers for Delta Dome Covered Stadium Papers, Oregon Historical Society, Portland, Oregon.

49. "Portlanders Confused on Stadium," *Oregonian* (Portland), 27 February 1966. Also, *Oregonian* (Portland), January and 11 February 1966; and *Oregon Journal* (Portland), 10 February 1966.

50. John Haviland to Terry Schrunk, 27 April 1966; Ford Montgomery to Terry Schrunk, 26 April 1966; and Building Owners and Managers Association to Terry Schrunk, 2 June 1966; all in Box 4, Schrunk Papers.

51. Sam Angeloff, "Are We Ready for the Big Leagues?" *Seattle Magazine*, January 1964, 10–16.

52. For examples, see Bellevue Chamber of Commerce to James R. Ellis et al., 18 June 1968; and Brewster Denny to Joseph Gandy, 20 June 1968; both in Box 18, Gandy Papers.

53. Portland voting record compiled from newspaper reports on elections; Seattle information from Banfield, *Big City Politics*, 144.

54. Roscoe C. Martin, *Metropolis in Transition: Local Government Adaptation to Changing Urban Needs* (Washington, 1963), 75–88; Mylon Winn, *A Model of Organizational Development: A Case Study of the Municipality of Metropolitan Seattle* (Ph.D. diss., University of Washington, 1982); and Municipality of Metropolitan Seattle, *Twenty-Year Report, 1959–79* (Seattle, 1979).

55. Ellis quoted Patrick Douglas, "Politics Forward Thrust," *Seattle Magazine*, January 1968, 29–32. Also see Forward Thrust Inc., *Developing a Capital Improvement Plan for a County*, 4 vols. (Seattle, 1967).

56. Stanley H. Brewer, *The Competitive Position of Seattle and Puget Sound Ports in World Trade*, University of Washington College of Business Administration, Management series No.7 (Seattle, 1963); and Padraic Burke, *A History of the Port of Seattle* (Seattle, 1976), 106, 110–11.

57. *Oregonian* (Portland), 20 June 1960; "Report on Dock Development Bonds" *Portland City Club Bulletin* 41 (28 October 1960).

58. Author's interview with Raymond Kell, Docks Commissioner and Port Commissioner, 11 June 1990, transcript in possession of author (hereafter Kell interview); Minutes of meeting of Metropolitan Planning Commission with Port of Portland and Commission of Public Docks, 20 August 1965, Box 2, David Eccles Papers, Oregon Historical Society, Portland, Oregon.

59. "Report on Port Management, Operation and Development in the Metropolitan Portland and Columbia River Area," *Portland City Club Bulletin* 45 (26 April 1965); and Kell interview.

60. Burke, *Port of Seattle*, 110–26; "The Maritime Industry's Magic Box," *Seattle Magazine*, May 1969, 52–55; Gordon Clinton to W. R. Norwood, 10 January 1963, in "Mayor's Maritime Advisory Committee" file, Box 27. Accession Group 239-2, Seattle Mayor's Papers, University of Washington Manuscripts Department, University of Washington, Seattle, Washington (hereafter Mayor's Papers); *Reporter* (Port of Seattle), 1 February 1967, in "Port Committee" file, Box 52, Mayor's Papers.

61. Averages calculated from total tonnages and total value of shipments reported in the monthly volumes of U.S. Department of Commerce, *U.S. Waterborne Exports and General Imports* (Washington, D.C.).

62. 1951 figures in Edward J. Taaffe, "Air Transport and United States Urban Distribution," *Geographical Review* 46 (April 1956): 219–38.

63. The *Official Airline Guide* indicates that Seattle in the 1970s and 1980s offered roughly 50 percent more direct and through flights to the east coast than did Portland. Passenger volumes are from John Tepper Marlin and James A. Avery, *The Book of American City Rankings* (New York, 1983). Lobbying efforts are discussed in *Seattle Business* 5 April 1966. Expansion of Seattle–Tacoma International Airport is treated in Burke, *Port of Seattle,* 124. Major planned expansion of Portland International Airport in the early 1970s was stopped by analysis of its negative environmental impacts.

64. In both 1960 and 1970, metropolitan Seattle had three and a half times as many employed engineers and technical workers as metropolitan Portland. *Eighteenth Census of the United States Vol. I: Characteristics of The Population,* Pt. 39, Table 74, and Pt. 49, Table 74 (Washington, D.C.); *Nineteenth Census of the United States Vol. I: Characteristics of the Population,* Pt. 39, Table 86, and Pt. 49, Table 86 (Washington, D.C.).

65. Enrollment data from American Council on Education, *American Colleges and Universities,* 4th through 13th editions, covering 1940 to 1986 at irregular intervals. Also Charles M. Gates, *The First Century at the University of Washington, 1861–1961* (Seattle, 1961), 216–19; Jane Sanders, *Into the Second Century: The University of Washington, 1961–1986* (Seattle, 1987); and Sale, *Seattle,* 208–10.

66. Edward Malecki, "Federal R & D Spending in the United States of America: Some Impacts on Metropolitan Economics," *Regional Studies* 16 (1982), 19–35. *Argus* (Seattle), 9 July 1965, reported that federal grants at the University of Washington nearly matched state general fund support by 1964.

67. Thomas Bolger, "The Forward Thrust Story," speech to Vancouver Rotary Club, 4 June 1968, in *Developing a Capital Improvement Plan, Vol 4: Selected Speeches on Forward Thrust,* 82, by Forward Thrust, Inc.

68. Gordon B. Dodds and Craig E. Wollner with the assistance of Marshall M. Lee, *The Silicon Forest: High Tech in the Portland Area, 1945 to 1986* (Portland, 1990).

69. *Seventeenth Census of the United States, Vol 2: Characteristics of the Population,* Pt. 37, Table 34, and Pt. 47, Table 34 (Washington, D.C.); *Eighteenth Census of the United States, Vol. 1: Characteristics of the Population,* Pt. 39, Table 73, and Pt. 49, Table 73 (Washington, D.C.); and *Nineteenth Census of the United States, Vol I: Characteristics of the Population,* Pt. 39, Table 83, and Pt. 49, Table 83 (Washington, D.C.).

70. Sale, *Seattle,* 212–15.

71. *Argus* (Seattle), 19 September 1958, 12 May 1961, 10 April 1964, and 7 August 1964.

72. Transcript of interview of James Ellis by Lorraine McConaghy, 13 October 1988, Seattle Parks Department, 1–2, transcript in possession of author. Also see Mechlin D. Moore, speech to Central Seattle Association, 10 May 1966, in "Central Association of Seattle" file, Box 38, Mayor's Papers.

73. Daniel J. Elazar, *American Federalism: A View from the States* (New York, 1972); Carl Abbott, "Urban Design in Portland, Oregon, as Policy and Process, 1960–1989," *Planning Perspectives* 6 (Winter, 1991): 1–18 examines the positive effects of the process orientation.

74. E. Kimbark MacColl, "Portland: First Class on a Steerage Ticket," *The New Pacific* 1 (Summer 1990): 41–49 explores Portland's ingrained conservatism. Portland attorney and political insider Raymond Kell contrasted the strong anti-tax sentiment in Portland with Seattle's willingness to "mortgage everything they had" to pursue economic development, Kell interview.

75. Green, *American Cities,* 189–92.

76. The same contrast between process and project orientations continued to characterize downtown development planning in the 1970s and 1980s. See Mark R. Bello,

"Urban Regimes and Downtown Planning in Portland, Oregon, and Seattle, Washington, 1974–1990" (Ph.D. diss. in progress, Portland State University). Seattleites reminded themselves of the city's go-getter heritage by purchasing thousands of copies of William C. Speidel, *Sons of The Profits, or There's No Business Like Grow Business: The Seattle Story, 1851–1901* (Seattle, 1967).

77. Abbott, *Portland*, 167–277.

78. William B. Beyers, "On Geographical Properties of Growth Center Linkage Systems," *Economic Geography* 50 (July 1974): 203–18, William B. Beyers, "Export Services in Postindustrial Society," *Papers of the Regional Science Association* 57 (1985): 33–48; and Pred, *City-Systems in Advanced Economies*.

79. *Banker*, March 1988, 37–61; "Japanese Investors Prefer California," *Chronicle* (San Francisco), 28 December 1989; and K. Leventhal and Co., *1988 Japanese Investment in U.S. Real Estate* (Los Angeles, 1989).

80. Diana Hooper, J. E. Simmons, and L. S. Bourne, *The Changing Economic Basis of Canadian Urban Growth, 1971–1981*, Center for Urban and Community Studies, Toronto, Research Paper 139, 1983.

81. In ways different from this essay, two recent books have taken on the question of city-level responses to the changing scale of the national economy. Don H. Doyle, in *New Men, New Cities, New South: Atlanta, Nashville, Charleston, Mobile, 1860–1910* (Chapel Hill, N.C., 1990), examines the successes and failures of the urban business class of the postbellum South in implementing the "New South" goals of integration into the national industrial economy. The focus of John T. Cumbler, *A Social History of Economic Decline: Business, Politics, and Work in Trenton* (New Brunswick, N.J., 1989) is the character of local responses to the shift from locally based "civic capitalism" to larger scale "national capitalism" or "bureaucratic corporatism." His model of the impacts of scale change on local decisions and decision-makers draws on Robert Merton's distinction between local and cosmopolitan leadership in Robert K. Merton, *Social Theory and Social Structure* (Glencoe, Ill., 1957).

82. Peter Hall, *The World Cities* (New York, 1966); R. S. Cohen, "The New International Division of Labor, Multinational Corporations, and Urban Hierarchy," in *Urbanization and Urban Planning in Capitalist Society*, ed. Michael Dear and Allan J. Scott (New York, 1981); John Friedmann and Goetz Wolff, "World City Formation: An Agenda for Research and Action," *International Journal of Urban and Regional Research* 6 (September 1982): 309–44; John Friedmann, "The World City Hypothesis," *Growth and Change* 17 (1986): 69–83; and Mattei Dogan and John D. Kasarda, eds., *The Metropolis Era: A World of Giant Cities*, Vol. I (Newbury Park, Calif., 1988).

INDEX

Abolitionist movement, 279–280. *See also* Slavery
Accent, as western characteristic, 21
Adams, Brooks, 25, 27
Adams, Henry, 25
Adams, Rev. John H., 290
Aerospace industry, 305, 312. *See also* Aircraft industry; Employment
AFL. *See* American Federation of Labor
African Americans. *See also* Minorities; Racism; Slavery
  "buffalo soldiers," 282–283, 285
  employment discrimination against, 240–246, 248, 253n48, 294n37
  Los Angeles riots, 274–275
Agricultural Adjustment Administration, 195, 232
La Aguila Mexicana, 126
Air pollution, 247, 251
Aircraft industry. *See also* Aerospace industry; Employment
  in World War II Los Angeles, 237–251, 252n11, 288–289
  racial discrimination in, 240–245, 289
  women's employment in, 242–243
Alabama, Great Depression effects, 227
Allen, William C., *Dakota Farmer* and, 180, 188, 189–190, 195–196, 197n24
Alvarado, Martina Castro, 67
American Federation of Labor (AFL), 205, 240. *See also* Labor
Americanization. *See also* Culture; Modernization
  role of frontier in, 28
El Amigo del Pueblo, 126
Anthony, Maj. Scott J., 154, 155
Anthrax, 109
Anza, Juan Bautista de, 60, 97–98, 112n1
Apache Indians, 98–112
Arapaho Indians, 98, 103, 104–105, 110
  Sand Creek Massacre, 147–159
Arballo y Gutiérrez, Dona Feliciana, 60
Archer, Branch, 126
Argentina. *See also* Brazil
  European immigration to, 44, 45, 54n24
  farm ownership in, 50, 51
  indigenous peoples of, 46

Argüello, Guadalupe Estudillo de, 66
Arista, Gen. Mariano, 123
Arizona, labor conflict and unionization, 203–218
Arizona Federation of Labor, 216, 218
Arkansas, inclusion in west, 20
Asano, Dorcas, 269
Ashley, William H., 87, 88, 91, 92
Astor, John Jacob, 87
Autobiography (Carson), 91, 96n19

Bandini, Isadora, 66
Bass, Charlotta, 249, 284
Baynes, James, 179
Becker, Carl, 33
Beckwourth, Jim, 84, 91
Bell, Philip A., 291
Belt, Elmer, 247
Bent, Charles, 91
Bent, William (fort), 105, 110, 111, 112
Beverly Hills (Calif.), 62, 71, 252n26
Big City Politics (Banfield), 306
Bisbee Deportation, 204
Bison. *See also* Environment; Native Americans
  consumption by Native Americans, 107–108, 111, 117n38
  drought affecting, 99–100, 101, 106, 111
  efficiency of, compared to cattle, 102, 114n15, 117n42
  populations, 101–102
  reproductive characteristics, 106, 116n31
Bison ecology, on Great Plains, 97–112
Bison robes, 99, 111, 118n49
Black Kettle, 154, 155, 159
Blacks. *See* African Americans
Bolger, Thomas, 312
Bolton, Herbert Eugene, 34–35
Book of the Fair (Bancroft), 135
Booth, Gov. Newton, 284
Borderlands, 34–35
Boronda, Tina, 64
Boulding, Kenneth, 296, 315n1
Bowron, Fletcher, 238–239
Boyce, Ed, 205
Brackett, Col. A. G., 92
Braddock, Betty, 20

Branch, Francis X., 67
Brazil. *See also* Argentina
   bandeirante tradition, 50–51, 55n25
   European immigration to, 41–43, 44,
      45, 46, 54n23
Brecht, Bertolt, 250
Brent, Charles, 105
Bridger, James "Old Gabe," 88
Briones, Juana, 64–65, 69
"Bronzeville," 245–246
Brown, Charlotte, 287
Brown, John, 279
Brown, Linda, 289
Brown, Oliver, 289
Brown v. Board of Education, 289,
   294n38
Bruce, Henry Clay, 280
Buffalo. *See* Bison
"Buffalo soldiers," 282–283, 285. *See
   also* African Americans
Burton, Ampara, 71
Bushnell, William F. T., *Dakota Farmer*
   and, 180, 181, 184–187
Business. *See also* Capitalism; Employ-
   ment; Entrepreneurialism; Imperi-
   alism; Trade
   fur-trapping as, 83–94
   mine owners' response to labor de-
      mands, 203–218
   in Seattle and Portland, compared,
      295–315
   women-owned and -operated, 64–65
   in World War II Los Angeles, 236–251
Byers, William N., 148, 150, 155–156,
   158, 159

Caldwell, Mayor Orville, 245–246
Calhoun, John C., 125
California. *See also* Los Angeles; San
   Francisco
   African American women in, 284, 286–
      287
   frontiers, 48–49
   inclusion in west, 16–17, 19
   Japanese World War II attacks, 238–
      239, 252n26
   Overland Trail immigration, 47–48,
      138
   population increases, 34, 251n2
   slavery in, 279
   Spanish law in, 59–80, 79n83
California Eagle (newspaper), 241–242,
   249
California Shipbuilding Corporation
   (Calship), 244
Campbell, Robert, 88
Canada
   European immigration to, 41, 44, 45,
      49
   frontiers, 49–50, 51, 54n21
   as part of west, 13, 15, 17, 45

Capitalism. *See also* Entrepreneurialism;
   Imperialism; Jacksonian man
   effect on bison herds, 105–106, 110–
      111
   European imperialism and, 35, 40–44,
      55nn26,29, 318n21
   Mormon rejection of, 137–138
   Western resentment against, 165
Carey, Sen. Joseph M., 283
Carlisle, Robert, 71
Carlon, Manuela, 67
Carson, Kit, 91, 96n19
Castro, Candida, 66
Castro, Josefa Romero de, 66
Central place theory, in comparison of
   cities, 298, 300
Chaboyo, Antonia, 66
Chancery courts, 73–74
Character, national, 28, 30
Cheyenne Indians, 98, 103, 104–105
   Sand Creek Massacre, 147–159
Chicago, 1880–1890 population, 183
Chicago World's Columbian Exposition,
   26, 135
Children. *See also* Education; Family;
   Women
   farm life and, 191–192
   on frontier, 47, 49
   Native American, 102, 115n18, 148
   Nisei, 257–258, 260, 263, 265–266
   parents' authority over, 64
China, 299
Chivington, Col. John M., 147–159
Chouteau, August Pierre, 104
Cities. *See also* Urbanization; *specific
   cities*
   Portland and Seattle, compared, 295–
      315
   network and regional cities, 299–301
   western, 285, 288
Civil rights movement. *See also* African
   Americans; Discrimination; Racism
   in World War II, 289–290
Civil War, 148–149, 278, 280–281, 291
   "buffalo soldiers," 282–283
Civil Works Administration, 226
Civilian Conservation Corps, 259
   in Idaho, 226, 231
Civilization
   at frontier, 26–27
   savagery and, 92, 158
Class and Community (Dawley), 207
Clifton-Morenci-Metcalf strike, 207–218
Climate. *See also* Drought; Precipitation
   dustbowl conditions, 187–188
   effect on bison herds, 101–102, 109–
      110, 114n10
Clinton, Gordon, 305
Cole, Cornelius, 279
Colonialism. *See also* Imperialism
   in west, 35–36, 226

Colorado. *See also* Mountain men; Rocky Mountains
    African Americans in, 287, 293n27
    cowboy strikes in, 171–175
    frontiers, 48–49
    Sand Creek Massacre, 147–159
Colorado River Aqueduct, 237
Colored Ladies Legal Rights Association, 284
Comanche Indians, 98–112
    protected by black cavalry, 282
Comité por Trabajadores en General, 213–214
Commentaries (Blackstone), 73
Community. *See also* Culture; Family; *Mutualistas;* Regionalism
    African American "race" organizations, 286
    "island communities," 296, 316n3
    Japanese American, 269–270, 272nn12,25
    local newspapers and, 183–185, 188, 190–191, 193–194, 199nn45,65
    rural, 184, 198n29
    Seattle and Portland, compared, 295–315
Comstock, Sarah, 237
Congress of Racial Equality (CORE), 289, 294n39
Consolidated Steel Corporation, 244
Copper industry, labor conflict and unionization in, 203–218
Cordley, Richard, 281
CORE. *See* Congress of Racial Equality
El Correo, 126
Couts, Cave, 66
Covington, Floyd C., 240
Cowboys. *See also* Great Plains; Ranching
    black, 284, 285
    strikes and unions, 164–175
Crime, in World War II Los Angeles, 246
Crocker, Edwin Bryan, 279
Culture. *See also* Community
    Native American, 46
    religious clash of, 134
    as western characteristic, 21

The Daily Tulean Dispatch, 264
Dakota Farmer. See also Farming; Media
    rural ideals and, 179–196
Dakota Farmers' Alliance, 186
Dana, Richard Henry, 64–65
Davis, William Heath, 62–63, 68, 77n21
Davis v. Beason, 143
De Haro Ranch, 68
Deaver, Clem, 282
Defense Plant Corporation (DPC), 237–238, 252n15
Democracy. *See also* Politics
    components of, 28

Demography, of frontier, 40, 53
Devin, William, 305
DeWitt, Lt. Gen. John L., 258
El Diario, 128
Dinesen, Isak, 46
Discrimination. *See also* Civil rights movement; Minorities; Racism; Slavery
    against African Americans, 240–246, 248, 253n48, 294n37
    in employment and housing, 240–241, 254n76
    in transportation, 281
Disease
    affecting bison and Indians, 109, 110, 111, 112, 147
    affecting urban dwellers, 247
Dodge City, 20
Dominguez Ranch, 67
"Double V" campaign, 241
Douglass, Lewis, 287
DPC. *See* Defense Plant Corporation
Drought. *See also* Climate; Precipitation
    effect on Great Plains, 187–188, 189, 195–196, 230–231
    effect on mountain states, 230
    effect on Plains Indians, 99–100, 101, 106, 111
Dunne, Finley Peter, 188

Eaton, John H., 93
Education. *See also* Children
    Japanese-American, 264–271, 272n25
    segregated, 276
El Rancho de las Pulgas, 68
Elazar, Daniel, 314
Ellis, James, 313
Employment. *See also* Business; Entrepreneurialism
    for African Americans, 285–286
    arson as aid to, 230
    cowboy strikes and unions, 164–175
    discrimination in, 240–246, 248, 253n48, 294n37
    in herding, 166–168
    for Japanese immigrant women, 257, 271n2
    in Japanese internment camps, 262
    migration for, 43, 44, 51, 221n27, 230–231, 249, 256–258
    women's self-employment, 64–65, 68–69
    in World War II Los Angeles, 237–251, 252n11
    World War II shortages, 262–263
Entertainment industry, 250
Entrepreneurialism. *See also* Business; Capitalism
    of California women, 64–65
    of cowboys, 172–174

Entrepreneurialism, *continued*
  of ex-mountain men, 88–94, 95n17
  of Mormons, 142
Environment. *See also* Land
  bison hunters' equilibrium with, 98–
    112
  in definition of westernness, 17, 31,
    35–36
  impacts of development on, 30, 247
Environmental movement, 34
El Estandarte Nacional, 129
Esteban, 276
Europe. *See also specific countries*
  colonial expansionism, 39–40, 51–52,
    55n29
  migration from, 41–44, 53n9
Evans, Gov. John, 148, 149–152, 158, 159
Evolution, of frontier, 29
Executive Order 9066, 258. *See also* Japa-
    nese Americans
Expansionism. *See also* Imperialism
  American, 127
  European, 39–40, 51–52, 55n29

Fair Employment Practices Committee
    (FEPC), 241, 249
Family. *See also* Children; Housing;
    Women
  change affecting farm families, 183–
    185, 188, 190–191, 193, 198n39
  economic survival with, 229
  Japanese American, 257–260, 263, 265,
    268–269, 271n3
  Mormon polygamy, 137, 143–144
  in New Spain, 59–64
  in World War II Los Angeles, 246
Farewell to Manzanar (Houston), 260
Farm Security Administration, 232
Farmers' Alliance, 164
Farming. *See also* Homesteading; Land;
    Ranching
  by ex-mountain men, 90–91
  by Native Americans, 102
  in Dakota territory, 179–196
  economic swings affecting, 183
  foreclosure auctions, 229–230
  at frontier, 29, 47–52
  Great Depression relief efforts, 225–
    233
  in Great Plains, 52
  in Idaho, 225–233
  migration of Europeans to, 41–43
Fashion, 250, 264
Federal government. *See also* Law; Poli-
    tics
  Great Depression spending in Idaho,
    225–233
  land ownership in West, 34
  Mormon Church and, 135, 136, 140–
    141, 143–144
  relation with Los Angeles, 236–251

FEPC. *See* Fair Employment Practices
    Committee
Fisher, Vardis, 232
Fiske, John, 25
Fitch, María Josefa Carrillo de, 66
Fite, Gilbert, 281
Fitzpatrick, Thomas, 108, 117n39
Fitzpatrick, Tom "Broken Hand," 88
Forbes, Jack, 282
Forest fires, 230
Forging the Copper Collar (Byrkit), 204,
    219n3
Fort Larned, 154
Fort Lyon, 148, 154–155, 156
Fowler, Jacob, 107, 116n35
France, 299
Franciscans, 65–66
Frontier. *See also* Pioneer period
  closing of, 135–136
  evolution of, 29
  historical study of, 29–30, 31–32
  as metaphor, 30
  relation to imperialism, 40, 44
  role of, 31–32
  shifting nature of, 12, 29, 47
  significance of, 24–25, 26–29
  typology
    Type I, 47–52
    Type II, 47–52
  values of, 135–136
  violence on, 140
Fur trade. *See also* Rocky Mountains
  mountain men and, 83–94

Gay, Peter, 250
Geography, as western characteristic, 21
Gerry, Elbridge, 91, 151
Gervais, Jean Baptiste, 88
Glenn, Evelyn Nakano, 268
Globe (Ariz.), miners' union, 205–206,
    212
Godkin, Edwin L., 27
Goetzmann, William, 12
Goggins, Ben, 212
Gold, in Great Depression, 227–228
Gold, Ernest, 250
Gorostiza, Manuel Eduardo de, 127
Grange, 164
Great Depression, 179–180
  British, 40, 53n2
  in Dakotas, 194–195
  in Idaho, 225–233
Great Plains. *See also* Horse; Native
    Americans; *specific states*
  bison ecology, 97–112
  colonization, 45, 52
  cowboy strikes and unions, 164–175
  drought affecting, 99–100, 101, 106, 111
  European immigration to, 41
  farming in, 52
  Great Depression effects, 227

The Great Plains (Webb), 35
Greeley, Millard F., 180, 188–189, 192–
    193
Grimsley, Thomas, 94
Growth. *See also* Modernization
    economic, 40–41
    in mining industry, 203–205
    regional vs. networked, 295–315

Hagerty, Father Thomas J., 211
Hancock, Henry, 71
Hardin, Samuel H., 276
Hardin, William Jefferson, 287
Harper's Ferry, 280
Harrison, Michael, 15
Heart Mountain, 260–261, 265
Henning, Commander B.S., 154
Henry, Andrew, 88
Henry, Buck, 238
Herrera, José Joaquin de, 120–123
Hickman, Willianna, 281
Historians
    compared to writers, 21–22, 25–26
    "old western," compared to "new west-
    ern," 11–12, 22, 27–28, 275–276
History
    American, 26
    scientific, 25–26
Homestead Act, 102
Homesteading. *See also* Farming; Land
    by ex-slaves, 281–282
    in Canada, 49
    Kinkaid Homestead Act of 1904, 282
    in South America, 50–51
    tenancy contracts and, 51
Hoover Dam, 237
Hopkins, Harry, 231
Hopkins, Mark, 279
Horiuchi, Shizuko, 256
Horse. *See also* Great Plains; Native
    Americans
    in Plains Indian culture, 98–99, 100–
    101, 103, 104–105, 107, 108–109,
    113n6, 117nn39–41
Housing
    in Japanese internment camps, 260–
    261
    in World War II Los Angeles, 249–250,
    254n76
Houston, Jeanne Wakatsuki, 260
Hunt, George P., 206, 213, 214–215

Idaho, Great Depression federal funding
    in, 225–233
Idaho Encyclopedia, 232
Immigrants. *See also* Migration
    Americanization of, 28
    in cultural and entertainment indus-
    try, 250
    in labor conflicts, 207–218
Immigration Act of 1924, 257

Imperialism. *See also* Business; Colonial-
    ism; Expansionism
    relation to frontiers, 40, 44–45
    urban, 317n11
Indian Wars. *See also* Native Americans;
    specific tribes
    Sand Creek Massacre and, 147–159
Industrial Workers of the World (IWW),
    in Arizona, 204, 210–211, 217
International Association of Machinists,
    240, 289
Irrigation. *See also* Farming; Ranching;
    Water
    in Dakota territory, 182–183
Irving, Washington, 84, 91, 95n
Italians. *See also* Immigrants
    in labor conflicts, 207–218, 221n22
IWW. *See* Industrial Workers of the
    World

Jackson, David, 88
Jacksonian man. *See also* Capitalism
    defined, 86–87, 94n
    mountain men and, 83–94
James, Thomas, 86, 88, 91, 92, 95n15
Japanese Americans. *See also* Minorities;
    Racism
    Japanese-American women in World
    War II, 255–271
    prewar background, 256–258
    resettlement, 264–271, 273n56
    World War II removal and internment,
    235, 239–251, 252nn21,22, 255–
    256, 258–259
Jefferson, Thomas, 30
Jerome (Ariz.), 218
Jésus Garcia, María de, 70
Jobs. *See* Employment
Johansen, Dorothy, 306

Kaiser, Henry J., 244, 248
Kansas. *See also* Great Plains; Native
    Americans
    African Americans in, 280, 284, 285,
    290
    cowboy unions in, 171
    inclusion in west, 19–20
    slavery in, 279–280
Kansas-Nebraska Act, 279
Katow, Smoot, 269
Kindelberger, J. H., 241
King, Rodney, 290–291
Kinkaid Homestead Act of 1904, 282
Kiowa Indians
    bison and, 98, 100, 103–105, 107, 108,
    110
    origin myth, 113n9
    protected by black cavalry, 282
Knights of Labor, 165, 170, 172
Korngold, Erich, 250
Kyogoku, Marii, 266, 268

Labor. *See also* Employment
  conflict and unionization in Arizona
    mines, 203–218
  cowboy strikes and unions, 164–175
  racial and gender discrimination in,
    240–241
Ladies Refugee Aid Society, 284
Land. *See also* Environment; Farming;
    Homesteading; Property rights;
    Ranching
  for European immigrants, 44, 47, 50,
    53, 139, 281
  squatters on, 71–72
  women's rights to, 61–80
Land grants, to Spanish women, 60–80
Lane, James H., 279, 280
Langlie, Arthur, 305
Lara, Lázaro Gutiérrez de, 211, 213, 217
Larkin, Thomas Oliver, 61
Lataillade, Dona María de la Guerra de,
    71
Law. *See also* Politics
  Mormon, 139
  Spanish, women's rights under, 63–80
Lawrence (Kans.), 280, 289
Lean Bear, 150
Lee, Dorothy, 305
Left Hand, 154, 160n28
Legacy of Conquest (Limerick), 12
Leonard, Zenas, 93, 96n26
Leonis, Espiritu, 71
Lester, Peter, 279
*Life and Adventures of James Beck-
    wourth* (Bonner), 91
Liga Protectora Latina, 214
Limerick, Frederick Jackson, 12
Literature, about mountain men, 91
Little, Frank, 210
Little Raven, 154, 155
Long, Stephen, 104
Lorenzanas, 60–61
Los Angeles, 91, 284. *See also* Califor-
    nia; Cities
  bilingual education, 34
  relation to greater west, 17, 19, 29n1
  riots, 274–275, 290–291
  Rodney King uprising, 290–291
  women's property rights, 60–61, 64
  World War II impact, 234–251
    African Americans, 288–289
    pre–World War II, 235–237
    post–World War II, 250–251
Los Angeles Castro, María de, 66
Los Angeles Sentinel, 242
Los Angeles Times, 238, 239, 251
Loucks, Henry L., 186
Love, Charles Norvell, 288
Luper, Clara, 284
Lytle, Lutie, 284

McCloy, John, 258
McCluskey, Henry S., 215, 216

McCombs, Pvt. Henry, 282
Macdonald, John A., 41
McGaa, William, 91
The Making of Urban Europe (Lees/
    Hohenberg), 299
Manifest destiny, 30
Mann, Thomas, 250
Mason, Biddy, 284, 293n27
Media. See also *Dakota Farmer*
  black newspapers, 241–242, 284, 286
  Japanese internment camp newspapers,
    263–264
  role in Arizona strikes, 222n41
  role in Mexican War, 122–124, 125,
    127–128, 131n17
Meining, D. W., 36
Meldrum, Robert, 90
The Mercedian, 264
Metaphor, self-fulfilling, 30–31
Mexican Americans. *See also* Immi-
    grants; Minorities
  labor conflict in Arizona mining com-
    munities, 203–218
  mutualistas, 204, 208–209, 214,
    219n2, 221n24
  in World War II Los Angeles, 235
  zoot suiters, 246, 254n66
Mexican War. *See also* California; Texas
  American racism and public opinion
    in, 120–130, 130n2
  legal and political changes following,
    69–80
  precursors, 93–94
Mexico
  frontiers, 54n10
  land grant secularization, 65–66
  as part of west, 13, 15, 17, 276–277
Miami (Ariz.), miners' unions, 210–218
Migration. *See also* Immigrants; Immi-
    gration
  African-American, 288–289
  bison, 102, 109–110, 113n7
  for employment, 43, 44, 51, 221n27
  in Great Depression/World War II,
    230–231, 249
  Japanese workers, 256–258
  into Seattle, 312–313
  Mormon, 141–143
Military, citizen militias, 147–159
Miller, Guy, 215
Miners' Magazine, 217
Mining
  Arizona labor conflict and unioniza-
    tion, 203–218
  black soldiers confront white strikers,
    282 283
  in Idaho, 227
Minorities. *See also* Discrimination; Ra-
    cism; *specific minorities*
  repression of, 30
Minoz, M. de J., 214
Miranda, Jose, 214

Mississippi, Great Depression effects, 227
Mississippi River, as boundary of west, 16, 17, 19, 20
Missouri, slavery in, 279–280
Missouri River, as boundary of west, 16, 17, 19
Modernization. *See also* Transportation
 affecting farming lifestyle, 180, 183–184, 188, 192, 193–194, 197n14
 affecting Portland and Seattle, 296–315
 homogenization and, 33
 pace of, 92–93
 of ranching, 175
 of transportation, 36
Montana. *See also* Great Plains
 Great Depression effects, 227
Montebello (ship), 238
Monterey (Calif.), founding and growth, 61
Montgomery, James, 279
Morgan, Neil, 306
Mormons. *See also* Religion; Utah
 deliverance of, closing of frontier and, 133–145
 emigration patterns, 47–48
 the "gathering," 137, 138, 143
Morrill Act, 143
El Mosquito Mexicano, 126, 127, 128
Mother Jones, 211
Mountain Meadows massacre, 140
Mountain men. *See also* Colorado; Rocky Mountains
 bison and, 109
 entrepreneurial adventures, 88–94
 as Jacksonian men, 83–94
 physical appearance, 83–84
 stereotypes of, 83–86
Moyer, Charles, 217, 224n82
Mun, Jules De, 104
Munras, Catalina Manzaneli de, 66
Mutual benefit societies, of immigrants, 204, 208–209
Mutualistas. See also Community
 at Arizona copper mines, 204, 208–209, 214, 219n2, 221n24

NAACP, 286
Napoleonic Wars, 40
National Association for the Advancement of Colored People (NAACP), 286
National Farmers' Alliance, 185
National Japanese American Student Relocation Council, 264–265
National Youth Administration, efforts in Idaho, 231
Native Americans. *See also* Bison; Minorities; Racism
 bison ecology and, 97–112
 European impacts on, 30, 44–47, 51–53

Five Indian Nations, 279
 Mormon relations with, 139–140
 religion, 112, 119n52
 Sand Creek Massacre, 147–159
 U.S. relations with, 125–126
Natural resources, misuse of, 135
Nebraska, inclusion in west, 19, 20
Negro Victory Committee, 241–242, 249
Nevada, labor organizing among miners, 212
New Deal, 195, 196, 226, 230. *See also* Great Depression
New England
 Great Depression effects, 227
 property rights, 73
New Mexico, 91, 148
 African Americans in, 279, 290
 bison hunting, 110
 cowboy unions, 173–174
 labor organizing among miners, 212
 Native Americans, 100, 103
 Santa Fe Trail, 110
 slavery in, 279
Newell, "Doc," 91
Newspapers. *See also* Media
 black, 241–242, 284, 286
 Dakota Farmer, 179–196
 in Japanese internment camps, 263–264
Neyera, Refugio, 214
Nieto, Dona Josefa Cota de, 71
North American Aviation, 241
North Dakota, Great Depression effects, 227
The North American Buffalo (Roe), 99

Odegaard, Charles, 312
Ogata, Elizabeth, 270
Ohio, westernness in, 13
Oklahoma
 African Americans in, 281–282, 290
 Great Depression effects, 227
 Native Americans of, 279
 slavery in, 281
Okubo, Miné, 256, 260, 270
Okumura, Mary, 259
Olsen, Gov. Culbert, 239
Olvera, Isabel de, 276, 283–284
100th meridian, as western boundary, 20
Oregon. *See also* Portland
 inclusion in west, 16–17
 Overland Trail immigration, 47–48, 138
 politics in, 314
 Portland and, 302, 318n26
Oregon Centennial Exposition, 307, 320n44
Ortega, Dona Soledad, 68
O'Sullivan, John O., 93, 96n31
Ota, Lillian, 266
Overland Trail, 47–48, 138
Owyhee Reclamation Project, 232

Pacific Appeal (newspaper), 286, 293n30
Pacific Northwest. *See also specific
     states and cities*
precipitation, 13
Paine, Lauran, 15
Pan American Federation of Labor, 218,
     224n95
Panic of 1907, 211
Paredes y Arrillaga, Gen. Mariano, 120,
     123
Parkman, Francis, 25
Parks, Rosa, 286–287
Parrott, William, 124
Partido Liberal Mexicano (PLM), in Ari-
     zona mining district, 211
Patriarchy, challenges to, 184
Pearce (Ariz.), labor conflicts, 205–206
Pearl Harbor, 237–238, 258. *See also*
     World War II
Peralta, Louis, San Pablo Ranch, 68
Perez, Juan, 70
Peterson, Fred, 305
Phelps-Dodge Corporation, 207
Pico, Pío and Andrés, 60, 68, 70
Pierce, Neil, 306
Pilcher, Joshua, 91
Pioneer period. *See also* Frontier
study of, 28–29
Place-versus-process issue
new western historians and, 12
survey responses about, 13–14
Pleasant, Mary Ellen, 284, 287
PLM. *See* Partido Liberal Mexicano
Police brutality, 290–291
Politics. *See also* Democracy; Federal gov-
     ernment; Law
at frontier, 45
Portland and Seattle, compared, 295–
     315, 319nn35,36
Polk, James K., 120, 121, 124
Pomeroy, Alan, 305
Pomeroy, Earl, 306
Population
of African Americans, 275, 294n35
contemporary increases, 34
of cowboys, 166
in Dakotas, 181–182
1850 census, 48
gender ratios in, 61
historical increases, 40
of Portland and Seattle, compared, 300–
     301, 304
of Southern Plains Indians, 102, 107,
     110, 111–112, 117n36, 118n50
Populism, 32, 284
Porter, Kenneth W., 275
Portland (Ore.). *See also* Oregon
compared to Seattle, 295–315
Delta Dome, 308
Poston Chronicle, 264
Powell, George, 215

Prather, Pvt. W. H., 283
Precipitation. *See also* Climate; Drought;
     Water
as western characteristic, 13, 281
Property rights. *See also* Land
of women in new Spain, 59–80
Protocol of Queretero, 69

Quakers. *See also* Religion
Japanese Americans and, 269–270

Racism. *See also* African Americans; Dis-
     crimination; Slavery; Violence
against indigenous people, 44–45
against Japanese Americans, 270–271
against Mexicans, 120–130, 246, 292n6
against minorities, 30, 240
against minority cowboys, 177
labor conflict in Mexican mining com-
     munities, 203–218
Railroads, 50, 52, 187, 204. *See also*
     Transportation
Canadian Pacific Railroad, 49
Southern Pacific Coast Railroad, 69
strikes, 282–283
trans-national, 41
underground, 279–280, 291
in Utah, 141
Rains, Dona Merced Williams, 71
Ranching. *See also* Farming; Irrigation
black cowboys, 285
cowboy strikes and unions, 164–175
Rancho Boca de la Canada de Pinole, 67
Rancho Cucamonga, 71
Rancho Guadalasca, 71
Rancho Huerta de Cuati, 62
Rancho Jamul, 71
Rancho Los Bolsas, 71
Rancho Nogales, 70
Rancho Paso de Bartolo, 70
Rancho Rodeo de las Aguas, 62, 71
Rancho Santa Ana Vieja, 68
Rancho Santa Gertrudis, 71
Rancho Santa Manuela, 67
Ranchos of California (Cowan), 67,
     76n15, 77n16
RAND Corporation, 250
Randolph, A. Philip, 241
Rattle Snake Island, 67
Ray (Ariz.), miners' unions, 210–216
Reagan, Ronald, 30
Reconstruction Finance Corporation
     (RFC)
in Idaho, 226, 232
in World War II, 237–238
*Recoplacion de leyes do los reynos de las
     Indias,* 63
Reeves, Richard, 13
Region, west as, 24–38
Regionalism. *See also* Community
defined, 12

manufacturers, 318n27
Portland and Seattle, compared, 295–315
sectionalism and, 32–35
Reid, Hugo and Victoria, 62
Religion. *See also* Mormons; Native Americans
African-American, 284, 286
cultural threats to, 127
Japanese-American, 263, 269–270
Native American, 112, 119n52
Quakers, 269–270
Religious persecution. *See also* Racism
against Mormons, 134–135, 136
Resa, Juan Guerra de, 276
RFC. *See* Reconstruction Finance Corporation
Rhodes, James Ford, 25
Riley, Earl, 305
Rio Grande River, as boundary, 16, 124
Rise of New York Port (Albion), 299, 317n19
Rocky Mountain Fur Company, 87–88
Rocky Mountain News, 148, 149, 150, 157, 161n
Rocky Mountains. *See also* Colorado; Native Americans
mountain men in, 83–94
Sage Brush Rebellion in, 31
as western boundary, 16
Roman Nose, 150
Roosevelt, Pres. Franklin Delano, 31, 196, 239, 241, 258
Roosevelt, Theodore, 25
Ross, Gov. C. Ben, 230
Rural communities. *See also* Community
relation to cities, 184, 198n29
Rural Electrification Administration, 226
Russell, Helen B., 191
Russell, Rev. Clayton D., 241–242

Sage Brush Rebellion, 31
St. Louis, as western boundary, 20
Salcido, C. L., 214
Salt Lake City, 139, 141, 142. *See also* Utah
San Francisco. *See also* California; Cities; Los Angeles
precipitation, 13
World War II impact, 245, 288
San Jose, founding and growth, 61
San Pablo Ranch, 68
Sanchez, Vincente, 62
Sand Creek Massacre, 147–159
Sandoval, José, 64
Sanitation, 41
Santa Ana, Gen. Antonio López de, 277
Santa Barbara. *See also* California
founding and growth, 61
Santa Fe Trail, 110. *See also* New Mexico

Savage, W. Sherman, 275
Schoenberg, Arnold, 250
Schools. *See* Education
Schrunk, Terry, 305, 308
Seattle. *See also* Washington
compared to Portland, 295–315
"Alaska thesis," 298
central place theory, 298
Seattle Magazine, 313
Sectionalism. *See also* Regionalism
at frontier, 32–34
Sepulveda, Ignacia, 64
Sepulveda, Joaquina, 70
Serrano, Florencio, 61
Shaw, Col. John, 92
Shipbuilding. *See also* Employment
in World War II Los Angeles, 237, 244–251, 288–289
Shoiji, Lily, 264
Shoshone Indians, 100
El Siglo Diez y Nueve, 128, 129
Silver, in Great Depression, 227–228
Sinoba, Casilda, 61
Slavery. *See also* African Americans; Racism
abolishment in South America, 50
among Native Americans, 102
in Southwest, 125, 127, 130n1, 276–277, 278–279, 291n3, 292nn9,11
Smith, Jedediah, 84, 88, 92, 93, 96nn23,24
Smith, John Simpson, 91
Smith, Joseph, Jr., 136–137
Smith, Pedro, 212
Smith v. Allwrigh, 288
Social services
in Great Depression, 195
in Idaho, 225–233
in Los Angeles, 237
Soledad, María de, 70
El Sol, 125, 126
Sonoda, Mary, 269
Soule, Cpt. Silas, 155, 156–157, 162n65
South America. *See* Argentina; Brazil
South Dakota. *See also Dakota Farmer*
Great Dakota Boom, 179, 181, 188, 196n1, 198n28
Great Depression effects, 227
inclusion of in west, 19, 20
Spanish colonial policy
borderlands, 34–35
law, 63–80
for women, 59–80
Squires, Charles W., 157
Stance, Sgt. Emanuel, 283
Stearns, Abel, 66, 71
Stimson, Henry, 258
Strong, Josiah, 27
Sublette, Milton "Thunderbolt," 88
Sublette, William L., 88, 90, 91, 93
Suffrage, for African Americans, 287–288

Sumner, Sen. Charles, 287
Sumner, William Graham, 27

Taxes. *See also* Federal government
  compared to federal spending, 232
Taylor, John, 142
Technology. *See also* Modernization
  effect on bison herds, 99–100
Texas. *See also* Mexican War
  African Americans in, 284, 288, 291
  cowboy strikes in, 168–175
  labor organizing among miners, 212
  role in Mexican War, 121–130, 276–
    279
  slavery in, 279, 291
  Spanish law in, 59–80, 276–277
Texas Freedman, 288
"Think tanks," 250
Thomas, W. H., 68
Three Years among the Indians (James),
  91
Timber, 227
Timeframe, in definition of west, 21
Tobacco, 61
Todd Shipyards, 244
Tornel y Mendivel, José María, 127, 277
Trade. *See also* Business
  among Native Americans, 103–104,
    105, 115n21, 116n33
  in bison robes, 99, 111, 118n49
  effect on bison herds, 99–100, 110–111
  with Mormons, 140–141
Transportation. *See also* Modernization;
  Railroads
  discrimination in, 281, 286–287
  modernization of, 36, 309–312, 322n63
Treaty of Fort Holmes, 110
Treaty of Gaudalupe Hidalgo, 60, 69, 74,
    99, 276. *See also* Mexican War
Tribolet, A. N., 214–215, 223n65
Turner, Emma J., 287
Turner, Frederick Jackson
  history with national context, 37–38,
    276
  sectionalism, 32–34
  significance of frontier, 24–25, 26–29,
    31–32, 135–136, 144
  West as process, 12
Tuttle, Gerald, 240

Underground Railroad, 279–280, 291.
    See also Slavery
Unions. *See* Labor
United Verde Copper Company, 206
Universal Negro Improvement Associa-
    tion, 286
University of Washington, 312
Urbanization. *See also* Cities
  western, 34, 235, 285, 288, 316n6,
    317n14

Utah. *See also* Mormons
  African American women in, 284
  Overland Trail immigration, 47–48,
    138
  slavery in, 279
  statehood, 144

Valencia, Manuel, 67
Vargas, Canuto A., 218
Vargas, Pascual M., 218
Vasquez, Louis, 91–92
Vegetation, bison herds and, 102, 114n17
Velarde, Fernando, 211
Verde, Cuerno, 98
Villa, María Rita Valdez de, 62, 71
Villa, Vincente, 62
Violence. *See also* Racism
  against labor leaders, 213
  against Native Americans, 147–159
  on frontier, 138, 140, 168
Voto, Bernard De, 13, 84, 91
Vultee Aircraft, 240

Wade, Sen. Ben, 156, 157–158
Wages
  farm income declines in, 227–228
  recovery of, 232–233
War Manpower Commission, 242
War Relocation Authority, 267
Warner, J. J., 91
Warren, Atty. Gen. Earl, 239
The War With Mexico (Smith), 121
Washington. *See also* Seattle
  inclusion in west, 16–17
  politics in, 314
Water. *See also* Irrigation; Precipitation
  irrigated farming in Dakotas, 182–183
  in relation to west, 34, 35
Waters, James, 91
Webb, Walter Prescott, 35, 275
Wenz, Alfred, 193
West
  boundaries, 15–19, 36–37
  defined, 11–12, 291n2
  as myth, 16
  as place, not process, 11–12
  as region, 24–25
West survey
  description, 12–13, 22nn5,6
  questionnaire, 14
  questions, 13–14, 15–22
    boundaries, 15–19
    characteristics, 21–22
    where do you have to go?, 19–21
  responses, 14–22
Western ethos, 37
Western Federation of Miners (WFM), in
    Arizona, 204, 205, 206, 209–212,
    216, 218n1, 224n82
Western History Association (WHA),

response to survey, 12, 14–22, 22–23n
Western Writers of America (WWA), response to survey, 14–22
White, Richard, 12, 113n4, 294n42
Wilburn, James, 242
Wilson, Benjamin, 91
Wilson, Benjamin D., 71
Wolf, bison and, 103, 106, 109, 115n20, 116n32, 118n44
Wolfskill, Sarchel, 90, 91
Women. *See also* Children; Family
  African-American, 281, 283–284, 293n26
  brenes parafernales, 63–64
  on frontier, 47, 49, 184–185, 192, 199n41, 271n2
  Japanese-American women in World War II, 255–271
  in Mormon society, 139
  Native American, 102, 115n18, 148
  property rights in Hispanic California, 59–80
  World War II employment, 240–241, 242–243, 248, 254n70, 268, 289

Works Progress Administration, 226
World War II
  African Americans in, 288–289
  impact on Los Angeles, 234–251, 251n1
  Japanese-American women in, 255–271
  Pearl Harbor, 237–238, 258
Writers
  compared to historians, 21–22, 25–26
  in WPA, 317n9
Wynkoop, Maj. Edward, 152–154, 158, 160n21
Wyoming, cowboy strikes, 168–175

Yellow Wolf, 112
Yorba, Ramon, 71
Yorba, Vincenta Sepulveda de, 68
Yoshino, May, 266
Young, Brigham, 139, 142
Yount, George, 91

Zabriskie, Joseph C., 279
Zoot suiters, 246, 254n66. *See also* Mexican Americans

WALTER NUGENT taught American history, including the West, at Indiana University from 1963 to 1984, and at the University of Notre Dame from 1984 to 1999. His books include *The Tolerant Populists: Kansas Populism and Nativism; Money and American Society, 1865–1880; Structures of American Social History; Crossings: The Great Transatlantic Migrations, 1870–1914;* and most recently, *Into the West: The Story of Its People.*

MARTIN RIDGE is past president of the Western History Association and of the Pacific Coast Branch of the American Historical Association. He is author of *Ignatius Donnelly: Portrait of a Politician; Atlas of American Frontiers; Bilingualism and Biculturalism: An American Dilemma;* and *Westward Journeys;* and co-author with Ray Allen Billington of *Westward Expansion.* He is the former editor of the *Journal of American History.*